T0299413

The Age of Decentralization

The Age of Decentralization talks about various decentralization technologies including Web3, decentralized identity, and decentralized storage, and how they can be incorporated in traditional tech architectures to improve technical and business performance.

In this book, the authors take us on a journey through the tech landscape, exploring how decentralized technologies, including Web3, are on the verge of becoming mainstream and offer a practical roadmap for understanding and embracing this shift. Web2 brought us "the great centralization" by centralizing not only data but also business processes, blurring the industry boundaries. So, payment platforms started offering e-commerce services and ride-hailing services started delivering food. Scale became the most effective moat. But, at the same time, these huge platforms became a magnet for security threats and started violating user privacy rights and consumer rights. The authors argue that the technological, regulatory, and social landscape is ready for the next evolution of technology systems as decentralization technologies get incorporated into traditional architectures.

This book serves as a guide for readers to understand the fundamentals of Web3 along with other decentralized technologies and creates a framework for incorporating them into traditional architectures. At the same time, the authors explore the organization level as well as the macro implications of decentralized technologies.

Sam Ghosh is an engineer, holds an MBA from the University of Calgary, and has completed all three levels of the CFA Program. He has been an entrepreneur in the FinTech domain. Sam has been teaching Web3 for the last three years to more than 26,000 students in 167 countries around the world.

Subhasis Gorai, a seasoned technology professional with over 19 years of experience, specializes in Enterprise and Web-Scale Applications, and Data Infrastructure. As Principal Engineer at Cloudera, he leads the Replication Manager team, managing diverse use cases like HA and Disaster Recovery. Previously, at Microsoft, Intuit, and Yahoo, he actively contributed to various platform development and Distributed Systems. Subhasis holds an MS in Software Systems from BITS, Pilani, and a Bachelor's degree from NIT, Durgapur.

The Age of Decentralization

How Web3 and Related Technologies
will Change Industries and our Lives

Sam Ghosh and Subhasis Gorai

A PRODUCTIVITY PRESS BOOK

First published 2025
by Routledge
605 Third Avenue, New York, NY 10158

and by Routledge
4 Park Square, Milton Park, Abingdon, Oxon, OX14 4RN

Routledge is an imprint of the Taylor & Francis Group, an informa business

Library of Congress Cataloging-in-Publication Data
Names: Ghosh, Sam, author. | Gorai, Subhasis, author.
Title: The age of decentralization : how Web3 and related technologies will change industries and our lives / Sam Ghosh and Subhasis Gorai.
Description: New York, NY : Routledge, 2025. | Includes bibliographical references and index. | Summary: "The Age of Decentralization talks about various decentralization technologies including Web3, Decentralized Identity, and Decentralized Storage, and how they can be incorporated in traditional tech architectures to improve technical and business performance. In this book, the authors take us on a journey through the tech landscape, exploring how decentralized technologies, including Web3, are on the verge of becoming mainstream and offer a practical roadmap for understanding and embracing this shift. Web2 brought us "the great centralization" by centralizing not only data but also business processes, blurring the industry boundaries. So, payment platforms started offering e-commerce services and ride-hailing services started delivering food. Scale became the most effective moat. But, at the same time, these huge platforms became a magnet for security threats and started violating user privacy rights and consumer rights. The authors argue that the technological, regulatory, and social landscape is ready for the next evolution of technology systems as decentralization technologies get incorporated into traditional architectures. This book serves as a guide for readers to understand the fundamentals of Web3 along with other decentralized technologies and creates a framework for incorporating them in traditional architectures. While at the same time the authors explore the organization level as well as the macro implications of decentralized technologies"-- Provided by publisher.
Identifiers: LCCN 2024027546 (print) | LCCN 2024027547 (ebook) | ISBN 9781032830230 (hardback) | ISBN 9781032830216 (paperback) | ISBN 9781003507352 (ebook)
Subjects: LCSH: Peer-to-peer architecture (Computer networks) | Computer network architectures. | Technological innovations--Economic aspects. | Industries--Technological innovations.
Classification: LCC TK5105.525 .G46 2025 (print) | LCC TK5105.525 (ebook) | DDC 004.6/52--dc23/eng/20240722
LC record available at https://lccn.loc.gov/2024027546
LC ebook record available at https://lccn.loc.gov/2024027547

ISBN: 978-1-032-83023-0 (hbk)
ISBN: 978-1-032-83021-6 (pbk)
ISBN: 978-1-003-50735-2 (ebk)

DOI: 10.4324/9781003507352

Typeset in Adobe Garamond Pro
by Deanta Global Publishing Services, Chennai, India

Sam Ghosh:

I dedicate this book to my nephew Pi (Ryan).

Subhasis Gorai:

I dedicate this book to my father, whose unwavering inspiration
and motivation have always guided me.

Contents

Acknowledgements

We would like to thank all the Web3 entrepreneurs and investors who did not give up through the testing times the Web3 ecosystem has been going through for the last few years.

We would also like to thank all those researchers and engineers who built and are building the conceptual and technical infrastructure that is helping new use cases emerge in the ecosystem.

Chapter 1

Introduction

Sam Ghosh

In the grand maze of human progress, moments of radical innovation often emerge as turbulent waves crashing against the shores of convention. These disruptive surges challenge the established norms, provoke regulatory scrutiny, and navigate tumultuous waters before eventually merging into the calm expanse of the mainstream. It is within this transformative ebb and flow that the narratives of innovation often find their genesis, revealing a cycle of evolution – of clashes, adaptations, and assimilations.

Okay, I ran out of my poetic abilities here – let us return to plain English.

Throughout technological history, many radical technologies emerged and clashed with the mainstream industry and regulations. These clashes sometimes resulted in truce and sometimes massacres.

Here, we are not talking about the truce but the massacres. While there were probably thousands of radical technologies that came throughout history and disappeared from our collective memory, there are some comparatively recent technologies that faced the wrath of the conventional.

So, did these "massacred" technologies just disappear?

We are at a similar juncture for Web3 technologies.

The failure of the Terra ecosystem in May 2022 rippled through the whole crypto ecosystem and caused a series of failures. The collapse of the FTX crypto exchange in November 2022 transformed the market downturn into a prolonged crypto winter resulting in capital flight from the Web3 sector.

But, capital flight is not the only problem for the crypto ecosystem. Regulators around the world are taking a harsher approach to crypto-assets, let that be the Biden administration's Roadmap to Mitigate Cryptocurrencies' Risks to the issuance of 146 alerts and warning lists for crypto-asset promotion by the UK's Financial Conduct Authority in October 2023.

Unfavorable market conditions are hindering investments in Web3 projects, evident from a significant decline in investments in Web3 projects. According to Crunchbase Web3 Tracker, investment in Web3 projects has dropped from US $10.4 billion in the first quarter of 2022 to just

DOI: 10.4324/9781003507352-1

US $1.2 billion in the last quarter of 2023. 2024 exhibited slight improvement with a $1.7 billion investment in Q1 and a $1.9 billion investment in Q2.

So, is this the end of the road for Web3?

To answer this question, we need to look into the radical technologies that came before Web3 and challenged the conventions. Maybe understanding what transpired for these radical technologies would shed some light on the fate of Web3.

1.1 Open Source Revolution

The concept of open-source software, gaining momentum in the late 20th century and particularly in the late 1990s and early 2000s, revolutionized traditional proprietary software models by emphasizing collaboration and transparency. Linux, created by Linus Torvalds in the early 1990s, served as a key example of this open-source movement.

Concerns about intellectual property rights, licensing, and legal issues related to open-source software were raised by regulatory bodies and certain tech companies. The collaborative nature of open-source development was perceived as a potential threat to proprietary models, leading to efforts to regulate or restrict the proliferation of open-source licenses.

Do you remember the SCO vs IBM lawsuit that was targeted to end Linux?

The SCO Group vs IBM lawsuit in the early 2000s was a major legal dispute challenging the legitimacy and usage of the Linux operating system. SCO Group, a software and services company, accused IBM of violating intellectual property rights and contractual obligations by integrating proprietary code into the Linux kernel.

The lawsuit, filed in 2003, persisted through SCO Group's bankruptcy and an unfavorable outcome in SCO vs Novell. It was reopened for ongoing litigation by a new judge on June 14, 2013.

The SCO Group accused IBM of incorporating SCO's UNIX code into Linux, violating intellectual property rights and copyright. SCO sought financial compensation, initially claiming US $1 billion, later revising it to US $3 billion, and then increasing it again to US $5 billion.

The lawsuit not only sought financial compensation but also raised concerns about the legal status of open-source software, particularly Linux. SCO aimed to assert control over Linux usage, creating uncertainty and fear within the open-source community and among businesses and individuals using or considering Linux. In May 2003, SCO Group issued warnings to companies, alleging liability for Linux usage.

Let us leave it here. We will get back to it later.

Who else wanted to hurt open-source?

Microsoft.

Microsoft, traditionally supportive of proprietary software, launched the "Get the Facts" campaign in 2003 to cast doubts on the security and total cost of ownership of open-source alternatives like Linux, discouraging organizations from adopting open source.

The campaign, costing over US $20 million, showcased various case studies to portray open-source Linux as less reliable and less secure.

Microsoft also employed a lock-in strategy, leveraging its dominance in the operating system and office software market. This created vendor lock-in, making it challenging for users to transition to open-source alternatives due to dependencies on proprietary ecosystems like Windows and Office.

So, did all this animosity against open-source end open-source?

The SCO-IBM case we talked about. Well, that only dragged SCO's impending bankruptcy, making it more and more painful. Ultimately in 2021, TSG Group, which represented SCO's debtors, settled with IBM and resolved all the remaining claims between TSG and IBM.

What happened to Microsoft's "Get the Facts"?

Shortly after Microsoft launched the campaign, a UK advertising standards body cautioned that Microsoft's "Get the Facts" campaign, asserting that Linux isn't cheaper than Windows, might be misleading.

The "Get the Facts" campaign by Microsoft received criticism for presenting facts in a misleading and biased manner. Critics highlighted the use of selective data and comparisons to downplay the advantages of open-source software, especially Linux.

The claims made by Microsoft's "Get the Facts" campaign were countered over time by the open-source community, analysts, and independent studies. These responses emphasized the benefits, security, and cost-effectiveness of open-source software, debunking many arguments presented in the campaign.

As the open-source ecosystem gained credibility and widespread adoption, the necessity for anti-open-source campaigns diminished. Microsoft, acknowledging this shift, also altered its approach toward open source.

In time, Microsoft adopted a more favorable approach to open-source. It actively contributed to open-source projects, released some of its technologies as open-source, and incorporated Linux functionalities into its ecosystem. This marked a notable change in Microsoft's perception and involvement with the open-source ecosystem.

As the industry dynamics evolved, the "Get the Facts" campaign lost its relevance, and Microsoft's approach toward open-source changed significantly, leading to the campaign's decline and eventual discontinuation.

So, where does Linux stand now?

- Linux is the preferred operating system for the top 500 of the world's supercomputers.
- 85% of smartphones run on Linux-based operating systems.
- Of the top 25 global websites, only two operate without Linux support.
- An extensive selection of over 600 Linux distributions (distros) is currently available.

Over the years we have seen integration of open-source initiatives with the mainstream.

1.1.1 Red Hat Acquired by IBM

In 2019, IBM purchased Red Hat, a leading open-source solutions provider, for approximately US $34 billion. This acquisition emphasized the significance of open source in IBM's cloud and hybrid cloud offerings, with Red Hat's enterprise Linux distribution playing a crucial role in its portfolio.

1.1.2 Google's Use of Open-source

Google strongly supports open-source, as seen in its adoption of the Linux kernel for Android, one of the most globally used mobile operating systems. Google actively contributes to numerous open-source projects and has open-sourced various tools and libraries, such as TensorFlow for machine learning.

1.1.3 Microsoft's Shift to Open-source

Microsoft, known for proprietary software, has made a big change by embracing open-source. They've open-sourced tools and frameworks and launched the Microsoft Windows Subsystem for Linux, allowing Linux to run on Windows.

1.1.4 Meta's Open-source Contributions

Meta (Facebook) is a major tech player supporting open-source. Contributions to projects like React and GraphQL have had a notable impact on web and software development.

1.1.5 Automotive Industry

Leading automotive companies, including Tesla, Volkswagen, and Toyota, have integrated open-source software into their vehicle systems. Tesla, for instance, employs open-source components in its infotainment system, enhancing flexibility and customization capabilities.

1.2 Torrent Technology

Now, another radical technology that received significant opposition was torrent technology. The rise of torrent technology gained momentum in the early 2000s, particularly with the launch of platforms like BitTorrent.

Torrent technology is a decentralized peer-to-peer file-sharing method that facilitates the distribution of large files over the internet. Instead of relying on a central server, files are divided into smaller pieces, and users (peers) download and upload these pieces simultaneously. Torrents use metadata and trackers in torrent files to guide peers to sources sharing the same files. Users act as both downloaders and uploaders, enhancing download speed. The technology employs cryptographic hashing for file integrity and magnet links for efficient file sharing without separate torrent files.

The problem is that peer-to-peer file sharing enabled the sharing of copyrighted material and it clashed with established copyright laws. Regulators and large companies tried to suppress torrent technology due to concerns about piracy, copyright infringement, and its impact on established business models.

The Pirate Bay, launched in 2003, is a prominent website for torrent-based peer-to-peer file sharing, known for distributing digital content, often copyrighted. It faced numerous legal actions and court orders in attempts to shut it down. Despite persistent attempts to shut it down, The Pirate Bay persevered, employing domain and server changes to evade legal actions.

In 2012, Pirate Bay co-founder Gottfrid Svartholm was arrested in Cambodia, extradited to Sweden, and later deported to Denmark. On October 31, 2013, he was sentenced to three and a half years in prison for computer hacking.

In 2012, the US introduced the Stop Online Piracy Act (SOPA) and the PROTECT IP Act (PIPA) to combat online piracy, targeting websites facilitating copyright infringement. Faced with substantial public opposition, both bills were ultimately postponed.

Torrent search engines experienced legal actions, resulting in limitations on their operations due to facilitating access to copyrighted content. Some were shut down, while others had to modify services to exclude copyrighted material. Some internet service providers (ISPs) have been known to throttle or limit P2P traffic, including torrents, on their networks. This wasn't solely about combating piracy but was often due to concerns about the strain of torrent traffic placed on network infrastructure, causing slowdowns or congestion for other users.

In some countries, authorities have taken measures to block or restrict torrent traffic and P2P sharing on a national level. This wasn't just about piracy but often due to concerns about the unregulated nature of P2P networks and their potential for sharing illicit or inappropriate content.

While torrenting received so much opposition, the utilization and acceptance of its underlying concepts have influenced various industries.

1.2.1 Content Distribution Networks (CDNs)

Several mainstream companies and services have adopted peer-to-peer concepts similar to torrent technology for content delivery. BitTorrent Inc, the company behind the BitTorrent protocol, established partnerships with CDN providers and media companies to distribute content using peer-to-peer methods.

1.2.2 Online Gaming and Software Updates

Some online gaming platforms and software developers use a torrent-like approach for distributing game updates and patches. For example, Blizzard Entertainment utilizes a peer-to-peer system to distribute updates for games like World of Warcraft.

1.2.3 Blockchain and Decentralized Technologies

The foundational principles of decentralization and peer-to-peer communication inherent in torrent technology have played a role in shaping and inspiring the development of blockchain and decentralized technologies. Although not directly linked, the decentralized nature of torrents has influenced similar structures in blockchain networks and distributed ledger technologies.

1.2.4 Legal Content Distribution Platforms

There are legal platforms that use similar technology to torrents for distributing content. For example, Tribler is a torrent-based software that aims to provide legal content distribution without relying on centralized servers.

1.2.5 Impact on Video Streaming Services

While not a direct adoption of torrent technology, some video streaming services have been influenced by its concepts. Concepts of distributed file sharing and efficient delivery methods inspired the development of peer-assisted video streaming in services like Netflix and Hulu.

1.2.6 Internet Service Providers (ISPs)

Some ISPs have implemented caching and peer-assisted distribution methods inspired by torrent technology to manage and optimize data delivery to customers.

Torrent technology, despite regulatory challenges and piracy associations, has indirectly influenced various industries. Its decentralized, peer-to-peer model has inspired alternative content distribution methods and influenced the development of decentralized technologies. Though not directly integrated into mainstream companies through acquisitions, its principles have had a significant impact on several sectors.

1.3 The Future of Web3

This book does not delve into speculation of what can happen to Web3 but rather proposes a framework on how we can integrate Web3 technologies in traditional architectures.

In this book, we will propose adding a Web3 layer to tech stacks as a Decentralization Layer. This layer would enable adding Web3 qualities such as immutability and decentralization to traditional tech architectures.

But, should we just propose the addition of decentralization layers and increase complexity just to ensure a future for Web3? Not really.

Additions of Decentralization Layer using Smart Contracts may solve some of the pressing technical problems in current centralized architectures. Smart contracts come with various qualities such as immutability (historical records cannot be manipulated), transparency (access records are auditable), automation (no manual intervention is required for smart contracts), and decentralization.

We will discuss all these qualities in detail in the book, but let's talk a little about the concept of decentralization here. So, what does decentralization mean?

Well, in Web3, decentralization is often referred to as the quality of Web3 networks that these networks are not controlled by any centralized entity.

But, if we look under the hood, there are two kinds of decentralization.

A. Blockchains, like all Distributed Ledger Technologies (DLTs), are decentralized, meaning they are served by multiple servers called nodes. These nodes run client software to participate in peer-to-peer blockchain networks. All active nodes maintain the same data record, including copies of smart contracts and data within them. Thus, even if some nodes go offline, the blockchain and smart contracts remain accessible and active. Let us call this **Technical Decentralization**.

B. But, there is another kind of decentralization in the context of Web3 networks – **Governance Decentralization**. DAOs (Decentralized Autonomous Organizations) empower Web3 platforms to be governed collectively by users, platform builders, and investors. The governance system's design and maturity determine the extent to which users can influence the platform's structure and rules.

In this book, our primary focus is to use the Technical Decentralization of Web3, rather than Governance Decentralization. We are not focusing on Governance Decentralization because it is more of a business and administrative tool rather than a technical concept.

Bibliography

Ad Watchdog Warns Microsoft to 'Get the Facts'. (2004, August 30). CNET. Retrieved December 13, 2023, from https://www.cnet.com/tech/services-and-software/ad-watchdog-warns-microsoft-to-get-the-facts/

Blizzard Entertainment. Retrieved December 13, 2023, from https://blizzard.com

Crunchbase Inc. (n.d.). *Web3 Tracker: News On Startups and Investors*. Crunchbase News. Retrieved June 7, 2024, from https://news.crunchbase.com/web3-startups-investors/

Deese, B., Prabhakar, A., Rouse, C., & Sullivan, J. (2023, January 27). *The Administration's Roadmap to Mitigate Cryptocurrencies' Risks | NEC*. The White House. Retrieved December 13, 2023, from https://www.whitehouse.gov/nec/briefing-room/2023/01/27/the-administrations-roadmap-to-mitigate-cryptocurrencies-risks/

FCA Issues 146 Alerts in First 24 Hours of New Crypto Marketing Regime | FCA. (2023, October 9). Financial Conduct Authority. Retrieved December 13, 2023, from https://www.fca.org.uk/news/statements/fca-issues-146-alerts-first-24-hours-new-crypto-marketing-regime

"The Ghost of SCO Dogs IBM Again." LinuxInsider, 7 June 2013, https://www.linuxinsider.com/story/the-ghost-of-sco-dogs-ibm-again-78287.html. Accessed 13 June 2024.

GraphQL | A Query Language for Your API. Retrieved December 13, 2023, from https://graphql.org

H.R.3261 - 112th Congress (2011-2012): Stop Online Piracy Act | Congress.gov | Library of Congress. (n.d.). Congress.gov. Retrieved December 13, 2023, from https://www.congress.gov/bill/112th-congress/house-bill/3261?q=hr3261

Hulu: Stream TV and Movies Live and Online. Retrieved December 13, 2023, from https://www.hulu.com

IBM Closes Landmark Acquisition of Red Hat for $34 Billion; Defines Open, Hybrid Cloud Future. (2019, July 9). Red Hat. Retrieved December 13, 2023, from https://www.redhat.com/en/about/press-releases/ibm-closes-landmark-acquisition-red-hat-34-billion-defines-open-hybrid-cloud-future

Is More P2P Always Bad for ISPs? An Analysis of P2P and ISP Business Models. Retrieved December 13, 2023, from http://people.se.cmich.edu/liao1q/papers/pid3220645.pdf

Lambert, F., & Johnson, P. (2018, May 19). *Tesla Releases Some of Its Software to Comply with Open Source Licences*. Electrek. Retrieved December 13, 2023, from https://electrek.co/2018/05/19/tesla-releases-softwar-open-source-licences/

Leahy, S. (n.d.). *Cosponsors - S.968 - 112th Congress (2011-2012): PROTECT IP Act of 2011*. Congress.gov. Retrieved December 13, 2023, from https://www.congress.gov/bill/112th-congress/senate-bill/968/cosponsors?r=23&s=1&q=%7B%22search%22%3A%22actionCode%3A%5C%2214000%5C%22%22%2C%22party%22%3A%22Independent+Democrat%22%7D

https://www.linux.org

Lohr, S. (2003, December 22). *SCO Sends Second Warning Letter to Linux Users (Published 2003)*. The New York Times. Retrieved December 13, 2023, from https://www.nytimes.com/2003/12/22/business/sco-sends-second-warning-letter-to-linux-users.html

Microsoft ad Campaign Takes Aim at Rivals. (2023, March 2). CNET. Retrieved December 13, 2023, from https://www.cnet.com/tech/services-and-software/microsoft-ad-campaign-takes-aim-at-rivals/

Microsoft's Open Source Program. (n.d.). Microsoft Open Source. Retrieved December 13, 2023, from https://opensource.microsoft.com/program/

Mobile Operating System. (2023, November 5). ScienceDirect. Retrieved December 13, 2023, from https://www.sciencedirect.com/topics/computer-science/mobile-operating-system

The Pirate Bay Cofounder: Prison Was 'Well Worth' it. (2023, March 2). Business Insider. Retrieved December 13, 2023, from https://www.businessinsider.in/tech/the-pirate-bay-cofounder-prison-was-well-worth-it/articleshow/47960428.cms#

React. Retrieved December 13, 2023, from https://react.dev

SCO Group, Inc. v. International Business Machines Corp. (n.d.). DBpedia. Retrieved December 13, 2023, from https://dbpedia.org/page/SCO_Group,_Inc._v._International_Business_Machines_Corp.

Stocker, S. H. (2020, July 31). *Linux Dominates Supercomputing*. Network World. Retrieved December 13, 2023, from https://www.networkworld.com/article/3568616/linux-dominates-supercomputing.html

https://www.terra.money

Tribler - Privacy Using our Tor-inspired Onion Routing. Retrieved December 13, 2023, from https://www.tribler.org/index.html

Usage Statistics and Market Share of Linux for Websites, December 2023. (n.d.). W3Techs. Retrieved December 13, 2023, from https://w3techs.com/technologies/details/os-linux

Vaughan, S. (2021, August 30). *That Linux Lawsuit: 20 Years Later, SCO vs IBM May Finally Be Ending*. ZDNET. Retrieved December 13, 2023, from https://www.zdnet.com/article/after-almost-20-years-the-sco-vs-ibm-lawsuit-may-finally-be-ending/

Weiss, T. (n.d.). *SCO Sues IBM for $1B in Intellectual Property Fight*. Computerworld. Retrieved December 13, 2023, from https://www.computerworld.com/article/2580723/sco-sues-ibm-for--1b-in-intellectual-property-fight.html

Chapter 2

Why Is Decentralization the Need of the Hour?

Sam Ghosh

The dot-com crash of the late 1990s marked a turning point, leading to the emergence of Web 2.0. This era is defined by user-generated content, expansive social networks, and a promise of democratization.

Despite advocating for decentralization, Web 2.0 unintentionally resulted in unprecedented centralization, reshaping the digital landscape and society in various ways.

Web 2.0 emphasized user participation and content sharing, leading to the rise of social media, content-sharing platforms, and online communities. Despite appearing democratic, these platforms relied heavily on centralized control and data accumulation.

Web 2.0 companies heavily relied on extensive user data accumulation, creating detailed profiles for targeted advertising and revenue maximization. Tech giants likely have more information about us than even our closest friends do. This centralized gathering of personal information not only raised privacy concerns but also granted these companies significant market and political influence.

With advanced algorithms, these platforms can shape news, opinions, and public conversation, potentially influencing political outcomes.

The implications are significant, prompting ethical and societal questions about the impact of such influence.

2.1 Rise of Large Centralized Architectures

The consolidation of vast amounts of data and networks, while profitable, poses risks. Centralized systems, as seen in events like the Cambridge Analytica scandal, are susceptible to breaches with far-reaching consequences, compromising the privacy and security of millions.

DOI: 10.4324/9781003507352-2

Centralization poses security risks and presents challenges in terms of availability, latency, and regulatory compliance. Relying on centralized networks can magnify the impact of disruptions, prompting the need for strict measures to ensure data protection and user privacy in response to emerging regulatory concerns.

In summary, Web 2.0, while promoting connectivity and user empowerment, concentrated power and information in the hands of a few tech giants. This has far-reaching implications across social, political, and technical contexts, giving rise to concerns about privacy, security, and the potential manipulation of public discourse.

CAMBRIDGE ANALYTICA SCANDAL

The Cambridge Analytica scandal marked a pivotal moment that highlighted substantial worries regarding data privacy and manipulation in the digital era.

In 2013, researcher Aleksandr Kogan developed a personality quiz app called "thisisyourdigitallife," operating on Facebook. The app not only collected data from quiz participants but also harvested information about their Facebook friends without obtaining explicit consent. This resulted in Cambridge Analytica gaining access to the personal data of millions of Facebook users.

Following this, Cambridge Analytica utilized the acquired data to construct detailed psychological profiles of users. These profiles were then employed for targeted political advertising and influence campaigns, notably during the 2016 US presidential election and the Brexit referendum in the UK.

The scandal prompted significant ethical and legal concerns about data privacy, user consent, and the unchecked use of personal information for political purposes. It led to heightened scrutiny and calls for more robust regulations concerning data protection and the responsible use of personal information by technology companies and political entities.

Let us understand the problems that arise due to large centralized architectures one by one.

2.1.1 Regulatory Challenges

The rise of centralized technology architectures, especially in the context of data storage, has created regulatory challenges. Concentrated pools of data within tech conglomerates raise privacy and security concerns while complicating regulatory efforts to ensure responsible data handling and user protection.

Centralized data storage poses regulatory challenges exemplified by the European Union's General Data Protection Regulation (GDPR) enacted in May 2018. While designed to establish data protection and privacy rules, the GDPR's implementation revealed specific issues associated with centralized tech architectures.

Enforcing regulations like GDPR in centralized systems is challenging due to compliance complexity. The extensive collection and processing of user data by centralized platforms make achieving full compliance difficult, leading to increased administrative burdens and costs for companies.

Further, the global nature of centralized data storage systems poses challenges for cross-border data flow and compliance with international protection standards. Global tech companies, operating in various countries, face a regulatory puzzle as they navigate legal complexities to comply with diverse international standards across multiple jurisdictions.

Dealing with data localization mandates adds complexity to centralized systems, as countries enforce laws requiring data storage within specific regions. This complexity arises in architectures optimized for efficiency across various regions, posing a challenge in meeting both data localization and privacy standards. It often necessitates adjustments to systems and protocols.

Another substantial hurdle for regulators is ensuring transparency and accountability within centralized systems. These platforms store large amounts of personal data, making it difficult to provide users with full visibility and control. Enforcing consent, data portability, and the "right to be forgotten" principles requires effective mechanisms within the complex structures of centralized systems.

The "right to be forgotten" is a privacy concept that allows individuals to request the removal or deletion of their personal information from online platforms or search engine results.

Anyway, regulators are refining strategies to adapt to the challenges of centralized data storage. Companies are also investing in compliance mechanisms and technologies to simplify adherence to data protection regulations while maintaining the functionality and convenience of centralized systems.

Now, apart from data centralization, these platforms often overreach to diverse industries.

Technology companies are not just technology companies anymore.

Accumulation of user data allowed tech platforms to expand services, leading to diverse offerings such as embedded payments in messaging apps (e.g. WeBank offers loans through WeChat and QQ app), payment/e-commerce firms venturing into banking, and edTech companies providing financial services (e.g. Byju's).

This hotchpotch leads to enormous regulatory complexity, especially when these tech companies start to enter highly regulated sectors such as financial services or healthcare.

In the recent past, we saw many payment companies enter financial services. At the outset, these businesses may look similar but they are fundamentally different businesses. Payment is a cash-flow-based business and financial services are balance-sheet-based businesses. Payment companies rarely have to deal with asset quality, a concept at the core of financial services companies taking deposits and offering loans.

So, when a payment company starts accepting deposits and giving loans, it may become very complex to regulate these entities. These companies may fail to keep the payment and the financial services entities isolated as observed in the case of India's PayTm. In February 2024, PayTm came under attack from the Indian Central Bank (RBI) for failing to keep their Payment Bank and other entities isolated.

The point is that centralization can result in enormous complexity from a regulatory perspective.

2.1.2 Security Issues

Centralized technology architectures, while enhancing connectivity and efficiency, pose security challenges due to the accumulation of vast amounts of data, making them susceptible to security breaches with serious consequences.

Data breaches in centralized systems, exemplified by the Equifax incident in 2017 affecting over 148 million Americans, raise significant concerns. The compromise of sensitive information led to substantial financial penalties, with Equifax settling for nearly $700 million.

The Yahoo breach in 2013, exposing over 3 billion user accounts and significant personal data, highlighted the far-reaching consequences of centralized system vulnerabilities. This incident impacted Yahoo's market value and led to substantial financial losses.

Cyber attacks on centralized systems, like the large-scale attack on Amazon Web Services (AWS) in 2020, caused major service disruptions, impacting websites and applications dependent on AWS. This outage incurred substantial financial losses, emphasizing the vulnerability of centralized cloud architectures and the necessity for improved security measures and contingency plans.

Cybersecurity Ventures estimated that global cybercrimes amounted to a staggering US $6 trillion in annual costs by 2021, with a significant portion linked to breaches and attacks on centralized systems.

2.1.3 Availability Issues

Centralized technology architectures have redefined connectivity and efficiency in the digital ecosystem. However, the concentration of critical infrastructure and services within these centralized systems has posed significant challenges in terms of availability, leading to instances of system outages with considerable financial repercussions.

System outages are a common challenge in centralized architectures. For instance, in 2017, Amazon Web Services (AWS) suffered a major outage, disrupting numerous websites and applications. The downtime, lasting hours, caused significant financial losses for affected companies, estimated to reach millions of dollars per hour.

Another substantial outage occurred in 2019, affecting Google Cloud services. The outage disrupted various Google services, including Gmail, YouTube, and Google Drive. This interruption not only inconvenienced users but also had financial implications for businesses that rely on these services.

The financial implications of these outages are substantial. While exact figures may not always be publicly disclosed, the general understanding is that such disruptions can cost companies millions of dollars per hour of downtime. The cumulative losses incurred due to these outages on centralized platforms are significant and can profoundly impact the revenue and operations of businesses reliant on these architectures.

To mitigate the risks associated with centralized platforms, businesses are adopting a multi-cloud approach, utilizing services from multiple cloud providers for redundancy and flexibility. However, this strategy doesn't eliminate the risk of a single point of failure, as the management systems coordinating multiple clouds could themselves become vulnerable, leading to widespread outages.

2.1.4 Disaster Recovery Inefficiencies

Recovering from system failures is a challenge for centralized architectures, often due to vulnerabilities like single points of failure. A single point of failure (SPOF) is a component in a system whose failure would cause the entire system to stop functioning. This susceptibility results in prolonged downtime, impacting productivity, revenue, and customer trust. The complexity of restoring these systems introduces inefficiencies, delays, and data loss risks, and limits scalability during recovery.

Decentralized architectures, characterized by distributed data and services, provide advantages in disaster recovery by minimizing the impact of failures and enabling faster, more resilient recovery.

2.1.5 Data Theft and Data Loss

Centralized architectures, consolidating data in one location, become attractive targets for cybercriminals aiming to steal sensitive information, as illustrated by the Yahoo data breach in 2013, compromising over 3 billion user accounts.

Breaches in centralized systems can go undetected for extended periods due to the complexity of monitoring large datasets. The Marriott data breach (2018), which exposed sensitive guest data, remained undetected for several years, emphasizing the difficulty in promptly identifying and mitigating breaches in centralized environments.

2.1.6 Section 230 and Handling of User-generated Content

Section 230 of the Communications Decency Act of 1996 is a subject of ongoing debate regarding online content moderation and tech platforms' responsibilities. Originally aimed at promoting a free and open internet, it has been criticized for allegedly shielding tech companies from liability for user-generated content. Recent concerns about its misuse by tech giants have sparked renewed attention to the controversy.

Section 230, often referred to as the *"26 words that created the internet,"* consists of two key provisions. The first part grants immunity to online platforms from being treated as the publisher or speaker of user-generated content. This means that platforms like social media sites are not held legally responsible for the content posted by their users. The second part protects these platforms from liability when they make good-faith efforts to moderate or remove content deemed objectionable.

Critics argue that some tech platforms have exploited the protections offered by Section 230 to avoid accountability for hosting harmful or false information. The misuse of Section 230 has been particularly evident in cases involving the spread of misinformation, hate speech, and other harmful content on various online platforms.

One notable example is the role of social media in disseminating misinformation during elections and public health crises. Critics argue that these platforms have not done enough to combat the spread of false information, citing Section 230 as a shield that allows them to escape legal consequences.

In 2020, the Department of Justice (DOJ) scrutinized Section 230, expressing concerns about its broad interpretation and potential misuse by tech platforms. The report recognizes the original intent to encourage online content moderation but emphasizes the necessity for a balanced approach that doesn't impede free speech or innovation.

The DOJ recommends refining Section 230's language to hold tech platforms accountable for their actions, aiming for a balance that protects users from harmful content without stifling the free exchange of ideas in the digital space.

But, it is not only the limitations of centralized architectures that necessitate the rise of decentralized architectures but also the rise of decentralized business models.

2.2 Rise of Decentralized Business Models

In recent times, various decentralized business models, such as the User Generated Gaming economy, peer-to-peer (P2P) e-commerce, ride-sharing, accommodation sharing, P2P lending, and gig economy platforms, have emerged, reshaping industries. These models revolutionize the way business is conducted and communities interact. However, centralized architectures present barriers that hinder these business models to achieve their full potential.

Let us briefly discuss some of these decentralized business models. We will have a detailed discussion on decentralized business models in the *Industry Case Studies* chapter.

2.2.1 User-generated Gaming Economy

Traditional gaming platforms, such as Steam or Apple's App Store, maintain control over content creation and distribution, restricting creative freedom for developers. This centralized approach affects the direct relationship between creators and players.

On the other hand, platforms like Roblox provide users the ability to create and share games, experiences, and items within the platform, offering higher flexibility and autonomy. Game developers on Roblox have significant creative freedom compared to centralized platforms.

Yet, is Roblox completely decentralized?

Roblox operates on a centralized architecture. Compare that with platforms like Decentraland which offer a relatively more decentralized framework with the use of blockchain technology. Here, developers have increased autonomy and players have ownership over in-game assets, fostering more engaged and collaborative gaming experiences.

In Roblox's centralized architecture, asset ownership depends on the platform's availability and governance. Users create and own assets within the centralized system. However, potential platform outages or changes may impact asset ownership and access until the platform's functionality is restored.

Decentraland, built on the Ethereum blockchain, operates in a decentralized manner across numerous nodes. The distributed nature of Ethereum ensures that data, including asset ownership, is replicated across nodes, enhancing resilience and availability.

2.2.2 Creator Economy Platforms

The creator economy is a dynamic environment where individuals leverage digital platforms to produce, monetize, and share content, skills, or products. Creators, ranging from artists to influencers, use their unique talents to connect with audiences, earn revenue, and build personal brands.

The rise of the creator economy is fueled by technological progress like social media and online marketplaces, enabling creators to connect directly with their audiences, circumvent traditional intermediaries, and generate independent income streams.

The creator economy's impact on the music industry signifies a significant shift, empowering individual artists with direct access to audiences and revenue streams, disrupting the traditional dominance of major labels and intermediaries.

The creator economy, supported by platforms like SoundCloud, has revolutionized artists' interactions with fans, offering greater autonomy and control over their careers and revenue streams. Through the direct-to-consumer model, artists have diversified their revenue streams, incorporating merchandise sales, live performances, streaming, and direct fan support via platforms like Patreon.

But, platforms like SoundCloud do not represent the pinnacle of decentralized music distribution rather decentralized platforms like Audius do.

Audius is a decentralized music streaming platform that allows artists to upload and monetize their music directly, offering them greater control and potential for increased revenue compared to traditional streaming platforms.

Let us compare SoundCloud and Audius.

SoundCloud uses a centralized architecture to store and serve content from its own servers, while Audius operates on a decentralized infrastructure, using blockchain technology to host and distribute music across a network of nodes, offering a more distributed system compared to SoundCloud's centralized approach.

Audius seeks to empower artists with greater control and increased revenue shares by leveraging blockchain technology to facilitate direct relationships between artists and listeners, minimizing the need for intermediaries.

SoundCloud provides various plans, including free and subscription-based models, enabling artists to monetize their music through subscriptions, advertising, and a direct monetization program for creators.

On the other hand, Audius uses its native token, AUDIO, to facilitate transactions and incentivize users. Artists can earn AUDIO tokens by engaging with the platform and accumulating a following.

But, it is not only the business model, the use of the Ethereum (and Solana) blockchain brings various advantages to Audius as well.

Audius utilizes blockchains for transparency, decentralization, and security in its music-sharing platform. Smart contracts automate crucial functions like royalty payments and copyright management, ensuring fair compensation for artists and reducing disputes

Audius employs content nodes to store audio files, while Ethereum manages metadata and serves as a decentralized content ledger, securely recording ownership changes and transactions. Discovery nodes enhance content discovery, and Ethereum's decentralization eliminates reliance on a central authority.

Audius' native token, AUDIO, operates on Ethereum and a wrapped version on Solana. It ensures network security, grants access to exclusive features, and supports decentralized governance. Node Operators stake (lock their) AUDIO tokens to secure the network, with larger stakes increasing their node's chances of being used by fans and artists. AUDIO also serves as collateral for additional artist tools such as artist tokens, badges, and earnings multipliers. Staking AUDIO gives users governance power, with each token staked equaling one vote. Blockchain technology, as utilized in platforms like Audius, guarantees the immutability and perpetual accessibility of ownership and IP records, even in the absence of the platform. This enables a cross-platform ecosystem where ownership and IP rights are recognized and validated across different services, fostering transparency and fairness for artists and content creators.

2.3 Economic Cost of Centralization

So, we have discussed how large centralized architectures introduce various challenges such as security challenges, availability issues, and data loss. Each of these challenges comes with a price tag.

Beyond internal organizational costs, there are additional economic implications in the form of negative externalities. These include regulatory hurdles related to privacy, data security challenges, socio-political concerns exemplified by incidents like the Cambridge Analytica Scandal, and the concentration of market power leading to the emergence of tech monopolies.

The last point deserves a little bit of discussion before we move forward.

Large tech players' centralization of data has resulted in a concentration of market power, often leading to the dominance of a few major players. This reduced competition can hamper innovation and restrict choices for consumers.

Data-driven market monopolization exacerbates regulatory challenges, security and privacy issues, and other aforementioned concerns.

The dominance of tech giants in the market hampers efficiency and deters smaller, innovative companies from market access, given the overpowering presence of established players.

Anyways, all these issues have economic costs associated with them and aggregate of all these costs would be the cost of centralization.

Understanding the economic cost of centralization is crucial for making an economic case for decentralization, as corporate decisions are primarily influenced by economic considerations.

What matters more is not the precise costs but the assessment of whether they are significant or not.

Another important point is that many costs may not be explicitly in monetary terms such as regulatory and political costs. However, these negative externalities show themselves as long-term compliance costs, legal costs, increased marketing costs, and lobbying costs.

Anyway, let us dive in.

2.3.1 Direct Economic Costs

2.3.1.1 Security Cost

Let us start with the security-related costs. The security-related costs of centralization include more than just economic impacts from breaches – they also include expenses for securing databases, compensating affected users for damages, fines, etc.

As per IBM Cost of a Data Breach Report 2023, the average cost of a data breach in 2023 was around US $4.45 million. This cost included costs related to lost business and post-breach responses. A staggering 82% of data breaches involved data stored in the cloud. This report also mentioned that 20% of organizations that experienced a data breach paid at least US $250,000 in fines.

At the same time, security budgets as a share of IT budgets are increasing steadily from 8.6% in 2020 to 11.6% in 2023 as per the IANS Security Budget Benchmark Report. Interestingly, tech firms spend the most on cybersecurity (19.4%) as a percentage of IT spending. So, the security-related costs for databases are significant and claiming more and more from the IT budgets.

In 2023, the average *cost per record* involved in a data breach was US $165, up from US $141 in 2017, according to the IBM report mentioned above. This metric is crucial as it reflects the financial impact of a data breach on an organization. The rising cost per record indicates an intensification of the overall economic impact of data breaches over time. Larger database breaches, compromising more records, significantly contribute to the financial burden on affected organizations.

Please note, that we did not consider the externalities of such security breaches here. These security breaches may affect user data and affect the users in many ways. Although fines may capture some cost related to these externalities, fines are often paid only for a small number of cases and after long legal battles. So, the economic cost for the users due to these security breaches can be much higher and may not be represented in financial terms right after the breach.

Okay, now, let us look into the economic cost of availability issues.

2.3.1.2 Availability Issues

As per a report from Ponemon Institute, the average cost per minute of unplanned outages is around US $8,851 as of 2016. This comes to around US $530,000 per hour.

This cost obviously varies from one industry to another. For some industries, cloud downtime may not impact the core business but for some industries (e.g. streaming services) an outage may not only cause revenue loss but can also cause long-term reputational damage. Who wants to subscribe to an OTT platform that is frequently not accessible?

Now, availability issues are not only about outages but also about high latency. While the adverse economic effects of outages are readily apparent immediately following an incident, latency inflicts gradual, long-term harm to the business through poor user experience.

Now, let us discuss the economic impact of data theft and data loss.

2.3.1.3 Cost of Data Theft and Data Loss

Data loss refers to the unintentional or accidental destruction, deletion, corruption, or inability to access and retrieve data from a storage system. Data loss, which can happen across personal devices, corporate networks, and data centers, carries significant consequences. It includes the loss of valuable information, operational disruptions, financial losses, and harm to an individual's or organization's reputation.

Data loss can result from various factors such as accidental deletion, unauthorized access, hardware failure, virus attacks, malware, natural disasters, and power outages.

According to a recent Verizon report, minor instances of data loss involving around 100 lost or compromised records result in an average cost ranging from US $18,120 to US $35,730 for businesses. The study also revealed that large-scale data loss involving over 100 million records incurs an average cost ranging from US $5 million to US $15.6 million.

Obviously, the economic cost of data loss varies across industries – for instance, the loss of media data can be critical for the streaming industry.

2.3.2 Indirect Economic Costs

2.3.2.1 Overview

Okay, now let us discuss the indirect economic impacts, i.e. the negative externalities.

These economic costs are borne by the society as a whole. Part of these economic costs might find their way back to the organization through compliance costs, litigations, lobbying costs, etc.

In 2019, the Federal Trade Commission imposed a staggering $5 billion penalty on Facebook, along with sweeping new restrictions on its business operations and multiple mandated compliance requirements. These penalties and restrictions were caused by Facebook's allegedly undermining of consumer choices.

In another case, Facebook settled a class action lawsuit at US $550 million. The lawsuit was regarding Facebook's use of facial recognition to collect and store biometric data without proper notice and consent from Facebook users in Illinois, US.

Centralized platforms, particularly social media platforms, have frequently invoked concerns regarding the safety of children. Leaked Meta documents reported by *The Guardian* indicate that approximately 100,000 children on Facebook and Instagram face daily online sexual harassment, including exposure to explicit images.

John Shehan, the head of the exploited children division at the National Center for Missing and Exploited Children, notes a significant surge in reports of child sexual abuse material on online platforms, escalating from 32 million in 2022 to a record high of over 36 million in 2023.

The implications of these findings are profound and have far-reaching consequences for our society.

2.3.2.2 Legal Framework for Data Protection and Privacy

Let us look into the provisions under various laws related to data protection and privacy etc.

2.3.2.2.1 General Data Protection Regulation (GDPR) – EU

GDPR, enforced since May 2018, imposes significant fines for non-compliance, with organizations facing penalties of up to €20 million or 4% of their global annual revenue, whichever is higher.

GDPR grants individuals in the EU enhanced rights over their personal data, including the right to access, rectify, and erase their data, as well as the right to data portability.

2.3.2.2.2 California Consumer Privacy Act (CCPA) – US

CCPA, established in 2020, imposes fines of up to US $7,500 for intentional violations and US $2,500 for unintentional violations. Additionally, consumers have the right to statutory damages in specific data breach instances.

CCPA grants California residents the right to be informed about collected personal information, to have their data deleted, and to opt out of the sale of their data.

2.3.2.2.3 Brazilian General Data Protection Law (LGPD) – Brazil

LGPD, enacted in September 2020, imposes penalties of up to 2% of an organization's revenue in Brazil, with a maximum penalty of BRL 50 million per violation.

LGPD grants individuals rights similar to those in GDPR, allowing them to access, correct, and delete their personal data.

2.3.2.2.4 Personal Information Protection Law (PIPL) – China

The Personal Information Protection Law (PIPL), which came into effect in November 2021, imposes fines of up to ¥50 million or 5% of an organization's annual revenue.

PIPL provides individuals in China with rights over their personal information, including the right to know, delete, and opt out of automated decision-making.

2.3.2.2.5 Data Protection Act 2018 – UK

The UK's Data Protection Act incorporates GDPR standards. The Information Commissioner's Office (ICO) can impose fines of up to £17.5 million or 4% of global turnover.

Similar to GDPR, UK citizens have rights over their personal data, including the right to access, correct, and delete information.

2.3.2.2.6 Personal Data Protection Act (PDPA) – Singapore

Under the PDPA, organizations in Singapore may incur fines up to 10% of their annual turnover or the higher of S $10 million, whichever is greater.

The PDPA provides individuals with rights to access, correct, and withdraw consent for the use of their personal data.

2.3.2.3 Regulatory Actions

Now, as mentioned before, centralized, data-driven market dominance can lead to inefficient and uncompetitive market economies.

Regulators globally have taken actions and conducted investigations against large centralized tech companies, focusing on allegations of uncompetitive behavior, data misuse, and concerns about centralized market power.

2.3.2.3.1 US Senate Judiciary Committee – Meta, TikTok, X, and other Social Media Companies

On 31st January 2024, CEOs of Meta, TikTok, X (formerly Twitter), and other social media companies faced the Senate Judiciary Committee and were asked to testify as lawmakers and parents grew increasingly concerned about the effects of social media on children.

The issues raised include the exploitation of children, addictive features, connections to suicide and eating disorders, unrealistic beauty standards, and bullying. Parents of victims held up pictures of their deceased children during the event.

In a tense session, the lawmakers raised whether Section 230 (of the Communications Decency Act of 1996) needed to be repealed.

2.3.2.3.2 European Union (EU) – Google

The European Commission has undertaken numerous anti-trust investigations targeting Google. Notably, in 2017, Google faced a €2.42 billion fine for purportedly prioritizing its own comparison shopping service over competitors in search results. Subsequent fines were imposed in 2018 and 2019 for additional antitrust violations.

2.3.2.3.3 United States – Facebook

In December 2020, the US Federal Trade Commission (FTC) and a coalition of state attorneys general filed antitrust lawsuits against Facebook, alleging anti-competitive practices and seeking remedies such as divestiture of acquired companies (Instagram and WhatsApp).

2.3.2.3.4 United States – Google

In October 2020, the US Department of Justice (DOJ) filed an antitrust lawsuit against Google, alleging the company unlawfully maintained a monopoly in search and search advertising. The lawsuit targets anti-competitive practices tied to agreements with device manufacturers and browser developers.

2.3.2.3.5 Australia – Digital Platforms Inquiry

In 2019, Australia conducted a Digital Platforms Inquiry investigating the market power of major platforms like Google and Facebook. The inquiry led to proposed legislation to address concerns about the bargaining power of these platforms in negotiations with news publishers.

2.3.2.3.6 China – Alibaba

In December 2020, the Chinese government launched an anti-trust investigation into Alibaba Group Holding, probing allegations of anti-competitive practices, including forced exclusivity agreements with merchants.

2.3.2.3.7 India – Competition Commission of India (CCI)

The CCI in India has initiated antitrust investigations into major tech companies, including Google and Amazon, focusing on allegations of abuse of dominance, anti-competitive agreements, and unfair business practices.

2.3.2.3.8 South Korea – Google

In 2021, South Korea's antitrust regulator, the Korea Fair Trade Commission (KFTC), fined Google ₩207 billion (approximately $177 million) for allegedly abusing its market dominance in the mobile operating system market.

So, the explicit costs and costs related to economic externalities for the centralized approach can be quite significant.

Now, the question arises -

2.3.3 How Can Decentralization Help?

Can decentralization help us deal with all these costs? We will look into this question in a later chapter after we understand the intricacies of Web3. Note that, the use of Web3 for decentralization may also introduce various costs. So, the discussion will be interesting.

In this chapter, we discussed the technical, business, and economic rationale for moving from centralized systems to decentralized systems.

Now, Subhasis will discuss traditional distributed architectures in the next chapter.

Bibliography

Antitrust: Commission Fines Google €2.42 Billion for Abusing Dominance as Search Engine by Giving Illegal Advantage to Own Comparison Shopping Service - Factsheet. (n.d.). European Commission. Retrieved December 13, 2023, from https://ec.europa.eu/commission/presscorner/detail/es/MEMO_17_1785

Audius.co. Retrieved December 13, 2023, from https://audius.co

Audius, Inc. (n.d.). *Welcome to the Audius Technical Documentation!* Audius Docs. Retrieved February 26, 2024, from https://docs.audius.org/welcome

Cadwalladr, C., & Graham, E. (2018, March 17). *Revealed: 50 Million Facebook Profiles Harvested for Cambridge Analytica in Major Data Breach.* The Guardian. Retrieved December 13, 2023, from https://www.theguardian.com/news/2018/mar/17/cambridge-analytica-facebook-influence-us-election

California Consumer Privacy Act of 2020. (2019, September 23). California Department of Justice. Retrieved December 13, 2023, from https://oag.ca.gov/system/files/initiatives/pdfs/19-0017%20%28Consumer%20Privacy%20%29.pdf

China Launches Antitrust Probe into Tech Giant Alibaba. (2023, March 2). Reuters. Retrieved December 13, 2023, from https://www.reuters.com/article/us-china-antgroup/china-launches-antitrust-probe-into-tech-giant-alibaba-idUSKBN28Y05T/

COMMUNICATIONS DECENCY ACT, 47 U.S.C. §230. Retrieved December 25, 2023, from http://www.columbia.edu/~mr2651/ecommerce3/2nd/statutes/CommunicationsDecencyAct.pdf

Cost of a Data Breach 2023. (n.d.). IBM. Retrieved December 13, 2023, from https://www.ibm.com/reports/data-breach

2015 Cost of Data Center Outages FINAL 5. (n.d.). Vertiv. Retrieved December 13, 2023, from https://www.vertiv.com/globalassets/documents/reports/2016-cost-of-data-center-outages-11-11_51190_1.pdf

Cybercrime Damages $6 Trillion by 2021. (2023, November 9). Cybercrime Magazine. Retrieved December 13, 2023, from https://cybersecurityventures.com/annual-cybercrime-report-2017/

Data Protection Act 2018. (n.d.). Data Protection Act 2018. Retrieved December 13, 2023, from https://www.legislation.gov.uk/ukpga/2018/12/contents/enacted

Department of Justice's Review of Section 230 oF The Communications Decency Act of 1996. (n.d.). Department of Justice. Retrieved December 25, 2023, from https://www.justice.gov/archives/ag/department-justice-s-review-section-230-communications-decency-act-1996

Digital Platforms Inquiry – Final Report. (2019, June 20). ACCC. Retrieved December 13, 2023, from https://www.accc.gov.au/system/files/Digital%20platforms%20inquiry%20-%20final%20report.pdf

EPIC - Equifax Data Breach. (n.d.). EPIC. Retrieved December 13, 2023, from https://archive.epic.org/privacy/data-breach/equifax/

Facebook Biometric Information Privacy Litigation. Retrieved December 13, 2023, from https://www.facebookbipaclassaction.com

Famous DDoS Attacks | Biggest DDoS Attacks. (n.d.). Cloudflare. Retrieved December 13, 2023, from https://www.cloudflare.com/en-in/learning/ddos/famous-ddos-attacks/

Fines / Penalties - General Data Protection Regulation. (n.d.). GDPR. Retrieved December 13, 2023, from https://gdpr-info.eu/issues/fines-penalties/

FTC Imposes $5 Billion Penalty and Sweeping New Privacy Restrictions on Facebook. (2019, July 24). Federal Trade Commission. Retrieved December 13, 2023, from https://www.ftc.gov/news-events/news/press-releases/2019/07/ftc-imposes-5-billion-penalty-sweeping-new-privacy-restrictions-facebook

FTC Sues Facebook for Illegal Monopolization. (2020, December 9). Federal Trade Commission. Retrieved December 13, 2023, from https://www.ftc.gov/news-events/news/press-releases/2020/12/ftc-sues-facebook-illegal-monopolization

Games - App Store Downloads on iTunes. (n.d.). App Store. Retrieved December 13, 2023, from https://apps.apple.com/us/genre/ios-games/id6014

General Data Protection Regulation (GDPR) – Official Legal Text. Retrieved December 13, 2023, from https://gdpr-info.eu

Google Cloud Service Health. (n.d.). Google Cloud Service Health. Retrieved December 13, 2023, from https://status.cloud.google.com/incidents/GC8EdsbcceGPryfoYfxy

The Guardian. (2024, January 18). *Meta Documents Show 100000 Children Sexually Harassed Daily on its Platforms.* The Guardian. Retrieved February 7, 2024, from https://www.theguardian.com/technology/2024/jan/18/instagram-facebook-child-sexual-harassment

Hosch, W. L. (n.d.). *Web 2.0 | Definition & Examples.* Britannica. Retrieved December 13, 2023, from https://www.britannica.com/topic/Web-20

Isaac, M. (2020, January 29). *Facebook to Pay $550 Million to Settle Facial Recognition Suit (Published 2020).* The New York Times. Retrieved December 13, 2023, from https://www.nytimes.com/2020/01/29/technology/facebook-privacy-lawsuit-earnings.html

It's Time to Update Section 230. (2021, August 12). Harvard Business Review. Retrieved December 25, 2023, from https://hbr.org/2021/08/its-time-to-update-section-230

Justice Department Sues Google for Monopolizing Digital Advertising Technologies. (2023, January 24). Department of Justice. Retrieved December 13, 2023, from https://www.justice.gov/opa/pr/justice-department-sues-google-monopolizing-digital-advertising-technologies

Lei Geral de Proteção de Dados Pessoais (LGPD). (2018, August 14). Planalto. Retrieved December 13, 2023, from http://www.planalto.gov.br/ccivil_03/_ato2015-2018/2018/lei/L13709compilado.htm

Mainland's Personal Information Protection Law. (n.d.). PCPD. Retrieved December 13, 2023, from https://www.pcpd.org.hk/english/data_privacy_law/mainland_law/mainland_law.html

The New York Times. (2018, April 4). *Cambridge Analytica and Facebook: The Scandal and the Fallout So Far (Published 2018).* The New York Times. Retrieved February 13, 2024, from https://www.nytimes.com/2018/04/04/us/politics/cambridge-analytica-scandal-fallout.html

PBS. (2024, January 31). *WATCH: Meta, TikTok and Other Social Media CEOs Testify in Senate Hearing on Child Exploitation.* PBS. Retrieved February 3, 2024, from https://www.pbs.org/newshour/politics/watch-live-ceos-of-meta-tiktok-x-and-other-social-media-companies-testify-in-senate-hearing

PDPA Overview - Singapore. (n.d.). Personal Data Protection Commission. Retrieved December 13, 2023, from https://www.pdpc.gov.sg/overview-of-pdpa/the-legislation/personal-data-protection-act

Penalties. (n.d.). ICO. Retrieved December 13, 2023, from https://ico.org.uk/for-organisations/law-enforcement/guide-to-le-processing/penalties/

Perlroth, N. (2017, October 3). *All 3 Billion Yahoo Accounts Were Affected by 2013 Attack (Published 2017)*. The New York Times. Retrieved December 13, 2023, from https://www.nytimes.com/2017/10/03/technology/yahoo-hack-3-billion-users.html

Public Version COMPETITION COMMISSION OF INDIA Case No. 07 of 2020 In re: XYZ (Confidential) Informant And Alphabet Inc. Oppos. (2022, October 25). CCI. Retrieved December 13, 2023, from https://www.cci.gov.in/images/antitrustorder/en/order1666696935.pdf

Reuters. (2024, February 8). *India c.bank Clampdown on Paytm Payments Bank Followed Persistent Non-compliance*. Reuters. Retrieved February 13, 2024, from https://www.reuters.com/world/india/india-cbanks-regulatory-action-paytm-payments-bank-due-persistent-non-compliance-2024-02-08/

Roblox. Retrieved December 13, 2023, from https://www.roblox.com

Rock, T. (n.d.). *The Truth About Data Loss in 2023*. Invenio IT. Retrieved December 13, 2023, from https://invenioit.com/continuity/cost-of-data-loss/

Satariano, A. (2018, November 30). *Marriott Hacking Exposes Data of Up to 500 Million Guests (Published 2018)*. The New York Times. Retrieved December 13, 2023, from https://www.nytimes.com/2018/11/30/business/marriott-data-breach.html

2023 Security Budget Benchmark Summary Report. (2023, October 2). IANS Research. Retrieved December 13, 2023, from https://cdn.iansresearch.com/Files/Marketing/2023SurveyContent/IANS+ArticoSearch-2023SecurityBudgetBenchmarkSummaryReport.pdf

South Korean Antitrust Regulator Fines Google $177M for Abusing Market Dominance. (2021, September 14). TechCrunch. Retrieved December 13, 2023, from https://techcrunch.com/2021/09/14/south-korean-antitrust-regulator-fines-google-177m-for-abusing-market-dominance/

Stream and Listen to Music Online for Free with SoundCloud. Retrieved December 13, 2023, from https://soundcloud.com

Summary of the Amazon S3 Service Disruption in the Northern Virginia (US-EAST-1) Region. (2017, February 28). AWS. Retrieved December 13, 2023, from https://aws.amazon.com/message/41926/

Vox.com. (2018, March 17). *Here's How Facebook Allowed Cambridge Analytica to Get Data for 50 Million Users*. Vox. Retrieved February 13, 2024, from https://www.vox.com/2018/3/17/17134072/facebook-cambridge-analytica-trump-explained-user-data

The Washington Post & Lima, C. (2024, January 28). *The Internet's CSAM Problem Keeps Getting Worse. Here's Why*. The Washington Post. Retrieved February 7, 2024, from https://www.washingtonpost.com/technology/2024/01/28/csam-ncmec-senate-hearing-child-porn/

Welcome to Decentraland. Retrieved December 13, 2023, from https://decentraland.org

Welcome to Steam. Retrieved December 13, 2023, from https://store.steampowered.com

Wiewiórowski, W. (n.d.). *Rights of the Individual | European Data Protection Supervisor*. European Data Protection Supervisor. Retrieved December 13, 2023, from https://edps.europa.eu/data-protection/our-work/subjects/rights-individual_en

Chapter 3

Decentralization without Blockchains

Subhasis Gorai

3.1 Traditional Distributed Systems

3.1.1 Introduction to Distributed Systems

By "traditional," I refer to distributed systems deployed in controlled environments such as private data centers or cloud infrastructures maintained by hyperscalers. This topic is extensive and intricate – a single chapter cannot possibly cover all its aspects. However, we will strive to keep this section relevant, concise, and informative.

First of all, why do we even need distributed systems? We need distributed systems because the end users of these systems are distributed and we need to make the system accessible to end users. Secondly, as the problem size and complexity increase, it becomes really hard to scale up a single system, i.e., the hardware upgrade of a single machine to solve the problem either does not exist, or the cost becomes prohibitively high. In such cases, it is judicious to employ a farm of mid-range, commodity hardware as long as the maintenance cost can be kept at bay by developing useful fault-tolerant software abstractions.

The type of distributed systems we are discussing here are shared-nothing systems. Each machine or virtual machine running the application is called a node and they are connected to an IP network (often Ethernet). The network is the only way those machines can communicate – each machine has its own processor, memory, and disk. We distribute the workload across these nodes. The shared-nothing approach has gained significant popularity in constructing internet services. Its appeal lies in its cost-effectiveness, as it eliminates the need for specialized hardware, utilizes readily available cloud computing services, and ensures robust reliability by employing redundancy across multiple geographically dispersed data centers.

DOI: 10.4324/9781003507352-3

Apart from shared-nothing, there are also shared-anything and shared-disk architectures. In a shared-anything (often more accurately termed "Shared Everything") architecture, all nodes in the system share access to all resources, such as CPUs, memory, and storage. In a shared-disk architecture, multiple nodes share a common storage infrastructure (disk or storage area network).

We need to understand that distributed systems are a significant paradigm shift from stand-alone computers. A single computer presents an idealized system model that operates with mathematical perfection that abstracts the fuzzy physical reality on which they are built – the computation outcomes from them are always deterministic. This does not remain the same when they are assembled as part of a distributed system, mainly due to the following reasons,

1. Flaky networks – packets could be arbitrarily delayed, dropped, or reordered.
2. Unreliable clocks due to drifting and syncing issues, non-availability of shared clocks, and shared memory only add to the complexity.
3. Nodes can sporadically and independently fail or be non-responsive for an indefinite period due to process pauses, context switching, etc.

Irrespective of the functional requirements of the system, reliability, scalability, and maintainability remain the touchstones for evaluating the acceptability of any system we will design.

3.1.2 Key Aspects of Traditional Distributed Systems

Here we will discuss certain key aspects of traditional distributed systems.

3.1.2.1 Replication

In traditional distributed systems, replication might be required for multiple reasons,

1. Fault-tolerance, back up, disaster recovery, and high availability,
2. Lower latency by placing the data close to the end user,
3. Scalability, by supporting a higher volume of read operations by allowing reads on replicas.

Replication can be done synchronously or asynchronously with a configured replication factor. Replica placement is quite crucial for high availability and fault-tolerance.

Contextually I would like to mention that replication is not the only way to resurrect data in the event of data corruption or hard disk failures. There are other techniques, i.e., Reed-Solomon Code. There are multiple approaches for replication, i.e., single-leader, multi-leader, and leaderless replication. Each approach has its pros and cons with multi-leader and leaderless replication having an inherent need for conflict resolution.

3.1.2.2 Sharding

Sharding is a process of partitioning large datasets into smaller subsets which can be due to –

1. You have massive data that can't fit in a single machine's storage
2. Spread the data by assigning shards across multiple nodes, to spread the traffic across these nodes evenly to avoid hot spots.

Traffic routing is another critical aspect for sharded data, commonly distributed systems rely on a coordination service to keep track of this metadata up-to-date. Whatever replication concept we came across in the last section that was applicable to individual machines is also applicable to individual shards as well.

3.1.2.3 Data Consistency

When data is distributed, it's a mammoth challenge to keep the replicas consistent. Strong consistency models like Linearizability can hit performance or availability. Implementation of an efficient linearizable data system is not quite possible, as the latency of read/write would at least be proportional to the uncertainty of the delays in the network. We have to settle with something less, i.e., causal consistency, which is still better than eventual consistency which is very vague. It is more pragmatic for most of the practical use cases as well.

3.1.2.4 Fault-tolerant Consensus

In distributed systems, consensus means several nodes unanimously agreeing on something. When multiple nodes propose values, the consensus algorithm decides on one of those values. The consensus algorithm must satisfy the following properties,

1. Uniform agreement – every node agrees to the same value,
2. Integrity – no node decides twice,
3. Validity – if a node decides on a value v, then v was proposed by some node,
4. Termination – every non-failing node eventually decides on some value.

Termination is a liveness property, while the other three properties are safety properties. Consensus systems need the majority of the nodes to operate.

Mutual exclusion, leader election, multicast, and total-order broadcast are all instances of the broader problem of consensus.

3.1.2.5 A Few Words About Scalability

Universal Scalability Law approximates the maximum relative throughput in relation to the number of load generators, or number of physical processors in the hardware configuration.

$$X(N) = \lambda N / \left(1 + \sigma(N-1) + \kappa N(N-1)\right)$$

λ is the slope, σ is the coefficient of serialization or contention, and the last bit (κ) is for the cross-talk penalty, also called the consistency or coherency penalty.

The Two Famous Impossibility Results

The following two famous impossibility results that greatly influence distributed system design and choosing the right system design among the available options.

The FLP Impossibility Result

Fischer, Lynch, and Paterson proved that there is no algorithm that is always able to reach consensus if there is a risk that a node may crash.

This is proved in the asynchronous system model, a very restrictive model where the deterministic algorithm is not allowed to use any clocks and timeouts.

If the algorithm is allowed to use timeouts, the consensus becomes solvable.

The CAP Theorem

When there is a network partition, the application may either choose to remain available or opt to linearizability.

Figure 3.1   The Two Famous Impossibility Results.

The crosstalk penalty grows rapidly. Due to its quadratic nature, it eventually surpasses the linear speedup of the ideal system we started with, regardless of how small κ is. This is what causes retrograde scalability to occur.

This is why it's rare to find distributed systems scaling well after adding dozens of nodes.

3.2 A Hitchhiker's Guide to the Blockchain

The next chapter will cover blockchains in detail but in this section, I would like to talk about blockchain from the context of distributed systems.

Blockchain is a distributed, decentralized ledger that is distributed across the nodes of a peer-to-peer network, where you can think of it as a chain of blocks added sequentially on top of each other one at a time. These blocks are immutable and contain a bunch of transactions bundled together as a package. Transactions can contain information like the amount of money, sender and receiver details, additional data, etc.

The specialty of these blocks is that they represent immutable (very close to being immutable) facts, i.e., no one can meddle with these records as they get materialized and enforce the following properties,

1. Censorship resistance – i.e., no single party or group of parties can manipulate them,
2. Inclusivity – i.e., it is accessible to everyone, no one can exclude anyone from using it, and this sets the stage for decentralization and transparency – as a result, no single point of failure thus improves the applications' availability and resiliency,

3. Security – the transactions are cryptographically secured through mechanisms like digital signatures and consensus, hence making it extremely difficult for unauthorized exploitation or counterfeiting,
4. Better traceability, auditability, hence enhanced supportability – every transaction recorded on blockchain can be traced back to its origin which is particularly important for critical use cases,
5. Efficiency – apparently it may look like it's not quite efficient compared to traditional systems but this is not true. We will discuss this in detail,
6. Self Sufficiency – it may not be a fundamental goodness of blockchain but often it is. We will discuss this as well.

We will try to understand the above concepts with a simple, fictitious example.

Suppose we have an online marketplace where participants can buy/sell stuff.

The most basic functional requirements of the platform should be,

1. Tokenization of assets – custom unique tokens can be used to represent ownership of various real-world assets, i.e., real estate, and artworks. Typically a Non-Fungible Token (NFT), a digital unique identifier, is used to tokenize a real-world asset on that platform and certify ownership.
2. Individuals should be able to trade and transfer ownership of these assets.

Now, assume in traditional systems, a single bookkeeping entity maintains and validates all the transactions happening on the platform. Most likely, the same entity also plays the role of the escrow, the intermediary to resolve all the disputes, etc. This is how a typical centralized system works; a lot of responsibility and unwarranted trust is imparted to a single entity. However, this has worked traditionally despite having the following shortcomings, but not limited to: a single entity can be unscrupulous and tamper with the books; being the escrow, it may have a significant amount of money at any time, which it can run away with in a worst-case scenario.

Let's, instead, think of a different kind of system where everybody keeps track of all things, i.e., all transactions in their systems. Now even if someone tries to alter something in a wrong and unauthorized manner, it will not be generally accepted provided he won't be able to influence the quorum with his misdeeds. It's computationally prohibitively expensive to alter the history. So he will be the only one ending up having a diverged copy of the ledger that can never be reconciled.

The second approach seems promising as it promotes *censorship resistance* and *inclusivity* but the explanation above is quite abstract, oversimplified, and raises further questions. While answering all such questions and implementation details are outside the scope of this chapter, we have upcoming chapters that will elaborate on these aspects. The second kind of system could be realized with the help of blockchain. Here we will briefly describe the process of transaction finalization on blockchain and try to answer a few fundamental questions.

The following outlines a generic scheme of things on blockchain,

1. Transaction propagation – when a user initiates a transaction, it is broadcasted to the network and propagated to multiple nodes. This ensures that the transaction is widely disseminated across the network. Each node maintains its copy of the distributed ledger and seeks to validate the transaction using its independent capacity,

2. Validation – transactions are validated by the nodes to check whether they abide by pre-defined validation rules, i.e., structural correctness, whether properly signed by the sender, whether the sender has enough funds, ensuring if the transaction is conflicting with any previous transactions (for example, *double spending*),

3. Transaction Pool – nodes maintain individual memory pools, AKA mempool, where they temporarily store the pending transactions after they are received until they are picked up for processing and included in a block,

4. Consensus mechanism – consensus is needed for ordering the transactions and materializing them. While the miners are responsible for proposing new blocks and appending them to the blockchain, the validity of the transactions is determined by the consensus of the participating nodes. If a particular transaction fails to get a quorum it will be discarded despite being included in a block proposed by a miner,

5. Propagation of valid blocks – once a miner successfully mines a block containing validated transactions, the block is broadcasted in the network. Each node verifies the validity of the block and its transactions before accepting it to be included in the blockchain. If any of the transactions or the block itself fails validation on any node, it will be rejected and not added to the node's copy of the blockchain.

6. Dealing with multiple versions of truth and Nakamoto Consensus – in a distributed decentralized blockchain network it is quite normal that nodes are off or forked in terms of the copy of the blockchain they are maintaining – resulting in multiple versions of truth. How are we going to reconcile these different versions? *Nakamoto Consensus* is the conflict resolution mechanism to determine the canonical version of the blockchain in a decentralized manner. It proposes the *longest chain rule* which considers the longest chain of blocks to be the valid version of the blockchain as it represents the chain with the most accumulated computational effort put into it by the miners,

7. Mempool management – once a transaction is included in a block and the block is successfully mined and finalized, it is removed from the pending transactions list of the node's mempool. Nodes may also remove transactions from their mempool if they become obsolete or fail to meet certain criteria. This enhances the efficacy of mempool and avoids duplicate processing of transactions.

We discussed how transactions are finalized in this second type of system. Now, let's introduce another intriguing aspect. In our fictitious platform, we will implement our own digital currency, eschewing the use of fiat currency. All transactions conducted on our platform must occur using this currency.

Let's discuss some of the fundamental questions we may have in this new platform.

In the new platform, everyone can participate, and nobody is excluded by anybody, hence the system promotes openness and non-excludability. Everyone has a copy of the data and may take part in decision-making. It's extremely difficult for an attacker to meddle with the record of truth because that will involve changing the majority of the participants' records of the transaction history. This becomes harder as more participants onboard on the system. That is the beauty of *decentralization*. In comparison to that, traditional systems, i.e., the first type are much more vulnerable to getting hacked.

This gives rise to a type of platform that has censorship resistance, up to the point where 51% of the participants are honest. It would be quite open, participants may enter or exit at their own will. Even if an attacker group gets 51% hash power, it can potentially jeopardize the censorship resistance, still, it would be computationally very expensive to go back to history, start altering the blocks, and start building an alternative chain.

But the fundamental question persists: why would anyone want to track all the transactions on this platform? It's a task that entails financial investment, time, and effort, which nobody desires. The answer is simple: we must incentivize them to remain on the platform and undertake the responsibility of maintaining and validating transactions. We propose compensating block producers with our currency, either through nominal transaction fees or by generating it.

What prevents the attacker from creating hundreds of fake accounts and influencing the system? This is known as the Sybil attack, where an attacker undermines the integrity of a peer-to-peer network by generating a large number of pseudonymous entities to wield a disproportionately large influence. However, this strategy may not be very advantageous due to the prohibitively expensive amount of computational power or stake that would be required.

We discussed the introduction of a custom currency, which could enhance the self-sufficiency of the system in various ways. However, won't there be challenges? For instance, defining monetary policy, which encompasses factors such as inflation, supply, distribution mechanisms, and governance. Indeed, these challenges will exist, but they are beyond the scope of this chapter.

How does such a system even run without an escrow entity?

We can simply replace a third-party escrow with a smart contract. Blockchain technology can streamline processes by automating tasks and reducing the need for intermediaries. Smart contracts, for example, enable self-executing contracts deployed on blockchain with predefined conditions, reducing the need for manual intervention and potentially saving time and costs making the system more efficient and robust.

3.3 Comparative Analysis

Traditional distributed systems often rely on centralized coordination mechanisms, where a designated central authority or server manages the system's operations and resolves conflicts. Blockchain platforms, on the other hand, aim for decentralization, distributing control and decision-making among multiple nodes in the network. The same considerations are even reflected in the consensus algorithms as well. Consensus algorithms in blockchains enable nodes to agree on the state of the system without the need for a central authority. Whereas consensus algorithms in traditional systems internally elect a leader during a term, they guarantee that within a term, the leader is unique.

Traditional distributed systems typically operate in environments where trust among participants is established or enforced through centralized control. Nodes may rely on pre-established trust relationships or a trusted third party to coordinate interactions. Blockchain platforms operate in trustless environments, where participants may be unknown or untrusted.

Both traditional distributed systems and blockchain platforms aim to be fault-tolerant and resilient to node failures and network disruptions. However, blockchain consensus algorithms often incorporate mechanisms specifically designed to tolerate Byzantine faults, where nodes may behave maliciously or fail arbitrarily, while traditional distributed systems may rely on assumptions of benign behavior.

Consensus algorithms in traditional distributed systems often prioritize performance and scalability, aiming to maximize throughput and minimize latency for a large number of transactions. Blockchain-based systems often prioritize decentralization and security over performance and scale.

Traditional distributed systems may prioritize immediate consistency and finality, where transactions are immediately committed and visible to all participants once agreed upon. Blockchain platforms often prioritize eventual consistency and probabilistic finality. Consensus algorithms in blockchains aim to ensure that transactions are eventually confirmed and committed to the ledger with a high degree of certainty, but immediate finality may not always be guaranteed.

Finally, blockchains are inherently quite slow.

Let's take an example. The average time it takes to mine a block on the Bitcoin network is approximately ten minutes (additionally it takes five more subsequent blocks to be validated for higher security and irreversibility) even with a network that has a high hash rate. So finalizing a block essentially takes an hour on average. With a 1MB block size, let's assume, it can hold a maximum of a few thousand transactions. So the eventual transactional throughput would be significantly lesser than traditional systems.

Is that bad?

Does it make the blockchain-based systems less attractive, probably not. If you observe traditional systems that involve financial transactions, the transaction settlement time is significantly high. As blockchain-based platforms remove the need for an intermediary, the transaction settlement time is much less compared to traditional systems and should be cheaper as well. Additionally, measures like second-layer scaling solutions or alternative consensus mechanisms like Proof-of-Stake (PoS) help achieve higher throughput.

Blockchain is a unified store that is not sharded and is ever-growing, the ever-increasing size of the blockchain may eventually start deterring the small-time participants in the network as it becomes difficult for them to afford the costs of data storage, electricity, and bandwidth, which is definitely not the objective. However, we can resort to techniques like transaction pruning to keep the size of the blockchain under control.

The concept of maintaining an append-only immutable log is not quite new, even in traditional system design we have seen the *Event Sourcing* pattern.

A decentralized system may have lower usability or accessibility compared to a centralized system, as it may require users to possess more technical knowledge or skills.

We need to understand that blockchain and traditional distributed systems are not competing technologies, rather they should be used to complement each other depending on the use cases. We should rather aspire for a hybrid or polyglot system where we judiciously choose blockchain to solve specific use cases. We also need to understand a bunch of things may need to happen off-chain as well.

Bibliography

Attiya, H. (2023, May 19). *Sequential Consistency vs Linearizability.* courses.csail.mit.edu. Retrieved February 18, 2024, from https://courses.csail.mit.edu/6.852/01/papers/p91-attiya.pdf

Fischer, M. J., Lynch, N. A., & Paterson, M. A. (n.d.). *Impossibility of Distributed Consensus with One Faulty Process.* groups.csail.mit.edu. Retrieved February 18, 2024, from https://groups.csail.mit.edu/tds/papers/Lynch/jacm85.pdf

Gunther, N. J. (2007). Univeral Scalability Law, *Guerrilla Capacity Planning.* Springer.

Kleppmann, M. (2017). *Designing Data-Intensive Applications: The Big Ideas Behind Reliable, Scalable, and Maintainable Systems.* O'Reilly Media, Sebastopol, California, United States

Microsoft. (n.d.). *Event Sourcing Pattern - Azure Architecture Center.* Microsoft Learn. Retrieved February 18, 2024, from https://learn.microsoft.com/en-us/azure/architecture/patterns/event-sourcing

Sybil Attack. (2023, May 19). ScienceDirect. Retrieved February 18, 2024, from https://www.sciencedirect.com/topics/computer-science/sybil-attack

Chapter 4

Primer on Web3 and Distributed Systems

Sam Ghosh

Okay, let us get back to our discussion on Web3 systems. In the last chapter, Subhasis discussed traditional distributed systems and blockchain from the perspective of traditional distributed systems.

So, how do we compare the traditional distributed systems with blockchain or other distributed ledger (DLT) based decentralized systems in terms of level of decentralization?

We will understand the decentralization that blockchains (and other DLTs) can enable in this and in the "Decentralization in Web3" chapter.

But, we need to address the comparison of traditional distributed systems with DLTs. In section 4.3.1 in this chapter, we will discuss distributed and decentralized systems and how they are different.

4.1 What is Web3?

Summing up Web3 in a single sentence is a challenging task, but we can attempt to define it through two distinct approaches.

4.1.1 First, as the Successor of Web 2.0

Simply put, Web 1.0 represents the read-only web (eg. blogs, etc.), Web 2.0 embodies the participatory web (eg. social media, e-commerce, etc.), and Web 3.0 envisions a decentralized web owned by users.

While Web 2.0 enhances user interaction through social networks and promotes user-generated content, Web 3.0 theoretically grants users ownership of decentralized networks through tokens and Decentralized Autonomous Organizations (DAOs).

DOI: 10.4324/9781003507352-4

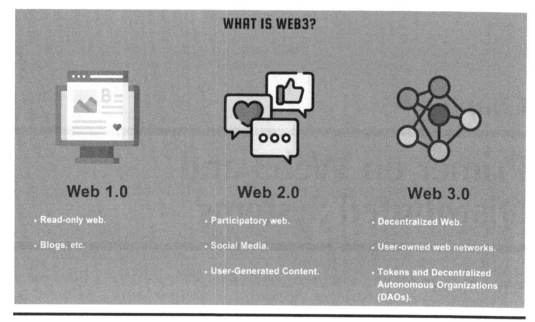

Figure 4.1   How Web 1.0, Web 2.0, and Web 3.0 are different.

In the subsequent sections of this chapter, we will delve into the emergence of Web3, exploring its roots in various technological and business trends. This discussion aims to provide a clearer understanding of what Web3 entails.

4.1.2 The Second Approach to Defining Web3 is Using the Fundamental Qualities of Web3

Web3 networks embody key principles such as openness, permissionlessness, trustlessness, automation, immutability, and decentralization.

- In Web3, networks are **open** to anyone, allowing easy participation. They are **permissionless**, eliminating the need for authorization to access services like DeFi protocols, in contrast to traditional financial systems that often involve stringent account opening procedures.
- **Truslessness** means that Web3 network participants do not need to trust each other for the system to work i.e. complete strangers can become part of the network without fearing adverse consequences. Trustlessness in Web3 networks is achieved through economic incentives rather than relying on trusted centralized authorities. To understand this concept, let us contrast a Web3-based decentralized finance (DeFi) system with the traditional financial system. In the traditional system, the absence of proper documentation to carry out trust-building processes such as know-your-customer (KYC) can prevent us from getting financial services. On the other hand, in DeFi there is no requirement for such documentation. Web3 replaces trust requirements with transparent transactions, consensus mechanisms, and sometimes collateral requirements.
- Web3 networks are **automated** systems because they leverage smart contracts and decentralized protocols to automate processes that traditionally require human intervention in centralized systems. These networks use code to execute predefined actions, such as transactions

and agreements, without the need for human intervention. This automation reduces the reliance on centralized authorities and streamlines operations, making the network more efficient and transparent.

■ **Immutability** is a core attribute of Web3 systems inherited from blockchains, ensuring that once data is part of a Web3 network, it cannot be altered. The uneditable nature of historical records in Web3 networks enhances credibility and transparency.

■ **Decentralization** is a pivotal feature of Web3, contrasting the centralized control seen in traditional tech platforms. In Web3, networks are served by numerous nodes, each running client software, making it challenging to take down or censor the network. Ownership and control are (theoretically) decentralized through tokens and voting mechanisms, providing higher availability and disaster recovery.

4.2 Emergence of Web3

To understand Web3, we need to explore the technological and industry trends that paved the way for its emergence. Let's start by examining the technology trends.

4.2.1 Technology Trends

Let us start with the open-source movement.

4.2.1.1 The Open-source Movement

The open-source movement, exemplified by projects like Linux and modern platforms like GitHub, has brought collaboration, transparency, and collective innovation to the technology sector.

GitHub revolutionized software development, enabling global collaboration, code-sharing, and contributions. Its infrastructure promotes transparency and collective innovation, democratizing software development and empowering a vast community of developers to collaborate and enhance codebases collectively.

Web3, characterized by openness, collaboration, and decentralization, is driven by a culture that frequently adopts open-source principles in various projects, including blockchain initiatives, decentralized applications (dApps), and distributed systems.

Web3 projects are dedicated to transparency, accessibility, community participation, decentralization, immutability, and iterative development. They adopt an open and transparent framework, inviting scrutiny of their codebases and encouraging contributions from a diverse community.

Active community engagement fosters a collaborative and inclusive ecosystem, while iterative development mirrors the continuous evolution seen in open-source software.

4.2.1.2 Peer-to-peer Networks

P2P networks like BitTorrent played a key role in shaping Web3 by revolutionizing data sharing and moving away from central server dependence. The decentralized values of P2P networks strongly influence Web3's decentralized nature.

BitTorrent revolutionized data sharing by creating a decentralized network, allowing direct file exchanges among users without a central server. This collaborative approach empowered users to actively contribute to content distribution, leading to more efficient and decentralized control over data.

This approach increased reliability, scalability, and resilience against potential failures, as data wasn't confined to a single point of control.

P2P networks like BitTorrent influence Web3 by promoting decentralization and peer-to-peer interactions. Web3 expands on these concepts with blockchain, smart contracts, and decentralized applications, reshaping digital asset creation, sharing, and access for a more decentralized, collaborative, and distributed web infrastructure.

Now, Web3 is not merely a set of technologies – it signifies a new way of doing business. To understand this, let us explore the business perspective.

4.2.2 Business Trends

This section focuses on how Web3 handles User-generated Content (UGC), setting itself apart from Web2 in this regard.

The widespread adoption of User-generated Content (UGC) has been a pivotal factor in the rapid expansion and monetization of website builders and online platforms.

User-generated content takes diverse forms – articles, images, videos, reviews – created by users rather than the platform's creators.

4.2.2.1 How has UGC Contributed to Platform Growth?

Several key elements contribute to the symbiotic relationship between user-generated content (UGC) and platform growth.

a. **Diverse and abundant content:** Platforms that enable UGC, such as social media sites and community forums, thrive on a continuous influx of diverse content. This constant flow of UGC fuels engagement, attracting more visitors and increasing their time spent on the platform.

b. **Network effects**: With an increasing number of users contributing content, the platform's appeal grows, fostering network effects. The greater the volume of content, the more valuable the platform becomes for users and advertisers alike, creating a self-reinforcing cycle of growth.

c. **Enhanced engagement and retention:** UGC often leads to heightened user engagement. This increased engagement contributes to longer user sessions and higher ARPU (average revenue per user).

d. **Monetization opportunities:** User-generated content creates various monetization opportunities, attracting advertisers to platforms with high user engagement and abundant content. This enables platforms to generate revenue through advertising, sponsorships, or premium services.

e. **Community building:** UGC-centric platforms build strong communities around shared interests, fostering a sense of belonging and brand loyalty. The loyal user base often becomes product advocates, attracting new users to the platform.

f. SEO and discoverability: Constantly refreshed user-generated content (UGC) can improve a platform's search engine rankings. Relevant content created by users increases the platform's visibility in search results, enhancing discoverability.

Online platforms have effectively leveraged these aspects of user-generated content to expand their user bases and generate revenue.

4.2.2.2 User-generated Content to User-owned Content

User-generated content (UGC) has been central to the growth and engagement of online platforms, raising a significant issue regarding ownership of UGCs. The question of who owns the content created by users gained prominence as the significance and quantity of UGCs increased over time.

The emergence of major platforms like YouTube (2005), Twitter (2006), and Facebook (2004) highlighted issues with content ownership. Initially, these platforms claimed broad usage rights over user-generated content (UGC) through their terms of service. By uploading content, users granted the platform a non-exclusive license to utilize the content for various purposes, including distribution and marketing within the platform.

Concerns and disputes over user ownership rights led to policy changes. Around 2010, YouTube clarified its stance on ownership, recognizing that users retained copyright over their content, while the platform retained usage rights for managing, distributing, and displaying the content on its site. In a similar move around 2012, Facebook revised policies, affirming user content ownership while granting platform usage and display rights within the social network.

Now, before we move forward, let us discuss the concept of ownership.

WHAT IS OWNERSHIP?

In accordance with natural law, the rights of an asset owner typically encompass:

I. **Right to possess**: *This gives an individual the authority to possess, control, and use a specific asset, seen as a natural extension of their right to personal autonomy.*
II. **Right to use**: *Owners can use the asset as they see fit, as long as it doesn't infringe upon the rights of others.*
III. **Right to transfer**: *Owners can transfer ownership interest to others through methods like sale, gift, or legal means.*
IV. **Right to exclude**: *Ownership includes the fundamental right to exclude others from using or accessing the property without consent.*
V. **Right to dispose**: *Owners have the right to dispose of their property, including the freedom to sell, destroy, or eliminate the asset as they see fit.*

Now, the question arises: Who holds a claim over any income generated from an asset?

According to natural law principles, an individual's rights to income from an asset align with broader property rights, encompassing possession, use, transfer, and exclusion of others. Income generated from an asset is considered belonging to the owner due to their ownership rights.

4.2.2.3 Conclusion

Now, returning to our discussion on user-generated content (UGC).

There's a conflict between how Web 2.0 platforms manage user-generated content and its alignment with natural law principles.

Ownership rights extend beyond income claims and platform trading, covering possession, transfer, exclusion, and disposal. Decentralized networks, such as blockchains, effectively implement these rights.

On Web2 platforms, user-generated content (UGC) faces significant limitations. Users cannot easily transfer their content between platforms due to restricted transfer rights and a lack of interoperability. As a result, accessing these assets outside of their original platform is difficult.

Web3, while not the pioneer in this respect, has acknowledged and respected user rights over user-generated content (UGC), notably in industries like gaming and creator economy platforms. Efforts to decentralize UGC ownership and trading without utilizing blockchains have faced limited success.

We will have a detailed discussion on this topic in the Industry Case Studies chapter.

4.3 Basics of Web3 Technology

The previous section offers a broad overview of Web3. This section will delve into fundamental Web3 concepts. Before that, let's familiarize ourselves with essential distributed systems concepts, which will be useful in the upcoming discussions.

Our journey starts by exploring distributed systems, followed by examining key blockchain principles and specific mechanisms within the Ethereum blockchain. Additionally, we will gain insights into how Ethereum processes smart contracts.

If certain concepts, especially those related to Ethereum, seem challenging now, don't worry. A complete understanding of these concepts isn't necessary to proceed to the next chapters. They are included as reference material.

4.3.1 Distributed Systems

4.3.1.1 What Is a Distributed System?

A distributed computing system comprises multiple software components that operate across multiple computers but function as a unified entity.

Computers in a distributed system can be physically close to each other connected by a local network or geographically distant linked by a wide area network. Configurations vary widely, including mainframes, personal computers, workstations, minicomputers, and more.

The primary goal of distributed computing is to make the network operate seamlessly as if it were a single computer.

Distributed systems are used in various areas such as datastores, messaging, computing, ledgers, file-systems, and applications.

With the increase in data volume and complexity, NoSQL databases (with distributed architecture) are now the preferred choice for datastores. Distributed messaging systems improve performance and scalability, offering features like publish-subscribe and point-to-point communication. Prominent examples of distributed ledgers are blockchains and alternative technologies like Hashgraph, Directed Acyclic Graph (DAG), Holochain, and Tempo (Radix). Noteworthy examples of distributed file systems include NFS and Hadoop.

4.3.1.2 Clients and Nodes

Distributed systems are composed of nodes, which are individual computing entities actively involved in the distributed network. These nodes, which can be in the same place or spread across different countries, include various types of computing entities like laptops, smartphones, IoT devices, and more.

Nodes participate in the distributed system by running client software, facilitating communication, and allowing the nodes to operate collectively as a unified entity.

4.3.1.3 Benefits of Distributed Systems

4.3.1.3.1 Scaling

Distributed systems provide the advantage of horizontal scaling, allowing for increased computing capacity by adding more machines to the system. This contrasts with standalone systems that rely on vertical scaling through the addition of hardware capacity.

Vertical scaling can be limited based on the prevailing technology and physical space limitations. In theory, horizontal scaling has no limits, but practical issues like latency and security may arise beyond a certain level.

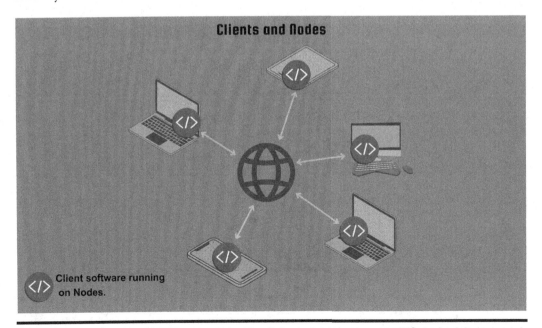

Figure 4.2 Clients and Nodes.

4.3.1.3.2 Fault-tolerance

Distributed systems contribute to higher availability as the entire system remains accessible even if one or more computers or nodes experience downtime.

4.3.1.3.3 Low latency

Distributed systems strategically position nodes to minimize latency. For example, if demand is anticipated from both New York and Sydney, having nodes in both cities ensures that the traffic reaches the nearest node, minimizing round-trip time within the physical constraints set by the speed of light.

4.3.1.4 Limitations of Distributed Systems

The **CAP Theorem** dictates that a distributed system can achieve only two of the three desired characteristics – consistency, availability, and partition tolerance.

4.3.1.4.1 Consistency

All clients, or users, perceive the same data simultaneously, irrespective of the node they connect to. To achieve consistency, any data written to one node must be instantly forwarded or replicated to all other nodes before the write is considered successful.

4.3.1.4.2 Availability

Users requesting data receive a response, even if one or more nodes are offline. In other words, all operational nodes in the distributed system provide a valid response for any request, without exceptions.

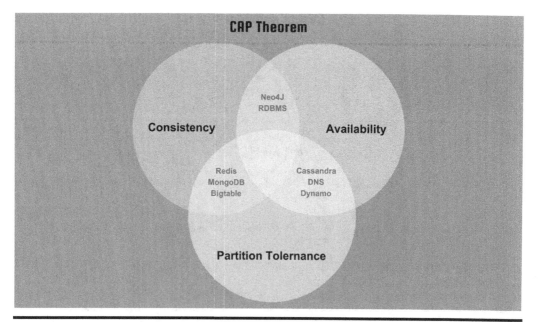

Figure 4.3 Cap Theorem.

4.3.1.4.3 Partition tolerance

The network must function seamlessly despite any communication breakdowns, or partitions, within the distributed system. A partition refers to a lost or temporarily delayed connection between two nodes.

Additionally, distributed systems face complexity and security risks. Managing diverse technical environments makes them complex, and the need for nodes to communicate poses security challenges, increasing vulnerability. The initial deployment cost for distributed systems is also higher.

4.3.1.5 Models of Distributed Systems – Master-slave and Peer-to-peer

There are two primary models of distributed systems: Master-slave and Peer-to-peer.

4.3.1.5.1 Master-slave:

In the Master-slave model, one node acts as the master, possessing comprehensive information and governing decision-making, while other nodes serve as slaves, executing tasks assigned by the master.

4.3.1.5.2 Peer-to-peer:

In the Peer-to-peer model, no single master is designated among nodes. All nodes equally share the responsibility of the master, fostering a decentralized and collaborative approach.

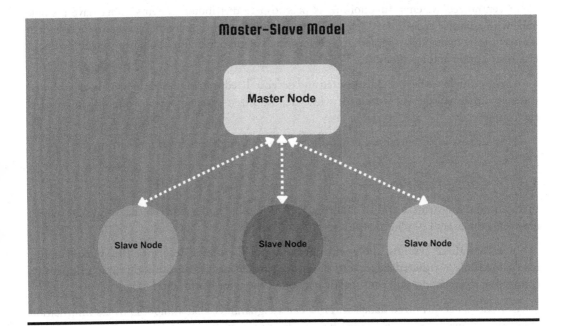

Figure 4.4   Master-slave model of distributed systems.

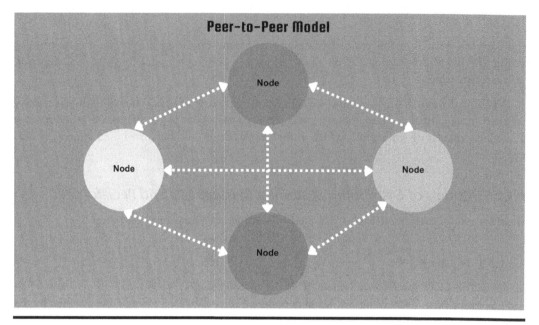

Figure 4.5 Peer-to-peer model of distributed systems.

4.3.1.6 Distributed vs Decentralized Systems

Distributed and decentralized systems are distinct concepts, with decentralized systems being considered a specialized form of distributed systems.

Decentralized systems, functioning as peer-to-peer distributed systems, don't have a single node with exclusive decision-making authority. In these systems, each node acts as an independent master server, managing transactions, performing calculations, and comparing results without task distribution among nodes.

The key difference between distributed and decentralized systems lies in their goals. Distributed systems aim to divide the workload, while decentralized systems seek to establish a trustless environment.

Trustlessness in decentralized systems is achieved through consensus mechanisms.

4.3.1.7 Consensus Process

In decentralized systems, a critical challenge is ensuring that nodes agree on the world state, which represents the overall system state at a specific moment.

In decentralized systems, the world state is a globally shared record of the system's status, maintained on a distributed ledger across network participants. This ensures that an outside entity, connecting to any node, will consistently encounter the same world state.

Consider a decentralized database. How can we guarantee that all nodes possess information about every transaction and no node is manipulating transaction records?

This is where the consensus process comes in.

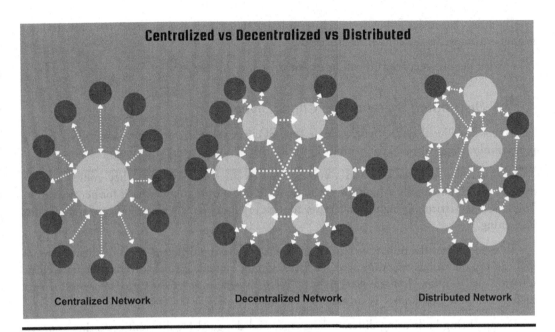

Figure 4.6 Schematic representation of centralized, decentralized, and distributed systems.

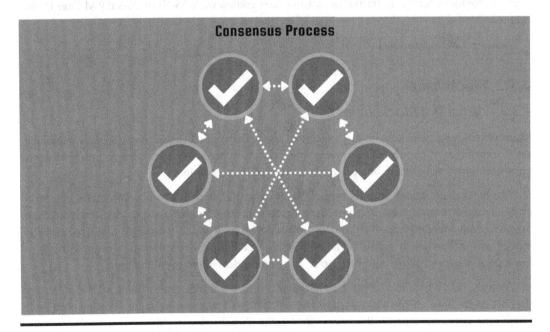

Figure 4.7 Simplistic representation of consensus process.

The consensus process in a decentralized database involves each node comparing transactions to ensure identical records. This builds confidence that all nodes are aware of every transaction, preventing malicious additions. Trust is established through the collective matching of data across nodes rather than relying on a central authority.

The rules that nodes follow to match records and agree on the world state in a decentralized system are known as the consensus processes.

Further details on consensus will be explored later in this chapter.

4.3.1.8 Distributed Systems and Client Diversity

Imagine a distributed system with a single type of client software, developed exclusively in one programming language and compatible only with the Windows operating system.

In this scenario, if hackers find a vulnerability in the client software, they could compromise all nodes, potentially taking the entire network down or manipulating it for personal gain. This threat is particularly significant in the context of blockchains with millions of transactions happening.

This emphasizes the importance of client diversity – having different types of client software that can run on various operating systems. Ethereum for example features diverse execution client software such as Besu, Nethermind, Erigon, and Go-Ethereum, as well as varied consensus clients such as Nimbus, Lighthouse, Teku, etc.

Despite being built using different languages and designed for different operating systems, these client software all implement the Ethereum Virtual Machine (EVM) and maintain consistent behavior in handling transactions and smart contracts. We will discuss EVM later in this chapter.

Now, let's delve into blockchains.

4.3.2 Blockchains

4.3.2.1 What is a Blockchain?

In simple language, blockchains are a specific type of distributed ledger. As previously explained, a distributed ledger is a form of a database where data is stored across multiple computing systems, known as nodes, which may be situated in various physical locations.

In a blockchain, nodes store encrypted copies of the database to ensure continued accessibility to the database, even if some nodes are temporarily offline. The number of nodes in a blockchain can vary from a few, perhaps 8–10 in the same physical location, to thousands dispersed globally, as seen with Ethereum. It should be noted that blockchains are decentralized systems as they follow a peer-to-peer structure and each node acts as an independent master server.

Alternatively, a blockchain can be viewed as a state machine comprised of nodes, indicating that all nodes have an identical state of the database at any given moment. Further details on "state" and state transitions will be discussed later in this chapter.

4.3.2.2 Understanding Blocks

But, how do blockchains get the name "blockchain"?

In blockchains, data is organized into blocks, and these blocks essentially serve as containers for batches of transactions. The creation of these blocks is designed to ensure that all nodes maintain an identical history of data.

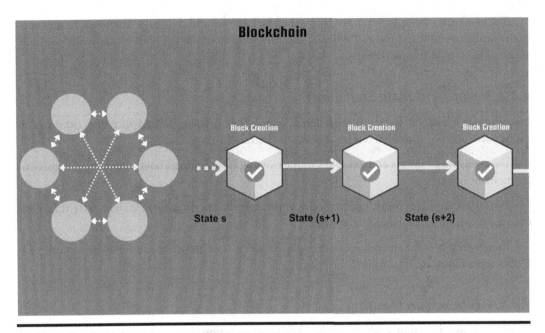

Figure 4.8 Blockchain – Storing data in blocks and acting as state machines.

Here's how it operates: At regular intervals, approximately every ten minutes in the case of Bitcoin and 12–15 seconds in the case of Ethereum, transactions occurring in the network since the last block creation are compiled and arranged according to predefined rules. Subsequently, these batches undergo verification and are then stored as blocks. It's important to note that the process of block creation and the specific data structure within a block can vary across different blockchains.

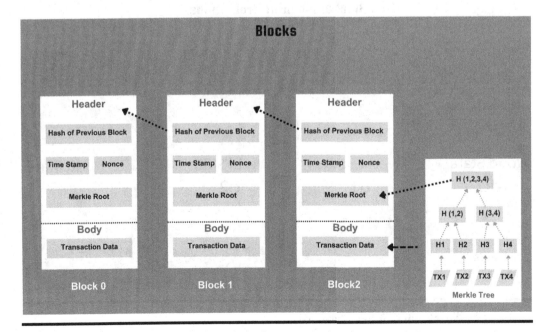

Figure 4.9 Simplistic representation of block structure.

Blocks consist of two key components – the block header and the body. The block header contains summarized data of the entire block, including a hash of the previous block, while the body contains encrypted transaction data.

4.3.2.3 State and State Transition

In computer science, a system is considered "stateful" if it is engineered to retain information about past events or user interactions, known as the system's state.

The term "state" in this context refers to the existing information about a network at a particular moment in time.

Transition, in this context, denotes a discontinuous change. In a blockchain, a state transition occurs every time a new block is accepted.

Therefore, a blockchain can be conceptualized as a state machine, and the creation of new blocks represents state transitions.

4.3.2.4 Blockchain Hashing

Now, understanding that nodes store blockchain transaction data in blocks raises the issue of ensuring uniformity across all nodes. Given each block may contain hundreds or thousands of transactions, verifying all of them across the nodes is computationally prohibitive.

To simplify this process, the data is organized in a hash table structure, and a hash root is computed for all the data within a block. This hash root is used to compare blocks across nodes, guaranteeing consistency in the stored data.

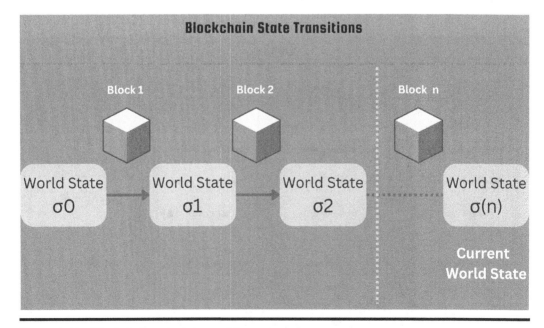

Figure 4.10 Blockchain as a state machine.

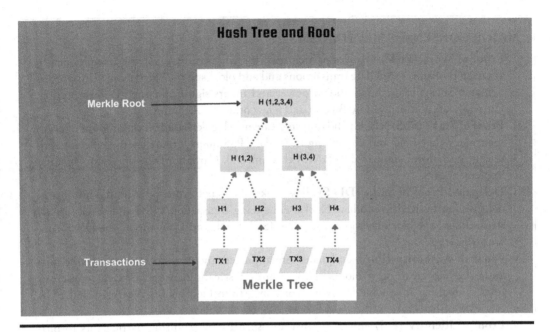

Figure 4.11   Hash Tree and Hash Root in blocks.

A hash table is a data structure that stores key-value pairs, using a hash function to quickly find the right location in an array where the value is stored. A hash function is an algorithm that transforms an input into a fixed-size string of characters, typically used to uniquely identify data. Now, the hash root is the top hash in a hash tree, representing the whole dataset and allowing for quick and secure data verification.

In Bitcoin, the data structure employed is the Merkle Tree, with the resulting hash root termed the Merkle Root. Ethereum, on the other hand, utilizes a modified data structure known as Patricia Merkle Tries.

4.3.2.5 *Consensus Process in Blockchains*

Before adding a block to a blockchain, nodes must achieve consensus on the validity of transactions to be included. This verification process, known as the consensus mechanism, ensures agreement among nodes on the validity of the transactions.

Consensus mechanisms serve multiple purposes, not only facilitating the addition of blocks but also enhancing the security of blockchain networks. They act as a deterrent against cyberattacks, such as 51% attacks, by increasing the cost of attack through the requirement of substantial computing power or staking crypto assets to participate in the consensus process.

There are various different types of consensus mechanisms, including Proof of Work, Proof of Stake, Delegated Proof of Stake, Proof of Authority, Proof of Identity, and others.

MAJOR CONSENSUS MECHANISMS

I. **Proof of Work (PoW)** involves participants, known as miners, solving complex mathematical problems to validate transactions and add blocks to the blockchain. This process demands substantial computational power and incurs significant energy consumption. Currently, PoW is utilized by Bitcoin and a few other blockchains.

II. **Proof of Stake (PoS)** selects validators to create new blocks based on the amount of cryptocurrency they hold and are willing to "stake." PoS offers a more energy-efficient consensus mechanism compared to PoW. Ethereum 2.0, Cardano, Polkadot, and Algorand implement PoS.

III. **Delegated Proof of Stake (DPoS)** allows token holders to vote for a limited number of delegates authorized to produce blocks, enhancing transaction speed and scalability by streamlining the block creation process. EOS, TRON, and Lisk employ the DPoS consensus process.

IV. **Proof of Authority (PoA)** designates pre-approved and trusted entities as validators authorized to create new blocks. PoA ensures a streamlined and efficient consensus process, making it suitable for private or consortium blockchains. VeChain and POA Network utilize PoA.

V. **Proof of Identity (PoI)** enhances trust and security by requiring participants to provide verifiable digital identities linked to real-world identity verification processes. This reduces the risk of fraudulent activities and Sybil attacks, contributing to a more secure blockchain network.

4.3.2.6 Blockchain Accounts

Crypto assets are virtual assets existing solely on blockchain networks (or other DLTs), recorded in the distributed ledgers supporting these networks.

To hold a crypto asset, we must maintain an account on the blockchain network, as all owned assets are associated with the respective user account.

A user account is represented by a public address and a private key. The public address is represented by a hash which is an alphanumeric string. The private key acts like a password.

The private key serves as an authentication mechanism proving ownership of crypto assets at a specific public address. Private keys are used for authorization of transactions involving crypto assets.

Now, let us discuss smart contracts and tokens.

4.3.3 Smart Contracts and Tokens

4.3.3.1 Smart Contracts

Smart contracts are autonomous programs on blockchains, acting as digital contracts with pre-established rules and conditions. They execute pre-programmed actions autonomously when specific criteria are met, eliminating the need for intermediaries.

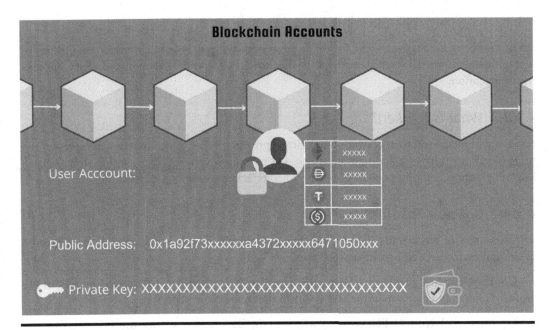

Figure 4.12   Visual representation of blockchain (externally owned) account.

Technically, smart contracts are a unique account type on a blockchain capable of holding crypto-assets and executing various tasks according to their programmed instructions.

4.3.3.2 Key Characteristics of Smart Contracts

4.3.3.2.1 Decentralized Execution

Smart contracts function in a decentralized environment, eliminating the need for a central authority to enforce or execute contract terms. This decentralization enhances trust by removing intermediaries. Coded in languages like Solidity, smart contracts are compiled into bytecodes. Once deployed on the blockchain, copies of the linked bytecode are stored across all active nodes.

The bytecode, consisting of Opcode instructions, allows each node (i.e., the Virtual Machine within the node) to independently and decentrally execute the smart contract. More details on this process will be covered later in this chapter.

4.3.3.2.2 Immutable Code

Once deployed on the blockchain, the code of a smart contract is usually immutable, preventing any alterations or tampering. This ensures that the agreed-upon terms remain secure and unchanged throughout the contract's execution.

4.3.3.2.3 Automatic Execution

Smart contracts stand out for their ability to autonomously execute predefined actions when specific conditions are met. Whether releasing funds, transferring ownership, or triggering other processes, smart contracts perform these operations without manual intervention.

4.3.3.2.4 Cryptographic Security

Smart contracts use cryptographic techniques for security, securing each transaction with cryptographic signatures. The transparency of the blockchain allows all participants to verify the contract's execution.

4.3.3.3 What is a Token?

A token within a blockchain network is a digital representation of value. Tokens can represent the value of various things, including the value of fiat currencies, commodities, voting rights, shares in DeFi platform liquidity pools, and usage rights for artworks, among other things.

4.3.3.4 Coins vs Tokens

In the context of blockchain and cryptocurrency, the terms "coins" and "tokens" have specific meanings, each representing distinct concepts.

Coins are native digital currencies specific to a blockchain, generated as an integral part of the protocol for use as a medium of exchange within that blockchain ecosystem.

For instance, Bitcoin (BTC) is a coin native to the Bitcoin blockchain, and Ether (ETH) is a coin within the Ethereum blockchain.

Unlike coins, tokens represent assets or utilities and can be created on existing blockchain platforms adhering to specific token standards.

For instance, tokens like USDT (Tether), following the ERC-20 standard, or CryptoKitties, using the ERC-721 standard, exemplify tokens created on the Ethereum blockchain. We will discuss these token standards later in this chapter.

4.3.3.5 Security and Utility Tokens

Tokens can be classified into two primary categories based on purpose: security tokens and utility tokens.

Security tokens are issued and treated as securities under the relevant regulatory framework. They represent ownership in an underlying asset and are subject to regulatory compliance.

Utility tokens, on the other hand, are tokens utilized within Web3 platforms to perform various functions. They can serve as a means of payment, confer governance rights in decentralized applications, represent liquidity provided to automated market making, and fulfill other utility-related roles within the blockchain ecosystem.

4.3.3.6 Fungible and Non-fungible Tokens

From a technical point of view, tokens can be classified into fungible tokens and non-fungible tokens (NFTs).

Fungible tokens have identical units, each with the same value, while the value of units in non-fungible tokens can vary.

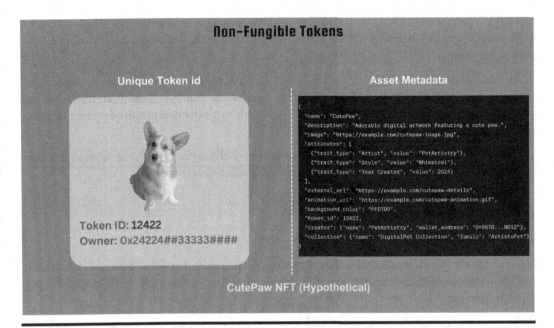

Figure 4.13   Unique token ID and asset metadata in NFTs.

On the Ethereum blockchain, the ERC-20 token standard is used to create fungible tokens, and the ERC-721 token standard is used for non-fungible tokens (NFTs).

Note that ERC stands for Ethereum Request for Comment.

Now, ERC-721 tokens introduce two significant differences from ERC-20:

■ *Unique Token ID*: Each token has a unique identifier, allowing for individual tracking of each unit.
■ *Ability to Attach Asset Metadata*: This feature enables the addition of specific details to the token, such as title, properties, and a link to an image representing the asset that the NFT signifies.

ERC-1155, a multi-token standard on Ethereum, consolidates fungible and non-fungible tokens in a single contract, introduced by Enjin for efficiency and cost reduction. Designed for applications like gaming and DeFi, it offers adaptability and gas efficiency, managing various token types within one smart contract for a more complex and customizable ecosystem.

4.3.3.7 Soulbound Tokens

Soulbound tokens or SBTs are a special case of NFTs.

SBTs are digital identity tokens that represent an individual's or entity's characteristics, traits, and achievements. Unlike regular NFTs, SBTs are non-transferable and permanently tied to an individual's private wallet, known as their "soul." This concept aims to establish a digital identity framework, encompassing personal data like age, qualifications, education, health records, and work achievements.

In May 2022, E. Glen Weyl, Puja Ohlhaver, and Vitalik Buterin published the whitepaper "Decentralized Society: Finding Web3's Soul" to propose the concept of soulbound tokens. The whitepaper explains how SBTs can be used as credentials in a fully decentralized society (DeSoc) governed by its users.

Web3 is not only about technology. A major part of Web3 is the underlying economic framework. So, to understand Web3, we must understand blockchain economics.

4.3.4 Blockchain Economics

4.3.4.1 Incentivizing Node Providers

In a centralized system, the central authority covers infrastructure costs like hosting, development, and maintenance, without users incurring expenses. Amazon, for example, bears these costs for Amazon.com and related sites.

In contrast, a blockchain network lacks a central authority, and node providers provide the necessary infrastructure for blockchain operation. To incentivize node providers, the native currency (i.e. coins) and the concept of network fees come into play.

Coins are created during block creation and rewarded to miners (in Proof of Work) or to validators (in Proof of Stake). The term "block creators" can be used as a generalized term for miners and validators.

In addition to the block rewards, the network fee is collected as a transaction fee to include a transaction in a block. This fee serves as an incentive for node providers and is distributed among them, encouraging their ongoing contributions to the network's infrastructure.

4.3.4.2 Network Fee

So, a network fee is the transaction fee that is collected to include a transaction in a blockchain.

The network fee is called the gas fee in Ethereum. Gas is the benchmark for computational resource usage on Ethereum. Gas is the unit measuring computational effort on Ethereum, representing the computational resources required for specific operations.

Various actions, such as deploying a smart contract, minting NFTs, or transferring tokens, involve a gas fee. The transaction cost (gas fee) equals the gas required multiplied by the gas price. The gas price, denominated in Gwei (one-billionth of an Ether and pronounced as "gway"), fluctuates based on network demand.

Unlike traditional transaction fees as a percentage of transaction value, gas fees depend on transaction complexity. Network fees are often associated with transaction speed, with faster transactions requiring higher fees.

EIP-1559, implemented in London Fork (August 2021), improves the Ethereum user experience with a dynamic base fee responsive to network demand. It replaces the traditional auction-based gas fee model, addressing scalability and introducing a deflationary mechanism by burning a portion of transaction fees.

EIP stands for Ethereum Improvement Proposal, serving as a design document for new features or improvements in the Ethereum blockchain. Vital for collaborative decision-making within the Ethereum community, EIPs guide the platform's evolution and development.

4.3.5 Ethereum

4.3.5.1 Emergence of Ethereum – from Distributed Ledger to World Computer

Ethereum plays a central role in the Web3 ecosystem, serving as the foundation for many programmable blockchains. Understanding Ethereum requires exploring its origins.

Bitcoin, launched in 2009, functions as a distributed ledger with a primary emphasis on serving as a payment system.

Around 2013, the potential of blockchains for applications beyond simple transactions became evident. Developers faced a choice between building on top of Bitcoin, with its constraints or creating a new blockchain. Building on Bitcoin meant dealing with limitations while starting a new blockchain required substantial effort in infrastructure development and testing.

The Mastercoin team, later known as Omni, was working on extending Bitcoin with a rudimentary smart contract overlay protocol. Vitalik Buterin, a young programmer, proposed a more generalized approach to enable flexible and scriptable contracts, surpassing the specialized contract language of Mastercoin. Although the Mastercoin team found the idea impressive, it deviated too much from their development roadmap.

In December 2013, Vitalik began sharing a whitepaper outlining the concept behind Ethereum – a Turing-complete, general-purpose blockchain.

In computer science, a Turing-complete machine can solve any computational problem with sufficient time, computational resources, and the necessary instructions.

Vitalik Buterin's proposal marked a notable departure from existing blockchain models, emphasizing versatility and programmability.

4.3.5.2 Difference between Bitcoin and Ethereum

The distinction between Bitcoin and Ethereum lies in their primary functions and design philosophies.

Bitcoin serves as a decentralized ledger primarily focused on being a payment platform. While it does allow some level of programming for specific use cases, Bitcoin's primary purpose is to facilitate peer-to-peer transactions.

In contrast, Ethereum is conceived as a generalized programming platform. Its founders envisioned a blockchain without a predefined purpose, capable of supporting a wide range of applications programmed directly on the blockchain.

The core idea behind Ethereum was to create a general-purpose blockchain, allowing developers to implement specific applications without dealing with the intricacies of peer-to-peer networks, consensus algorithms, and other underlying mechanisms. Ethereum abstracts these complexities, offering a deterministic and secure programming environment for decentralized blockchain applications, making it versatile for a wide range of decentralized applications beyond simple transactions.

4.3.5.3 What Is Ethereum, exactly?

From the book *Mastering Ethereum* – co-authored by Gavin Wood – one of the co-founders of Ethereum.

The following excerpt is taken from *Mastering Ethereum* by Andreas M. Antonopoulos, and Gavin Wood, released under the Creative Commons Attribution-ShareAlike 4.0 International License (CC-BY-SA 4.0).

"Ethereum is a deterministic but practically unbounded state machine, consisting of a globally accessible singleton state and a virtual machine that applies changes to that state.

From a more practical perspective, Ethereum is an open-source, globally decentralized computing infrastructure that executes programs called smart contracts. It uses a blockchain to synchronize and store the system's state changes, along with a cryptocurrency called ether to meter and constrain execution resource costs.

The Ethereum platform enables developers to build powerful decentralized applications with built-in economic functions. While providing high availability, auditability, transparency, and neutrality, it also reduces or eliminates censorship and reduces certain counterparty risks."

In computer science, "deterministic" describes a system where the future state is entirely determined by the prior state, meaning that the same operational steps in the same order will lead to exactly the same state.

Now, in the context of Ethereum being described as a *"deterministic but practically unbounded state machine, consisting of a globally accessible singleton state,"* we can refer back to the discussion on decentralized systems.

In decentralized systems, each node processes all transactions and computations and then compares the results with all other nodes. For a blockchain to achieve this, it needs to be deterministic.

This means that if each node starts from the same initial state and processes the same transactions and smart contracts, they should all reach the same final state. If nodes reach even slightly different states, the consensus will fail. Block creation in Ethereum signifies a transition of the world state, and regardless of the consensus protocol used, nodes must unanimously agree on the new world state at each block creation. Nodes that do not agree will diverge from the chain.

4.3.5.4 Ethereum from a High-level

Okay, let us talk about Ethereum at a high-level. Now, this can be esoteric. So, if you are not completely clear about it right now – do not worry.

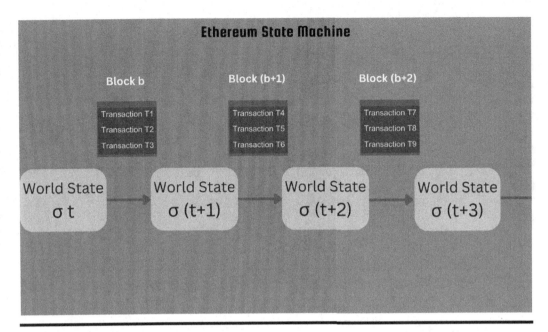

Figure 4.14 Ethereum state machine.

Ethereum nodes maintain a unified world state, ensuring consistency. Connecting to any node offers identical information about the entire system.

Unlike distributed systems where nodes split the workload, in a decentralized system, all nodes process all transactions and perform all computations, maintaining the world state individually. There is no external world state – each node holds its version.

To ensure nodes maintain an identical state, the block creation and consensus process come into play. At regular intervals (around 12–15 seconds for Ethereum), all active nodes create blocks by aggregating transactions since the last block creation and matching them with a Patricia-Merkle root. It's crucial to note that blocks contain transactions, not account balances.

Block creation represents a state transition, and the current world state in Ethereum is the cumulative result of all state transitions from the genesis block. It's analogous to your bank account balance being the sum of all transactions involving your account.

During each block creation, all nodes update their copy of the world state, and the Ethereum Virtual Machine (EVM) plays a key role in this process, which will be discussed later.

When an external actor connects to any Ethereum node, they access the most recently saved world state of the Ethereum network.

4.3.5.5 Ethereum Accounts

In Ethereum, there are two types of accounts: "Externally Owned Accounts" (EOA) or "User-owned Accounts" and "Contract Accounts" (CAs) (Figure 4.16).

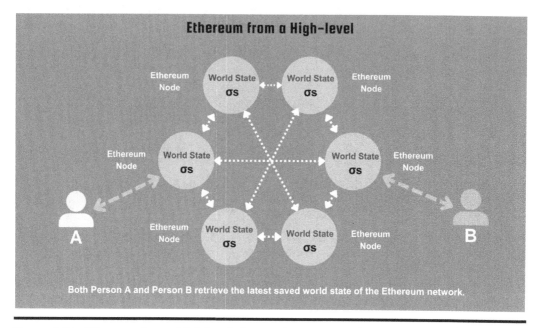

Figure 4.15 Ethereum from a high-level. Connecting to any node gives the same world state.

I. Externally Owned Account (EOA):
   – Consists of a cryptographic pair of keys: public and private keys.
   – Are user-controlled, with transactions requiring the user's private key for authorization.
   – The creation of user-owned accounts does not incur transaction fees.
   – Can receive, hold, and send Ether, the native currency of Ethereum.
   – Can interact with deployed smart contracts.
II. Contract Account (CA):
   – Represents a smart contract deployed to the network, controlled by code.
   – Are not controlled by any user – operations are determined by the programmed code.
   – The deployment of contract accounts involves transaction fees due to network storage usage.
   – Can receive, hold, and send Ether.
   – Can interact with other deployed smart contracts.
   – Can be triggered by various actions, such as receiving tokens or creating another contract account through transactions from external accounts.

In summary, both Externally Owned Accounts (EOAs) and Contract Accounts (CAs) can manage Ether transactions and engage with deployed smart contracts. EOAs are user-controlled and do not incur fees for creation, while Contract Accounts, controlled by code, involve deployment transaction fees and respond to actions from external accounts.

4.3.5.6 Account Abstraction and Smart Contract Wallets

Account abstraction proposes improvements to Ethereum account management, aiming for greater flexibility. Presently, users use private keys to interact with Externally Owned Accounts (EOAs), and only EOAs can initiate transactions. When interacting with smart contracts, users

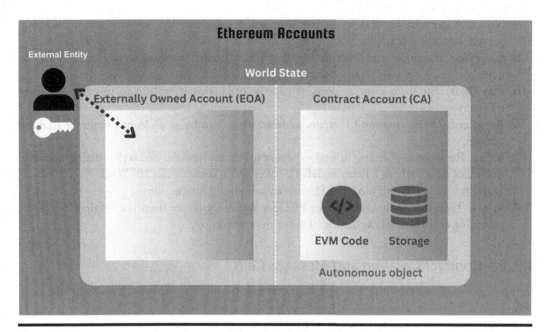

Figure 4.16   Two types of Ethereum accounts – EOA and CA.

must go through EOAs, introducing limitations like the need to maintain an ETH balance for gas fees.

The proposal introduces Smart Contract Wallets, such as ERC-4337, operating based on Contract Accounts (CAs) instead of EOAs. Smart Contract Wallets allow users to interact with smart contracts without managing private keys for EOAs or holding Ether in those accounts. This innovation simplifies the user experience, addressing challenges related to forgetting or losing seed phrases. Seed phrases in the context of Ethereum accounts are a series of words generated by your cryptocurrency wallet that grant access to your wallet and funds, acting as a backup to recover your account if needed.

Smart Contract Wallets, facilitated by Account Abstraction, offer notable enhancements to Ethereum. They allow for batch transactions, multi-step operations, social recovery for lost keys, sponsored transactions (where others cover gas costs), and the utilization of alternative crypto assets for gas, extending beyond the native coin (ETH). The implementation of Account Abstraction through Smart Contract Wallets aims to enhance the user-friendliness and versatility of blockchain interactions.

4.3.5.7 Ethereum Transactions

Transactions in Ethereum are cryptographic signed data messages that contain a set of instructions, which can involve sending Ether from one Ethereum account to another or interacting with a smart contract deployed on the blockchain. These transactions are the sole triggers for a change of state or the execution of a contract in the Ethereum Virtual Machine (EVM).

An ethereum transaction, in its serialized binary message form, includes the following key data:

I. **Nonce**: A sequence number issued by the originating Externally Owned Account (EOA) to prevent message replay.
II. **Gas price**: The amount of Ether (in wei) that the originator is willing to pay for each unit of gas.
III. **Gas limit**: The maximum amount of gas the originator is willing to purchase for this transaction.
IV. **Recipient**: The destination Ethereum address, which can be an EOA or a contract account address.
V. **Value**: The amount of Ether (in wei) to be sent to the destination. Wei is the smallest denomination of Ether, where 1 Ether equals 10^{18} Wei and 1 Gwei equals 10^9 Wei.
VI. **Data**: A variable-length binary data payload containing instructions.
VII. **V, r, s**: The three components of an ECDSA digital signature from the originating EOA, providing cryptographic authentication for the transaction.

4.3.5.8 Contract Creation and Message Calls

In Ethereum, there are two primary types of transactions: contract creation transactions and message calls.

4.3.5.8.1 Contract Creation Transaction

■ A smart contract account is deployed on the Ethereum blockchain through a contract creation transaction initiated from an Externally Owned Account (EOA).

4.3.5.8.2 Message Call Transaction

■ A message call transaction, initiated by an Externally Owned Account (EOA), facilitates interaction with another EOA or an existing contract account on the Ethereum blockchain.
■ Examples of message call transactions include sending Ether from one account to another or interacting with a smart contract (e.g., executing a trade on the decentralized exchange Uniswap).

4.3.5.9 Account State and World State

The primary objective of transaction processing in Ethereum is to update the world state through the creation of blocks.

Accounts serve as the fundamental components of the world state in Ethereum, and they consist of various elements.

An account is technically defined as the mapping between the public address of an account and its account state. The account state comprises the following components:

I. **Nonce**: The number of transactions initiated from that account.
II. **Ether Balance**: The amount of Ether held by that account denominated in Wei (equal to 10^{-18} Ether).
III. **Storage Hash**: Relevant for Contract Accounts, it is a 256-bit hash of the root node of a Merkle-Patricia trie that encodes the storage contents of the account. In simple terms, storage hash is where the data relevant to a contract account lives.

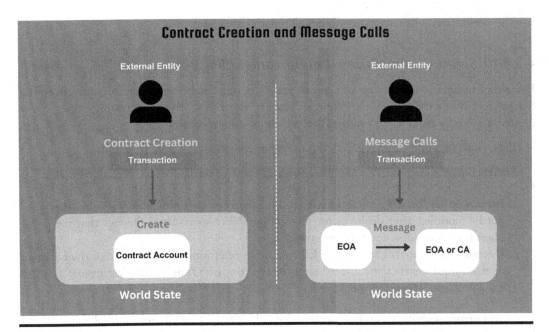

Figure 4.17 **Ethereum transaction types – contract creation and message calls.**

IV. **Code Hash**: Also specific to Contract Accounts, it refers to the binary code of Ethereum smart contracts. This code is immutable and executed by the Ethereum Virtual Machine (EVM) in response to message calls.

It's important to note that the account state in Ethereum does not include information about tokens owned by a particular address, such information is managed by respective smart contracts.

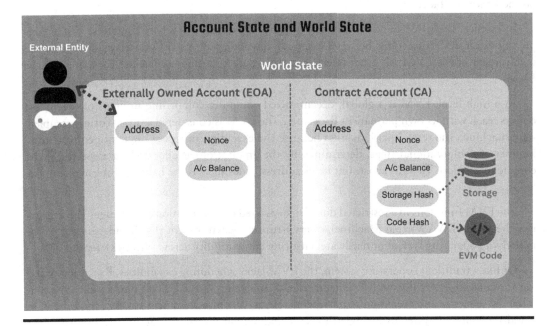

Figure 4.18 **Account state for EOA and CA.**

The world state in Ethereum aggregates all the account states.

4.3.5.10 Smart Contracts on Ethereum and Solidity

Ethereum introduced the concept of contract accounts and, consequently, smart contracts on the blockchain. While the term "smart contract" existed since the 1990s, Ethereum brought a new dimension to it by making it a fundamental feature of its blockchain.

Ethereum is a world computer and like any other computer, it is programmable.

Smart contracts are programs for Ethereum and exhibit several distinctive characteristics:

1. **Immutability**: Smart contracts deployed on Ethereum are immutable, meaning they cannot be modified after deployment. This immutability stems from the fact that the Code Hash for a contract account is unchangeable.
2. **Determinism**: Smart contracts on Ethereum are deterministic, ensuring that the outcome of executing a smart contract is the same for everyone who runs it. This deterministic nature enhances consistency and reliability.

Ethereum smart contracts are crafted using high-level languages such as Solidity and Vyper. These languages provide developers with the tools to create programmable, self-executing contracts that automate and enforce predefined rules and conditions.

4.3.6 Ethereum Virtual Machine (EVM)

4.3.6.1 Introduction to EVM

Ethereum nodes are equipped with Ethereum Virtual Machines (EVMs) to process smart contracts. The EVM functions as the runtime environment responsible for executing smart contracts on the Ethereum blockchain.

In essence, the EVM handles the deployment and execution of smart contracts. While simple value transfer transactions between externally owned accounts (EOAs) may not require the involvement of the EVM, all other operations that result in a state update are computed by the EVM.

At a high level, EVM is a global, decentralized computer comprising millions of executable objects, each with its own permanent data store. The EVM is considered a quasi-Turing-complete state machine. The term "quasi" is used because the execution processes are confined to a finite number of computational steps, determined by the amount of gas allocated for a specific smart contract execution. This gas constraint helps address issues such as the halting problem or infinite loops.

The EVM functions in a restricted domain, dedicated to computation and storage. This design, like the JVM (JAVA Virtual Machine), offers a runtime environment that is independent of the underlying operating system or hardware, ensuring compatibility across various systems.

Unlike a traditional operating system, the EVM lacks scheduling capabilities. Execution ordering is managed externally, with Ethereum clients analyzing verified block transactions to determine the sequence and execution requirements for smart contracts. In this context, the Ethereum world computer operates in a single-threaded manner, similar to JavaScript. Additionally, the

EVM lacks a "system interface" or "hardware support" since it doesn't interact with physical machines – it is a completely virtual entity.

4.3.6.2 Role of EVM in Ethereum

The primary function of the Ethereum Virtual Machine (EVM) within Ethereum is to calculate state transitions based on transactions involving smart contracts.

While each Ethereum node runs its local instance of the EVM, it's important to note that all instances of the EVM operate on the same initial state and produce an identical final state. This collective behavior effectively transforms the Ethereum network into a unified "world computer."

The EVM plays a crucial role in managing all account state transitions, and by extension, it contributes to the overall transition of the world state in the Ethereum blockchain.

4.3.6.3 Smart Contract Compilation

The Ethereum Virtual Machine (EVM) operates at a low level and doesn't comprehend smart contracts written in high-level languages like Solidity. Instead, it understands machine-readable instructions known as Opcodes (operation codes).

Programmers use compilers, such as Solc for Solidity, to translate their high-level code into bytecode. Bytecode consists of a sequence of Opcode instructions, which are then executed by the EVM.

Let us see what a few simple lines of code on Solidity look like in Opcodes (Figure 4.19). We can now understand why we are not programming in Opcodes.

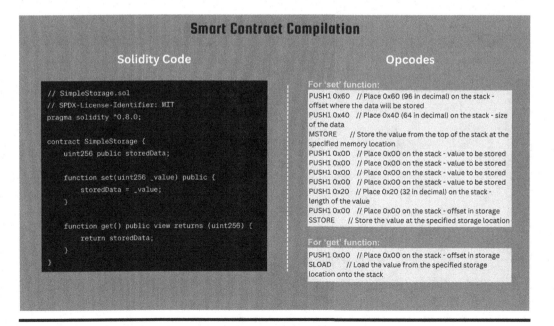

Figure 4.19 Solidity Code and respective Opcodes.

EVM performs diverse tasks, including arithmetic, logic, blockchain interaction, smart contract execution, and data access through specific opcodes, each serving a unique purpose in enhancing its functionality.

4.3.6.4 EVM Architecture

The Ethereum Virtual Machine (EVM) operates on a stack-based architecture, where all in-memory values are stored on a stack (Figure 4.20). It uses a word size of 256 bits, primarily to support native hashing and elliptic curve operations.

The EVM encompasses various addressable data components:

1. **Immutable Program Code (ROM)**: This carries the bytecode of the smart contract intended for execution.
2. **Volatile Memory**: Each location in memory is explicitly initialized to zero and is temporary during the execution of a smart contract.
3. **Permanent Account Storage**: A component of the Ethereum state, this storage is zero-initialized and endures across multiple executions of a smart contract.

4.3.6.5 Stack and Stack Machine

The Ethereum Virtual Machine (EVM) utilizes a stack-based architecture. The stack, in computer science, is an abstract data type characterized by two main operations:

1. **Push**: This operation adds an element to the collection.
2. **Pop**: This operation removes the most recently added element that has not yet been removed.

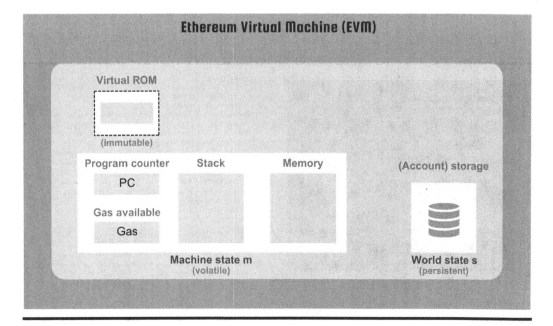

Figure 4.20   Visual representation of EVM architecture.

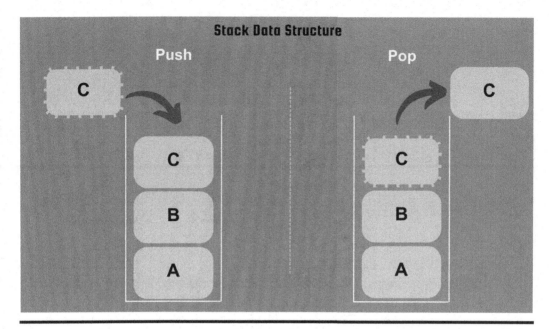

Figure 4.21   Push and Pop in Stack Data Structure.

A real-life analogy for a stack is a stack of plates (Figure 4.21). You can only take a plate from the top of the stack, and you can only add a plate to the top. If you want to access a plate not on the top, you must remove all the plates above it. Similarly, in a stack data structure, you can only interact with the element on the top, and the last-added element is the first one to be removed.

4.3.6.6 EVM Code and Smart Contract Execution

Recall our discussion on Ethereum accounts, particularly the "Code Hash" associated with contract accounts.

The Ethereum Virtual Machine (EVM) Code is essentially the bytecode of the smart contract linked to the contract account. As previously mentioned, there are two main types of transactions in Ethereum – Contract Creation and Message Call transactions.

To create a new contract, a contract creation transaction is required (Figure 4.22). In this transaction, the "to" field is set to the special 0x0 address, and the "data" field contains the contract's initiation code. When processed, this transaction initializes a new contract account with the code specified in the "data" field. The Ethereum Virtual Machine (EVM) is instantiated, and the execution output of the deployment code becomes the code for the new contract account. This allows new contracts to be programmatically initialized, leveraging the Ethereum world state at the time of deployment.

Subsequent message calls to the contract address invoke the "EVM code," and the account state is updated accordingly.

Importantly, the "EVM code" is immutable, meaning the "Code Hash" can never be changed for a deployed smart contract. Only the "Storage Hash" is updated, along with the nonce and balance if applicable.

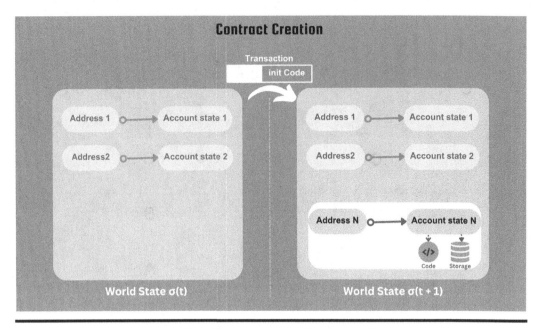

Figure 4.22 Visual representation of a contract creation transaction.

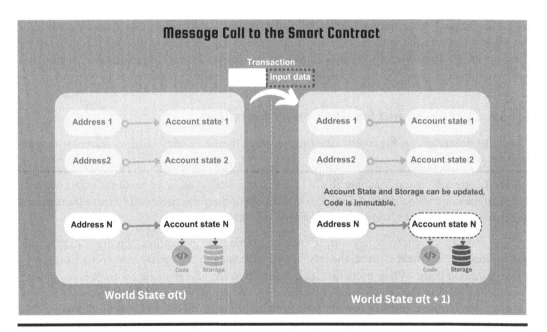

Figure 4.23 Visual representation of a message call to a smart contract.

4.3.6.7 EVM Compatible Blockchains

You probably hear the term "EVM Compatible" all the time. So, What does it mean?

The term "EVM Compatible" refers to a blockchain network or platform that is specifically designed to execute applications and smart contracts written in the same bytecode as Ethereum, utilizing the Ethereum Virtual Machine (EVM).

An EVM-compatible blockchain is engineered to run applications and execute smart contracts using the same bytecode as Ethereum. It ensures that smart contracts developed for Ethereum can be deployed and run on the EVM-compatible blockchain with minimal or no modifications to the code.

EVM Compatibility brings various benefits such as smart contract compatibility as Ethereum-compatible smart contracts can also run on these blockchains and interoperability as existing decentralized applications or token projects can be migrated to these blockchains. Apart from that, developers can leverage existing Ethereum-based frameworks, debugging tools, and other resources to develop decentralized applications for these blockchains.

In DeFi, EVM compatibility makes it easier for projects to migrate their tokens between different blockchain networks, which can be important for strategic reasons or to tap into different liquidity pools.

EVM compatibility plays a crucial role in fostering a more interconnected blockchain ecosystem, enabling developers to create and deploy applications across multiple platforms that adhere to Ethereum's bytecode standards.

Now, some major EVM-compatible blockchains are Binance Smart Chain (BSC), Polygon (formerly Matic), Avalanche, Harmony, and Optimistic Ethereum (Optimism).

BSC offers fast block times (around three seconds) and low transaction fees. Polygon aims to provide scalable and interoperable solutions for Ethereum. Avalanche supports the creation of custom blockchain networks with various consensus mechanisms. Harmony focuses on scalability with fast transaction confirmations and low fees. Optimism is designed to bring layer 2 scaling solutions to the Ethereum network.

Please note that we are not talking about Web3 governance here. That will be covered in the "Decentralization in Web3" chapter.

Okay, now that we (hopefully) have a solid base in Web3, let us cover some technologies that can act as the bedrock of our decentralized future.

We discussed the problems with centralized technical systems in the previous chapters. Most of the problems with centralized systems arise from

1. **Centralized user authentication** – Centralized authentication involves gathering user data, leading to privacy and security concerns.
2. **Centralized storage of data** – Centralized storage gives way to data breaches, data loss, and availability issues.
3. **Centralized analytics** – Despite being the norm, data science doesn't have to be centralized. Big tech often justifies data centralization for analytics benefits, but this approach raises privacy, security, and ethical concerns.

Now, we will discuss three technological trends that are leading us towards decentralization of each aspect mentioned above – 'Decentralized Identity Solutions', 'Decentralized Storage', and 'Decentralized Data Science'.

Bibliography

Antonopoulos, A. M., & Wood, G. (n.d.). *ethereumbook/ethereumbook: Mastering Ethereum, by Andreas M. Antonopoulos, Gavin Wood*. GitHub. Retrieved December 13, 2023, from https://github.com/ethereumbook/ethereumbook

BitTorrent | The World's Most Popular Torrent Client. Retrieved December 13, 2023, from https://www.bittorrent.com

Buterin, V. (n.d.). *Ethereum: A Next-Generation Smart Contract and Decentralized Application Platform.*. Retrieved February 29, 2024, from https://ethereum.org/content/whitepaper/whitepaper-pdf/Ethereum_Whitepaper_-_Buterin_2014.pdf

Buterin, V. (2021, September 29). *ERC 4337: Account Abstraction without Ethereum Protocol Changes | by Vitalik Buterin | Infinitism*. Medium. Retrieved December 13, 2023, from https://medium.com/infinitism/erc-4337-account-abstraction-without-ethereum-protocol-changes-d75c9d94dc4a

Chandrakant, K. (2023, March 20). *Fundamentals of Distributed Systems*. Baeldung. Retrieved December 13, 2023, from https://www.baeldung.com/cs/distributed-systems-guide

Consensys. (n.d.). *Consensys/teku: Java Implementation of the Ethereum 2.0 Beacon Chain*. GitHub. Retrieved February 13, 2024, from https://github.com/Consensys/teku

EIP-1559: Fee Market Change for ETH 1.0 Chain. (2019, April 13). Ethereum Improvement Proposals. Retrieved December 26, 2023, from https://eips.ethereum.org/EIPS/eip-1559

Erigon. (n.d.). *ledgerwatch/erigon: Ethereum Implementation on the Efficiency Frontier*. GitHub. Retrieved February 13, 2024, from https://github.com/ledgerwatch/erigon

ethereumbook/07smart-contracts-solidity.asciidoc at develop · ethereumbook/ethereumbook. (n.d.). GitHub. Retrieved December 13, 2023, from https://github.com/ethereumbook/ethereumbook/blob/develop/07smart-contracts-solidity.asciidoc

ethereumbook/13evm.asciidoc at develop · ethereumbook/ethereumbook. (n.d.). GitHub. Retrieved December 13, 2023, from https://github.com/ethereumbook/ethereumbook/blob/develop/13evm.asciidoc

GitHub, Inc. (n.d.). GitHub: Let's Build from Here · GitHub. Retrieved December 13, 2023, from https://github.com

Go Ethereum. (n.d.). *ethereum/go-ethereum: Official Go Implementation of the Ethereum Protocol*. GitHub. Retrieved February 13, 2024, from https://github.com/ethereum/go-ethereum

Holochain | Distributed App Framework with P2P Networking. Retrieved December 26, 2023, from https://www.holochain.org

Home | Solidity Programming Language. Retrieved December 26, 2023, from https://soliditylang.org/

Hon. Joseph C. Hutcheson,Jr. (1951). *Natural Law and the Right to Property*. Retrieved December 13, 2023, from https://scholarship.law.nd.edu/cgi/viewcontent.cgi?filename=6&article=1004&context=naturallaw_proceedings&type=additional

Hyperledger Besu. (n.d.). Welcome | Besu Documentation. Retrieved February 13, 2024, from https://besu.hyperledger.org

Installing the Solidity Compiler. (2023, October 30). docs.soliditylang.org. Retrieved December 26, 2023, from https://docs.soliditylang.org/en/develop/installing-solidity.html

Liang, Y.-C. (n.d.). *(PDF) Blockchain for Dynamic Spectrum Management*. ResearchGate. Retrieved February 28, 2024, from https://www.researchgate.net/publication/337306138_Blockchain_for_Dynamic_Spectrum_Management

Lighthouse. (n.d.). *sigp/lighthouse: Ethereum Consensus Client in Rust*. GitHub. Retrieved February 13, 2024, from https://github.com/sigp/lighthouse

Linux Org. (n.d.). Linux.org. Retrieved December 13, 2023, from https://www.linux.org

Nethermind. (n.d.). Nethermind | Blockchain Research & Software Engineering. Retrieved February 13, 2024, from https://www.nethermind.io

Nikolaidis, F. (2019, May). *Figure 1.7 -CAP Theorem*. ResearchGate. Retrieved December 26, 2023, from https://www.researchgate.net/figure/CAP-Theorem-is-a-concept-that-a-distributed-storage-system-can-only-have-2-of-the-3_fig5_338689219

Nimbus. (n.d.). Nimbus | Nimbus. Retrieved February 13, 2024, from https://nimbus.team/index.html

Opcodes for the EVM | ethereum.org. (2023, June 19). Ethereum. Retrieved December 13, 2023, from https://ethereum.org/en/developers/docs/evm/opcodes/

Peh, B. (2017, September 15). *Solidity Bytecode and Opcode Basics | by Bernard Peh.* Medium. Retrieved December 13, 2023, from https://medium.com/@blockchain101/solidity-bytecode-and-opcode-basics-672e9b1a88c2

Radix DLT | Radically Better Web3. Retrieved December 13, 2023, from https://www.radixdlt.com/

Tani, T. (n.d.). *Ethereum EVM Illustrated.* GitHub. Retrieved February 29, 2024, from https://github.com/takenobu-hs/ethereum-evm-illustrated

Vyper — Vyper Documentation. Retrieved December 26, 2023, from https://docs.vyperlang.org/

Weyl, G., Kennith, S., Manivel, R., & Shruthi, K. (2022, May 11). *Decentralized Society: Finding Web3's Soul by E. Glen Weyl, Puja Ohlhaver, Vitalik Buterin: SSRN.* SSRN Papers. Retrieved December 26, 2023, from https://papers.ssrn.com/sol3/papers.cfm?abstract_id=4105763

Chapter 5

Decentralized Identity Systems

Sam Ghosh

If someone asks your identity, you would probably respond with your name or profession. This is often an acceptable response in casual settings. However, in formal settings such as in a job application, you might need to provide proof to validate such claims.

Traditional identity validation methods conducted by external entities expose individuals to risks such as identity theft and surveillance, particularly as personal data becomes more accessible online.

Decentralized identity solutions empower individuals to regain control over their digital identities and personal data in the interconnected digital world.

Let us learn how.

5.1 Basics of Identity Systems

Our identity in the world relies on entities that validate our claims about who we are, what we have done, and our capabilities. These validating entities are referred to as identity systems.

An identity system typically consists of the following elements:

1. **Identity**: The core aspect of who an individual or entity is, encompassing personal attributes, characteristics, and information.
2. **Identifier**: A unique designation or set of data used to distinguish and reference an individual within the identity system.
3. **Attestation**: Verification or confirmation provided by external entities validating specific aspects of an individual's identity.
4. **Role**: The designated function, position, or responsibilities associated with an individual within a particular context or community.

Together, these elements constitute the foundational structure of an identity system, facilitating the governance, verification, and control of identities.

 DOI: 10.4324/9781003507352-5

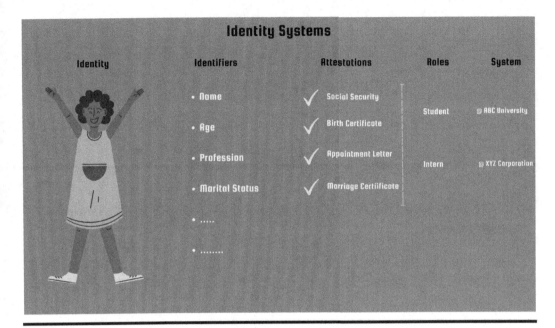

Figure 5.1   Broad Overview of Identity Systems.

Now, let's delve deeper into each of these components.

5.1.1 Identity

In an identity system, "identity" refers to a comprehensive set of attributes and data that uniquely establish an individual or entity, forming a detailed profile outlining distinctive characteristics. The concept of "identity" covers a wide range of personal information that sets one entity apart from another.

Identity information includes various details:

- *Personally Identifiable Information (PII)*: PII refers to essential personal information such as full name, date of birth, social security number, address, contact details, and government-issued IDs, crucial for uniquely identifying individuals.
- *Additional Attributes*: An identity goes beyond PII, encompassing diverse attributes like education, employment history, financial records, and other relevant details, collectively contributing to an individual's uniqueness and depth.
- *Digital Persona*: The concept of identity extends beyond the physical attributes into the digital space. It encapsulates online behavior, internet usage patterns, social media interactions, digital footprints, and preferences, forming an individual's digital persona.

An individual's identity is a multidimensional portrayal comprising personal data, physical and digital attributes, and a digital persona. This collective of these elements distinguishes one person from another within an identity system.

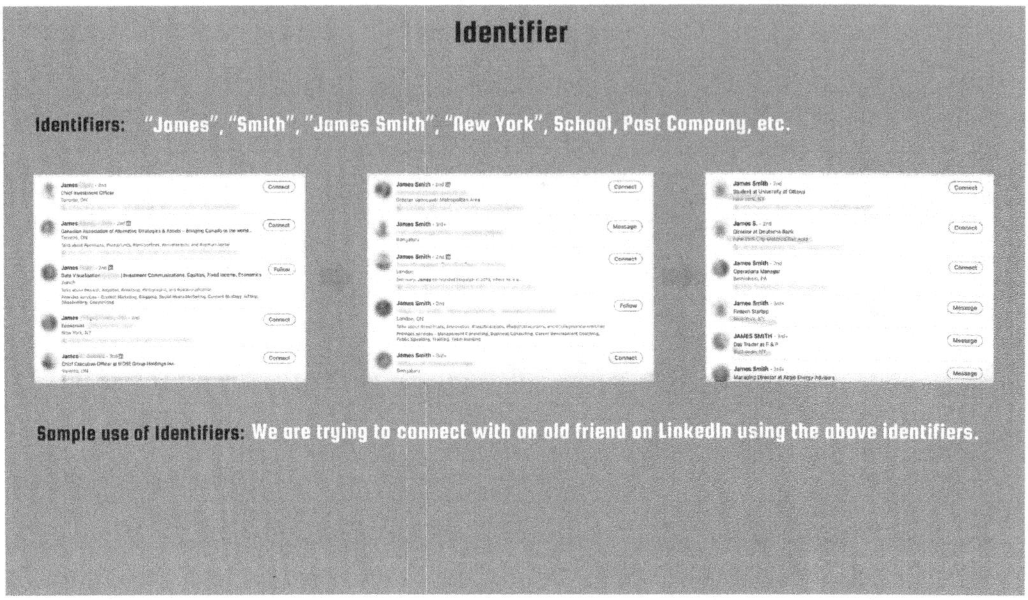

Figure 5.2   Illustration of how identifiers are used with the example of a LinkedIn search.

5.1.2 *Identifier*

In identity systems, an identifier serves as a unique digital code or token intricately linked to an individual's identity. It functions as a distinct label, locating and distinguishing a specific identity within a specific context.

Identifiers play a pivotal role in digital systems by facilitating the management, access, and referencing of identities. They are fundamental in the process of identifying and differentiating individuals, enabling systems to accurately recognize and interact with specific identities.

5.1.3 *Attestation*

In the context of identity systems, attestation is a fundamental process that involves presenting evidence or proof to substantiate specific attributes or claims associated with an identity.

In identity systems, validation is often done through trusted entities using methods like digital signatures or formal attestations to confirm the accuracy of information linked to an individual's identity.

5.1.4 *Role*

In identity systems, a "role" refers to the specific function, responsibility, or access rights assigned to an individual or entity within a given context, outlining the scope of actions or information access within that setting.

Roles are pivotal in defining the capabilities and authorizations of an identity within a system, determining their level of access and permissions. For example, in an organization's SAP system, roles like "employee," "manager," or "administrator" grant varying levels of access and permissions based on job responsibilities.

Roles within an identity system are crucial for managing access rights and permissions. Aligned with an entity's duties, roles determine who can access specific information and perform authorized actions based on assigned responsibilities or functions.

A methodical approach to roles in an identity system establishes clear access levels, guaranteeing that each identity only has access to pertinent information and functionalities. This systematic regulation of access rights through assigned roles not only strengthens security but also ensures that individuals possess appropriate permissions aligned with their responsibilities in a specific system or organization.

5.1.5 Who Owns your Identity?

In a centralized system, the centralized authority controls the identities, meaning the authority owns the identities. This is where decentralized identity systems differ.

Decentralized identity systems leverage decentralized identifiers (DIDs), unique identifiers that empower individuals with control over their digital identity across platforms. DIDs act as portable and universal keys, allowing users to manage and utilize their identity information across diverse applications and services.

5.2 Introduction to Digital Identity Systems

Digital identity systems are frameworks designed to manage, authenticate, and verify the digital identities of individuals or entities across various online platforms. It's important to highlight that these systems are not limited to humans and can also be extended to objects within the Internet of Things (IoT) and even to organizations.

Digital identity systems are essentially databases storing verified information about individuals or objects.

Given that these systems store and secure verified information related to individuals or objects, these databases can function as single sources of truth regarding various claims about the individuals or the objects.

5.2.1 Types of Digital Identity Systems

5.2.1.1 Centralized Systems

Government-issued IDs: Traditional identity systems managed by governmental authorities, including driver's licenses, passports, and national identification cards.

Corporate identity systems: Organizations and corporations manage digital identities for employees and clients through centralized databases and proprietary systems.

5.2.1.2 Decentralized Systems

Self-sovereign identity (SSI): Empowers individuals to control their digital identities. Platforms like Sovrin and uPort enable users to manage identity information through decentralized and verifiable credentials.

    Blockchain-based systems: Platforms like Civic and SelfKey leverage blockchain technology for secure and decentralized identity management, offering users control over their digital identities.

5.2.1.3 Federated Identity Systems

Single sign-on (SSO): Systems like OAuth and OpenID enable users to access multiple services using a single set of credentials. This is often managed by major tech companies such as Google, Facebook, or Twitter.

    Social login and federated identity providers: Services like "Login with Facebook" or "Sign in with Google" utilize users' existing social media accounts as credentials for various platforms and applications.

5.3 Evolution of Digital Identity

Digital identity has undergone significant transformations over the years, shaped by technological advancements, evolving societal needs, and the proliferation of online interactions.

    Let's explore the key phases in the evolution of digital identity.

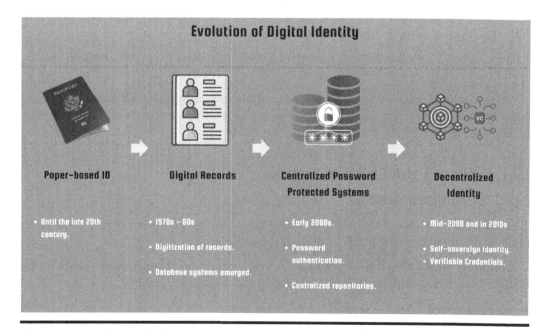

Figure 5.3 Evolution of digital identity over the years.

5.3.1 Pre-digital Era

In the pre-digital era, identity records were paper-based, relying on documents like passports and driver's licenses. This persisted until the late 20th century before the widespread adoption of digital records.

5.3.2 Emergence of Digital Records

During the 1970s and 1980s, there was a significant shift from paper to digital records, with the development of organizational database systems. This marked the initial transition from manual, paper-based record-keeping to computerized data storage, improving the efficiency of data management.

5.3.3 Rise of Centralized Digital Identity Systems

In the late 20th century and early 2000s, basic username-password systems for online authentication emerged. Companies adopted centralized database repositories for digital identities, storing user credentials and personal information. This facilitated centralized access to individual identities across various online services.

5.3.4 Blockchain and Decentralized Identity

Decentralized identity technologies gained prominence in the mid-2000s, especially with the growth of blockchain and related technologies in the 2010s. We will explore these technologies in the following sections.

5.4 Types of Digital Identities

Digital identities are not limited to human identity.

5.4.1 Individual Digital Identity

Pertains to a person's online presence, personal information, and digital footprint in various systems and platforms.

5.4.2 Corporate Digital Identity

Represents an organization, encompassing its legal identity, structure, roles, and access rights for its members.

5.4.3 Device Digital Identity

Refers to the identity and authentication of machines, gadgets, or IoT devices, enabling secure interactions and data exchange.

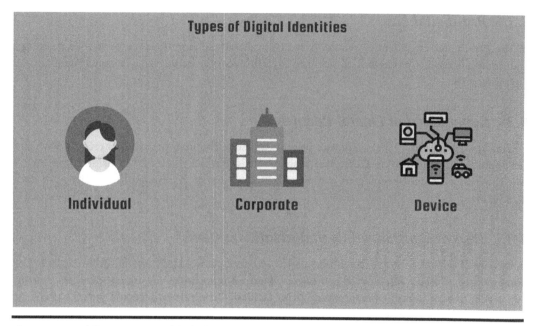

Figure 5.4   Different types of digital identities.

5.5 Why Talk about Digital Identity now?

But, why talk about digital identity now? What is the urgency?

The increasing significance of digital identity stems from the exponential growth of personal data moving online. This shift isn't limited to government agencies and regulatory bodies. It also extends to the corporate sector, where extensive user data is being collected to construct large information repositories.

Applications often request extensive permissions to access contacts, images, and emails, frequently without users fully grasping the implications. Onboarding processes are designed to collect maximum data with minimal resistance, putting user privacy and control of personal information at risk.

It is crucial to address these digital identity issues to regain control, ensure transparency, and safeguard user privacy in our swiftly digitizing world.

5.5.1 Data Privacy Concerns

Let me explain how vulnerable user privacy is in this digital age with one example.

The BBC documentary "The Trap: India's Deadliest Scam" investigates Chinese-operated loan apps that ensnare users in debt cycles. These apps utilize aggressive tactics via call centers to recover loans, resulting in distress and over 60 reported suicides.

These loan apps typically target economically vulnerable groups like students and informal workers, offering small loan amounts ranging from $100 to $1000.

Besides charging exorbitant interest rates, these apps pose a threat by collecting extensive user information, including contacts, call history, and images. Harassment begins even before the due payment date, manifesting in repeated abusive calls not only directed at the borrower but also at individuals in their contact list.

In a disturbing case, manipulated pornographic images of a female debtor were distributed to her entire contact list, which included colleagues, acquaintances, and her own daughter.

Recounting her experience, the victim expressed profound shock and considered suicide, revealing the emotional toll inflicted by the invasive tactics: "I was numb, shocked. I thought of suicide but did not have the courage…Morphed photos showing me nude were sent to everyone in my contact list, including my daughter, my father's acquaintances, and children for whom I am like a mother."

Users may face privacy threats not only from voluntarily shared data but also from hacked databases. Governments and corporations, in recent years, have amassed massive databases with inadequate security measures, raising concerns about unauthorized access and potential misuse.

For example, the Indian Aadhar database faced a data breach in October 2023, affecting the personal information of 815 million individuals.

These vulnerabilities underscore the broader threats individuals encounter in the digital age.

However, concerns related to digital identity systems extend beyond just privacy.

5.5.2 Exclusion and Digital Divide

A significant issue in identity systems stems from the exclusion of certain demographics due to limited access to technology or documentation.

Substantial portions of the population, particularly in developing nations, lack formal identification, leading to their exclusion from various services and opportunities. This digital disparity exacerbates social and economic inequalities, impeding their access to essential resources such as healthcare, education, and financial services.

5.5.3 Centralized Control and Single Point of Failure

Conventional identity systems, relying on centralized databases, face the risk of a single point of failure. Compromises in these databases can lead to widespread identity theft, fraud, and data breaches, affecting millions of individuals.

5.5.4 Complex Identity Verification Processes

The existing procedures for identity verification are often burdensome, time-intensive, and complex. This challenge is particularly pronounced in cross-border identity verification or interactions between diverse systems.

Authenticating identity across various platforms, especially without a universal standard, is challenging and requires extensive paperwork and authentication procedures.

The evolution of digital ecosystems has given rise to interconnected digital identities, encompassing both physical attributes and online personas and activities.

Efficiently managing and safeguarding digital identities has become crucial as individuals engage in diverse online platforms and activities. Growing concerns include potential risks of impersonation, hacking, and fraud in digital ecosystems.

Addressing these identity-related challenges demands innovative solutions and a fundamental rethinking of how identity is both managed and verified.

Let us now explore decentralized identity solutions.

5.6 Introduction to Decentralized Identity

Decentralized identity enables individuals, organizations, or entities to control and own their digital identities, removing the need for a central authority. This departure from traditional identity management empowers entities to securely handle and authenticate their identities in a decentralized manner.

5.6.1 Key Characteristics of Decentralized Identity

5.6.1.1 User Control and Ownership

Entities, whether they are individuals or organizations, have full control over their digital identities, managing and presenting identity attributes autonomously without relying on centralized authorities.

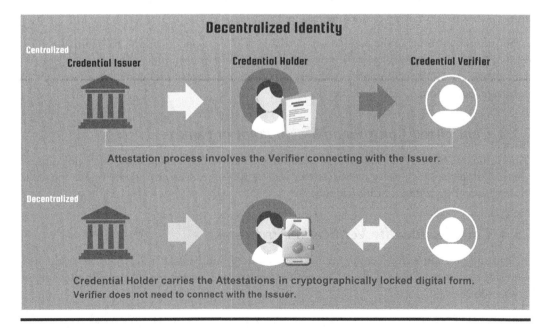

Figure 5.5 Visual representation of how decentralized identity works differently from centralized identity solutions.

5.6.1.2 Decentralization

Decentralized identity operates on a distributed architecture, often utilizing technologies like blockchain or other distributed ledger systems. This ensures that identity data is stored across a network in a distributed manner, enhancing security and resilience.

5.6.1.3 Privacy and Selective Disclosure

Decentralized identity empowers users to selectively disclose specific identity attributes without revealing unnecessary personal information, enhancing privacy and security in identity verification.

5.6.1.4 Interoperability and Portability

Decentralized identity systems prioritize interoperability, ensuring that identities are portable and applicable across diverse platforms and services, fostering seamless integration.

5.6.1.5 Verifiable and Trustworthy Credentials

Decentralized identity systems use verifiable credentials and cryptographic proofs to ensure secure and tamper-resistant identity verification, eliminating reliance on centralized authorities.

Now that we have gained some insight into decentralized identity, let's delve into self-sovereign identities, an implementation of decentralized identity principles.

5.7 Self-sovereign Identity (SSI)

Self-sovereign identity (SSI) empowers individuals with full control over their identities, allowing them to manage and disclose personal information based on their preferences, without relying on central authorities or intermediaries.

SSI aims to empower individuals with the autonomy to securely and privately own, manage, and present their digital identities across diverse interactions and contexts.

5.7.1 Three Pillars of Self-sovereign Identity (SSI)

5.7.1.1 Decentralized Identifiers (DIDs)

Decentralized identifiers (DIDs) are unique, self-owned identifiers that empower entities to manage their identities across various systems and contexts.

5.7.1.2 Verifiable Credentials (VCs)

Verifiable credentials (VCs) are digital proofs validating identity attributes, issued by trusted entities, and cryptographically secured for verification.

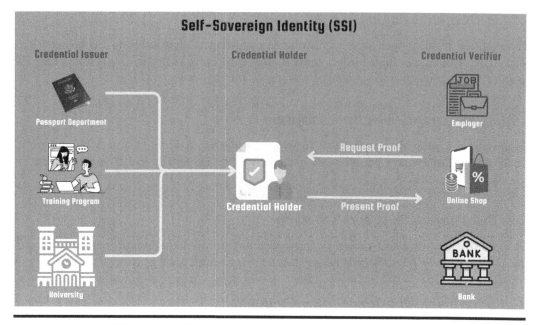

Figure 5.6 Visual illustration of the self-sovereign identity (SSI) process.

5.7.1.3 Blockchain or Distributed Ledger Systems

These serve as the infrastructure supporting secure and decentralized storage of identity data and transactions. They establish a trusted and tamper-resistant environment.

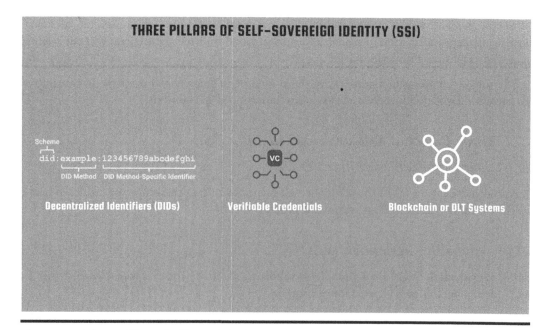

Figure 5.7 Three pillars of self-sovereign identity (SSI).

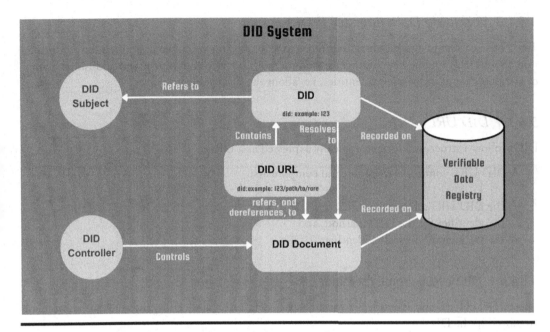

Figure 5.8 **Visual illustration of how a DID system works.**

5.8 Decentralized Identifiers (DIDs)

Decentralized identifiers (DIDs) are essential components of self-sovereign identity systems, serving as unique and persistent identifiers for individuals, organizations, and devices within decentralized identity frameworks.

Decentralized identifiers (DIDs) empower entities to establish and control their identities, eliminating the need for reliance on central authorities or intermediaries.

5.8.1 DID System

Decentralized identifier (DID) systems encompass various components including DID subject, DID controller, verifiable data registry, DID URLs, DID documents, and other related elements.

5.8.1.1 DID Subject

The DID subject is the real-world entity associated with the decentralized identifier, representing individuals, organizations, devices, or any entity identified by the DID.

5.8.1.2 DID Controller

The DID controller has authority over the associated DID, making decisions and managing the identifier. It is responsible for updating the DID document, and handling public keys, authentication methods, and service endpoints. The controller may or may not be the same as the subject.

5.8.1.3 Verifiable Data Registry (VDR)

The VDR is a secure and decentralized repository for storing verifiable data, including information about DIDs (public keys, authentication methods, service endpoints), and additional claims or attributes about individuals or entities, i.e. about the DID subject.

5.8.1.4 DID URL

DIDs follow a structured format, typically expressed as a URL.

A DID URL comprises three integral components:

1. The DID URI scheme identifier,
2. The identifier for the DID method, and
3. The DID method-specific identifier.

5.8.1.4.1 DID URI Scheme Identifier

The DID URI scheme identifier is the first part of a DID, indicating the scheme or protocol employed in the DID.

The URI scheme identifier defines how the identifier should be interpreted and accessed, specifying the type of decentralized identifier and its resolution process.

Common examples include "did:" as the prefix for many DIDs, signaling the start of the identifier, followed by the specific DID method, which is the next component in the DID structure.

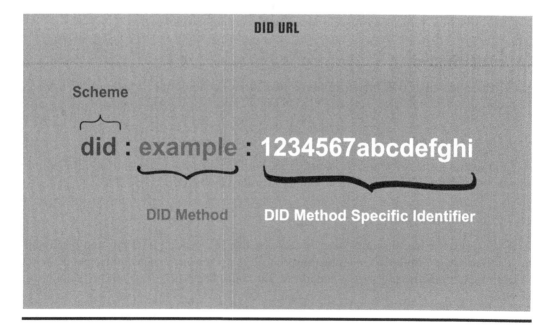

Figure 5.9   Visual illustration of the DID URL components.

5.8.1.4.2 DID Method Identifier

The identifier for the DID method is the second component of a DID, providing information about the method used to create, update, and manage the DID. Each DID is associated with a specific method, outlining the rules and processes governing the identifier's lifecycle.

For example, in the DID "*did:example:123456*," the "*example*" part represents the Identifier for the DID method, indicating that the DID follows the rules and processes defined by the "*example*" method.

Different DID methods may handle identifier creation, resolution, and updates in distinct ways, enhancing the flexibility and diversity of the decentralized identity ecosystem.

5.8.1.4.3 Method-specific Identifier

The DID method-specific identifier, the third component in the DID structure, is unique to each DID and specific to the chosen DID method.

The DID method-specific identifier is the part of the DID that distinguishes one identifier from another within the same method and is determined by the specifications of the chosen DID method.

For example, in the DID "*did:example:123456*,'"the "*123456*" part represents the DID method-specific identifier, and it is specific to the "*example*" DID method. The combination of the DID URI scheme identifier, identifier for the DID method, and DID method-specific identifier creates a unique and decentralized identifier for a specific entity within the chosen decentralized identity framework.

5.8.1.5 DID Document

A DID document is an essential part of decentralized identity systems, offering standardized information about the associated DID entity. It includes key details like public keys, authentication methods, and associated services.

Key elements commonly found in a DID document include:

- **Context and purpose**: Information about the DID's context and the DID's intended purpose.
- **ID**: The unique identifier for the DID.
- **Public keys:** Public keys associated with the DID, which are crucial for cryptographic operations, including authentication and establishing secure communication. Each key has an *ID, type, controller*, and the *actual key material*.
- **Authentication methods**: Details on the methods that can be employed to authenticate the entity linked to the DID.
- **Service endpoints:** Information about services offered by the entity, including endpoints for interactions or communications.
- **Proofs and signatures**: Cryptographic proofs or signatures that can be used to verify the authenticity and integrity of the DID document.

DID Document (Sample)

```
{
  "@context": "https://www.w3.org/ns/did/v1",
  "id": "did:example:123456789abcdefghi",
  "publicKey": [
    {
      "id": "#key1",
      "type": "Ed25519VerificationKey2018",
      "controller": "did:example:123456789abcdefghi",
      "publicKeyBase58":
"zxy7iXuFeA1i6NjMbfTowS5SKC6z9BvHkeTcJ4kMk4Wb",
      "proof": {
        "type": "Ed25519Signature",
        "created": "2022-02-07T12:34:56Z",
        "proofPurpose": "authentication",
        "verificationMethod": "#key1",
        "jws":
"eyJhbGciOiJFZERTQSIsImI2NCI6ZmFsc2UsImNyaXQiOlsiYjY0Il19..
(signature)"
      }
    }
  ],

  "authentication": [
    {
      "type": "Ed25519SignatureAuthentication2018",
      "publicKey": "#key1"
    }
  ],

  "service": [
    {
      "id": "#service1",
      "type": "LinkedDomains",
      "serviceEndpoint": "https://example.com/linked-domains"
    }
  ],
  "proof": {
    "type": "Ed25519Signature",
    "created": "2022-02-07T12:34:56Z",
    "proofPurpose": "assertionMethod",
    "verificationMethod": "#key1",
    "jws":
"eyJhbGciOiJFZERTQSIsImI2NCI6ZmFsc2UsImNyaXQiOlsiYjY0Il19..
(signature)"
  }
}
```

Figure 5.10 Sample DID document to illustrate the components of a DID document.

5.8.1.6 DID Resolution Process

Resolving a decentralized identifier (DID) involves the coordinated interaction between the DID and its associated DID document.

5.8.1.6.1 A General Overview of How the Process Works

5.8.1.6.1.1 DID creation   The process starts with an entity creating a unique identifier and selecting a DID method that governs the identifier's lifecycle.

5.8.1.6.1.2 DID document creation   Simultaneously with DID creation, the entity generates a DID document containing vital information about the associated entity, formatted for machine-readability and interoperability. The DID document contains information on public keys, authentication methods, service endpoints, additional metadata, etc.

5.8.1.6.1.3 Publishing the DID document   The entity publishes the DID document to a location accessible by others. This location can be specified in the DID document itself, and it could be on a decentralized storage system, a distributed ledger (e.g. blockchain), or any other appropriate medium.

5.8.1.6.1.4 Resolving the DID   Resolving a DID involves retrieving the associated DID document by querying the specified location, such as a blockchain or decentralized storage system, to obtain the latest information about the entity.

5.8.1.6.1.5 Verifying and trusting the DID document   During the resolution process, the entity validating the retrieved DID document employs cryptographic methods to ensure integrity.

This involves checking signatures, verifying public keys, and, if successful, establishing trust in the information contained within the document.

5.8.1.6.1.6 Interacting with the Entity   After validating the DID document, the entity gains access to information about associated public keys, authentication methods, and service endpoints. This facilitates secure interactions, including authentication and communication, between the resolving entity and the one associated with the DID.

The process emphasizes trust established via cryptographic verification of the DID document. DIDs' decentralized nature and standardized DID document format enhance security, privacy, and interoperability in decentralized identity systems. This setup reduces reliance on central authorities and intermediaries in identity management.

5.8.2 W3C Standard for Decentralized Identifiers

The World Wide Web Consortium (W3C) has established a standard for decentralized identifiers (DIDs) to ensure consistency and interoperability. This specification defines the structure, methods, and governance of DIDs, ensuring their security, decentralization, and universal applicability.

5.8.2.1 Key Aspects of W3C DID Standard

5.8.2.1.1 Method Specification

The W3C standard provides guidelines for creating method specifications governing the generation and management of DIDs. Examples include "did:op" for the Ocean Protocol and "did:webs" for web-based DIDs. The below table shows a sample of the DID methods currently in development by W3C.

5.8.2.1.2 DID Document Structure

The W3C standard specifies the structure and content of DID documents to ensure consistency, which is crucial for verification and authentication.

5.8.2.1.3 Interoperability

The W3C standard promotes interoperability among DIDs, facilitating collaboration across various decentralized identity systems.

The W3C DID standard sets a universal framework for creating, managing, and using DIDs, ensuring consistent and secure identity representation in decentralized systems. It aims to foster trust, security, and interoperability in decentralized identity management.

Now, let's explore verifiable credentials.

Table 5.1 Sample DID Method Specifications Currently Being Developed by W3C

DID Method	Registry	Contact
dns	Domain Name System (DNS)	Danube Tech
dock	Dock	Dock.io
ethr	Ethereum	uPort
example	DID Specification	W3C DID Working Group
health	DID Health	support
hedera	Hedera Hashgraph	Hedera Hashgraph, Swisscom Blockchain AG
holo	Holochain	Holo.Host
hpass	Hyperledger Fabric	IBM
hsk	PlatON	HashKey DID
ibmdc	Hyperledger Fabric	IBM Digital Credentials
id	ID Service	Mastercard
ion	Bitcoin	Various DIF contributors
iota	IOTA	IOTA Foundation
op	Ocean Protocol	Ocean Protocol
uport	Ethereum	uPort
webs	Web, and Key Event Receipt Infrastructure (KERI).	Trust over IP (ToIP) DID Method webs Task Force.
zkme	EVM compatible chains. Primary on Polygon	zkMe

5.9 Verifiable Credentials (VCs)

Verifiable credentials (VCs) are digital credentials that can cryptographically authenticate specific information about an entity, be it a person, organization, or object, without needing a central authority.

These credentials are portable attestations with cryptographic proofs commonly associated with decentralized identifiers (DIDs).

In a self-sovereign identity (SSI) framework, individuals can possess and present verifiable credentials as evidence of specific attributes, protected by cryptographic mechanisms for integrity and authenticity. The incorporation of verifiable credentials (VCs) with decentralized identifiers (DIDs) adds a decentralized layer, allowing individuals to manage their identity-related data independently of central authorities.

In summary, verifiable credentials serve as portable, cryptographically supported attestations, often linked with DIDs in decentralized identity systems.

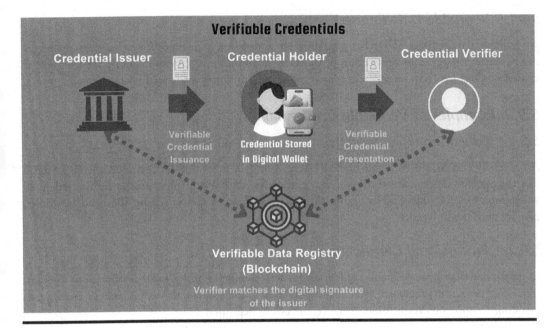

Figure 5.11 Visual illustration of verifiable credentials.

5.9.1 *Components of Verifiable Credentials*

5.9.1.1 *Issuer*

The issuer is the entity responsible for creating and signing a verifiable credential, asserting the authenticity of the information it contains.

Issuers, trusted within specific ecosystems, are entities like governmental bodies, educational institutions, or employers, authorized to make claims about individuals or subjects through verifiable credentials.

5.9.1.2 *Subject or Holder*

The subject of a verifiable credential is the entity for whom the credential provides attestations. This can be an individual, organization, or any entity that the credential is meant to represent.

5.9.1.3 *Claims*

Claims are statements within the verifiable credential that convey specific information about the subject. These claims are the assertions or attributes being attested to. For example, a claim might include information about a person's age, citizenship, or educational qualifications.

5.9.1.4 *Proofs and Signatures*

Proofs and signatures are cryptographic mechanisms used to validate the authenticity and integrity of the verifiable credential. These components ensure that the information within the credential has not been tampered with and that the credential was issued by a trusted and authorized party. Signatures are often generated using public-private key pairs, providing a secure and verifiable means of proving the origin and integrity of the credential.

5.9.1.5 Verifiable Data Registry

A verifiable data registry (VDR) is a secure and tamper-resistant repository that participates in the issuance, storage, and verification of verifiable credentials. It ensures decentralized storage of credentials and may handle cryptographic proofs and signatures associated with them.

5.9.2 Examples of Verifiable Credentials

5.9.2.1 Educational Credentials

A university can issue a verifiable credential certifying an individual's degree, containing details like the person's name, earned degree, and graduation date. Recipients can share this credential with employers for independent verification of its authenticity, eliminating the need for direct contact with the university.

5.9.2.2 Professional Certifications

Organizations can issue verifiable credentials for an individual's professional certifications in fields like IT or project management. Recipients can share these credentials with clients or employers, enabling autonomous verification of the certifications' legitimacy.

5.9.2.3 Identity Documents

Verifiable credentials may be found in digital identity documents, such as government-issued IDs, driver's licenses, or passports. Rather than carrying physical documents, individuals can utilize digitally verifiable credentials, securely sharing and verifying them without divulging unnecessary personal information.

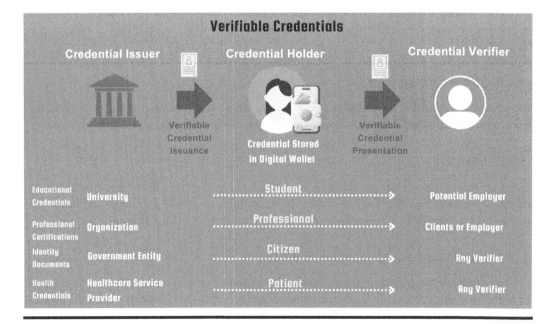

Figure 5.12   Various use cases of verifiable credentials.

5.9.2.4 Health Credentials

In the context of digital health records, verifiable credentials may play a role in authenticating vaccination records, test results, or other medical information. These credentials can be securely shared with healthcare providers, employers, or for travel purposes, all while upholding privacy and data security.

5.9.3 W3C Verifiable Credential Data Model

The W3C verifiable credentials data model, developed by the World Wide Web Consortium (W3C), serves as a standardized framework for secure, interoperable, and privacy-respecting creation, exchange, and verification of digital verifiable credentials. It outlines the structure and procedures for managing and utilizing these credentials, especially within decentralized and self-sovereign identity systems.

5.10 Impact of Decentralized Identity

5.10.1 Benefits of Decentralization of Identity Management

The integration of decentralized identifiers (DIDs) and verifiable credentials transforms the user experience in digital identity management, enhancing privacy, security, and user autonomy.

5.10.1.1 Enhanced User Control

DIDs and verifiable credentials empower users to control their digital identities, enabling selective disclosure for enhanced privacy. This allows users to present specific credentials, ensuring personalized and controlled information-sharing in various interactions.

5.10.1.2 Improved Security

Verifiable credentials, secured by cryptographic proofs, offer tamper-proof identity attribute representations. The integration of DIDs and verifiable credentials enhances security by removing dependence on centralized authorities, reducing the risk of single points of failure.

5.10.1.3 Simplified Identity Interactions

Verifiable credentials simplify identity verification, facilitating easy sharing and verification across different services. The ability to reuse credentials across contexts minimizes redundant data sharing and repeated authentication.

5.10.1.4 Privacy-centric Experience

DIDs and verifiable credentials empower users to have control over how they share data, enhancing online privacy through selective disclosure of specific attributes only when needed, and reducing unnecessary personal information exposure.

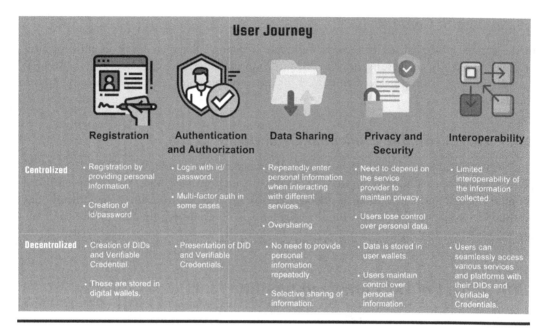

Figure 5.13   Contrasting the user journey in decentralized identity systems with that of centralized identity systems.

5.10.1.5 Portable and Interoperable Identities

Users can easily transfer digital identities across platforms, creating a portable and flexible experience. Standardized DIDs and verifiable credentials allow identities to be used and verified across various systems, fostering a user-friendly and interoperable environment.

5.10.2 User Journey

Let's contrast the user experience in centralized identity systems with decentralized identity systems, emphasizing the crucial distinctions and benefits inherent in each approach.

5.10.2.1 User Registration

In centralized systems, users register with a service provider, submitting personal information to be stored on central servers. Authentication involves creating usernames and passwords.

In decentralized systems, users establish a decentralized identifier (DID) owned and controlled by them. Verifiable credentials, confirming identity attributes, are generated and securely stored in the user's digital wallet for privacy.

5.10.2.2 Authentication and Authorization

In centralized systems, users access services through login credentials like usernames and passwords. The provider validates and authorizes access, sometimes using multi-factor authentication (MFA) for increased security.

In decentralized systems, users present their DIDs and verifiable credentials to access services, eliminating the need for usernames and passwords. Services can independently verify credentials without relying on a central authority.

5.10.2.3 Data Sharing

In centralized systems, repetitive entry of personal information is common when using various services, with limited control over data sharing.

Decentralized systems allow users to selectively disclose attributes via verifiable credentials, sharing only necessary information. No repetitive entry of personal data is needed, as users carry identity attributes in their digital wallets.

5.10.2.4 Privacy and Security

In centralized systems, users rely on service providers to secure data, risking breaches and privacy concerns. Control over shared data is often limited.

Decentralized systems securely store data in the user's wallet, minimizing vulnerability to breaches. Users have greater control over their data and can manage privacy preferences for each interaction.

5.10.2.5 Interoperability

In the case of decentralized systems, users seamlessly access diverse services and platforms using their DIDs and verifiable credentials, fostering a user-centric and convenient experience.

Decentralized identity systems offer enhanced control, privacy, security, and streamlined interactions compared to centralized systems. Users actively manage their identities, selectively share data, and enjoy increased portability across various contexts, aligning with the principles of self-sovereign identity.

5.11 Decentralized Identity Framework in Ethereum

The decentralized identity framework in Ethereum enables self-sovereign, secure, and decentralized management of identity information. Leveraging the Ethereum blockchain and adhering to existing standards, it empowers individuals to control their identity data.

5.11.1 Components of Decentralized Identity Framework in Ethereum

5.11.1.1 Decentralized Identifiers (DIDs)

DIDs are crucial in the Ethereum decentralized identity framework, acting as unique identifiers that empower individuals to represent and control their identities. Aligned with the W3C DID specification, Ethereum-based DIDs enable decentralization, allowing individuals to self-generate identifiers without centralized control.

5.11.1.2 Verifiable Credentials

Verifiable credentials are employed to present and verify identity attributes. On Ethereum, these credentials can be stored on the blockchain and secured cryptographically according to the W3C verifiable credentials standard.

5.11.1.3 Public Key Infrastructure (PKI)

Ethereum utilizes PKI to furnish the requisite cryptographic keys (public and private) for authentication, ownership, and verification of digital assets. DIDs within Ethereum often intertwine with public and private keys, facilitating cryptographic proofs for authentication.

5.11.1.4 Smart Contracts and Attestations

The functionality of Ethereum's smart contracts comes into play for the management and interaction with identity-related data. Smart contracts take on the responsibility of storing and managing attestations linked to DIDs, ensuring their authenticity and fostering interaction within the decentralized identity ecosystem.

5.11.2 Framework Implementation

5.11.2.1 Decentralized Identifiers on the Blockchain

DIDs are stored on the Ethereum blockchain, facilitating their resolution, verification, and interaction with identity-related data. These decentralized identifiers are cryptographically secured, ensuring their tamper-proof nature and independent verifiability.

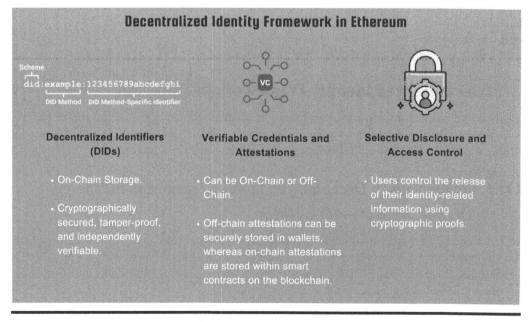

Figure 5.14 Components of decentralized identity framework in Ethereum.

5.11.2.2 Verifiable Credentials and Attestations

Attestations, or verifiable credentials, in the Ethereum-based decentralized identity framework, can be stored either on-chain or off-chain. Off-chain attestations, encrypted and signed by issuers, are securely kept in wallets, while on-chain attestations reside within smart contracts on the blockchain for easy verification while protecting sensitive information. On-chain refers to data recorded directly on the blockchain, whereas off-chain refers to data stored outside the blockchain.

5.11.2.3 Selective Disclosure and Access Control

Users wield control over the release of their identity-related information through cryptographic proofs. Decentralized identifiers and verifiable credentials facilitate selective disclosure, empowering users to unveil specific attributes without divulging their entire personal information. This mechanism enhances both privacy and security.

5.11.3 Types of Attestations on Ethereum

The Ethereum decentralized identity ecosystem includes various methods for managing attestations, which are verifiable claims about an entity. In other words, attestations are a form of verifiable credentials. These methods include off-chain attestations, off-chain attestations with persistent access, on-chain attestations, and the use of soulbound tokens for identity management.

5.11.3.1 Off-chain Attestations

Off-chain attestations in Ethereum's decentralized identity framework are stored within digital wallets, signed with the issuer's DID, and presented as JSON Web Tokens. These attestations include the issuer's digital signature, ensuring the verification of off-chain claims.

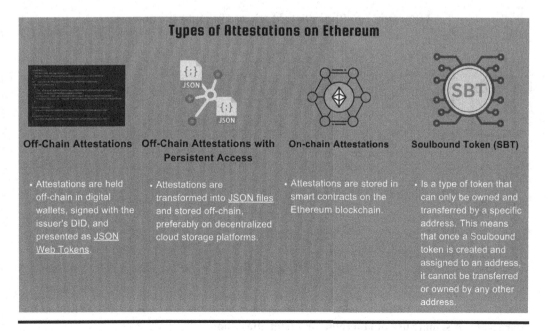

Figure 5.15   Different types of attestations used in Ethereum decentralized identity framework.

For instance, a university (issuer) creates an academic certificate for James (identity owner), shared with a potential employer (verifier) from a mobile wallet. The verifier confirms attestation validity by verifying the issuer's DID (public key on Ethereum).

5.11.3.2 Off-chain Attestations with Persistent Access

Attestations are converted into JSON files and stored off-chain, preferably on decentralized cloud storage platforms. A hash of the JSON file is stored on-chain, linked to a DID through an on-chain registry.

This approach ensures persistence on the blockchain while encrypting and verifying claims information. Selective disclosure is facilitated, allowing the private key holder to decrypt the information.

5.11.3.3 On-chain Attestations

Attestations are stored in Ethereum smart contracts, serving as a registry that links attestations to on-chain decentralized identifiers (public keys).

For example, a company planning to sell ownership shares using a smart contract may only allow buyers who have undergone a background check.

Another company performs background checks and issues on-chain attestations on Ethereum, certifying that an individual has passed the background check without exposing personal information.

The smart contract selling shares can then check the registry for screened buyers' identities, determining who is eligible to purchase shares.

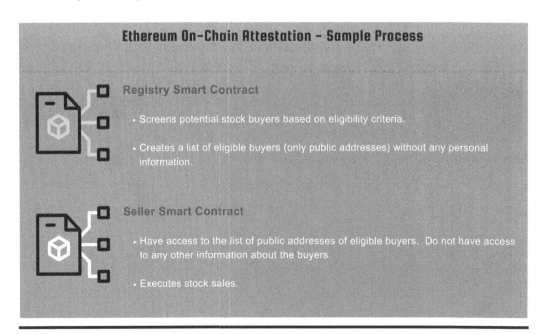

Figure 5.16   A sample use of Ethereum on-chain attestation.

5.11.3.4 Soulbound Tokens and Identity

Soulbound tokens (SBTs) serve as digital identity tokens representing an individual's or entity's characteristics, traits, and achievements. Unlike regular NFTs, SBTs are non-transferable, permanently tied to an individual's private wallet, known as their "soul."

Once an SBT is created and assigned to an address, it cannot be transferred to any other address. For instance, these tokens might represent course completion or game scores, acting as unique identifiers for specific achievements or engagements.

Soulbound tokens have the potential to accumulate distinctive information linked to a specific wallet, establishing a one-of-a-kind on-chain identity attached to a particular Ethereum address. This identity may include tokens representing achievements, such as course completions or game scores, serving as distinctive markers for specific accomplishments or engagements.

Each approach within the Ethereum-based decentralized identity framework offers distinct features and applications, providing various means of storing, accessing, and verifying attestations while upholding privacy, security, and verifiability within the decentralized ecosystem.

5.12 Sign-in with Ethereum

"Sign-in with Ethereum" is an authentication method enabling users to log in or access various services using their Ethereum accounts for identity verification, moving away from traditional username and password systems.

Sign-in with Ethereum can be applicable for both decentralized applications (dApps) and conventional online services.

The use of Ethereum accounts and cryptographic signatures enhances security by eliminating reliance on password-based authentication and mitigating associated risks. Users retain control over their identities, accessing online services without reliance on third-party providers. Ethereum blockchain provides decentralization in authentication, reducing dependence on centralized authorities.

Sign-in with Ethereum has the potential for universal implementation across diverse platforms and services.

5.12.1 Workings of Sign-in with Ethereum

5.12.1.1 Decentralized Identity

Ethereum accounts function as decentralized identifiers (DIDs), with each account linked to a unique identifier created through public-private key pairs.

5.12.1.2 Decentralized Authentication

Sign-in with Ethereum substitutes traditional username-password pairs, employing users' Ethereum accounts for authentication. Users establish their identity by signing messages with their private keys, confirming ownership without the need for a password.

5.12.1.3 Cryptographic Signatures

During the login process, users are prompted to sign a message using their Ethereum account's private key. The service verifies the signature against the associated public key, ensuring the user's authenticity.

5.13 Ethereum-based Decentralized Identity Projects

Numerous ambitious initiatives are leveraging Ethereum as the backbone for the development of decentralized identity solutions.

1. **Ethereum name service (ENS)** is a decentralized naming system facilitating on-chain, machine-readable identifiers such as Ethereum wallet addresses, content hashes, and metadata.
2. **SpruceID** is a decentralized identity project empowering users to manage their digital identity via Ethereum accounts and ENS profiles, eliminating the need for reliance on third-party services.
3. **Ethereum attestation service (EAS)** is a decentralized ledger/protocol designed for creating on-chain or off-chain attestations about various subjects.
4. **Proof of Humanity (PoH)** is a social identity verification system, PoH, constructed on the Ethereum blockchain.
5. **BrightID** is a decentralized and open-source social identity network aiming to revolutionize identity verification through the establishment and analysis of a social graph.
6. **Proof-of-personhood passport** is a decentralized digital identity aggregator.
7. **Walt.id** is an open-source decentralized identity and wallet infrastructure empowering developers and organizations to harness self-sovereign identity along with NFTs/SBTs.

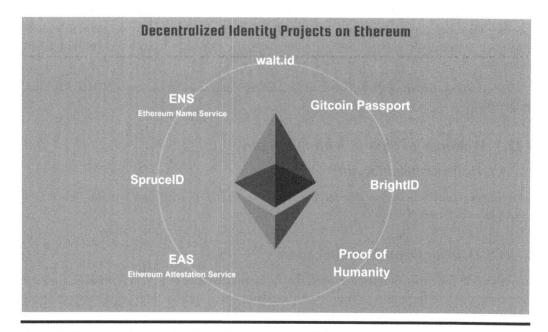

Figure 5.17   Major decentralized identity projects on Ethereum.

5.14 PolygonID

Polygon ID represents a significant advancement in the field of decentralized identity within the Polygon network. It introduces a self-sovereign, decentralized, and private identity solution with a focus on the following key features.

5.14.1 Zero-knowledge (ZK) Cryptography

As the pioneer identity platform utilizing ZK cryptography, Polygon ID enhances user privacy and facilitates blockchain scaling. This technology ensures the confidentiality and security of user data.

5.14.2 Decentralized and Self-Sovereign Identity

Polygon ID empowers users with control over their identity and personal data, adhering to the principles of decentralized identity. Users can independently manage and govern their digital identities.

5.14.3 On-Chain Verification

Emphasizing on-chain verification, Polygon ID facilitates the creation of novel reputation structures for diverse applications within the Web3 ecosystem.

Polygon ID enables various applications such as decentralized credit scores, social payments in DeFi, decentralized sybil scores, voting power and delegation, reputation for DAOs, player profiles for Web3 games, and private P2P communication for social apps.

5.14.4 Open Ecosystem

Polygon ID embraces existing standards and ecosystem development, providing a foundation for developers and organizations to construct trust management services within the Polygon network.

5.15 Other Decentralized Identity Solutions

A. Built on the Ethereum blockchain, **uPort** facilitates self-sovereign identity through user-controlled identity creation, management, and attestation. Users can securely manage identity data, share attestations, and engage with Ethereum-based applications.

B. Operating on a permissioned distributed ledger, **Sovrin** offers a self-sovereign identity framework. It supports verifiable credentials, enabling individuals and organizations to exchange trusted data in a private and secure manner.

C. **Microsoft's ION** operates as a decentralized identity network on the Bitcoin blockchain. It empowers users to own and control their identifiers independently, eliminating the need for centralized authorities.

D. Under the Hyperledger umbrella, **Hyperledger Indy** is an open-source project providing tools, libraries, and reusable components for creating and utilizing independent digital identities based on distributed ledgers.

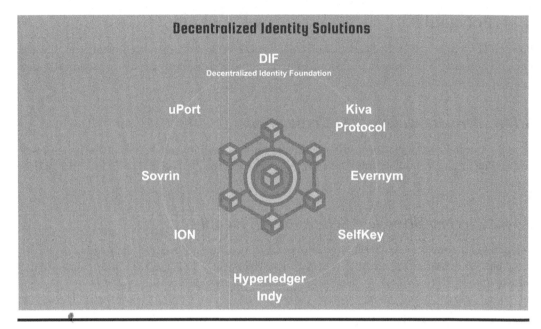

Figure 5.18   Some major decentralized identity projects.

E. **SelfKey** is a blockchain-based digital identity system designed to grant users ownership and control over their digital identities. It features a marketplace where users can securely manage and share their identity attributes.

F. **Evernym** offers a decentralized identity platform utilizing blockchain and verifiable credentials. It focuses on creating self-sovereign digital identities for both businesses and individuals.

G. **Kiva Protocol** is a decentralized identity system leveraging blockchain technology for self-sovereign identity management. Users can own, control, and securely share their identity attributes.

H. **DIF (Decentralized Identity Foundation)** is an organization dedicated to developing open standards for decentralized identity systems. They collaborate on technical standards and best practices to enhance interoperability across a variety of solutions.

Although decentralized identity solutions offer sophisticated alternatives to centralized identity systems, there are still a few areas that need improvement for these solutions to effectively replace traditional identity systems.

5.16 Limitations of Current Decentralized Identity Solutions

5.16.1 Usability Challenges

Simplifying user experience is a major challenge, especially for those who aren't tech-savvy. Making cryptographic key management, navigating decentralized interfaces, and dealing with blockchains more user-friendly is crucial for widespread adoption.

5.16.2 Scalability Challenges

Scalability challenges arise as decentralized identity solutions encounter limitations when accommodating a large user base. Blockchains, with constraints like block size and time, face scalability concerns that need to be addressed.

5.16.3 Interoperability Challenges

Achieving seamless interaction between different decentralized identity systems remains an ongoing challenge. Establishing standards for secure data sharing across various systems without compromising security is essential but not yet fully realized.

5.16.4 Regulatory Compliance Complexity

Adhering to diverse regional and industry-specific regulations while upholding decentralized identity principles is complex. Compliance with regulations like Know Your Customer (KYC) and Anti-Money Laundering (AML) can be a significant hurdle.

5.16.5 Cost and Infrastructure Barriers

Developing and maintaining decentralized identity systems demands technical expertise and infrastructure investment, posing challenges for smaller entities and users with limited resources.

5.16.6 Data Recovery and Revocation

Recovering or revoking identities or data when cryptographic keys are lost or compromised can be challenging. It is crucial to balance security with effective recovery mechanisms.

5.16.7 Adoption and Network Effects

Achieving widespread adoption necessitates a paradigm shift in how users, organizations, and governments perceive and engage with digital identities. The network effects and endorsement by key stakeholders are pivotal for the success of these systems.

Addressing these limitations is paramount for the broader adoption and successful implementation of decentralized identity solutions across various industries and user groups. Ongoing development and collaborative efforts aim to overcome these challenges, enhancing the effectiveness and usability of decentralized identity systems.

Bibliography

BBC. (2023, October 10). *The Trap: Inside the Blackmail Scam Destroying Lives Across India - BBC World Service Documentaries.* YouTube. Retrieved January 3, 2024, from https://www.youtube.com/watch?v=JilJhn_tP-c

BrightID. (n.d.). BrightID. Retrieved January 3, 2024, from https://www.brightid.org

Civic Technologies,Inc. Civic ID: Your identity, evolved, https://www.civic.id/. Accessed 12 June 2024

Decentralized Identifiers (DIDs) v1.0. (n.d.). W3C. Retrieved December 13, 2023, from https://w3c.github .io/did-core/

DIF. (n.d.). Decentralized Identity Foundation: DIF. Retrieved January 3, 2024, from https://identity. foundation

EAS. (n.d.). Ethereum Attestation Service: EAS. Retrieved January 3, 2024, from https://attest.sh

ENS. (n.d.). Ethereum Name Service. Retrieved January 3, 2024, from https://ens.domains

Ethereum. (n.d.). *Decentralized Identity | ethereum.org.* Ethereum. Retrieved January 3, 2024, from https:// ethereum.org/en/decentralized-identity/

Ethereum. (n.d.). Sign-In with Ethereum. Retrieved January 3, 2024, from https://login.xyz

Evernym Inc. (2022, March 2). Evernym: Blog - Digital Identity, Privacy, & Compliance. Retrieved January 3, 2024, from https://www.evernym.com/blog/

Gitcoin. (n.d.). *Gitcoin Passport - Proof-of-Personhood Tools.* Alchemy. Retrieved January 3, 2024, from https://www.alchemy.com/dapps/gitcoin-passport

Hyperledger Foundation. (n.d.). *Indy.* Hyperledger. Retrieved January 3, 2024, from https://www .hyperledger.org/projects/hyperledger-indy

Kiva Microfunds, Inc. "Kiva Protocol." kivaprotocol.com, 2021, https://kivaprotocol.com/ Accessed 2024 June 8.

Microsoft. (2021, March 25). *ION – We Have Liftoff! - Microsoft Community Hub.* Microsoft Tech Community. Retrieved January 3, 2024, from https://techcommunity.microsoft.com/t5/security -compliance-and-identity/ion-we-have-liftoff/ba-p/1441555

OpenID Foundation. OpenID - OpenID Foundation, https://openid.net/. Accessed 12 June 2024.

Parecki, Aaron. "OAuth 2.0 — OAuth." OAuth.net, https://oauth.net/2/. Accessed 12 June 2024.

Proof of Humanity. (n.d.). Proof of Humanity. Retrieved January 3, 2024, from https://proofofhumanity.id

SelfKey. (n.d.). SelfKey: Self-Sovereign Identity for More Freedom and Privacy. Retrieved January 3, 2024, from https://selfkey.org

Sovrin. (n.d.). Home - Sovrin. Retrieved January 3, 2024, from https://sovrin.org

SpruceID. (n.d.). SpruceID. Retrieved January 3, 2024, from https://spruceid.com

uPort. (n.d.). uPort. Retrieved January 3, 2024, from https://www.uport.me

W3C. (2022, March 3). *Verifiable Credentials Data Model v1.1.* W3C. Retrieved January 3, 2024, from https://www.w3.org/TR/vc-data-model/

W3C. (2023, January 18). *Decentralized Identifier Resolution (DID Resolution) v0.3.* W3C Credentials Community Group. Retrieved February 4, 2024, from https://w3c-ccg.github.io/did-resolution/

Walt.id. (n.d.). walt.id | Powerful Digital Identity and Wallet Infrastructure. Retrieved January 3, 2024, from https://walt.id

Weyl, G. (2022, May 11). *Decentralized Society: Finding Web3's Soul by E. Glen Weyl, Puja Ohlhaver, Vitalik Buterin :: SSRN.* SSRN Papers. Retrieved January 3, 2024, from https://papers.ssrn.com/sol3/papers .cfm?abstract_id=4105763

World Wide Web Consortium (W3C). (n.d.). *Software and Document License - 2023 Version | Copyright.* W3C. Retrieved February 24, 2024, from https://www.w3.org/copyright/software-license-2023/

ZKID Labs AG. (n.d.). Polygon ID | Trusted Digital Identity for Your Next Big Idea. Retrieved January 3, 2024, from https://polygonid.com

Chapter 6

Decentralized Storage

Sam Ghosh

The DOMO – Data Never Sleeps Report 10.0 indicates that global data creation, capture, copying, and consumption reached approximately 97 zettabytes in 2022. Projections suggest this figure will rise to 181 zettabytes by 2025. For context, one zettabyte equals one trillion gigabytes.

Annually, an astounding 1.81 trillion photos are taken globally, equivalent to 57,000 per second or 5.0 billion per day. This intense data creation aligns with a rapid growth in content sharing, with YouTube users adding 500 hours of content per minute and Instagram users sharing 66,000 images every minute in 2022.

The surge in data generation and sharing is driving the widespread adoption of cloud services. By 2025, cloud-stored data is projected to reach 100 zettabytes, comprising 50% of the world's data, a significant rise from around 25% in 2015.

However, the accelerated growth in cloud adoption is not without its challenges. Key challenges to widespread cloud adoption include costly outages and security breaches.

In this chapter, we will explore the potential role of blockchain and Web3 technologies in addressing these challenges, introducing decentralization, transparency, and immutability to current cloud architectures.

6.1 Understanding Cloud

6.1.1 What is Cloud Computing?

Cloud computing is often described as using someone else's computing resources, but it's crucial to understand that cloud providers may not necessarily own and manage the infrastructure, a point we'll explore later.

Cloud computing is better defined as the use of shared computing resources, delivering IT resources over the internet on demand and typically employing a pay-as-you-go pricing model.

DOI: 10.4324/9781003507352-6

So, instead of buying, owning, and maintaining physical data centers and servers, you can access technology services, such as computing power, storage, and databases, on an as-needed basis from a cloud provider.

Generally, the responsibility of maintaining the resources lies with the cloud provider, while users leverage them on a need basis.

Cloud computing is made possible by virtualization. Virtualization involves crafting a software-based or "virtual" representation of a computer, commonly known as a virtual machine. This virtual machine is equipped with allocated portions of CPU, memory, and storage resources, sourced from a physical host computer. The host computer may be a personal computer or a distant server, such as one located in a data center provided by a cloud service provider.

Hypervisors, or virtual machine monitors (VMMs), enable virtualization by managing and creating virtual machines (VMs). They allow a single host computer to support multiple guest VMs by virtually sharing resources like memory and CPU.

6.1.2 Cloud Service Models

Cloud computing operates through three service models: Infrastructure as a Service (IaaS), Platform as a Service (PaaS), and Software as a Service (SaaS), each offering varying levels of shared infrastructure to users.

6.1.2.1 Infrastructure as a Service or IaaS

Iaas is comparable to acquiring a new laptop, potentially without an operating system and without any application installed. In the context of virtualization, IaaS provides virtual machines created

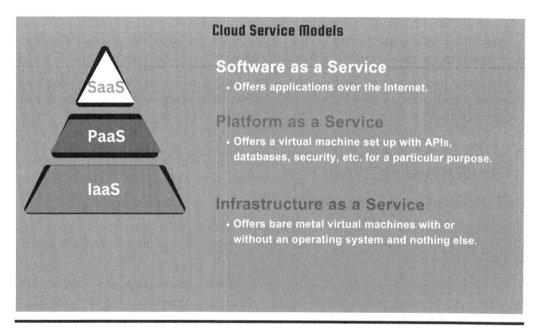

Figure 6.1   Cloud service models – IaaS, PaaS, and SaaS.

through a hypervisor, mirroring the concept of a new computer with designated virtual computing resources.

6.1.2.2 Platform as a Service or PaaS

PaaS goes beyond Infrastructure as a Service, offering pre-configured virtual machines customized for specific purposes. PaaS includes various capabilities, including APIs for distribution, caching, queuing, messaging, storage, workload management, user identity, and analytics. Users are only required to develop or migrate application code.

6.1.2.3 Software as a Service or SaaS

SaaS provides users with both infrastructure and the application layered on top of it. Users can access the application over the internet without dealing with technical intricacies.

I believe it's crucial to delve deeper into the differences among IaaS, PaaS, and SaaS.

One way to conceptualize this progression is that as we move from IaaS to SaaS, the level of abstraction increases, implying a reduction in the technical complexities users need to concern themselves with. Simultaneously, the utilization of the infrastructure becomes progressively more specialized.

For instance, AWS EC2 is an example of IaaS. Managing an EC2 instance involves considerations like the operating system, storage, etc. Say, you want to host a Node.js app on EC2. You will need to install dependencies, configure databases (e.g., MySQL), handle firewall settings, and ensure security even before deploying the application code.

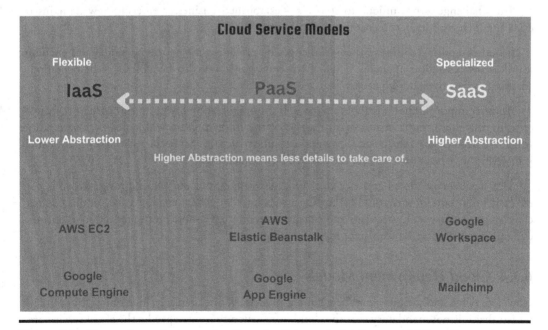

Figure 6.2 Figure shows how moving from IaaS towards SaaS means higher abstraction but lower flexibility.

AWS Elastic Beanstalk, a Platform as a Service (PaaS), simplifies deployment by handling infrastructure complexities. Users upload code, and the service manages the underlying infrastructure. While it reduces complexity, it may limit flexibility compared to Infrastructure as a Service (IaaS) like EC2. For complex setups such as running a hybrid application served using both Node.js and Apache servers, multiple Beanstalk environments might be needed.

SaaS presents a distinct paradigm where users don't need to engage in any building process – they simply access the application over the internet and utilize its functionalities.

Examples of SaaS include Google Workspace, Mailchimp, Salesforce, and Slack, among others.

Note that many cloud providers provide a range of services covering both IaaS and PaaS. For instance, AWS offers EC2 as an IaaS option and Elastic Beanstalk as a PaaS alternative. In the context of Google Cloud, Compute Engine and Cloud Storage exemplify IaaS, while Cloud Run and App Engine serve as examples of PaaS.

6.1.3 Benefits of Cloud Computing

Consider you're a startup founder embarking on the journey of building a web app for your customers. At this initial stage, uncertainties loom large – you're unsure if the app will gain traction, the speed at which it might do so, and what resources would be necessary for scaling the application.

Acquiring and managing infrastructure not only ties up capital that could be invested in business growth but also requires significant manpower. Additionally, if infrastructure changes are needed due to shifts in the tech stack or market requirements, additional investment becomes unavoidable.

This challenge is not unique to startups – established businesses entering new domains or updating their tech stack can encounter similar situations.

Cloud computing addresses these challenges by providing a pay-per-use model and enabling seamless infrastructure upgrades. This empowers organizations to be agile in their operations, adapting swiftly to changing needs.

Another important point is about finances. If the organization invests in infrastructure instead of using the cloud, the cost related to the use of the infrastructure will appear as depreciation which is a fixed cost. As the cloud is pay-per-use, infrastructure cost becomes a variable cost which is more intuitive because it reflects the reality of infrastructure use.

This flexible cost model creates a clear link between income and expenditures, which is particularly important for scenarios like hosting a web app that generates ad revenue. In this context, cloud expenses vary with user visits and engagement, offering a more precise reflection of business dynamics and supporting consistent financial margins.

6.1.4 Cloud Deployment Models

Now, let's delve into various cloud deployment models. While defining cloud computing, I mentioned that it is not mandatory that the cloud infrastructure is managed by the cloud service provider. This is where the difference between public and private clouds comes in.

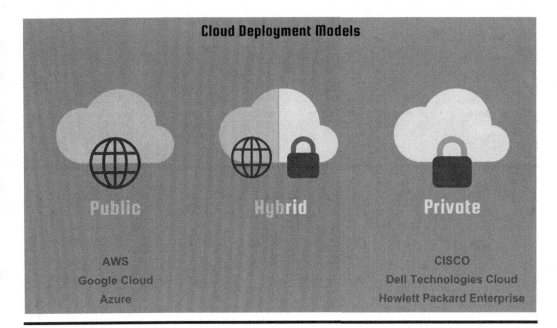

Figure 6.3   Different cloud deployment models.

6.1.4.1 *Public Cloud*

In a public cloud, the cloud service provider (e.g., AWS, Google Cloud, or Azure) owns and manages computing resources, providing standardized user experiences and workflows with pay-per-use billing.

6.1.4.2 *Private Cloud*

Contrastingly, a private cloud is a dedicated infrastructure for a single organization, serving multiple business units within that organization. Ownership, management, and operation can be handled by the user organization, the cloud service provider, or a combination, and the infrastructure may be located on or off premises.

The key distinction lies in control and customization. Public clouds are standardized, with the cloud provider controlling the infrastructure, while private clouds offer customization aligned with the specific needs of a single organization, allowing the organization to maintain control over the infrastructure.

Notable private cloud providers include Cisco, Dell, and HPE, among others.

6.1.4.3 *Virtual Private Cloud*

A Virtual Private Cloud (VPC) is a public cloud service that allows organizations to create a secure and private computing environment within a segmented portion of a shared public cloud.

Using a VPC enables organizations to leverage the advantages of dynamic scalability, high availability, and cost-effectiveness in a public cloud, all while customizing infrastructure and

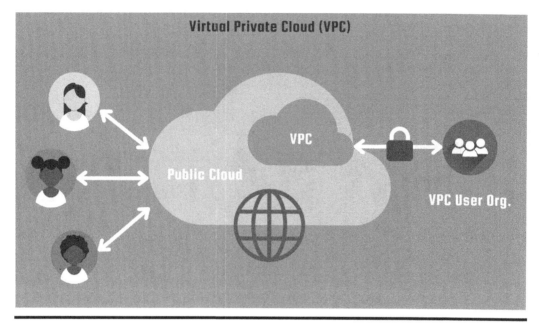

Figure 6.4   Virtual Private Cloud (VPC).

security to meet the specific needs of the organization. Leading public providers like AWS and Google Cloud offer VPC services.

6.1.4.4 Hybrid Cloud

A hybrid cloud is a mixed computing environment utilizing a combination of public and private clouds, along with on-premises data centers or "edge locations" for running applications, storing data, and accessing services.

Hybrid cloud environments provide flexibility by incorporating on-premises private cloud services while leveraging the diverse storage and application options offered by public cloud providers such as Google Cloud.

Currently, the hybrid cloud stands as the most prevalent cloud model.

Now, let us discuss cloud storage.

6.1.5 Cloud Technology – Cloud Storage

Cloud storage allows you to save data in the cloud. There are multiple types of cloud storage: some require attachment to a compute node before accessing the data, while others can be accessed directly through the public Internet or a dedicated private network connection. Cloud providers host, secure, manage, and maintain cloud storage and its infrastructure, ensuring data accessibility. Users can scale their storage needs and pay based on capacity on a "per gigabyte" basis. Costs vary depending on storage type, often linked to read/write speeds, with faster speeds incurring higher per-gigabyte costs.

6.1.5.1 Classification of Cloud Storage

Cloud storage can be classified into direct attached, file storage or NFS, block storage, and object storage.

6.1.5.1.1 Direct Attached Storage or "Local Storage"

Attached directly to a cloud-based server, this type of storage offers higher read/write speeds and is primarily utilized for storing a server's operating system. Typically ephemeral, this storage lasts only as long as the attached compute resource and is not shareable with other nodes.

6.1.5.1.2 File Storage or NFS

Attached to compute nodes via network file system (NFS) over a standard Ethernet network, file storage solutions offer file-level access.

6.1.5.1.3 Block Storage

Block storage system operates by breaking files into separate data chunks (blocks) and assigning each block a unique address. Block storage is connected to compute nodes through high-speed fiber connections and is typically provisioned in volumes that can be mounted onto a compute node.

6.1.5.1.4 Object Storage

This storage solution is not tied to a specific compute node and does not require direct attachment. Provisioned as an object storage service instance, it utilizes APIs for tasks such as data upload, download, and management. Its compatibility with any system supporting API calls eliminates the need for an underlying compute node.

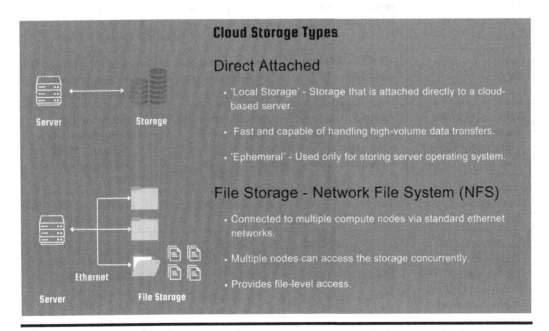

Figure 6.5   Cloud storage types (1 of 2) – Direct attached and network file system (NFS).

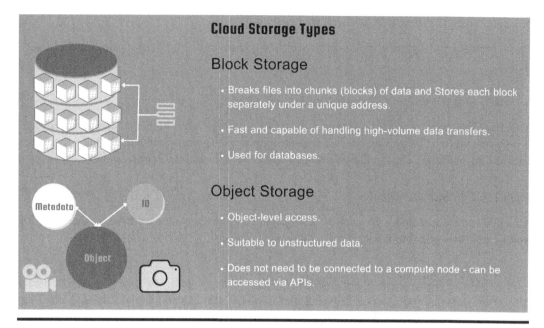

Figure 6.6   Cloud storage types (2 of 2) – Block storage and object storage.

Table 6.1   Comparison of Different Types of Cloud Storage

Direct Attached	File Storage	Block Storage	Object Storage
Used for single-instance VMs. Directly attached to a single virtual machine.	Shared file access – Suitable for multi-instance applications.	High-performance – Used for databases and applications.	Scalable, distributed storage.
Low latency, high I/O.	Scalable and highly available.	Ideal for databases and applications requiring high I/O.	Ideal for storing large amounts of unstructured data.
Data is tied to the instance – Not suitable for shared use.	Multiple instances can access the same data simultaneously.	Typically attached to a single VM.	Highly durable, redundant data storage – HTTP/HTTPS access via APIs.
Provides block-level access.	Provides file-level access.	Provides block-level access.	Provides object-level access.
E.g. Amazon EBS (Elastic Block Store), Google Persistent Disk, Azure Managed Disks.	E.g. Google Cloud Filestore, Azure Files.	E.g, Google Persistent Disk, Azure Managed Disks	Amazon S3 (Simple Storage Service), Google Cloud Storage, and Azure Blob Storage.

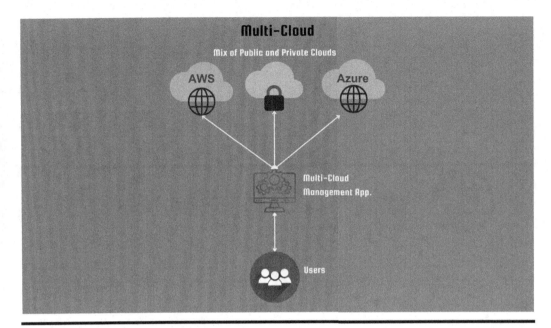

Figure 6.7   Visual representation of a multi-cloud system.

6.2 Trends in Cloud Computing

6.2.1 Rise of Multi-cloud

A multi-cloud strategy involves an organization concurrently utilizing cloud computing services from at least two different cloud providers to operate their applications. Rather than relying on a single-cloud stack, multi-cloud environments typically incorporate a mix of two or more public clouds, two or more private clouds, or a combination of both.

According to a recent report, more than 80% of enterprises have adopted a multi-cloud strategy, with 78% utilizing more than three public clouds.

The primary driver behind the increasing adoption of multi-cloud strategies is the concern over public cloud outages. Such outages can lead to significant losses in revenue and damage to an organization's reputation. According to a report by the Uptime Institute, over 60% of cloud failures incurred costs exceeding US $100,000 in 2022.

Enterprises favor multi-cloud solutions to avoid the financial burden associated with relying solely on a single public cloud provider.

Multi-cloud management tools streamline the implementation of multi-cloud strategies by providing procedures and utilities for monitoring and securing applications across diverse public cloud environments. These tools offer a unified interface, supporting platforms like AWS, Azure, and Kubernetes, enabling efficient oversight by IT teams.

6.2.2 Hybrid vs Multi-cloud

Multi-cloud and hybrid cloud are distinct strategies that are sometimes confused.

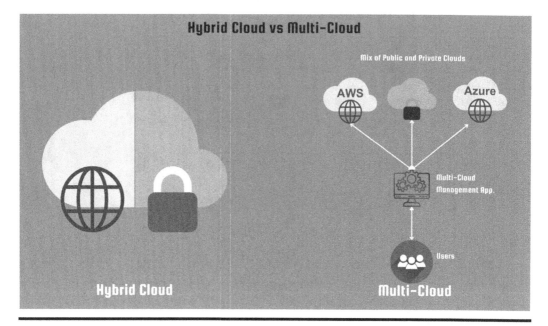

Figure 6.8   Difference between a multi-cloud strategy and a hybrid-cloud strategy.

A hybrid cloud is characterized by the storage location of data, involving a combination of a private cloud designed for the user organization and a public cloud.

In contrast, a multi-cloud strategy revolves around the utilization of services from multiple cloud service providers.

When a multi-cloud deployment is combined with an on-premises data center (private cloud), it becomes a hybrid multi-cloud strategy.

6.2.3 Cloud Security Concerns

As previously discussed, the surge in cloud adoption comes with its set of challenges.

The rise of cloud technology coincides with an increase in challenges related to cloud security. According to the Ermetic State of Cloud Security 2021 Report, 98% of companies encountered at least one cloud data breach in the previous 18 months.

According to a market.us report, the Cloud Security market is projected to exhibit growth at a CAGR (Compound Annual Growth Rate) of 22.5%, reaching US $148 billion by 2032.

6.3 What Can Web3 Bring to Cloud Technology?

So, we understood the challenges associated with cloud computing. So, how can Web3 help?

6.3.1 Decentralization

On April 26, 2023, Google Cloud faced a shutdown affecting Western Europe, Japan, India, Indonesia, and South Carolina in the US. The cause was attributed to fire and water damage to the data centers. This incident marked the second major outage in 2023, with a prior occurrence disrupting millions of users' access to Outlook and Teams.

The estimated cost of such outages for businesses is around US $365,000 per hour of downtime.

The root cause of these outages lies in centralized data storage.

Cloud services, dependent on centralized data management and data centers, can face widespread issues impacting millions of users due to problems within these data centers. Power failures in data centers are a common cause of cloud outages.

Web3, with its inherent decentralized structure, offers a potential solution to this problem. By creating decentralized cloud architectures, it reduces dependence on centralized data centers.

While storing data in blockchains presents challenges, as discussed later in this book, blockchains, and other distributed ledgers can handle metadata and indexes, facilitating automated cloud management through smart contracts.

6.3.2 Security

How can Web3 enhance cloud security?

Web3 can contribute to heightened cloud security through increased transparency. All transactions on (public) blockchains are publicly visible, facilitating the detection of any system attacks.

Another way of enhancing cloud security with Web3 is decentralized identity management, replacing traditional credentials such as IDs/passwords. This digital identity can serve as authentication to access cloud resources.

Blockchains can also maintain access control lists for cloud resources. Access permissions and policies are stored on a blockchain ledger, with smart contracts automatically enforcing these policies. This may ensure that only authorized users can access specific resources.

More sophisticated approaches may involve utilizing non-fungible tokens (NFTs) for access control. These tokens grant temporary access to specific cloud resources without exposing sensitive access credentials. Access is automatically revoked once the token expires, enhancing security measures.

6.3.3 Increased Privacy

Enhanced privacy for cloud users is a key advantage of decentralized identity management.

Web3 empowers users with decentralized, self-sovereign identities, granting individuals greater control over their personal information. This diminishes dependence on centralized identity providers, allowing users to selectively share only the necessary identity attributes for cloud services without divulging excessive information.

In Web3 systems, characterized by trustlessness, users aren't required to demonstrate trustworthiness through personal information. Instead, tokens can be employed for access control, and smart contracts can effectively enforce access rules. This shift ensures a more privacy-centric and secure approach to identity management in cloud services.

6.3.4 Censorship Resistance

One facet of decentralization involves resistance to censorship. In a centralized system, censorship can be achieved by simply taking down one of the few connected servers.

On the other hand, disrupting a decentralized system is highly complex, if not impossible, due to the redundancy and diversity of nodes. With identical information across all active nodes, the removal of one or a few nodes has minimal impact on the entire network.

Nevertheless, censorship resistance presents a double-edged sword. Implementing legitimate censorship becomes challenging in a decentralized network. Such networks may be exploited for criminal activities, making it difficult for authorities to effectively censor unlawful actions.

6.3.5 Immutability

Blockchains are immutable, meaning that once data is added to the network, it cannot be altered. The interconnected blocks through hash functions ensure that any modification in historical data cascades through all subsequent blocks. Nodes attempting alterations get forked out from the blockchain network as their chain becomes different from the majority. A blockchain fork is a divergence in the blockchain network that occurs when a single blockchain splits into two separate chains.

This immutability characteristic finds application in various cloud use cases where the credibility of historical data and transparency are paramount. For instance, in cloud applications for supply chain or inventory management, blockchain can be leveraged to meticulously trace the origin and journey of products. Every transaction related to a product, spanning manufacturing to distribution, is securely recorded on the blockchain, ensuring transparency and authenticity. Immutability plays a pivotal role in preventing the infiltration of counterfeit goods into the supply chain, empowering participants to validate product authenticity at each stage.

Additionally, immutability proves valuable in other cloud applications, such as Anti-money Laundering (AML) and Know Your Customer (KYC) processes, land ownership records, intellectual property records, etc.

6.4 Potential Issues with using Blockchain with the Cloud

6.4.1 Inefficient Storage

Certainly, blockchains come with several advantages, but they also have inherent limitations. Notably, blockchains exhibit inefficiency when used for storage.

The need to store every transaction across all nodes in a blockchain significantly increases storage requirements, making blockchains impractical for large volumes of data.

Major public blockchain networks, such as Bitcoin and Ethereum, face significant scalability challenges. Issues like transaction throughput constraints and block size limitations hinder the efficient processing of a large volume of data transactions. With block sizes typically limited to a few hundred kilobytes and block time restrictions, these blockchains can only handle a very restricted amount of data within a given time interval. We will discuss more on these concepts when we discuss blockchain scaling in the Web3 Architectures chapter.

6.4.2 *Latency*

Blockchains inherently introduce latency, primarily attributed to block time and the consensus process. Latency is the delay between a request and the response, often measured as the time taken for data to travel from the source to the destination in a network.

In a blockchain network, transactions are grouped into batches called blocks at scheduled intervals, adhering to predefined rules. The time between the creation of one block and the next is termed block time. As a result, data isn't instantly added to the blockchain upon transaction initiation. Depending on block time, users may have to wait seconds or minutes for data to be officially included. Moreover, when dealing with large data volumes, the uncertainty regarding whether the data will be added to the blockchain is a common concern.

Another source of latency is the consensus process, where a majority of active nodes must agree on the inclusion of a block in the blockchain. Depending on the consensus process – proof-of-work, proof-of-stake, etc. – block confirmation time can be significant and thus increases the latency.

As network congestion rises, the time required for block confirmation also increases. This escalating latency poses practical challenges, making the use of blockchain in various cloud applications impractical.

6.4.3 *Cost*

As mentioned earlier, blockchain network fees often rise with transaction complexity and surge during network congestion. Increased demand for network resources leads to higher fees. This makes using blockchains for cloud applications cost-prohibitive and accurately forecasting transaction expenses becomes challenging.

As cloud applications expand and generate a larger volume of transactions, the cumulative transaction fees can become substantial. This phenomenon has the potential to undermine the cost-effectiveness of blockchain utilization. Furthermore, scalability issues can worsen network congestion, leading to increased fee inflation.

6.4.4 *Technical Complexity*

A less-explored aspect is the technical complexity associated with incorporating blockchains into cloud applications. Web3, being an emerging technology, is still evolving in areas such as access management, security, and handling upgrades.

Developing a cloud application using blockchains demands significant technical expertise, as various aspects of Web3 are in a state of ongoing development. For instance, smart contracts pose challenges for editing due to the immutable nature of blockchains, making modifications to blockchain-based cloud applications particularly challenging.

Moreover, the public accessibility of smart contract bytecodes and transactions in public blockchains introduces security concerns for blockchain-based cloud applications. The integration of blockchain with existing cloud infrastructure and systems adds another layer of complexity, potentially requiring the development of custom middleware and APIs to ensure seamless communication between blockchain-based components and traditional databases or services.

6.4.5 Regulatory Challenges

Due to data localization and privacy laws, there are constraints on how and where data can be stored.

Data Privacy and GDPR Compliance – Adherence to data privacy regulations, such as the General Data Protection Regulation (GDPR) in the EU, imposes stringent requirements for "personal data" handling. Blockchain's transparency and immutability may pose challenges for GDPR compliance, making it challenging to erase or rectify personal data once recorded on the blockchain.

Blockchain networks often function globally, and cloud applications may involve data transfer across borders. Navigating compliance with data transfer regulations and ensuring data doesn't cross specific jurisdictions without proper authorization can be complex.

Anti-money Laundering (AML) and Know Your Customer (KYC) – Regulations mandate user identity verification. On public blockchains, where user identities are often pseudonymous, complying with AML and KYC regulations becomes complex, especially for cloud applications dealing with financial data.

Blockchain technology is evolving rapidly, and regulatory frameworks are struggling to keep pace, creating uncertainties for blockchain projects as regulations continue to evolve.

6.5 Decentralized Storage

One prominent business case for leveraging Web3 technologies in the cloud is decentralized storage. Protocols such as Filecoin, Arweave, Safe Network, and Storj are active participants in this domain.

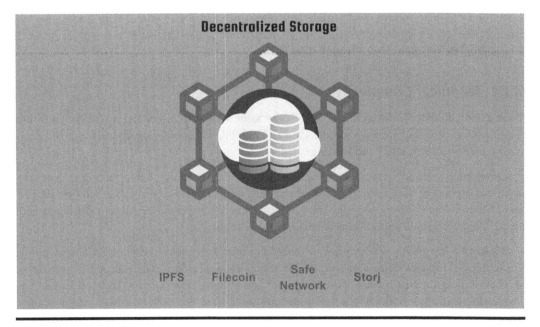

Figure 6.9   Decentralized storage.

The primary objective of these networks is to eliminate the reliance on centralized data centers and substitute them with decentralized storage providers. Consequently, these networks transform into decentralized marketplaces for storage, incorporating automated economic rules encoded in smart contracts. Crypto tokens serve as the currency for transactions within these marketplaces, and the pricing for storage adjusts dynamically based on demand and supply.

For a detailed discussion, let's delve into the example of IPFS and Filecoin, where Filecoin is constructed upon the IPFS infrastructure.

6.5.1 IPFS

IPFS, short for InterPlanetary File System, operates as a protocol facilitating peer-to-peer file sharing. At its core, IPFS is grounded in principles of decentralization, immutability, and content addressing.

6.5.1.1 Decentralization

IPFS employs a peer-to-peer network of nodes for content distribution and retrieval, minimizing the risk of a single point of failure and censorship.

6.5.1.2 Immutability

Once data is added to IPFS, it attains immutability. Modifications to the data generate a new cryptographic hash, preserving the integrity of previous versions.

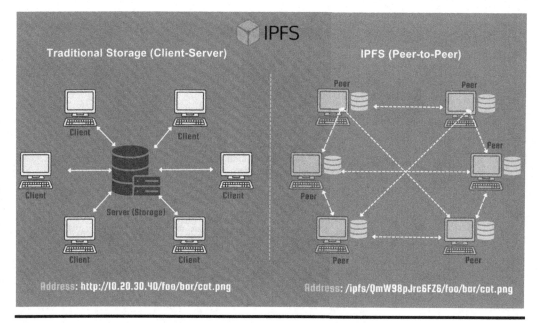

Figure 6.10   How IPFS is different from traditional centralized storage.

6.5.1.3 Content Addressing

In contrast to traditional systems using location-based addressing, IPFS adopts content addressing. Files are identified and accessed based on their content, utilizing a unique cryptographic hash, known as the Content Identifier (CID), derived from the file's contents.

However, a notable deficiency in IPFS was the lack of an economic incentive system for storage providers. In this regard, IPFS shares similarities with BitTorrent, an open-source file-sharing network where peers offer storage voluntarily without economic motivation. Yet, scalability requires an economic incentive system.

6.5.2 Filecoin

Filecoin plays a crucial role in addressing this gap by establishing an economic incentive layer on the top of IPFS.

Filecoin introduces a decentralized storage market for IPFS storage, where users (clients) can compensate storage providers (miners) for the storage provided.

Operating as a blockchain with a proof-of-storage consensus mechanism, Filecoin utilizes **FIL** as its native coin. In the Filecoin network, miners store and retrieve data for clients. To become a miner, participants need to pledge a specific amount of **FIL** as collateral and demonstrate their storage capacity. Miners compete for storage deals by offering competitive pricing and maintaining a high quality of service.

Filecoin employs distinctive proof mechanisms, namely "proof-of-replication" and "proof-of-spacetime," to verify that miners genuinely store the data they claim to store. These proofs necessitate miners to demonstrate the reservation and commitment of storage space for a particular piece of data.

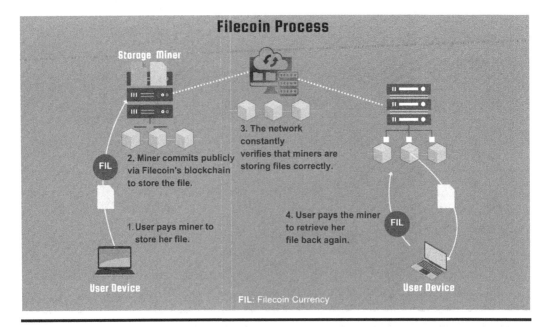

Figure 6.11   Illustrative process flow for Filecoin.

Clients can retrieve their stored data from the Filecoin network at any time, and miners receive **FIL** tokens as rewards for successful data retrieval. This retrieval market ensures ongoing data accessibility and fair compensation for miners' services.

So, we have explored the advantages of decentralized storage. Now, let us now discuss the limitations of existing blockchain-based decentralized storage systems.

6.5.3 Limitations of Current Blockchain-based Decentralized Storage Systems

6.5.3.1 Storage Availability/Sustainability

Many blockchain-based storage networks claim "permanent storage." This can be a misleading claim. Voluntary participation by storage providers means availability of storage space and availability for retrieval primarily depends on the incentive for the storage providers. For example, IPFS lacked an incentive layer. As a result, data uploaded by a node was only stored on that node and not shared with other IPFS nodes, undermining the core principle of decentralized storage. The claim of permanent storage is futile – "permanent storage" till the node providers are incentivized.

6.5.3.2 Budgeting Issues

As the pricing for storage changes dynamically, this makes it impossible to budget for storage costs. Most of the decentralized storage providers depend on the supply and demand of storage space to dynamically update the price of storage. Apart from that, the use of crypto tokens for payment makes pricing volatile and budgeting very difficult.

6.5.3.3 Possible Illegal Use

Many decentralized storage providers claim to be censorship-resistant. This can open up a crackdown by regulators in the future as censorship resistance can lead to the use of storage services for illegal purposes.

Bibliography

Amazon. (n.d.). *Private Cloud - Amazon Virtual Private Cloud (VPC)*. AWS. Retrieved January 4, 2024, from https://aws.amazon.com/vpc/

Arweave Org. (n.d.). Arweave - A Community-driven Ecosystem. Retrieved January 4, 2024, from https://www.arweave.org

AWS. (n.d.). *Amazon EC2 Instances Featuring AMD EPYC Processors*. AWS. https://aws.amazon.com/pm/ec2-amd/

AWS. (n.d.). Cloud Computing Services - Amazon Web Services (AWS). Retrieved January 4, 2024, from https://aws.amazon.com

AWS. (n.d.). *Cloud Object Storage - Amazon S3*. AWS. https://aws.amazon.com/pm/serv-s3

AWS. (n.d.). *Web App Deployment - AWS Elastic Beanstalk*. AWS. Retrieved January 4, 2024, from https://aws.amazon.com/elasticbeanstalk/

AWS. "Cloud Block Storage - Amazon EBS - AWS." Amazon AWS, https://aws.amazon.com/ebs/. Accessed 13 June 2024.

Cisco. (n.d.). *Cisco Private Cloud Solutions*. Cisco. Retrieved January 4, 2024, from https://www.cisco.com/c/en_in/solutions/cloud/private-cloud.html

Claburn, T. (2023, April 26). *Google Cloud Suffers Outage in Europe Amid Water Leak, Fire.* Theregister. Retrieved December 14, 2023, from https://www.theregister.com/2023/04/26/google_cloud_outage/

Computer Weekly. (2023, February 27). *Advanced Digital Resiliency Can Save Organisations Millions.* Computer Weekly. Retrieved January 4, 2024, from https://www.computerweekly.com/news /365531915/Advanced-digital-resiliency-can-save-organisations-millions

Cybercrime Magazine. (2020, June 3). *The World Will Store 200 Zettabytes Of Data By 2025.* Cybercrime Magazine. Retrieved January 4, 2024, from https://cybersecurityventures.com/the-world-will-store -200-zettabytes-of-data-by-2025/

Dell. (n.d.). *Private Cloud.* Dell. Retrieved January 4, 2024, from https://www.dell.com/en-in/blog/tags/ private-cloud/

DOMO. (n.d.). *Data Never Sleeps 10.0.* Domo. Retrieved January 4, 2024, from https://www.domo.com/ data-never-sleeps

Ermetic and IDC. (2021, July 1). *State of Cloud Security: Examining Cloud Footprints - Tenable Cloud Security.* Ermetic. Retrieved January 4, 2024, from https://ermetic.com/blog/cloud/state-of-cloud -security-2021-more-aware-yet-very-exposed/

Filecoin. (n.d.). Filecoin: A Decentralized Storage Network for Humanity's Most Important Information. Retrieved January 4, 2024, from https://filecoin.io

Filecoin. (n.d.). *The FIL Token.* Filecoin Docs. Retrieved January 4, 2024, from https://docs.filecoin.io/ basics/assets/the-fil-token

General Data Protection Regulation (GDPR) – Official Legal Text. Retrieved December 14, 2023, from https://gdpr-info.eu

Google. (n.d.). *Business Apps & Collaboration Tools.* Google Workspace. Retrieved January 4, 2024, from https://workspace.google.com/intl/en_in/

Google. (n.d.). *Cloud Storage.* Google Cloud. Retrieved January 4, 2024, from https://cloud.google.com/ storage

Google. (n.d.). *Filestore: Fully Managed Cloud File Storage.* Google Cloud. Retrieved January 4, 2024, from https://cloud.google.com/filestore?hl=en

Google. (n.d.). Google Cloud: Cloud Computing Services. Retrieved January 4, 2024, from https://cloud .google.com

Google. (n.d.). *Hybrid And Multicloud Application Platform.* Google Cloud. Retrieved January 4, 2024, from https://cloud.google.com/solutions/hybrid-and-multicloud-application-platform

Google. (n.d.). *Persistent Disk: Durable Block Storage.* Google Cloud. Retrieved January 4, 2024, from https://cloud.google.com/persistent-disk?hl=en

Google. (n.d.). *Virtual Private Cloud (VPC).* Google Cloud. Retrieved January 4, 2024, from https://cloud .google.com/vpc

Hewlett Packard. (n.d.). Hewlett Packard Enterprise (HPE). Retrieved January 4, 2024, from https://www .hpe.com/us/en/home.html

Google Cloud. "Compute Engine." Google Cloud, https://cloud.google.com/products/compute.Accessed 13 June 2024.

Google Cloud. "Cloud Storage." Google Cloud,https://cloud.google.com/storage#object-storage-for-com-panies-of-all-sizes.Accessed 13 June 2024.

Google Cloud. "Cloud Run."Google Cloud, https://cloud.google.com/run.Accessed 13 June 2024.

Google Cloud. "App Engine Application Platform." Google Cloud, https://cloud.google.com/appengine .Accessed 13 June 2024.

IPFS. (n.d.). IPFS: An Open System to Manage Data without a Central Server. Retrieved January 4, 2024, from https://ipfs.tech

Mailchimp. (2022, August 30). *Intuit Mailchimp.* mailchimp.com. Retrieved January 4, 2024, from https:// mailchimp.com/?currency=USD

Market.us. (2023, March 22). *Cloud Security Market Growth ($148.3 Bn by 2032 at 22.5% CAGR) Global Analysis by Market.us, North-America Dominates with 42.4% of the Market Share.* GlobeNewswire. Retrieved January 4, 2024, from https://www.globenewswire.com/en/news-release/2023/03/22 /2632736/0/en/Cloud-Security-Market-Growth-148-3-Bn-by-2032-at-22-5-CAGR-Global-Analysis -by-Market-us-North-America-Dominates-with-42-4-of-the-Market-Share.html

Microsoft. (n.d.). *Azure Blob Storage.* Microsoft Azure. Retrieved January 4, 2024, from https://azure.microsoft.com/en-in/products/storage/blobs

Microsoft. (n.d.). Microsoft Azure: Cloud Computing Services. Retrieved January 4, 2024, from https://azure.microsoft.com/

Microsoft. (2023, October 12). *Azure Disk Storage Overview - Azure Virtual Machines.* Microsoft Learn. Retrieved January 4, 2024, from https://learn.microsoft.com/en-us/azure/virtual-machines/managed-disks-overview

Microsoft. (2022, April 26). *Introduction to Hyper-V on Windows 10.* Microsoft Learn. Retrieved January 4, 2024, from https://learn.microsoft.com/en-us/virtualization/hyper-v-on-windows/about/

Microsoft. (2023, January 20). *Introduction to Azure Files.* Microsoft Learn. Retrieved January 4, 2024, from https://learn.microsoft.com/en-us/azure/storage/files/storage-files-introduction

Oracle. (n.d.). MySQL. Retrieved January 4, 2024, from https://www.mysql.com

Oracle. (n.d.). Oracle VM VirtualBox. Retrieved January 4, 2024, from https://www.virtualbox.org

Oracle. (n.d.). *Oracle VM Overview.* Oracle. Retrieved January 4, 2024, from https://www.oracle.com/virtualization/technologies/vm/

Photutorial. (2023, November 24). *How Many Photos Are There? (Statistics & Trends in 2024).* Photutorial. Retrieved January 4, 2024, from https://photutorial.com/photos-statistics/

PR Newswire. (2022, May 18). *Virtana Research Finds More Than 80% of Enterprises Have a Multi-Cloud Strategy and 78% Are Using More Than Three Public Clouds.* PR Newswire. Retrieved January 4, 2024, from https://www.prnewswire.com/news-releases/virtana-research-finds-more-than-80-of-enterprises-have-a-multi-cloud-strategy-and-78-are-using-more-than-three-public-clouds-301548266.html

Safe Network. (n.d.). Safe Network. Retrieved January 4, 2024, from https://safenetwork.tech

Salesforce. (n.d.). Salesforce: The Customer Company - Salesforce.com US. Retrieved January 4, 2024, from https://www.salesforce.com

Slack Technologies, LLC. (n.d.). Slack Is Your Productivity Platform | Slack. Retrieved January 4, 2024, from https://slack.com/

Storj Labs Inc. (n.d.). Globally Distributed Cloud Object Storage. Retrieved January 4, 2024, from https://www.storj.io

Uptime Institute. (n.d.). *Uptime Institute's 2022 Outage Analysis Finds Downtime Costs and Consequences Worsening as Industry Efforts to Curb Outage Frequency Fall Short.* Uptime Institute. Retrieved January 4, 2024, from https://uptimeinstitute.com/about-ui/press-releases/2022-outage-analysis-finds-downtime-costs-and-consequences-worsening

What is IPFS? The hard drive for Blockchain. (2023, July 28). iCommunity Labs. Retrieved January 4, 2024, from https://icommunity.io/en/what-is-ifps-the-hard-drive-for-blockchain/

Chapter 7

Decentralized Data Science

Sam Ghosh

ChatGPT, a product of OpenAI, has garnered attention for its groundbreaking nature and significant impact in the field of machine learning. Its success is prompting an AI race – the emergence of similar AI-based products.

However, the excitement around machine learning is not devoid of concerns – especially about privacy.

Recently, researchers, primarily from Google's DeepMind, successfully prompted ChatGPT to disclose portions of its training data using a novel attack prompt. This prompt instructed ChatGPT to endlessly repeat specific words, revealing substantial amounts of personally identifiable information (PII). Additionally, evidence suggests that ChatGPT sometimes outputs training data verbatim.

This problem isn't exclusive to ChatGPT – researchers reveal that similar risks exist with other language models, including open-source models like Pythia or GPT-Neo, semi-open models like LLaMA or Falcon, and closed models like ChatGPT.

Earlier, concerns around machine learning were primarily associated with unauthorized access to training data in centralized data processing. However, it is now evident that centrally trained models can also inadvertently disclose sensitive information.

As major tech players enter the AI race, the question arises: What data will be used to train these models? Likely, they will use data on you and me – even our personal information, biometric data such as facial recognition, speech patterns, and browsing histories.

This is where decentralized data science becomes relevant.

Decentralized data science marks a departure from traditional centralized data processing structures. Its objective is to distribute the power of data analysis and machine learning across a network of devices, enabling collaborative insights without compromising user privacy and security.

Various technologies collectively contribute to the field of decentralized data science.

DOI: 10.4324/9781003507352-7

Let's delve into some of these technologies in this chapter. However, before we do that, let's take a moment to understand data science and machine learning.

7.1 Primer on Data Science

7.1.1 What is Data Science?

Data science is an interdisciplinary field utilizing statistical methods, algorithms, and systems to derive meaningful insights from structured and unstructured data.

Inherently interdisciplinary, data science combines statistical methods, algorithms, and domain-specific knowledge to analyze data, identify patterns, and facilitate informed decision-making.

Encompassing the entire data lifecycle, data science involves processes such as data collection, data cleaning, exploratory data analysis, statistical modeling, machine learning, and effective communication of results through data visualization and comprehensive reporting.

Data science includes various classes, including descriptive analytics (examining and summarizing historical data), diagnostic analytics (identifying causes behind past events), predictive analytics (making predictions based on historical data), natural language processing (analyzing textual data), machine learning (building models for predictions or classification), and big data analytics (analyzing large volumes of data), etc.

While data science is a vast discipline, our focus here is on machine learning.

7.2 Primer on Machine Learning

Despite being named "machine learning," it doesn't necessarily entail training machines but rather focuses on training models.

Let's return to our conversation about ChatGPT.

7.2.1 So, What Is ChatGPT exactly?

ChatGPT falls under the category of machine learning models known as an LLM, or large language model, created by OpenAI using the GPT (generative pre-trained transformer) architecture. The GPT architecture is a neural network design specifically crafted for efficient processing of sequential data.

An LLM, or large language model, is a type of sophisticated natural language processing model distinguished by its extensive size, intricate structure, and capacity to comprehend and produce human-like text on a large scale.

You can read "Improving Language Understanding by Generative Pre-Training" by the OpenAI team for a better understanding of the technical side of ChatGPT.

Now, imagine you want to develop an application similar to ChatGPT, but without utilizing machine learning. Consider the diverse range of tasks that ChatGPT can handle, and think about the multitude of scenarios that must be incorporated into your code.

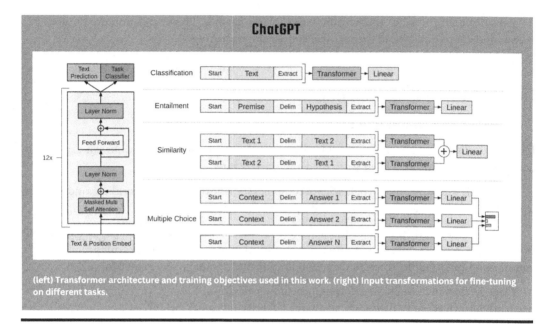

Figure 7.1   Transformer architecture and training objectives behind ChatGPT. From the paper "Improving Language Understanding by Generative Pre-Training" written by OpenAI team members Alec Radford, Karthik Narasimhan, Tim Salimans, and Ilya Sutskever.

How many scenarios do you have to deal with?

Potentially billions, or even trillions of scenarios.

The biggest problem is probably that we will not be able to imagine and evaluate all the scenarios.

7.2.2 So, How Does Machine Learning Do That?

Machine learning involves creating models that can learn from data without explicit programming. Machine learning algorithms can identify patterns, extract insights, and make predictions based on training data.

7.2.3 Machine Learning Models

Machine learning models are at the core of machine learning systems.

Distinguishing themselves from traditional software, which operates on rule-based principles, machine learning models are driven by data. Essentially, a machine learning model is a mathematical representation or a set of algorithms designed to learn patterns and relationships from data. Its purpose is to make predictions, classifications, or decisions without the need for explicit programming for the given task.

Machine learning models demonstrate adaptability, a key distinction from traditional software that tends to be rigid. Unlike traditional software, machine learning models can adapt to changes in the environment or input data, generalizing patterns learned from training data to function

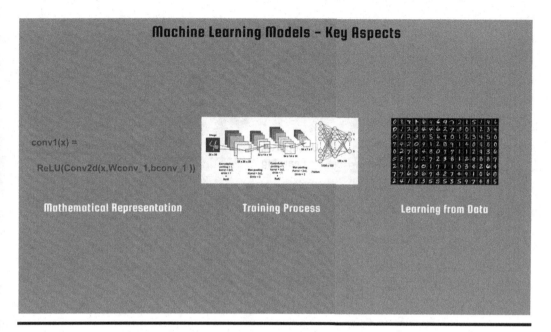

Figure 7.2 Key aspects of machine learning models.

effectively in new, unseen scenarios. This adaptability is a significant strength of machine learning models.

The key aspects of machine learning models are mathematical representation, training process, and learning from data.

A machine learning model, when depicted mathematically, expresses relationships between input features and the target output. This representation takes various forms, including equations, decision trees, neural network weights, or other mathematical structures.

Machine learning models, trained on datasets with input-output pairs, adjust internal parameters to align with patterns in the data, minimizing disparities between predictions and real outcomes. The model gains knowledge through generalization from training data, capturing underlying patterns to make predictions or decisions with new, unseen data.

7.2.4 Types of Models by Training

7.2.4.1 Supervised Learning

Supervised learning involves training a model on labeled datasets, and associating input data with corresponding output labels. The goal is to learn a mapping from inputs to outputs for predicting on new, unseen data, as seen in tasks like object recognition where labeled images help associate objects with their labels.

7.2.4.2 Unsupervised Learning

Unsupervised learning involves training algorithms on unlabeled data to identify patterns, group similar data points, or reduce dataset dimensionality without predefined output labels.

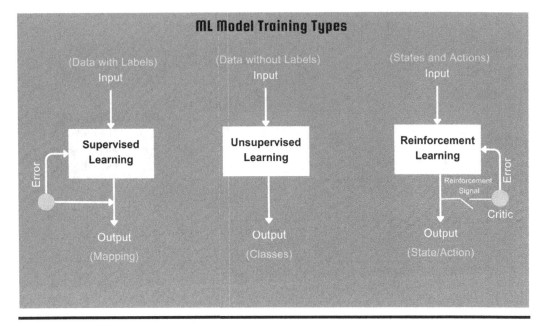

Figure 7.3   Different types of machine learning model training.

Unsupervised Learning tasks include clustering and dimensionality reduction. In fraud detection, unsupervised learning, using algorithms like K-Means clustering or DBSCAN, helps identify fraudulent activities without explicit guidance.

7.2.4.3 Reinforcement Learning

Reinforcement learning involves agents making decisions through interactions with an environment and receiving feedback in the form of rewards or penalties. This trial-and-error learning, akin to human learning, is exemplified in training computer programs to play games, where they acquire effective strategies over time through points for correct moves and penalties for incorrect ones.

Let us learn about machine learning frameworks that play key roles in decentralized data science.

7.2.5 Machine Learning Frameworks

Machine learning frameworks are software tools and libraries designed to provide a structured and efficient environment for the development, training, and deployment of machine learning models. These frameworks come with a range of abstractions, APIs, and pre-implemented algorithms, streamlining the machine learning development process.

Some major ML frameworks are TensorFlow, PyTorch, Keras, Scikit-learn, MXNet, Caffe, and Theano, etc.

■ **TensorFlow**, developed by Google, stands out as one of the most widely used open-source machine learning frameworks. It caters to an array of tasks, spanning traditional machine learning to deep learning.

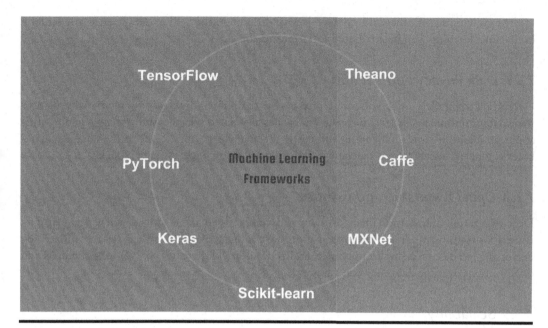

Figure 7.4   Various machine learning frameworks.

Known for its flexibility, scalability, and expansive ecosystem, TensorFlow finds applications in image recognition, natural language processing, and other various diverse fields.

■ **PyTorch**, an open-source machine learning framework from Facebook's AI Research Lab (FAIR), finds applications in deep learning research, especially in computer vision and natural language processing.

■ Initially designed as a high-level API for constructing neural networks atop other frameworks, **Keras** has become an integral component of TensorFlow (as of TensorFlow 2.x). It is commonly employed for building and training neural networks across various tasks.

■ **Scikit-learn** is built on top of scientific computing libraries like NumPy and SciPy. Offering a simple and consistent interface, it addresses various machine-learning tasks, including classification, regression, clustering, and dimensionality reduction.

■ **MXNet** is used for deep learning tasks, including image and speech recognition, as well as natural language processing.

■ **Caffe**, a deep learning framework developed by the Berkeley Vision and Learning Center, is utilized for image classification, object detection, and image segmentation.

■ **Theano**, a numerical computation library, enables developers to define, optimize, and evaluate mathematical expressions.

These frameworks possess distinct strengths, with the choice influenced by factors such as ease of use, community support, performance, and specific task requirements.

7.3 Why Does Data Science Need to Be Decentralized?

In the context of data science and machine learning, decentralization refers to the dispersion of computation, data, and decision-making processes across multiple nodes or entities instead of depending on a centralized system.

The growing significance and value of decentralization in the field of data science, particularly in machine learning, can be attributed to various reasons.

7.3.1 Data Privacy and Security

Decentralized models offer enhanced privacy by enabling individuals to retain control over their data, minimizing the risk of privacy breaches associated with centralized aggregation. This approach makes it more challenging and costly for malicious actors to access the complete databases compared to centralized repositories, which are prime targets for cyberattacks.

7.3.2 Data Ownership and Control

Decentralization allows individuals to own and control their data, crucial when personal data is used for training models. This ensures users have influence over how their data is utilized. By decreasing reliance on a single entity, decentralization provides greater control to individuals and organizations over the data they contribute.

7.3.3 Scalability

Decentralized systems distribute processing across multiple nodes, improving resource utilization and scalability for machine learning models. This enables model deployment on edge devices, reducing dependence on centralized cloud processing, especially valuable in applications where low latency is essential.

7.3.4 Robustness and Fault-tolerance

Centralized systems are susceptible to a single point of failure. In contrast, decentralized systems exhibit greater robustness and resilience, as failures or attacks on one node do not compromise the entire system.

Decentralized architectures are adept at recovering from node failures more gracefully. This proves crucial for sustaining the availability of machine learning services in dynamic and unpredictable environments.

7.3.5 Fairness and Bias Mitigation

Decentralized models can take into account local contexts and nuances inherent in various data sources. This aids in mitigating biases that might arise when training models on centralized, homogeneous datasets.

Centralized models trained on biased datasets may unintentionally worsen existing biases. Decentralized approaches enable the utilization of more diverse data sources, potentially minimizing the risk of bias amplification.

7.3.6 Regulatory Compliance

Certain jurisdictions mandate the local storage of data, and decentralization facilitates data localization by dispersing data across various geographical locations while still enabling model training and deployment.

Decentralized systems can be structured to adhere to privacy laws and regulations by reducing the transfer of sensitive data across borders.

7.3.7 Cost Effective

Decentralized processing of data on user devices eliminates the need for extensive centralized storage infrastructure, offering significant cost-effectiveness through reduced maintenance and scalability expenses.

Also, decentralized processing minimizes the need for frequent and large-scale data transfers to centralized servers, reducing bandwidth requirements and associated costs, particularly in internet-transmitted data scenarios.

In summary, decentralization in data science and machine learning addresses challenges in privacy, security, scalability, fairness, and regulatory compliance, offering economic benefits.

Now, let's delve into the tools that facilitate decentralized data science, starting with federated learning.

7.4 Federated Learning

7.4.1 What is Federated Learning?

You've likely encountered autocomplete or text prediction while typing on your cellphone keyboard. For instance, when you type "th," various options like "thanks," "this," "thank," etc., are suggested.

Text prediction relies on a machine learning system that learns from your typing patterns and provides recommendations based on that data.

Figure 7.5 **Text prediction on cell phone keyboard.**

There are two crucial aspects to consider:

I. **Privacy:** Typing on a cellphone keyboard involves entering sensitive information such as passwords and bank account numbers. Sending typing data to a centralized database for training the text prediction model may lead to significant privacy breaches.

II. **Personalization:** Effective text prediction requires a high level of personalization for individual users. Typing behavior varies widely. For example, non-native English speakers may use the English alphabet for their native languages. Additionally, individual preferences influenced by social circles, hobbies, culture, etc., make building a unified prediction model less useful for personalized text prediction.

Addressing privacy and personalization requirements demands processing data directly on the device, avoiding the need to send it to a central database. This is where federated learning comes in.

Federated learning is a machine learning approach in which a model is trained across multiple decentralized edge devices (like smartphones, IoT devices, or other endpoints) without the exchange of raw data.

In federated learning, instead of sending data to a central server for training, the model is sent to individual data sources. Local training occurs on each device, and only model updates or aggregated information are transmitted back to the central server.

Federated learning relies on various technologies. One of these technologies is TensorFlow Federated (TFF).

7.4.2 TensorFlow Federated (TFF)

TFF, developed by Google, is a framework for implementing federated learning. It extends TensorFlow to enable machine learning models to train across decentralized devices, addressing the complexities of distributed learning across edge devices.

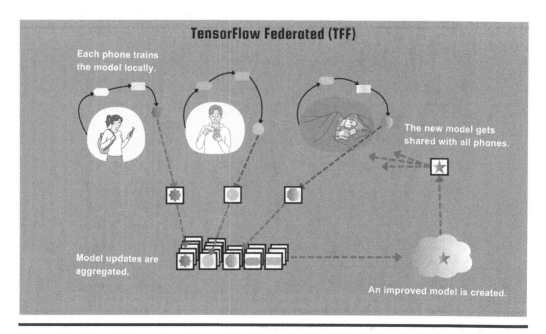

Figure 7.6 Visual illustration of Tensorflow Federated (TFF).

TFF incorporates federated learning algorithms, including federated averaging, enabling efficient and privacy-preserving model training.

TFF seamlessly integrates with TensorFlow and other frameworks, allowing the use of existing TensorFlow models and components in federated learning scenarios.

Let us refer to the Python code below. The provided code utilizes TensorFlow Federated (TFF) to train a model on the Extended MNIST (EMNIST) dataset. The federated learning approach involves training the model on ten clients, representing individual devices or entities, showcasing the decentralized nature of federated learning.

```python
import tensorflow as tf
import tensorflow_federated as tff

# Define a simple model
def create_federated_model():
    return tf.keras.models.Sequential([
        tf.keras.layers.Input(shape=(784,)),
        tf.keras.layers.Dense(10, activation=tf.nn.softmax)
    ])

# Create a sample dataset
mnist_train, mnist_test = tf.keras.datasets.mnist.load_data()
emnist_train = mnist_train[0], mnist_train[1]
emnist_test = mnist_test[0], mnist_test[1]

# Preprocess the data
def preprocess(dataset):
    return dataset.reshape((-1, 784)).astype('float32') / 255.0

emnist_train = preprocess(emnist_train)
emnist_test = preprocess(emnist_test)

# Define the Federated Learning Task
def create_federated_task():
    emnist_train = tff.simulation.datasets.emnist.load_data()
    sample_clients = emnist_train.client_ids[:10] # Use only 10
      clients for simplicity

    def model_fn():
        model = create_federated_model()
        return tff.learning.from_keras_model(
            model,
            input_spec=emnist_train.element_type_structure,
            loss=tf.keras.losses.SparseCategoricalCrossentropy(),
            metrics=[tf.keras.metrics.SparseCategoricalAccuracy()])

    return tff.learning.build_federated_averaging_process(
        model_fn,
        client_optimizer_fn=lambda: tf.keras.optimizers.SGD(learning_
          rate=0.02),
        server_optimizer_fn=lambda: tf.keras.optimizers.SGD(learning_
          rate=1.0))
```

```
# Train the federated model
federated_task = create_federated_task()
state = federated_task.initialize()
for round_num in range(5):
    state, metrics = federated_task.next(state, [emnist_train.create_
      tf_dataset_for_client(client) for client in sample_clients])
    print('Round {}: loss={}, accuracy={}'.format(round_num, metrics.
      loss, metrics.sparse_categorical_accuracy))
```

7.4.3 Federated Averaging (FedAvg)

FedAvg is a frequently used federated learning algorithm, playing a crucial role within TFF. This algorithm aggregates model updates originating from decentralized devices to enhance a global model with up-to-date data.

In FedAvg, local model training occurs on individual devices, and only the resulting model updates are sent to a central server for aggregation. The aggregation involves weighted averaging of model parameters, considering each device's contribution based on the number of data points it provides.

7.4.4 Secure Aggregation

Secure aggregation is crucial in federated learning, ensuring the aggregation of model updates without revealing individual contributions.

Certain federated learning implementations leverage homomorphic encryption (which will be discussed later) to execute secure aggregation on encrypted model updates.

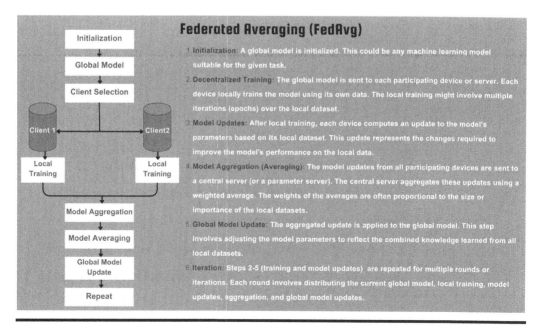

Figure 7.7   General process in federated averaging.

7.4.5 *TensorFlow Lite*

TensorFlow Lite, a lightweight version of TensorFlow for mobile and edge devices, is commonly used to deploy federated learning models locally. This allows for inference on edge devices without the need for constant communication with a central server. Inference here means the model giving an output either as a prediction or a classification.

We will discuss TensorFlow Lite in detail later in this chapter.

7.4.6 *Federated Datasets*

TFF introduces federated datasets, allowing developers to work with distributed datasets across decentralized devices or clients.

Each client possesses its local dataset, and federated learning tries to collaboratively train a machine learning model across these localized datasets without centrally accumulating raw data.

In TFF, federated datasets are frequently represented using the *tff.FederatedType*.

This allows developers to define the type of data distributed across clients.

For instance, *tff.FederatedType(tf.float32, tff.CLIENTS)* represents a federated dataset containing float32 numbers distributed across clients.

7.4.7 *Federated Optimization*

Federated optimization techniques involve modifying conventional optimization algorithms to suit the federated learning environment. These techniques encompass variations of SGD (stochastic gradient descent) specifically designed for situations where data is decentralized across multiple devices.

Please refer to the pseudocode below to get a sense of federated optimization.

```
# Input: Initial model x[0]; ClientOpt, ServerOpt with learning rate
η, ηs;
T - number of rounds

for t in range(T):
    # Step 1: Sample a subset S(t) of clients
    S_t = randomly_select_clients()

    # Step 2: Initialize local models on selected clients
    local_models = {i: x[t].copy() for i in S_t}

    # Step 3: Local training on selected clients
    for i in S_t:
        # Step 3.1: Iterate for τ_i rounds of local training
        for k in range(τ_i):
            # Step 3.2: Compute local stochastic gradient
            g_i = compute_local_gradient(local_models[i])

            # Step 3.3: Perform local update using the ClientOpt
              function
            local_models[i] = ClientOpt(local_models[i], g_i, η, t)
```

```
# Step 4: Compute local model changes
local_changes = [local_models[i] - x[t] for i in S_t]
Δ_t = sum(local_changes) / len(local_changes)

# Step 5: Update the global model on the server using the
  ServerOpt function
x[t + 1] = ServerOpt(x[t], -Δ_t, ηs, t)
```

Now, let us end our discussion on federated learning with some use cases.

7.4.8 Federated Learning Use Cases

7.4.8.1 Predictive Text and Keyboard Suggestions

As previously discussed, mobile keyboards leverage federated learning to enhance text prediction and suggestion features. The model is sent to users' devices, learning from individual keystrokes without transmitting sensitive information. Model updates, like new word predictions or corrections, are aggregated to improve the global keyboard model.

7.4.8.2 Speech Recognition and Virtual Assistants

Federated learning can benefit speech recognition on mobile devices. Virtual assistants like Siri or Google Assistant deploy models updated based on users' voice commands. Federated learning enables improvements in these models without sending audio recordings to a central server – instead, only model updates reflecting enhanced speech recognition are shared.

7.4.8.3 Health and Fitness Apps

Mobile health and fitness apps can employ federated learning for personalized health recommendations. The app sends a machine learning model to users' devices to analyze local health data, such as step counts, heart rate, or sleep patterns. The model is collaboratively updated to provide personalized insights without exposing individual health information.

7.4.8.4 Camera and Image Processing

Federated learning can enhance image processing for mobile cameras. For instance, a camera app might use federated learning to improve image recognition for specific scenes or objects. The model is locally trained on users' devices using their photos, and only aggregated model updates are sent to the central server.

7.4.8.5 Autonomous Vehicles and Traffic Prediction

Mobile devices within vehicles can contribute to traffic prediction models, allowing the system to adapt to local traffic patterns without sharing real-time location data. Model updates help improve route planning and traffic management.

7.4.8.6 Language Translation Apps

Language translation apps on mobile devices can leverage federated learning to enhance translation models. The app sends the translation model to users' devices, and as users translate text, the model learns from diverse language usage patterns. Only model updates are transmitted back to enhance the overall translation model.

Apart from the above use cases, federated learning can be used to build personalized advertising and recommendation systems on mobile devices to optimize mobile network parameters and enhance Quality of Service (QoS).

In the above scenarios, federated learning enables collaborative model training on mobile devices without compromising user privacy. By keeping data on the device and sharing only aggregated model updates, it enhances machine learning models while maintaining user trust in the privacy and security of their personal information.

7.5 Decentralized Data Marketplaces

7.5.1 Introduction

While federated learning addresses one aspect of decentralized data science, the decentralized accessibility of training data constitutes the other aspect.

Prominent centralized technology platforms utilize extensive user data to establish a competitive advantage, leading to substantial market dominance. Beyond privacy-related issues, the aggregation of data leads to data monopolies and diminishes market efficiency. It makes it practically impossible for new players to enter a market without spending exorbitant amounts to gain market access.

Democratization of data availability can only democratize industries.

Credible and useful data may already exist with various entities but might be confined to silos, such as health service organizations possessing health-related data and retail chains holding data on consumer buying habits.

Decentralized data marketplaces have the potential to liberate data from these silos by offering monetization opportunities to offline data holders.

These marketplaces revolutionize data exchange dynamics by eliminating the need for central authorities and promoting transparent, secure, and efficient transactions. Through the utilization of blockchain technology and decentralized networks, these marketplaces redefine the processes of buying and selling data.

But, there is still a pickle – how can we ensure user privacy while buying and selling user data?

This is where differential privacy comes in.

Before delving into differential privacy, let's explore decentralized marketplaces a little more comprehensively.

7.5.2 How do Decentralized Data Marketplaces Work?

Blockchain plays a crucial role in decentralized data marketplaces by ensuring transaction transparency and security. Smart contracts, like those in Ethereum, automate and enforce data agreements.

Tokens, like those in the Ocean Protocol, act as currency in these marketplaces, representing value, ownership, or access rights and incentivizing data contributors.

Platforms such as Streamr facilitate peer-to-peer interactions, reducing costs and enhancing privacy.

Smart contracts enforce access controls, ensuring data is shared only with authorized parties, thereby improving security and privacy. Contributors can monetize their data through automated smart contract-based payments. Smart contracts automate licensing and usage terms, guaranteeing transparent and enforceable data agreements.

Common data formats and protocols, as seen in the Streamr platform, enhance interoperability for seamless data exchange. Decentralized identity solutions provide secure and private authentication, empowering users with control over their identity information.

Reputation systems, such as those on platforms like Ocean Protocol, validate the accuracy and reliability of data sources, ensuring high data quality.

Platforms like Arweave feature community-driven governance, allowing participants to influence marketplace decision-making processes.

Decentralized data marketplaces find applications in healthcare, where platforms like Hu-manity.co enable patient data sharing for research. In finance, alternative data platforms like Numerai (numer.ai) facilitate the exchange of datasets for investment strategies. In IoT, Streamr (streamr.network) supports the sharing of sensor data for smart cities.

7.6 Differential Privacy

Now, as promised, let us discuss differential privacy.

In simple terms, differential privacy is a method that introduces noise to data to safeguard individual privacy while retaining the ability to conduct meaningful statistical analysis.

However, why is it termed differential privacy?

The term "differential privacy" originates from a privacy attack known as a "differencing attack". This attack is employed to de-anonymize individual user information by analyzing seemingly isolated datasets. A differencing attack involves removing an individual entry from the data and comparing the result of a function with and without the said entry to reveal information about that specific individual representing that entry.

Arvind Narayanan and Vitaly Shmatikov from the University of Texas demonstrated in their paper titled "Robust De-anonymization of Large Sparse Datasets" that apparently anonymous datasets, such as the Netflix subscriber dataset, could be de-anonymized using external knowledge sources like the IMDb dataset.

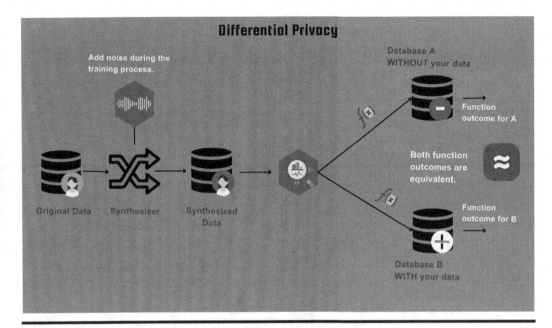

Figure 7.8   Process flow for differential privacy.

When an entity shares data with external parties, whether through data marketplaces, for research purposes, or for other reasons, anonymization alone is not sufficient.

This is where differential privacy becomes crucial.

Differential privacy serves as a privacy-preserving framework for crafting algorithms and systems that enable the collection and examination of data while safeguarding the privacy of individuals whose data is part of the analysis. The primary objective of differential privacy is to ensure that whether an individual's data is included or excluded, does not significantly influence the overall analysis outcome.

While we won't delve into the intricate details of this framework here, those interested in the mathematical aspects of differential privacy can explore "The Algorithmic Foundations of Differential Privacy" by Cynthia Dwork and Aaron Roth, which serves as an excellent starting point.

7.7 Homomorphic Encryption

In addition to anonymization, another method of safeguarding privacy is through encryption. However, the challenge arises in processing encrypted data.

This is where homomorphic encryption becomes relevant.

Homomorphic encryption is a cryptographic technique that enables computations to be conducted on encrypted data without the need for decryption.

The underlying concept of homomorphic encryption is to facilitate operations on encrypted data in such a way that the decrypted results are equivalent to the outcomes of the same operations performed on plaintext data.

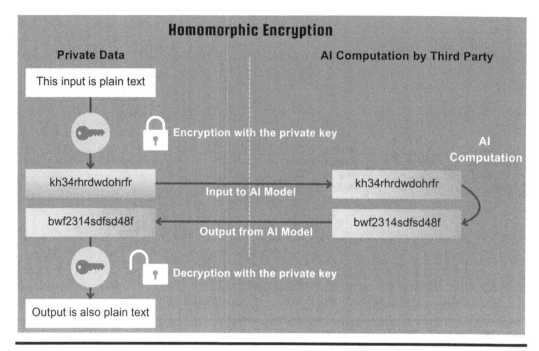

Figure 7.9   Process flow for homomorphic encryption.

Homomorphic encryption comes in different forms, such as partially homomorphic and fully homomorphic encryption, each offering different capabilities regarding the types of operations that can be performed on encrypted data.

Homomorphic encryption can be used in various use cases such as in secure cloud computing to process sensitive data, in privacy-preserving data analytics to process healthcare and financial services data, in privacy-preserving machine learning where models are trained on encrypted datasets, in secure multi-party computation scenarios allowing multiple parties to jointly compute a function over their inputs without revealing those inputs to each other, in privacy-preserving search enabling users to search for specific information in an encrypted database without revealing the search query or the contents of the database, in IoT data processing, and in encrypted messaging, etc.

You can refer to the below papers to get into depth in homomorphic encryption:

■ "A Fully Homomorphic Encryption Scheme," by Craig Gentry
■ "Homomorphic Encryption: Cryptography's Holy Grail," by David J. Wu

7.8 Edge Computing and Edge Analytics

7.8.1 Introduction

An alternative distributed data processing paradigm, distinct from federated learning, is edge computing and edge analytics. Edge computing focuses on processing data near its source, at the

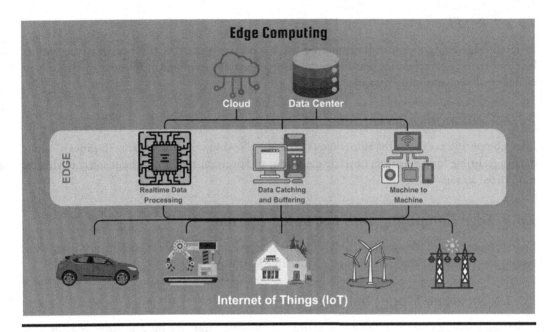

Figure 7.10   Edge computing.

network edge where it originates. This approach aims to minimize latency, optimize bandwidth, and enable real-time or near-real-time data processing.

In edge computing, data processing happens on local devices or edge nodes, eliminating the need to send data to centralized cloud servers. This enhances autonomy for edge devices and reduces dependence on central infrastructure.

7.8.2 Use Cases of Edge Computing and Edge Analytics

Typical applications of edge computing include real-time analytics, Internet of Things (IoT) implementations, industrial automation, and other situations where rapid data processing is essential.

7.8.2.1 Smart Cities

Smart cities use edge computing in traffic management, processing data from intersection sensors and cameras locally for real-time traffic analysis, optimization, and adaptive signal control.

7.8.2.2 Industrial Internet of Things (IIoT)

In industrial applications, edge computing is employed for predictive maintenance. On-site sensors gather machinery data, and edge nodes analyze it to predict maintenance requirements, minimizing downtime.

7.8.2.3 Healthcare

Edge computing enables real-time patient monitoring in healthcare. Wearable devices with sensors process health data locally, and edge nodes analyze it to provide immediate feedback or alerts.

7.8.2.4 Retail

In retail, edge computing can be employed for in-store analytics. Local processing of customer behavior data by cameras and sensors optimizes store layouts, improves customer experience, and enables real-time inventory management.

7.8.2.5 Autonomous Vehicles

Edge computing is crucial for autonomous vehicles, allowing onboard systems to process sensor data in real-time for navigation, obstacle detection, and decision-making without solely relying on centralized servers.

7.8.3 Edge Computing with Federated Learning

Edge computing and federated learning can synergize to establish a robust and privacy-preserving system for distributed data processing and machine learning.

7.8.3.1 Localized Model Training

Federated learning enables collaborative training of machine learning models across edge devices without centralizing raw data. Edge devices autonomously train and refine models with local data, contributing to personalized models while safeguarding individual data privacy.

7.8.3.2 Decentralized Model Inference

Deploying trained machine learning models on edge devices through edge computing enables decentralized model inference, empowering local predictions without data transmission to a central server. This reduces latency and conserves bandwidth.

7.8.3.3 Privacy-preserving Machine Learning

Federated learning ensures that raw data remains decentralized, aggregating only model updates centrally. This aligns with the privacy-centric principles of edge computing, where data is processed locally, safeguarding users' sensitive information on their devices.

7.8.3.4 Real-time Personalization

Federated learning allows personalized model creation from individual edge device data, enabling real-time, context-aware predictions and recommendations at the edge without relying on centralized servers.

7.8.3.5 Optimized Edge AI

Edge computing facilitates deploying machine learning models on edge devices, optimizing models trained through federated learning for local inference. This is especially valuable for real-time decision-making in applications like autonomous vehicles and smart cameras.

7.8.3.6 *Secure Multi-party Computation (SMPC)*

Combining secure multi-party computation with federated learning allows for secure collaborative computations across edge devices. This ensures that computations involving model updates are conducted securely, preserving the privacy of individual contributions.

Further details on SMPC will be discussed later in this chapter.

7.8.3.7 *Dynamic Model Updating*

Federated learning supports dynamic model updating based on evolving data distributions across edge devices. Edge devices can adapt their machine learning models in response to local changes, enhancing the model's accuracy and relevance over time.

7.9 Secure Multi-party Computation (SMPC)

7.9.1 *Introduction*

Secure multi-party computation (SMPC) is a cryptographic technique enabling multiple parties to jointly compute a function over their inputs while preserving input privacy. It ensures that computations on sensitive data are performed in a distributed and secure manner, safeguarding each party's private information and upholding privacy during collaborative computations.

While SMPC and homomorphic encryption share the goal of enabling privacy-preserving computation, they differ in application contexts and scenarios. SMPC exhibits greater versatility, emphasizing the collaboration of multiple parties.

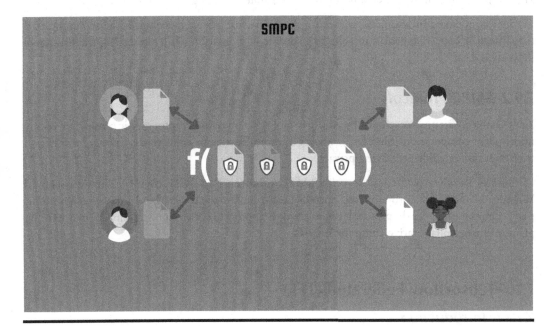

Figure 7.11   Visual illustration of SMPC.

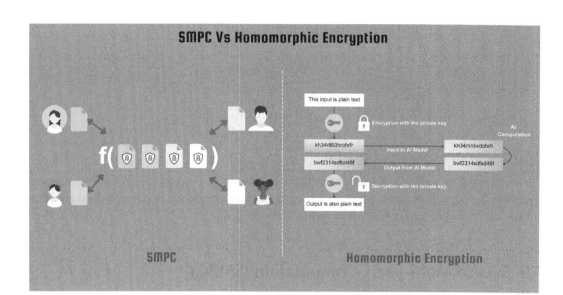

Figure 7.12   Comparison of SMPC with homomorphic encryption.

In contrast, homomorphic encryption is more specialized and effective for particular types of computations. Typically, homomorphic encryption entails a single party processing encrypted data.

Secure multi-party computation (SMPC) is utilized in collaborative data analysis, machine learning on sensitive datasets, and privacy-preserving computations. By employing cryptographic protocols and zero-knowledge proofs, SMPC ensures the confidentiality of each party's input during computations, allowing accurate validation without revealing input information.

SMPC operates in scenarios without a single trusted party, distributing trust among participants. The collective goal is to achieve a specific computation while preserving the privacy of individual data.

7.9.2 SMPC Protocols

Yao's Garbled Circuits, developed by Andrew Yao, is a pioneering cryptographic protocol in secure multi-party computation (SMPC). It allows multiple parties to collectively compute a function over their inputs while preserving privacy.

Besides Yao's Garbled Circuits, other SMPC protocols like BGW (Ben-Or, Goldwasser, and Wigderson) and SPDZ (pronounced "Speedz") contribute to the diverse landscape of secure multi-party computation. Each protocol offers unique approaches and applications in maintaining privacy during collaborative computations.

7.10 Tensorflow Federated (TFF)

7.10.1 Introduction

Earlier, we touched upon TFF, and now let's delve a bit deeper into its functionalities.

TFF, or TensorFlow Federated, is a versatile open-source framework designed to explore machine learning and computations on decentralized data. It extends TensorFlow's capabilities to meet the unique requirements of federated learning.

Functioning as an open framework, TFF allows for the local simulation of decentralized computations and provides a suite of APIs tailored for federated learning.

7.10.2 TensorFlow Federated APIs

TensorFlow Federated offers two primary APIs:

- Federated learning (FL) API, and
- Federated core (FC) API.

7.10.2.1 Federated Learning (FL) API

The federated learning (FL) API is tailored for collaborative training of machine learning models across decentralized devices, ensuring privacy. Ideal for scenarios with multiple participating devices, it allows training a central model without revealing raw data, making it valuable for privacy-sensitive applications or when central data aggregation is impractical.

Please refer to the below code that uses TensorFlow Federated (TFF)'s federated learning (FL) API to implement a simple federated learning process.

This federated learning process is utilized in a sample training loop, where the model is trained on federated data for multiple rounds, showcasing the integration of TFF's FL API for distributed machine learning.

```
import tensorflow as tf
import tensorflow_federated as tff

# Define a simple model and compile it
model = tf.keras.Sequential([tf.keras.layers.Input(shape=(784,)), tf.
  keras.layers.Dense(10, activation='softmax')])
model.compile(optimizer='sgd', loss='sparse_categorical_crossentropy',
  metrics=['accuracy'])

# Load federated data (dummy data for illustration)
@tff.tf_computation(tf.int32)
def generate_dummy_data(client_id):
    return tf.data.Dataset.from_tensor_slices({'x': tf.constant([1.0]
      * 784, dtype=tf.float32), 'y': tf.constant(1, dtype=tf.int32)}).
      repeat(10)

# Wrap the model and data into Federated Types
model_type = tff.framework.type_from_tensors(model)
data_type = tff.to_type(generate_dummy_data.type_signature)

# Define a federated computation for forward pass
@tff.federated_computation(model_type, data_type)
```

```
def forward_pass(model, data):
    return tf.reduce_mean(tf.nn.sparse_softmax_cross_entropy_with_
    logits(logits=model(data['x']), labels=data['y']))

# Wrap the forward pass in a Federated Learning Process
federated_algorithm = tff.learning.from_compiled_keras_model(model,
  compile_model=lambda m: m)

# Sample usage of federated learning
federated_data = [generate_dummy_data(client_id) for client_id in
  range(10)]
state = federated_algorithm.initialize()
for round_num in range(5):
    state, metrics = federated_algorithm.next(state, federated_data)
    print(f'Round {round_num}: {metrics}')
```

7.10.2.2 Federated Core (FC) API

The federated core (FC) API in TensorFlow Federated offers essential primitives for a diverse range of decentralized computations, expanding its applicability beyond machine learning to other scenarios. This API acts as a versatile toolkit for expressing decentralized computations in TensorFlow Federated.

The FC API is valuable for developers needing to execute a wide range of decentralized computations beyond typical federated learning tasks. It enables the expression of diverse computations on distributed datasets.

Let us refer to the code below. The code utilizes TensorFlow Federated (TFF) Federated Core API to implement a simple federated learning scenario for linear regression. It defines a linear regression model and dummy federated data using TFF constructs. The Federated Core API is then employed to define federated computations for local training (*local_train*) and federated averaging (*federated_averaging*) functions.

```
import tensorflow as tf
import tensorflow_federated as tff

# Define a simple linear regression model
def create_model():
    return tf.keras.Sequential([tf.keras.layers.Input(shape=(1,)),
      tf.keras.layers.Dense(1)])

# Define a federated dataset (dummy data for illustration)
@tff.tf_computation
def generate_dummy_data():
    return tf.data.Dataset.from_tensor_slices({'x': tf.constant([1.0],
      dtype=tf.float32), 'y': tf.constant([2.0], dtype=tf.float32)})

# Wrap the model and data into Federated Types
model_type = tff.to_type(create_model().to_flattened_type())
data_type = tff.to_type(generate_dummy_data.type_signature.result)
```

```
# Define a federated computation for local training
@tff.federated_computation(model_type, tf.float32, data_type)
def local_train(model, learning_rate, data):
    optimizer = tf.keras.optimizers.SGD(learning_rate)
    model.compile(optimizer, loss='mse')
    model.fit(data['x'], data['y'], epochs=1, verbose=0)
    return model

# Define a federated computation for federated averaging
@tff.federated_computation(tff.type_at_server(model_type), tff.
type_at_clients(tf.float32), data_type)
def federated_averaging(server_model, learning_rate, client_data):
    server_weights = tff.federated_map(local_train, [tff.federated_
       broadcast(server_model), learning_rate, client_data])
    return tff.federated_mean(server_weights)

# Sample usage of Federated Core API
initial_model = create_model()
federated_data = [generate_dummy_data() for _ in range(10)]
learning_rate = 0.1

server_model = federated_averaging(initial_model, learning_rate,
  federated_data)

# Print the updated server model
print("Updated Server Model Weights:", server_model.trainable_
  variables)
```

7.11 Tensorflow Lite (TFLite)

7.11.1 Introduction

TensorFlow Lite (TFLite) is a lightweight version of TensorFlow designed for mobile and edge devices, playing a crucial role in decentralized data science. It enables the integration of machine learning at the edge, supporting on-device inference and promoting privacy, efficiency, and low-latency applications.

The below code shows a sample use of TFLite. The code demonstrates the usage of TensorFlow Lite (TFLite) to convert a simple Keras model into the TFLite format for deployment on resource-constrained devices. It converts the model using the TFLiteConverter, saves it to a file, and loads it using the TFLite Interpreter. The code then prepares input data, sets the input tensor, runs inference, and prints the input and output results, showcasing the integration of TFLite for deploying lightweight models on edge devices.

```
import tensorflow as tf
from tensorflow import lite

# Create a simple model
model = tf.keras.Sequential([
```

```
        tf.keras.layers.Input(shape=(4,), name='input'),
        tf.keras.layers.Dense(2, activation='softmax', name='output')
])

# Convert the model to TensorFlow Lite format
converter = lite.TFLiteConverter.from_keras_model(model)
tflite_model = converter.convert()

# Save the TensorFlow Lite model to a file
with open('model.tflite', 'wb') as f:
    f.write(tflite_model)

# Load the TensorFlow Lite model
interpreter = lite.Interpreter(model_content=tflite_model)
interpreter.allocate_tensors()

# Get input and output details
input_details = interpreter.get_input_details()
output_details = interpreter.get_output_details()

# Prepare input data (assuming a 4-dimensional input)
input_data = tf.constant([[1.0, 2.0, 3.0, 4.0]], dtype=tf.float32)

# Set input tensor
interpreter.set_tensor(input_details[0]['index'], input_data)

# Run inference
interpreter.invoke()

# Get the output
output_data = interpreter.get_tensor(output_details[0]['index'])

print("Input:", input_data.numpy())
print("Output:", output_data)
```

7.11.2 Key Features of TensorFlow Lite

7.11.2.1 Edge Computing

TensorFlow Lite is tailored for edge computing, enabling the execution of machine learning models on mobile, IoT, and other edge devices. This aligns with decentralized data science principles, emphasizing local computation near data sources and reducing dependence on centralized processing.

7.11.2.2 Model Efficiency

TFLite models prioritize efficiency in size and computation, crucial for deployment on resource-constrained devices in decentralized scenarios with limitations in computational power and storage capacity.

7.11.2.3 Privacy Preservation

TensorFlow Lite, through on-device inference, plays a role in preserving privacy. Instead of transmitting raw data to a central server, data remains on the device, with only model inferences or updates being shared.

7.11.2.4 Low Latency

On-device inference with TensorFlow Lite ensures low-latency processing, particularly beneficial for applications requiring real-time or near-real-time predictions. In decentralized data science, especially in scenarios like edge analytics, low latency is crucial for timely decision-making.

7.11.2.5 Compatibility with TensorFlow

TensorFlow Lite models seamlessly transition from TensorFlow models, facilitating a unified machine learning workflow. This compatibility ensures a smooth journey from centrally training models to deploying them on decentralized devices.

7.11.3 Role of TFLite in Decentralized Data Science

7.11.3.1 Federated Learning on Edge Devices

TensorFlow Lite (TFLite) facilitates federated learning on edge devices by enabling local model execution and supporting on-device training and inference. This decentralized approach allows collaborative model training across multiple devices without centralizing sensitive data, making it pivotal for federated learning.

7.11.3.2 Edge Analytics

In decentralized data science, TFLite enhances edge analytics by executing machine learning models directly on edge devices, emphasizing analytics proximity to the data source. This is crucial for applications such as predictive maintenance, anomaly detection, and real-time decision-making in edge environments.

7.11.3.3 Privacy-preserving Applications

TFLite's on-device inference enhances privacy in decentralized scenarios by keeping data localized. This is crucial for privacy-sensitive applications like healthcare diagnostics or personalized recommendations, where user data security concerns are prevalent.

7.11.3.4 Resource-efficient Deployment

TFLite's lightweight design enables deployment on devices with diverse computational capabilities, making it ideal for decentralized environments with varying hardware profiles. This resource efficiency is crucial for successful machine learning deployment in decentralized settings.

In the last three chapters, we have discussed three exciting new disciplines towards our decentralized future – decentralized identity, decentralized storage, and decentralized data science.

So, what does it mean for us, the users?

These technologies collectively empower users by providing control over their privacy and data, demonstrating the feasibility of constructing systems that safeguard user rights while delivering a comparable user experience. This improves user agency and autonomy in digital interactions, creating a transparent and user-friendly environment.

These technologies pave the way for a future where users have complete control over sharing their data and its recipients. Users could autonomously capture the economic value of their data, directly monetizing the data they generate without relying on centralized intermediaries.

Bibliography

[2311.17035] Scalable Extraction of Training Data from (Production) Language Models. (2023, November 28). arXiv. Retrieved December 14, 2023, from https://arxiv.org/abs/2311.17035

Apache. (n.d.). Apache MXNet | A Flexible and Efficient Library for Deep Learning. Retrieved January 5, 2024, from https://mxnet.apache.org/versions/1.9.1/

Asharov, Gilad, and Yehuda Lindell. "A Full Proof of the BGW Protocol for Perfectly-Secure Multiparty Computation." Cryptology ePrint Archive,https://eprint.iacr.org/2011/136. Accessed 13 June 2024.

Berkeley AI Research. (n.d.). Caffe | Deep Learning Framework. Retrieved January 5, 2024, from https://caffe.berkeleyvision.org

Dwork, C., & Roth, A. (n.d.). *The Algorithmic Foundations of Differential Privacy.* UPenn CIS. Retrieved January 5, 2024, from https://www.cis.upenn.edu/~aaroth/Papers/privacybook.pdf

EleutherAI. (2022, February 25). *EleutherAI/gpt-neo: An Implementation of Model Parallel GPT-2 and GPT-3-style Models Using the Mesh-tensorflow Library.* GitHub. Retrieved January 5, 2024, from https://github.com/EleutherAI/gpt-neo

Gentry, C. (n.d.). *A Fully Homomorphic Encryption Scheme a Dissertation Submitted to The Department of Computer Science and the Committee on Gradua.* Applied Cryptography Group. Retrieved January 5, 2024, from https://crypto.stanford.edu/craig/craig-thesis.pdf

Google. (n.d.). Federated Learning. Retrieved January 5, 2024, from https://federated.withgoogle.com

Google. (n.d.). Keras: Deep Learning for Humans. Retrieved January 5, 2024, from https://keras.io

Google. (n.d.). Scikit-learn: Machine Learning in Python — Scikit-learn 1.3.2 Documentation. Retrieved January 5, 2024, from https://scikit-learn.org/stable/

Google. (n.d.). *TensorFlow Federated: Machine Learning on Decentralized Data.* TensorFlow. Retrieved January 5, 2024, from https://www.tensorflow.org/federated

Google. (n.d.). TensorFlow.org. Retrieved January 5, 2024, from https://www.tensorflow.org

Google. (n.d.). *TensorFlow Lite | ML for Mobile and Edge Devices.* TensorFlow. Retrieved January 5, 2024, from https://www.tensorflow.org/lite

Google. (2019, March 6). *Introducing TensorFlow Federated — The TensorFlow Blog.* The TensorFlow Blog. Retrieved January 5, 2024, from https://blog.tensorflow.org/2019/03/introducing-tensorflow-federated.html

Homomorphic Encryption Standardization. (n.d.). Homomorphic Encryption Standardization. Retrieved January 4, 2024, from https://homomorphicencryption.org/introduction.

Hu-manity.co.Hu-manity.co – Restoring Trust in Digital, https://hu-manity.co/. Accessed 13 June 2024.

IEEE. (2023, October 21). What Is Homomorphic Encryption? IEEE Digital Privacy. Retrieved February 2, 2024, from https://digitalprivacy.ieee.org/publications/topics/what-is-homomorphic-encryption.

IEEE. (2023, October 21). What Is Multiparty Computation? IEEE Digital Library. Retrieved February 2, 2024, from https://digitalprivacy.ieee.org/publications/topics/what-is-multiparty-computation.

Keller, M. (n.d.). *MP-SPDZ: A Versatile Framework for Multi-Party Computation*. Cryptology ePrint Archive. Retrieved January 5, 2024, from https://eprint.iacr.org/2020/521

The Linux Foundation. (n.d.). PyTorch.org. Retrieved January 5, 2024, from https://pytorch.org

McSwine, D. (2023, November 7). *Secure Multi-Party Computation: Theory, Practice and Applications*. ScienceDirect. Retrieved January 5, 2024, from https://www.sciencedirect.com/science/article/abs/pii/S0020025518308338

Meta. (n.d.). *LLaMA: Open and Efficient Foundation Language Models - Meta Research*. Meta Research. Retrieved January 5, 2024, from https://research.facebook.com/publications/llama-open-and-efficient-foundation-language-models/

Narayanan, A., & Shmatikov, V. (n.d.). *Robust De-anonymization of Large Sparse Datasets*. UT Computer Science. Retrieved January 5, 2024, from https://www.cs.utexas.edu/~shmat/shmat_oak08netflix.pdf

Numerai.",https://numer.ai/. Accessed 13 June 2024.

Ocean Protocol. (2020, August 19). *Ocean Protocol Whitepaper V3 & V4*. Ocean Protocol. Retrieved January 5, 2024, from https://oceanprotocol.com/tech-whitepaper.pdf

Ocean Protocol Foundation Ltd. (n.d.). Meet Ocean: Tokenized AI & Data — Ocean Protocol. Retrieved January 5, 2024, from https://oceanprotocol.com

OpenAI. (n.d.). ChatGPT. Retrieved December 14, 2023, from https://chat.openai.com

Price, Jonathon, et al. "Stochastic gradient descent." Cornell University Computational Optimization Open Textbook, 21 December 2020.

PYTHIA. (n.d.). PYTHIA 8.3 - PYTHIA 8.3. Retrieved January 5, 2024, from https://pythia.org

Radford, A., Narasimhan, K., Salimans, T., & Sutskever, I. (2018, June 11). *Improving Language Understanding with Unsupervised Learning*. paperswithcode. Retrieved January 5, 2024, from https://paperswithcode.com/paper/improving-language-understanding-by

Streamr. (2020, August 20). *The Streamr Network: Performance and Scalability*. Whitepaper. Retrieved January 5, 2024, from https://streamr-public.s3.amazonaws.com/streamr-network-scalability-white-paper-2020-08-20.pdf

Technology Innovation Institute. (n.d.). Falcon LLM. Retrieved January 5, 2024, from https://falconllm.tii.ae

TensorFlow. "emnist."TensorFlow, https://www.tensorflow.org/datasets/catalog/emnist. Accessed 13 June 2024.

TensorFlow. "Federated Core." TensorFlow, https://www.tensorflow.org/federated/federated_core.Accessed 13 June 2024.

TensorFlow. "Federated Learning." TensorFlow, https://www.tensorflow.org/federated/federated_learning. Accessed 13 June 2024.

The Arweave Project."Snapshot on Arweave: Governing the Future." arweave.medium.com, 20 December 2020, https://arweave.medium.com/snapshot-on-arweave-governing-the-future-68f64c3affe4. Accessed 13 June 2024.

Theano/Theano: Theano Was a Python Library That Allows You to Define, Optimize, and Evaluate Mathematical Expressions Involving Multi-dimensional Arrays Efficiently. It is Being Continued as Aesara: www.github.com/pymc-devs/aesara. (n.d.). GitHub. Retrieved January 5, 2024, from https://github.com/Theano/Theano

Streamr. Streamr: The decentralized real-time data network, https://streamr.network/. Accessed 13 June 2024.

Wu, D. J. (n.d.). *Fully Homomorphic Encryption: Cryptography's Holy Grail*. UT Computer Science. Retrieved January 5, 2024, from https://www.cs.utexas.edu/~dwu4/papers/XRDSFHE.pdf

Yakoubov, S. (n.d.). A Gentle Introduction to Yao's Garbled Circuits. Retrieved January 5, 2024, from https://web.mit.edu/sonka89/www/papers/2017ygc.pdf

Chapter 8

Decentralization in Web3

Sam Ghosh

In the chapter "Primer on Web3 and Distributed Systems," we mentioned the qualities of Web3 networks –

open, permissionless, trustless, automated, immutable, and decentralized.

In this section, we will delve into one specific quality of Web3 networks – decentralized.

Understanding the decentralized nature of Web3 is important to understand how we can bring decentralization to traditional architectures.

8.1 Centralized vs Decentralized Systems

As we mentioned earlier, decentralized, in simple words, means that an entity is not controlled by any central authority.

8.1.1 So, What Does It Mean by Control?

Control may show itself in various forms:

8.1.1.1 Control Over Access

Centralized systems strictly control who can join the system and who can remain in the system.

Decentralized systems should be open and censorship-resistant.

8.1.1.2 Control Over Identity

Trust plays an important role in centralized systems and trust is built by providing personal credentials. Centralized systems control your role in the system based on who you are or at least who you appear to be.

 DOI: 10.4324/9781003507352-8

Decentralized systems need to be trustless i.e. what role you can take should not matter based on who you are but what you bring to the table.

8.1.1.3 Control Over the Flow of Resources

Centralized systems exert tight control over the inflow, outflow, and access to resources within the system. The economic model of these platforms relies on maintaining control, as seen in ride-hailing apps handling payments to drivers and food delivery apps managing payments to restaurants.

The control over the flow of resources gives the tech platforms control over the economic incentive structure on the platform and these platforms almost always prioritize their own economic welfare.

In the case of decentralized systems, the flow of resources should be transparent and fair. This fairness needs to be reached through market economics and consensus, not unilateral decisions.

8.1.1.4 Control Over the Flow of Information

Centralized systems also strictly control the flow of information. For example, ride-hailing apps often do not share all the information about a booked ride with the drivers. This control enables platform authorities to enforce rules advantageous to them in economic terms.

Decentralized systems need to be completely transparent while preserving necessary privacy. So, in the case of a decentralized system, no entity should have any undue advantage arising out of any information asymmetry.

8.1.1.5 Control Over the Future Direction

In the case of centralized systems, any system participants, other than the platform authority, practically have no control over the future direction of the system. The central authority "reserves all rights" over the future direction of the system.

In the case of a decentralized system, all platform participants with any stake in the system should have meaningful control over the future direction of the system.

8.2 What is Decentralization?

Decentralization is the process of cultivating the qualities of decentralized networks into technical or business systems.

Decentralization is a matter of scale. Even most Web3 networks are NOT completely decentralized – well, the voting power in DAOs is often concentrated in the hands of platform builders, giving them considerably more control over the governance of the platforms.

8.3 Types of Decentralization

A. Blockchains, like all Distributed Ledger Technologies (DLTs), are decentralized, relying on multiple servers (nodes) instead of a single server. Nodes run client software in a peer-to-peer network, ensuring that all active nodes maintain identical records of data, including copies of smart contracts. This decentralized structure ensures continued accessibility and activity even if some nodes go offline. Let us call this **"Technical Decentralization"**.

B. But, there is another kind of decentralization in the context of Web3 networks – **"Governance Decentralization"**. The use of DAOs or Decentralized Autonomous Organizations (and other decentralized governance mechanisms) allows Web3 platforms to be governed by their users along with the platform builders and investors. Based on the design and maturity of the governance system, platform users can have a significant say in how the platform is structured and what rules govern the platform.

We will discuss governance on Web3 platforms in this chapter. But, before that, let us understand the governance of tech platforms a little.

8.4 Governance of Tech Platforms

8.4.1 Introduction

In the context of tech platforms, governance refers to the set of regulations, processes, and structures dictating decision-making, policy implementation, and overall management of the platform. It includes mechanisms for user interactions, content moderation, feature development, and other aspects of platform functionality.

So, how centralized or decentralized the governance of the major tech platforms are?

As a user (or service provider on these platforms) how much control do you think you have on –

- What criteria do social media platforms use to determine which content to retain and which content to remove?
- How do social media platforms differentiate between content that should be promoted virally and content that should be suppressed?
- What algorithms do e-commerce platforms employ to prioritize search rankings for merchants?
- How do e-commerce platforms establish their commission rates?
- What factors influence the tariff decisions of ride-sharing platforms?
- How do ride-sharing platforms determine the commission rates charged to drivers?

The reality is that users often do not have much control and knowledge regarding the decision-making processes behind content moderation, platform economics, and various algorithms governing platform operations.

Over the years, these platforms have transformed from mere sources of entertainment to integral components of our daily lives. Video-sharing and social media platforms support the livelihoods of numerous content creators, ride-sharing platforms sustain drivers, and e-commerce platforms serve as crucial distribution channels for small businesses.

Considering the substantial influence these platforms exert over our lives, it seems reasonable for users to have a say in the design and operation of these platforms.

Shouldn't these platforms also bear responsibility for the externalities they generate? In many instances, platforms have neglected these responsibilities, leading to legal battles.

Examples of such legal battles include Facebook's Cambridge Analytica Scandal, Apple's disputes over App Store policies, and Airbnb's legal challenges related to discrimination on its platform.

It is pertinent to mention Section 230 and related issues in this context.

8.4.2 User-generated Content and Section 230

We have already mentioned Section 230 in the chapter "Why is decentralization the need of the hour?" Let us discuss a little more here.

Many critics have raised concerns about the potential misuse of Section 230 of the Communications Decency Act of 1996. This legislation, a cornerstone of Internet law in the US, grants liability protections to online platforms regarding user-generated content. Section 230 has significantly influenced the legal and governance landscape of the internet.

Under Section 230, online platforms are not treated as publishers of user-generated content. This legal framework shields them from being held accountable for the content posted by their users. It empowers platforms to moderate or restrict access to content they find objectionable or that violates their policies, without facing legal repercussions.

However, critics argue that some platforms abuse the immunity provided by Section 230. They allege that this broad immunity allows platforms to evade accountability for harmful content or for unfair content moderation practices. Section 230's broad protections have raised concerns about the potential lack of accountability among platforms on issues like misinformation, hate speech, and harmful content.

In response to these concerns, the US Department of Justice conducted a review of Section 230, proposing widespread reforms to address the challenges associated with its implementation.

Okay, we understand the need for governance reform for the tech platforms and Web3 platforms offer an alternative governance structure. But, before delving into governance models for Web3 platforms, it's important to establish a framework for understanding governance systems.

8.5 Framework for Governance Systems

8.5.1 Transparency

Transparency is a foundational principle of any governance system, involving the open accessibility of information, decisions, and processes to all participants. It fosters trust and enables stakeholders to comprehend the reasoning behind decisions.

8.5.2 Fairness and Equity

Fairness is crucial in governance, emphasizing impartiality and equitable representation. All participants, regardless of their stake or influence, should have a fair opportunity to express opinions and contribute to decision-making.

8.5.3 Protection of Minority Rights

Governance models should safeguard the rights and interests of minority stakeholders to prevent their marginalization. Decision-making processes should not lead to the neglect of minority views in favor of majoritarian approaches.

8.5.4 Inclusivity and Consensus Building

Governance systems should encourage broad participation to incorporate diverse perspectives, fostering community ownership and legitimacy. Effective consensus-building processes are essential, considering a variety of opinions and preferences within the community.

8.5.5 Accountability

Clear lines of accountability are vital, with participants being answerable for their actions. Governance structures should outline consequences for the misuse of power or violation of rules to maintain system integrity.

8.5.6 Rule of Law and Compliance

Governance systems should be grounded in clear and enforceable rules, defining decision-making parameters and establishing a stable environment. Alignment with legal frameworks and regulatory requirements is essential for legitimacy and risk reduction in governance systems.

8.5.7 Incentive Structures

Governance mechanisms should align incentives to promote positive contributions to the ecosystem, fostering a thriving and collaborative community.

8.5.8 Continuous Improvement

Governance is a dynamic process. Regular evaluations and opportunities for improvement ensure responsiveness to community needs.

8.5.9 Flexibility and Adaptability

Effective governance allows for flexibility and adaptability to changing circumstances. Updating rules, incorporating feedback, and responding to emerging challenges are crucial for long-term success.

8.5.10 *Decision Efficiency and Conflict Resolution*

Governance processes should prioritize efficiency without compromising inclusivity or decision quality. Robust governance mechanisms should include efficient processes for resolving disputes or conflicts within the community, contributing to a healthy and sustainable ecosystem.

8.6 Transitioning towards Decentralization

Social media platforms are recognizing the limitations of their governance structures in recent times.

For instance, Meta introduced an oversight board with the aim *"to promote free expression by making principled, independent decisions regarding content on Facebook and Instagram and by issuing recommendations on the relevant Meta content policy."*

While steps toward inclusive governance are appreciable, this approach has notable limitations.

Firstly, the oversight board's authority is limited to reviewing individual content decisions and making recommendations on specific policies, lacking the power to enforce broader policy changes or address systemic concerns.

Secondly, despite the inclusion of many prominent figures like Nobel Peace Prize winner Tawakkol Karman and Former Prime Minister of Denmark Helle Thorning-Schmidt, the question arises: Can these few high-profile individuals truly represent the diverse global user base of billions?

Thirdly, while the oversight board may oversee content removal, it appears to have no influence over other governance aspects. Actions like limiting the reach of content or profiles (shadow banning) can be as impactful as content removal.

The focus should not only be on content removal or reach limitations for specific accounts but also on algorithms determining content reach on the platforms and the economic policies for advertisers and sellers.

There are various aspects that just cannot be incorporated into a centralized governance system.

8.7 Decentralized Governance

Okay, now let us discuss decentralized governance.

Imagine if Facebook (Meta) were to announce tomorrow that every user would now possess voting rights. They decide to make all governance policies and algorithms publicly accessible and establish a system where any user can propose changes to the governance process. These proposals undergo a voting procedure, and if a proposal secures a majority of votes, it is adopted and put into effect.

Certainly, there could be various possible scenarios based on factors such as whether all users are granted equal votes or if their votes differ based on their contributions (such as engagement on the platform), the definition of a majority (more than half, two-thirds, one-fourth of votes, etc.), along with minimum quorum requirements (indicating the minimum number of votes needed for proposal adoption), etc.

This encapsulates the essence of decentralized governance – transparent, dynamic, and inclusive.

8.8 Decentralized Governance in Web3

8.8.1 Introduction

Let me clarify right from the start – depending on the maturity and design of the governance process, the governance of a Web3 platform can be fully centralized, partially decentralized, or fairly decentralized. Complete decentralization is often more of a concept than a reality.

Even for many advanced DAOs (Decentralized Autonomous Organizations), there are challenges that prevent them from achieving complete decentralization. One entity or a group of related entities may gain control over the DAO by accumulating voting rights, potentially ignoring the rights of other voting members, as seen in the case of Uniswap in 2020.

In October 2020, Dharma, which acted as a portal to Uniswap, proposed reducing the votes required to create and pass a proposal in the Uniswap governance system. This proposal raised concerns that if the proposal had passed, it could have made it easier for Dharma and another major proponent, the blockchain simulation company Gauntlet, to pass any proposal by colluding.

Fortunately, the community rejected this proposal.

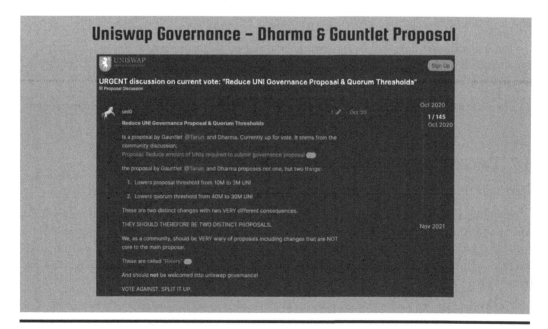

Figure 8.1 Dharma and Gauntlet proposal to change the quorum requirements for proposing and passing a proposal.

Anyways, let's delve into DAO and token-based governance. Although DAO-based governance is the most popular, it's not the sole Web3 governance structure. Other governance mechanisms will be discussed later in this chapter.

8.8.2 DAO and Token-based Governance

The primary elements of DAO-based governance processes are DAOs, i.e. decentralized autonomous organizations and governance tokens.

8.8.2.1 So, What is a DAO?

In simple terms, a DAO is an internet-native organization collectively owned and managed by its members.

Let's delve a little deeper.

Consider the corporate governance of a traditional publicly traded company. The company is owned by equity shareholders, legally termed as members, and their shares carry voting rights, allowing them to influence the governance of the company.

However, shareholders, or more precisely voting rights holders, often lack significant control over asset allocations within the company. They must rely on the decisions of board members and managers who control operations, and these board members and managers may prioritize their own interests over those of the shareholders, leading to what is known as an agency problem in corporate governance.

Now, imagine an organization where all asset allocations occur automatically according to pre-approved rules sanctioned by the majority of its members. The entire governance structure is encoded as smart contracts on a blockchain network.

Because blockchain networks are immutable, the governance system cannot be arbitrarily modified. Any changes must go through a proposal and voting mechanism, and even the voting process is pre-programmed. Consequently, all fund allocations within the organization take place in an automated and auditable manner.

This encapsulates the essence of a DAO.

8.8.2.2 DAO Classification

DAOs come in various forms both based on the industry they serve and their internal workings.

Standard DAOs, charity DAOs, venture capital DAOs, social DAOs, art DAOs, and DeFi DAOs, etc. are examples of DAO classification based on the sector they serve.

8.8.2.2.1 DAOs can also be classified based on what purpose they solve on Web3 systems.

a. **Protocol DAOs** are specialized entities designed to oversee various functions within Web3 protocols, such as borrowing and lending. These DAOs assist platforms in efficiently executing their operations and decision-making processes.

E.g. MakerDAO for the Maker liquidity protocol that issues the stablecoin DAI.

b. **Grant DAO**s are established to empower enterprises strategically utilizing capital resources obtained from charitable donations across the Web3 ecosystem. Their primary goal is to provide financial support to projects driving meaningful change.

E.g. GitCoin DAO facilitates open-source ecosystem growth and distributes millions in funding to various projects.

c. **Philanthropic DAOs** aim to advance social responsibility within the Web3 space by uniting around a common mission to create a positive impact.

E.g. UkraineDAO is used for fundraising to support the Ukrainian Army in collaboration with PleasrDAO, Trippy Labs, and the musical group Pussy Riot.

d. **Social DAOs** provide platforms for like-minded individuals to come together for learning, collaboration, and project engagement, often with entry barriers like token ownership or NFT possession.

E.g. Developer DAO comprises Web3 enthusiasts and developers working together to shape the future of Web3.

e. **Collector DAOs** pool resources to collectively invest treasury funds into NFT art and collectibles, allowing members to gain exposure to high-value investments.

E.g. FlamingoDAO focuses on collective investment in blue-chip NFT art.

f. **Venture DAOs** bring together capital from various sources to fund initiatives related to early-stage Web3 startups, protocols, and off-chain investments, democratizing investment processes.

E.g. MetaCartel provides finances and operational guidance to emerging decentralized applications (dApps).

g. **Media DAOs** produce content directed by the community, reimagining traditional media platforms and allowing participants to share profits.

E.g. BanklessDAO promotes banking-free money systems through media, culture, and education.

h. **SubDAOs** are specialized DAOs that manage specific tasks within a broader DAO, improving decentralization while enhancing specialization and efficiency.

E.g. Balancer protocol that utilizes subDAOs to handle decision-making and implementation efficiently within the larger balancer DAO.

8.8.2.3 Governance Tokens

Governance tokens are cryptographic tokens that empower holders to actively participate in shaping the future of a Web3 network by proposing and voting on governance-related matters.

Holders of governance tokens typically have the right to initiate change proposals, cast votes on proposed changes, or delegate their voting authority to another member of the Web3 platform. However, it's important to note that governance tokens can also be freely traded, and their value is determined independently by demand and supply forces.

Several popular governance tokens include UNI on the Uniswap network, AAVE on the Aave network, MKR on the Maker network, and COMP on the Compound network.

To ensure true decentralization of Web3 protocols, it is crucial to widely distribute ownership of governance tokens rather than concentrated holding. Consequently, these tokens are often distributed to various market participants as incentives. For instance, in the case of Compound, both lenders and borrowers receive COMP tokens, fostering a broader and more decentralized governance structure.

8.8.3 Alternative Web3 Governance

In addition to DAO-based governance, alternative governance models like quadratic voting, liquid democracy, futarchy, and others have emerged.

- A. **Quadratic voting** in DAO-based systems introduces a quadratic relationship between the number of tokens and voting power, addressing issues of voting power centralization and promoting a more balanced distribution of influence. Unlike traditional one-token-one-vote models, quadratic voting allows participants to allocate more tokens to express their preferences intensively, enhancing the nuance in decision-making
- B. **Liquid democracy** combines direct and representative democracy, enabling participants to either vote directly on proposals or delegate their voting power to trusted individuals in a fluid and adaptable system. This dynamic approach allows participants to make informed choices, either directly participating in areas of expertise or delegating their votes to trusted experts, with the flexibility to adjust delegations as issues or circumstances change.
- C. **Futarchy** is a governance concept that combines elements of futurism and democracy. In futarchy, decision-making involves voting on broadly defined goals, while market mechanisms, such as prediction markets, are used to determine the best policies to achieve those goals based on expected outcomes.

Let us end this chapter with some case studies on Web3 governance.

8.9 Web3 Governance Case Studies

8.9.1 Curve Governance

Curve serves as a decentralized exchange facilitating stablecoin trading across various blockchain networks like Ethereum, Avalanche, Polygon, Arbitrum, Fantom, Harmony, and more.

One of the distinctive features of Curve is providing low fees and minimal slippage in transactions. Slippage refers to the disparity between the requested order price and the actual execution price during asset trading.

Curve's governance is governed by CurveDAO. The governance system employs a time-locked voting mechanism.

Participation in voting requires CRV tokens (Curve DAO tokens) to be vote-locked, resulting in the receipt of "vote-escrowed CRV" or veCRV tokens. The duration of the lock-in period directly influences the magnitude of voting power, with longer lock-in periods corresponding to greater influence. The weight of veCRV gradually diminishes as escrowed tokens approach the expiration of their lock-in period.

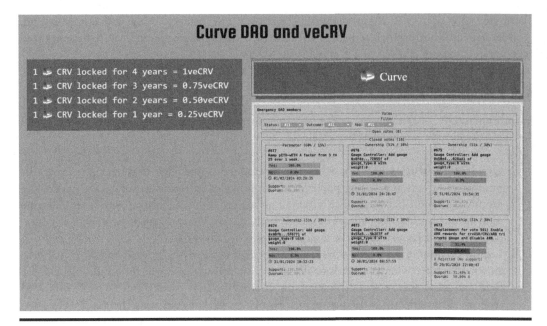

Figure 8.2   Governance on Curve using veCRV tokens.

8.9.2 Uniswap Governance

Uniswap is one of the largest decentralized exchanges, operating on the Ethereum blockchain and various layer 2 (L2) solutions such as Polygon, Optimism, and Arbitrum. The governance token for the Uniswap platform is the ERC-20 token UNI.

Participation in voting on Uniswap requires delegation. Delegating UNI entails linking the voting power of tokens to a specific address, enabling it to be used for voting purposes. This address may belong to the token owner or a trusted party chosen by the token owner, deemed capable of voting in the best interest of Uniswap Governance.

There is a minimum UNI token delegation requirement for both proposing and passing a proposal. To initiate a proposal, an address must have a minimum of one million UNI delegated to their address (reduced from 2.5 million which was reduced from ten million). For a proposal to be passed a minimum of 4% of all UNI (40 million) votes are required to support the proposal.

8.9.2.1 The Uniswap Governance Process Involves Three Steps

8.9.2.1.1 Temperature Check

This initial step gauges the willingness to alter the existing state. It requires securing 25,000 UNI yes-votes within a span of two days.

18.9.2.1.2 Consensus Check

This stage involves a formal discussion regarding a potential proposal. To progress, a minimum of 50,000 UNI yes-votes must be attained within a five day period.

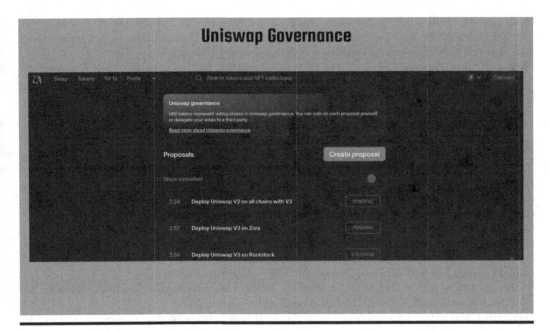

Figure 8.3   Uniswap governance.

8.9.2.1.3 Governance Proposal

The final step involves creating a proposal based on the outcome of the consensus check. The proposal can include one or multiple actions, with a maximum of ten actions per proposal. The entity initiating the proposal must code for implementing the proposal, and the code undergoes scrutiny by a professional auditor before being subjected to voting through any governance portal.

Additionally, at least one million UNI should be delegated to the address raising the proposal for it to proceed.

With this, we conclude this chapter here.

Bibliography

Aave Price Today, AAVE to USD Live Price, Marketcap and Chart. (n.d.). CoinMarketCap. Retrieved December 27, 2023, from https://coinmarketcap.com/currencies/aave/

Balancer DeFi Liquidity Protocol. Retrieved December 27, 2023, from https://balancer.fi

BanklessDAO Community. Retrieved December 27, 2023, from https://www.bankless.community

Campbell, J., Casella, A., Lara, L. D., Mooers, V. R., & Ravindran, D. (2023, November 7). *Liquid Democracy. Two Experiments on Delegation in Voting.* NBER. Retrieved December 27, 2023, from https://www.nber.org/papers/w30794

Clemence, S. (2022, December 18). *Black Travelers Say Home-Share Hosts Discriminate, and a New Airbnb Report Agrees (Published 2022).* The New York Times. Retrieved December 27, 2023, from https://www.nytimes.com/2022/12/13/travel/vacation-rentals-racism.html

COMMUNICATIONS DECENCY ACT, 47 U.S.C. §230. Retrieved December 27, 2023, from http://www.columbia.edu/~mr2651/ecommerce3/2nd/statutes/CommunicationsDecencyAct.pdf

Compound Price Today, COMP to USD Live Price, Marketcap and Chart. (n.d.). CoinMarketCap. Retrieved December 27, 2023, from https://coinmarketcap.com/currencies/compound/

Confessore, N. (2018, April 4). *Cambridge Analytica and Facebook: The Scandal and the Fallout So Far (Published 2018).* The New York Times. Retrieved December 27, 2023, from https://www.nytimes.com/2018/04/04/us/politics/cambridge-analytica-scandal-fallout.html

Curve DAO: Vote-Escrowed CRV — Curve 1.0.0 Documentation. (n.d.). Curve. Retrieved December 27, 2023, from https://curve.readthedocs.io/dao-vecrv.html

Department of Justice's Review of Section 230 of the Communications Decency Act of 1996. (n.d.). Department of Justice. Retrieved December 27, 2023, from https://www.justice.gov/archives/ag/department-justice-s-review-section-230-communications-decency-act-1996

Developer DAO. Retrieved December 27, 2023, from https://www.developerdao.com

ERC-20 Token Standard | ethereum.org. (2023, May 30). Ethereum. Retrieved December 27, 2023, from https://ethereum.org/en/developers/docs/standards/tokens/erc-20/

Flamingo DAO. Retrieved December 27, 2023, from https://flamingodao.xyz

Gauntlet. (n.d.). gauntlet.xyz. Retrieved December 27, 2023, from https://www.gauntlet.xyz/

Gitcoin Governance. Retrieved December 27, 2023, from https://gov.gitcoin.co

Governance. (n.d.). Uniswap. Retrieved December 27, 2023, from https://uniswap.org/governance

Hanson, R., Lohr, S., Leibovich, M., & Barrett, G. (n.d.). *Futarchy: Vote Values, But Bet Beliefs.* Robin Hanson. Retrieved December 27, 2023, from https://mason.gmu.edu/~rhanson/futarchy.html

Home | Uniswap Protocol. Retrieved December 27, 2023, from https://uniswap.org/

It's Time to Update Section 230. (2021, August 12). Harvard Business Review. Retrieved December 27, 2023, from https://hbr.org/2021/08/its-time-to-update-section-230

MakerDAO. MakerDAO | An Unbiased Global Financial System, https://makerdao.com/en/. Accessed 13 June 2024.

Maker Price Today, MKR to USD Live Price, Marketcap and Chart. (n.d.). CoinMarketCap. Retrieved December 27, 2023, from https://coinmarketcap.com/currencies/maker/

Meet the Board. (n.d.). Oversight Board. Retrieved December 27, 2023, from https://www.oversightboard.com/meet-the-board/

MetaCartel.org. Retrieved December 27, 2023, from https://www.metacartel.org

Nicas, J. (2021, April 30). *Apple's App Store Draws Antitrust Scrutiny in European Union (Published 2020).* The New York Times. Retrieved December 27, 2023, from https://www.nytimes.com/2020/06/16/business/apple-app-store-european-union-antitrust.html

PleasrDAO. Retrieved December 27, 2023, from https://pleasr.org

Proposals - Curve Resources. (n.d.). Curve Resources. Retrieved December 27, 2023, from https://resources.curve.fi/governance/proposals/

Quadratic Voting as Efficient Corporate Governance. (2013, October 3). Chicago Unbound. Retrieved December 27, 2023, from https://chicagounbound.uchicago.edu/cgi/viewcontent.cgi?article=1642&context=law_and_economics

Trippy Labs. Trippy Labs, https://www.trippylabs.com/. Accessed 13 June 2024.

UkraineDAO (UA, UA) (@Ukraine_DAO). (n.d.). X. Retrieved December 27, 2023, from https://twitter.com/Ukraine_DAO

Umar, A., & O'Donnell, C. (2024, January 27). *Lower Onchain Proposal Threshold.* app.uniswap.org. Retrieved February 10, 2024, from https://app.uniswap.org/vote/2/55

Uniswap Price Today, UNI to USD Live Price, Marketcap and Chart. (2020, September 16). CoinMarketCap. Retrieved December 27, 2023, from https://coinmarketcap.com/currencies/uniswap/

Uniswap. "Process |Uniswap." Uniswap Docs, https://docs.uniswap.org/concepts/governance/process .Accessed 13 June 2024.

URGENT Discussion on Current Vote: "Reduce UNI Governance Proposal & Quorum Thresholds". (2020, October 13). Uniswap Governance. Retrieved December 27, 2023, from https://gov.uniswap.org/t/urgent-discussion-on-current-vote-reduce-uni-governance-proposal-quorum-thresholds/7117

Chapter 9

Decentralization with Token or without Tokens

Sam Ghosh

If you've been keeping tabs on the cryptocurrency market, you've witnessed its significant fluctuations in recent years.

Before the 2021 crypto winter started, the cryptocurrency market cap reached approximately US $3 trillion in September 2021, with a peak daily trading volume of US $300 thousand in May 2021.

In the next few years, significant changes occurred in the cryptocurrency landscape.

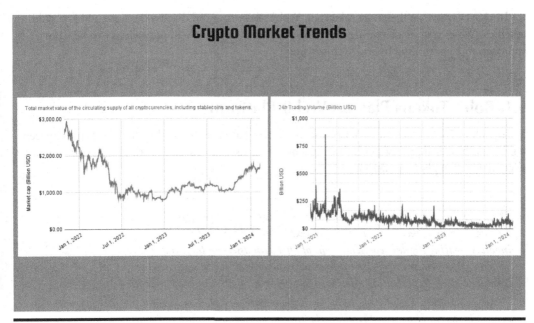

Figure 9.1   Crypto-asset market trends.

DOI: 10.4324/9781003507352-9

The Terra ecosystem breakdown in May 2022 had widespread repercussions, triggering a series of failures across the crypto landscape. The downfall of the FTX crypto exchange in November 2022 worsened the market conditions, leading to an extended period of crypto winter, with prices struggling to recover since April–May 2022.

The crypto ecosystem faced challenges beyond capital flight, as global regulatory bodies adopted a stringent stance. Initiatives like the Biden administration's Roadmap to Mitigate Cryptocurrencies' Risks and the issuance of 146 alerts on crypto-asset marketing and warning lists by the UK's Financial Conduct Authority (FCA) added pressure. Deteriorating market conditions impacted Web3 project investments, leading to a sustained decline from Q2 2022 to Q1 2024. According to Crunchbase Web3 Tracker, investment in Web3 projects has dropped from US $10.4 billion in the first quarter of 2022 to just US $1.2 billion in the last quarter of 2023. 2024 exhibited slight improvement with a $1.7 billion investment in Q1 and a $1.9 billion investment in Q2.

Despite challenges, the Alchemy Q2/2023 Web3 Development Report indicated that Web3 was gaining strength. Despite decreases in NFT and DeX trading volume and stagnant Bitcoin/Ethereum prices, EVM Smart Contract creation surged by an impressive 1,106% YoY.

Surprisingly, the subdued values of crypto assets may have been conducive to the growth of Web3. How?

Through the reduction in gas prices in dollar terms. Gas, serving as the fuel for Web3, is priced in Gwei on Ethereum, equivalent to one billionth of an Ether. The Gwei-based Gas price fluctuates on demand, while the Gas price in dollar terms is influenced by both demand and the Ether price. The Gas price determines transaction costs on programmable (EVM-compatible) blockchains.

The point is that the Web3 ecosystem continued to grow even when crypto assets weren't appealing to investors. This shows that the growth of the Web3 ecosystem is not really dependent on the high returns typically associated with crypto assets.

In this chapter, we'll explore tokens on Web3 platforms and discuss the potential for building tokenless Web3 systems. Creating Web3 platforms that operate without tokens can be a powerful approach to constructing hybrid architectures.

9.1 Roles Tokens Play on Web3 Platforms

Tokens play diverse roles on Web3 platforms, serving as currency within the platform, representing ownership in liquidity pools, and incentivizing users to interact with the platform in ways aligned with the platform design.

> *We are only evaluating the need for utility tokens here and not tokenized assets and stablecoins. Tokenization in the context of blockchain and crypto-assets involves creating digital representations of off-chain assets on blockchain networks. Tokenization can be categorized into security tokens (acting as securities) or tokenized assets (representing assets without being explicitly issued as securities).*
>
> *A stablecoin, on the other hand, is a cryptocurrency that maintains a value pegged to an external reference like the US dollar, the British pound, or the price of gold.*
>
> *A utility token refers to a type of cryptocurrency or digital token designed primarily to fulfill a specific purpose or function within a decentralized network.*

Token Roles on Web3 Networks

Use Case	Platform	Token	Utility
Token as Currency	Decentraland	MANA	Users can buy virtual assets on the platform.
Token as share in a liquidity pool	Uniswap	Uniswap V3 Positions NFT	Each NFT corresponds to a distinct liquidity position.
Governance token	Curve	veCRV	Allows token holders to participate in governance.
User Acquisition/ Engagement Tool	Axie Infinity	Smooth Love Potion (SLP)	Incentivizes engagement on the platform.
Equity for platform builders	Uniswap	UNI	Act as economic incentives for the platform builders.
Synthetic Tokens	Synthetix	sUSD	Offers "synthetic" exposure to the underlying physical or abstract assets.
Stablecoins	MakerDAO	DAI	Maintains a stable value relative to an external reference.

Figure 9.2 Different roles played by tokens on Web3 networks.

9.1.1 Token Roles

9.1.1.1 Token as Currency

9.1.1.1.1 MANA on Decentraland

Decentraland is a leading Metaverse project on the Ethereum blockchain, providing users with a virtual reality platform to create, explore, and monetize various content and applications within its virtual world.

The MANA token, an ERC-20 fungible token on the Ethereum blockchain, is central to the Decentraland economy, acting as the primary currency for transactions within the Decentraland ecosystem.

MANA tokens in Decentraland allow users to acquire NFTs such as LAND and ESTATE, representing ownership of virtual real-estate. Additionally, MANA is used for transactions within the Decentraland marketplace for items such as avatars, virtual wearables, names, etc.

9.1.1.2 Token as Share in a Liquidity Pool

9.1.1.2.1 cTokens in Compound DeFi Lending platform

Liquidity pools are an integral part of decentralized finance (DeFi) protocols, facilitating automated market making. A market maker is an intermediary that provides liquidity (assets available for trading) to the market by holding assets and continuously offering buy and sell quotes. As DeFi platforms lack such intermediaries, market-making must be automated, known as automated market-making.

To function effectively, automated market makers require consistent and reliable liquidity sources, which is where liquidity pools come in. Liquidity providers are incentivized to supply liquidity (cryptoassets in this case), receiving rewards such as interest, a share of trading fees, or governance tokens. DeFi platforms issue liquidity pool tokens to liquidity providers to track their share in the liquidity pools and calculate repayment when they wish to withdraw their contributions.

Compound, a decentralized finance (DeFi) lending platform, issues cTokens (CErc20 for ERC-20 tokens and CEther for Ether deposits) to users who supply cryptocurrency assets as collateral to the Compound protocol.

cTokens represent a user's stake in Compound's lending pool and appreciate over time due to interest accrual. Despite a fixed number of cTokens in a user's wallet, their value grows steadily as each cToken becomes convertible into an increasing amount of the underlying asset.

cTokens can be used for multiple purposes – they can act as collateral for borrowing from the Compound protocol, can be burned to retrieve the asset they represent in the liquidity pool, and can be transferred to other accounts like any other ERC-20 token.

Similar concepts exist in other DeFi platforms, such as aTokens in AAVE and LP tokens in Pancakeswap.

9.1.1.2.2 Uniswap V3 NFTs

Uniswap v3 introduces a unique approach by using non-fungible tokens (NFTs) to represent shares in liquidity pools, known as Uniswap Position NFTs. Unlike its predecessors, V1 and V2, which used fungible ERC-20 tokens for liquidity positions, V3 adopted Positions NFTs (ERC-721 tokens). Each NFT corresponds to a distinct position and includes a piece of on-chain generative art. Notably, these positions NFTs are tradable on NFT platforms like OpenSea.

9.1.1.3 Governance Token

We have already discussed governance tokens in the "Decentralization in Web3" chapter, delving into examples such as veCRV (vote-escrowed CRV) and UNI of Uniswap. These governance tokens play an important role on Web3 platforms, empowering token holders to initiate governance proposals and participate in the voting process.

9.1.1.4 User Acquisition/Engagement Tool

9.1.1.4.1 SLP token on Axie Infinity

Axie Infinity is a well-known play-to-earn Game developed by Vietnamese studio Sky Mavis. Axie Infinity employs two ERC-20 utility tokens, Smooth Love Potion (SLP) and Axie Infinity Shard (AXS).

Users need SLP tokens to breed new Axies. Axies are the central character of the gaming ecosystem and are represented by NFTs. Owning more Axies helps earn more rewards.

AXS tokens in Axie Infinity serve multiple purposes – acting as the governance token, enabling transactions in the Axie NFT marketplace, and playing a crucial role in the breeding process to get more Axies. Furthermore, players can stake AXS tokens on the platform to earn yields.

Due to the higher utility of AXS tokens compared to SLP tokens, players aim to accumulate more AXS tokens. However, obtaining AXS tokens necessitates acquiring more SLP.

While players can initiate gameplay by purchasing the least expensive Axies, success in player vs player (PvP) gameplays requires powerful Axies. Winning PvP gameplays is required to get AXS rewards.

This mechanism drives demand for tokens, promoting play-to-earn incentives and attracting new players to the network.

9.1.1.5 Equity for Platform Builders

In Web3 platforms, tokens often have multiple roles – can play transactional roles and can also carry voting rights at the same time.

These tokens are frequently traded in public markets, experiencing price increases as the issuing platforms gain popularity through effective tokenomics, marketing strategies, or speculative forces. An example of such a token is UNI from Uniswap.

The platform builders and contributors often primarily receive these tokens as their compensation. As these tokens carry voting rights, the influence of the platform builders on the platform governance directly correlates with the tokens they hold. With tokens holding market value, the platform builders have an economic incentive to push token prices high similar to that of startup founders holding unlisted stocks or stock options.

9.1.1.6 Synthetic Tokens

Synthetic tokens enable us to have "synthetic" exposure to the physical or abstract goods that they represent without requiring one-to-one backing. For example, a synthetic gold token representing one ounce of gold would be tradable for the price of one ounce of physical gold. Synthetic tokens can be issued either by a centralized entity, like a bank whose credit "backs" the token, or a decentralized network whose incentives ensure that the synthetic token is always redeemable for the asset's price.

An example is the Synthetix protocol, which captures price movements of various crypto-assets, fiat-assets, and commodities with zero slippage, without actual ownership of the asset. This is achieved through the creation of Synth synthetic tokens. Synths are denoted in an sAsset format, such as sUSD, sLINK, and sBTC, tracking the prices of USD, LINK tokens, and Bitcoin, respectively.

9.1.1.7 Stablecoins

9.1.1.7.1 DAI from Maker

A stablecoin is a cryptocurrency designed to maintain a stable value relative to an external reference, using different mechanisms for price stability.

DAI is a stablecoin pegged to the US dollar, aiming to maintain a value of US \$1. Users can mint DAI by depositing collateral into decentralized smart contracts (Maker Vaults) within the Maker Protocol.

DAI stablecoins are issued as loans and are backed by the provided collateral. Borrowers can retrieve their collateral by repaying the borrowed DAI along with a fee referred to as a stability fee. This stability fee must be paid exclusively in DAI and is calculated as an annual yield.

9.2 Problems with Using Tokens on Web3 Platforms

Okay, tokens contribute value to Web3 systems in various ways, but it's important to acknowledge that they also introduce certain limitations to Web3 platforms.

9.2.1 Price Volatility

Crypto tokens face a significant challenge due to their inherent price volatility. Listing tokens on crypto exchanges, essential for using them as economic incentives, also exposes them to speculative forces and pump-and-dump schemes. Malicious actors can artificially inflate token prices, and then sell their holdings, causing substantial losses for other token holders.

For platform builders, the situation remains favorable as long as token prices increase, enhancing user incentives and simplifying user acquisition. However, complications arise when speculators engage in mass token dumping. A sudden crash in token prices diminishes user incentives to join or continue using the Web3 platform. At the same time, platform developers may lose motivation to maintain the platform as the value of their token holdings declines.

In the worst case, these situations can lead to a bank run, with users hastily withdrawing their crypto assets, potentially leading to the failure of the entire Web3 platform. DeFi platforms are particularly susceptible to such crises, but any Web3 platform issuing tokens could face similar challenges.

9.2.2 Regulatory Challenges

As previously discussed, governments globally are preparing to regulate crypto-assets. When Web3 platforms issue tokens, they expose themselves to regulatory uncertainties surrounding crypto-assets.

Web3 introduces a fundamental transformation for numerous industries, and regulations crafted for traditional systems frequently conflict with the principles of Web3. Tokens commonly become a focal point of contention in this context.

9.2.3 Token Frauds

Token frauds do not help with the regulatory skepticism surrounding crypto-assets.

The inherent anonymity of Web3 may facilitate different types of token fraud. A major example of token fraud is a rug-pull, where anonymous platform developers introduce new projects, and attract funds from prospective users with promises of significant returns, only to abandon the project on the launch date and abscond with the collected funds.

Other forms of token fraud include Ponzi schemes, and pump-and-dump schemes among others.

9.2.4 Financial Security Regulations

Web3 platforms often face regulatory uncertainty about whether or not tokens should be considered financial securities, such as equity or any other type of security. The Howey Test evaluates whether a contract constitutes an investment contract based on criteria like the investment of money and the expectation of profits from the efforts of others. Depending on the token's design, many tokens could be considered investments in financial securities, subjecting them to various capital market regulations in various jurisdictions.

Capital market regulations impose constraints on the manner, timing, and sources of capital raised. They frequently intersect with Anti-money Laundering (AML) laws, requiring investor identification and verification. The anonymity in blockchain transactions presents a challenge for AML compliance, causing a fundamental conflict between crypto-assets and existing regulatory structures.

Another pertinent issue revolves around the timing of fundraising activities. Traditional capital market regulations typically demand that issuer entities demonstrate financial stability before engaging in a "public placement," i.e., raising funds from the general public. If crypto tokens are classified as financial securities, adherence to due process and stability requirements becomes crucial before issuing them to the broader public on web3 platforms.

9.2.5 Technical Difficulties

Understanding the characteristics of tokens on Web3 platforms can be challenging, given their multifaceted roles in platform access, governance, investments, and many other possible roles.

Understanding how to effectively use tokens often requires a combination of technical and economic knowledge, presenting a potential challenge for many users.

9.3 Can Web3 Technology Evolve beyond Reliance on Tokens?

We discussed the distinction between coins and tokens in the "Primer on Web3" chapter. Now, we are going to solely focus on crypto-tokens here and not on coins.

Why?

Engaging with a blockchain necessitates the use of the crypto coin of that blockchain. Every blockchain transaction involves a transaction fee paid in the native coin. For EVM-compatible blockchains, this fee is called the gas fee, as previously discussed. While Ethereum's Account Abstraction may allow gas fees to be paid with crypto assets other than ETH, the service provider handling account abstraction must still deal with ETH.

Please note that we discussed Account Abstraction in the "Primer on Web3" chapter.

So, dealing with the native crypto coin of a blockchain, in which a Web3 platform is built, is not optional. On the other hand, dealing with crypto tokens remains an option.

9.3.1 Web3 without Tokens

Will building Web3 platforms without tokens pose a challenge in maintaining the core characteristics that define Web3 systems?

■ Web3 platforms embody **openness** and **permissionlessness**, allowing anyone to join without seeking approval or creating accounts with the platform (in theory).

- **Trustlessness** is a core tenet of Web3, where platforms operate on economic incentives, minimizing reliance on trusted third parties.
- **Automation** is also a basic characteristic of Web3 and it is achieved through smart contracts which are automated programs on blockchains that operate seamlessly without human intervention.
- The **immutability** of Web3 platforms mirrors the immutability of blockchains, ensuring historical records remain unchanged.
- **Decentralization**, a key attribute of Web3, implies that platforms are not controlled by any centralized authority, making censorship challenging.

We will discuss this later but before that let us now discuss ways to achieve the functionalities provided by tokens on Web3 platforms without the use of tokens.

9.3.1.1 Platform Currency

As previously mentioned, Web3 platforms often utilize tokens for transactions within the platform. However, these tokens can be replaced with the native coin of the underlying blockchain, such as ETH for platforms on Ethereum, MATIC for platforms on Polygon, and SOL for platforms on Solana.

This strategy helps mitigate the impact of speculative forces on the platform, as the native coins have a larger capital base, making it more challenging to manipulate their prices. Additionally, using native crypto-assets can reduce the risk of various token-related frauds.

This approach also enhances user accessibility, as individuals can transact using widely available native assets like ETH, MATIC, or SOL on the Web3 platform, eliminating the need to acquire specific tokens, which may have limited availability based on exchange listings.

9.3.1.2 User Acquisition and Retention

As previously mentioned, tokens are commonly employed for user acquisition and incentivizing user behavior on Web3 platforms.

While utilizing the blockchain native asset is an alternative for achieving similar objectives, there are methods to attract and engage users without relying on such incentives.

Firstly, creating platforms that genuinely fulfill users' needs and desires. For instance, while play-to-earn gaming is gaining popularity, traditional pay-to-play games still have a presence. Although more challenging, designing products that resonate with users can be highly effective.

Moreover, user engagement can be maintained through access-based incentives, such as unlocking additional levels as users interact more with the platform (particularly relevant for gaming applications) or reducing transaction fees as users increasingly engage with the platform.

Implementing a reputation system based on factors like past contributions and behavior is another approach to engaging users without the use of tokens.

9.3.1.3 Governance

Is it mandatory to employ tokens for voting?

Certainly not! Token-less governance is not just a concept but a reality.

Take the example of DAOStack's Reputation-based governance.

In the DAOstack ecosystem, Reputation is a key concept representing a member's standing within the DAO. Unlike a token, Reputation lacks a financial value and is not a tradable asset. Instead, it is earned through a member's contributions, endorsements from peers, and the member's overall activity within the DAO. A member's influence and voting power within the DAO directly correlates with her Reputation. The greater a member's Reputation, the more substantial her vote becomes in the decision-making process.

Members have the ability to propose initiatives, and throughout the voting period, fellow members express their preferences by casting votes proportionate to their Reputation. The ultimate decision is determined by the aggregated Reputation-based votes.

A notable feature of this system is that, unlike governance tokens, Reputation cannot be transferred. This characteristic serves as a safeguard against various issues such as vote buying and bribery that can plague governance systems.

Furthermore, a Reputation-based model promotes continued engagement with Web3 platforms, preventing users from acquiring tokens solely for voting and quickly selling them after influencing a specific proposal. Leveraging Reputation-based voting mechanisms enables Web3 platforms to align users more effectively with the platform's long-term objectives.

In addition to Reputation-based governance, there are various other token-less governance systems.

One such system is quadratic voting, which is not exclusive to Web3 but is a broader voting mechanism. The fundamental concept behind quadratic voting is to emphasize the degree of preference, not just the preference itself.

A typical quadratic voting system operates as follows: Each participant receives a fixed number of voting credits or votes to distribute across various options in a given decision-making scenario. Participants can allocate their votes in a non-linear manner. Specifically, quadratic voting enables voters to allocate votes quadratically, meaning that the cost increases quadratically for each additional vote assigned to an option. For example, casting one vote may cost one credit, while casting two votes might cost four credits, three votes might cost nine credits, and so forth.

Quadratic voting can be implemented without tokens, perhaps in conjunction with a Reputation system. Users accrue Reputation points through increased engagement with the platform and spend them by proposing and voting on relevant proposals. The associated cost of voting in terms of Reputation points can act as a deterrent against governance manipulations.

There are also other tokenless governance processes like Sortition, where the system randomly selects individuals from a community to participate in decision-making. This approach does not necessitate token ownership and ensures broad participation and diversity of perspectives.

Participatory budgeting offers an alternative for token-less governance, particularly in the context of budget allocation. Communities or organizations can collectively decide on resource allocation without the reliance on tokens.

The key takeaway is that platform developers have the flexibility to design diverse strategies for tokenless governance.

9.3.1.4 Equity for Platform Builders and Fundraising

Now, consider two interconnected functions that tokens typically serve on Web3 platforms – fundraising and functioning as equity for platform builders. How can we fulfill these two requirements without the use of tokens?

Let us start with equity for platform builders. One alternative to issuing tokens to platform builders is issuing performance-based payments in the form of annuities. Web3 platforms primarily generate revenue from transaction fees and sales of virtual assets. A system can be designed to track the contributions of the platform developers and investors to the development of the platform. This process will not define how much the platform builders will receive but rather the percentage share in future net profits. Say, it is defined that "x"% of future profits for "y" years will be used to pay back the platform developers and investors. Platform builders and investors can decide their slice in the future profit pool through governance voting. As previously suggested, Web3 platforms can utilize the native asset of the blockchain they are built on, the transaction fee is collected in that same blockchain native asset and the vesting of the profit share also happens in that blockchain native asset.

Now, coming to fundraising. Instead of tokens, platforms can issue bond-like instruments, making coupon payments to fund providers from the collected transaction fees. This approach ensures a prolonged commitment from both platform developers and fund providers.

Implementing token-less fundraising helps safeguard the platform from pump-and-dump scams and provides a level of protection for fund providers against rug-pulls. However, it's important to note that regulatory challenges may still arise, depending on jurisdiction.

Another issue with the proposed system is that while sharing profits may be easier, transfer of control may be more difficult without tokens.

To address this, segregating claims to future profits from claims to voting rights may offer some protection against regulatory scrutiny depending on jurisdiction.

Now, through the previously outlined mechanisms, we seek to sidestep regulatory scrutiny.

Alternatively, a more proactive approach involves embracing regulations rather than avoiding them. A Web3 platform can opt to issue security tokens – resembling stock options but in the form of tokenized assets – to developers and fund providers, adhering to capital market regulations. Several jurisdictions permit the issuance of security tokens and have defined streamlined processes to do that. The acceptance of security tokens within regulatory frameworks is not a recent development in the US. Notably, in 2020, North Capital obtained regulatory approval to launch an alternative trading system for security tokens.

However, this means that the platforms need to follow the capital market regulations and will lose any regulatory arbitrage.

9.3.1.5 Tracking Share in Liquidity Pools

Is it possible to generate liquidity without relying on LP tokens? Before delving into that topic, it's crucial to acknowledge that LP tokens, or liquidity provider tokens, backed by liquidity positions, may not share all the challenges associated with other utility tokens.

LP tokens represent proportional ownership in a liquidity pool, exhibiting greater stability relative to the price movements of underlying assets. Linked directly to providing liquidity in specific trading pairs, LP tokens help facilitate trades and mitigate the typical pump-and-dump schemes witnessed with individual tokens. Their value aligns more evenly with fluctuations in the underlying assets, contributing to a more balanced representation.

Unlike utility tokens, LP tokens involved in liquidity provision generally present fewer regulatory challenges. They operate within the decentralized exchange and liquidity pool framework, focusing on providing a service (liquidity) rather than functioning as speculative assets or investment vehicles.

LP tokens may offer exposure to a portfolio of assets in a liquidity pool. This diversified exposure can provide a form of risk management and hedging against specific asset price volatility, offering a balanced approach to market movements.

However, LP tokens come with their own set of risks, such as impermanent loss. Liquidity providers may experience impermanent loss due to shifting prices of assets in the pool, in contrast to simply holding the assets. This risk is inherent in providing liquidity in automated market makers (AMMs) on DeFi platforms.

Now, am I suggesting that liquidity mining is not possible without tokens?

No, I am not.

Liquidity mining can be made possible without using tokens through a reward-based system, rather than a token-based system.

Similar to the reputation system discussed earlier, the platform can establish an internal credit or point system. Credits are earned by providing liquidity and can be redeemed for shares in future profits, Reputation points, reduced fees, access to premium features, and more.

9.3.2 Can Web3 Platforms Retain their Qualities without Tokens?

9.3.2.1 Open and Permissionless Systems

Is it possible to establish open and permissionless Web3 systems without tokens? Yes, it can be accomplished through the implementation of identity-based access. By integrating decentralized identity systems or utilizing social verification for access, tokenless systems can achieve openness and permissionlessness.

9.3.2.2 Trustless Systems

Before addressing this, it's essential to note that trustlessness and censorship resistance may not always be desirable qualities. As mentioned earlier, censorship resistance in a Web3 platform may attract illegal activities and regulatory attention. However, incorporating decentralized identity can help preserve trustless qualities for the Web3 platform even in the absence of tokens.

9.3.2.3 Automated Systems

Web3 platforms attain automation through the utilization of smart contracts, where the existence of tokens becomes irrelevant.

9.3.2.4 Immutability

Immutability is an inherent quality of blockchains, and the presence or absence of tokens does not impact this characteristic.

9.3.2.5 Decentralized Systems

Decentralization can be categorized into two types:

- **Technical decentralization**, achieved through the existence of multiple nodes, ensures the availability of the Web3 platform even if one or more nodes go offline. This is an inherent quality of blockchains and is not contingent on the use of tokens.
- **Governance decentralization**, typically facilitated by governance tokens, can be replicated using the token-less governance mechanisms discussed earlier in this book.

The above discussion doesn't suggest an immediate halt to token use on Web3 platforms. Instead, it encourages considering the concept of a token-less Web3. It underscores the importance of critically evaluating the core of Web3, asking whether its primary purpose is issuing tokens for quick financial gains or employing smart contracts to integrate qualities like immutability and decentralization into existing technological frameworks.

Token-less Web3 represents a crucial step towards establishing hybrid architectures.

These architectures would facilitate the integration of immutability, decentralization, and other Web3 attributes into traditional technological systems without necessitating engagement with the economic, regulatory, and technical challenges associated with crypto assets.

Bibliography

Axie Infinity. (n.d.). Axie Infinity - Battle, Collect, and Trade Collectible NFT Creatures. Retrieved December 27, 2023, from https://axieinfinity.com/

AAVE. AToken | v3 |Developers, https://docs.aave.com/developers/tokens/atoken.Accessed 13 June 2024.

CoinMarketCap."Decentraland price today, MANA to USD live price, marketcap and chart."CoinMarketCap, https://coinmarketcap.com/currencies/decentraland/. Accessed 13 June 2024.

CoinmarketCap. "sUSD price today, SUSD to USD live price, marketcap and chart." CoinMarketCap,https://coinmarketcap.com/currencies/susd/. Accessed 13 June 2024.

CoinmarketCap. "Dai price today, DAI to USD live price, marketcap and chart." CoinMarketCap, https://coinmarketcap.com/currencies/multi-collateral-dai/. Accessed 13 June 2024.

Compound Finance. (n.d.). Compound Finance. Retrieved December 27, 2023, from https://compound.finance/

Compound. "Compound v2 Docs | cTokens." Compound Finance, https://docs.compound.finance/v2/cto-kens/.Accessed 13 June 2024.

Curve DAO: Vote-Escrowed CRV — Curve 1.0.0 documentation. (n.d.). Curve. Retrieved December 27, 2023, from https://curve.readthedocs.io/dao-vecrv.html

DAOstack. (n.d.). Reputation - DAOstack Arc Docs. Retrieved December 27, 2023, from https://daostack.github.io/arc/contracts/controller/Reputation/

DAOstack End-of-road Update, and the Common Open Development Program Announcement | Built with Notion. (n.d.). Notion. Retrieved December 27, 2023, from https://daostack.io/

Decentraland. (n.d.). Welcome to Decentraland. Retrieved December 27, 2023, from https://decentraland .org/

Decentraland."Marketplace." Decentraland, https://decentraland.org/marketplace/lands.Accessed 13 June 2024.

Deese, B., Prabhakar, A., Rouse, C., & Sullivan, J. (2023, January 27). *The Administration's Roadmap to Mitigate Cryptocurrencies' Risks | NEC.* The White House. Retrieved December 27, 2023, from https://www.whitehouse.gov/nec/briefing-room/2023/01/27/the-administrations-roadmap-to-miti-gate-cryptocurrencies-risks/

ERC-4337: Account Abstraction Using Alt Mempool. (2021, September 29). Ethereum Improvement Proposals. Retrieved December 27, 2023, from https://eips.ethereum.org/EIPS/eip-4337

FCA Issues 146 Alerts in First 24 Hours of New Crypto Marketing Regime | FCA. (2023, October 9). Financial Conduct Authority. Retrieved December 27, 2023, from https://www.fca.org.uk/news/statements/fca -issues-146-alerts-first-24-hours-new-crypto-marketing-regime

Framework for "Investment Contract" Analysis of Digital Assets1. (n.d.). SEC.gov. Retrieved December 27, 2023, from https://www.sec.gov/files/dlt-framework.pdf

Global Live Cryptocurrency Charts & Market Data. (n.d.). CoinMarketCap. Retrieved December 27, 2023, from https://coinmarketcap.com/charts/

Interconnected DeFi: Ripple Effects from the Terra Collapse. (2023, June 29). Board of Governors of the Federal Reserve System. Retrieved December 27, 2023, from https://www.federalreserve.gov/econres /feds/files/2023044pap.pdf

Introducing Uniswap v3. (2021, March 22). Uniswap Blog. Retrieved December 27, 2023, from https://blog .uniswap.org/uniswap-v3

Learn About PB. (n.d.). Participatory Budgeting Project. Retrieved December 27, 2023, from https://www .participatorybudgeting.org/about-pb/

MakerDAO. (n.d.). MakerDAO | An Unbiased Global Financial System. Retrieved December 27, 2023, from https://makerdao.com/en/

Nelson, D. (2020, April 27). *US Regulator Clears Security Token Trading System to Launch.* CoinDesk. Retrieved December 27, 2023, from https://www.coindesk.com/markets/2020/04/27/us-regulator -clears-security-token-trading-system-to-launch/

OpenSea. (n.d.). OpenSea, the Largest NFT Marketplace. Retrieved December 27, 2023, from https:// opensea.io/

PancakeSwap. Pancake LPs (Cake-LP),https://pancakeswap.finance/info/token/0x36a0c612f986a0b15e66 5f574d971bad71998977.Accessed 13 June 2024.

Q2 2023 - Web3 Development Report. (n.d.). Cloudinary. Retrieved December 27, 2023, from https://res .cloudinary.com/alchemyapi/image/upload/v1691086454/web3-developer-report-q2-23-updated.pdf

Quadratic Voting as Efficient Corporate Governance. (n.d.). The University of Chicago Law Review. Retrieved December 27, 2023, from https://lawreview.uchicago.edu/print-archive/quadratic-voting-efficient -corporate-governance

sDao: Sorition-based DAO. (n.d.). ETHGlobal. Retrieved December 27, 2023, from https://ethglobal.com/ showcase/sdao-sorition-based-dao-gjcbr

Synthetix. (n.d.). Synthetix.io. Retrieved December 27, 2023, from https://synthetix,io/

Uniswap. (n.d.). Home | Uniswap Protocol. Retrieved December 27, 2023, from https://uniswap.org/

Web3 Tracker: News On Startups and Investors. (n.d.). Crunchbase News. Retrieved June 13, 2024, from https://news.crunchbase.com/web3-startups-investors/

Chapter 10

Web3 Architectures

Sam Ghosh

In this chapter, we will cover a high-level overview of the architectures of Web3 systems.

While it is often thought that Web3 systems are completely based on blockchain (or other DLTs), it is rarely so.

As discussed in the "Decentralized Storage" chapter, blockchains come with inherent limitations. Insufficient storage capacity, high latency, and higher costs are among the challenges that can impede the scalability and practicality of deploying a comprehensive system solely on-chain (i.e. on a blockchain). While the blockchain excels in enabling trustlessness and immutability, these limitations necessitate a more thoughtful and hybrid approach.

Pure on-chain Web3 systems can be viable but only for limited use cases. For example, a decentralized voting system that requires absolute transparency, immutability, and censorship resistance might opt for a pure on-chain implementation. In this scenario, the data volume is relatively low, and the immutability of blockchain is crucial.

Before we discuss elements of Web3 architecture, let us look at how Web3 systems are different from Web2 systems at a high level.

10.1 From Platform Thinking to Network Thinking

Web 2.0, characterized as the participatory web, facilitates user interaction through social and other kinds of digital networks, giving rise to user-generated content and the emergence of digital platforms.

Digital platforms are online ecosystems that utilize digital technologies to connect users, businesses, and developers. They provide frameworks for exchanging information, services, and products, streamlining interactions, and serving as foundations for various online activities.

In the last two decades, large digital platforms have emerged in various industries such as retail (e-commerce), education (ed-tech), food services (food delivery), and transportation (ride-hailing platforms).

DOI: 10.4324/9781003507352-10

Digital platforms are the epitome of centralization. With the help of network effects and various economic incentives, these platforms acquire a huge number of users fairly rapidly and then standardize processes and economics for the whole industry. Over time, these platforms started to integrate seemingly different industries. Say, ride-hailing platforms started to deliver food, and fintech platforms started hosting e-commerce services.

But, centralization did not only occur at a business level but also led to technological centralization. These platforms evolved into complex systems leveraging a barrage of different technologies, built around large databases.

Web3 systems differ not only in user experience but also in their fundamental architecture. Unlike Web 2.0 platforms with distinct technology layers, Web3 adopts a network-centric approach. It consists of diverse components, blending decentralized and centralized elements to form a dynamic and interconnected ecosystem.

Web3 system architecture extends beyond blockchain and distributed ledger technologies (DLTs). While blockchain (or other DLT) stays at the center, Web3 architecture includes various other components including decentralized storage, decentralized identity, and various peer-to-peer protocols. This networked approach enhances resilience, transparency, and collaboration among diverse technical components. Contrasting to the rigid layering of Web 2.0 architectures, Web3's emphasis on a networked model enables interoperability and adaptability.

In simple words, building Web3 systems requires embracing network thinking, a departure from the platform-centric approach of Web2.

10.1.1 What Is Network Thinking?

"Network thinking" is a conceptual approach that emphasizes the comprehension and analysis of systems, structures, or phenomena as interconnected networks rather than isolated entities. It represents a philosophy that acknowledges the significance of relationships, interactions, and dependencies among various components within a system.

Network thinking is not limited to technology, and its applicability extends to various fields, including social sciences and business.

Now, let's explore some key characteristics of network thinking.

10.1.2 Key Aspects of Network Thinking

10.1.2.1 Interconnected Systems

Network thinking views systems as interconnected networks rather than isolated entities, recognizing that the actions of one element can influence and be influenced by others within the network. For example, in a social network, individuals represent nodes, and their relationships or interactions form edges. Comprehending this network structure is crucial for deciphering information flow, influence, and community formation dynamics.

Applying this concept to Web3 networks reveals a complex structure. Blockchain ecosystems, central to Web3, are seen as networks where each node signifies a participant in decentralized transactions. However, Web3 systems are more than just technically uniform blockchain nodes. Other crucial components like oracles and decentralized identity systems are also vital to Web3 networks. In the Web3 interconnected framework, the collaboration of various systems enhances the network's overall robustness and adaptability, aligning with the principles of network thinking.

10.1.2.2 Emergent Properties

Network thinking acknowledges that the collective behavior of a network can result in emergent properties not apparent when examining individual components. Emergent properties are characteristics or behaviors that manifest in the system as a whole, arising from interactions between components. They are not predetermined by individual elements but emerge from the collective interactions within the system.

For example, in a social media network, trends or patterns emerge from cumulative user interactions, offering valuable insights. In Web3, network thinking applies to blockchain networks, leading to emergent properties like decentralized governance using decentralized autonomous organizations (DAOs) and community-driven decision-making, etc.

10.1.2.3 Resilience and Redundancy

Network thinking emphasizes the importance of building resilient systems by incorporating redundancy and interconnectedness. This strategy enables systems to adapt to disruptions or failures in individual components.

Consider the design of internet infrastructure, which incorporates redundancy to enable data to pass through multiple paths. In the event of a route failure, the network can dynamically adapt, ensuring continuous functionality.

In Web3 networks, resilience is achieved through redundancy, mitigating the risk of a single point of failure. This is exemplified by the presence of multiple nodes dedicated to validating transactions, ensuring redundancy in the overall network structure.

10.1.2.4 Holistic Understanding

Network thinking calls for a holistic understanding of systems by considering the relationships and dependencies among components.

For example, in a supply chain network, recognizing dependencies between suppliers, manufacturers, and distributors is essential for optimizing logistics and improving efficiency.

In the context of Web3 systems, understanding the complex dynamics of the entire Web3 ecosystem involves analyzing the dynamic interactions among various elements like blockchains, identity systems, decentralized storage, and data oracles, etc.

10.1.2.5 Feedback Loops

Network thinking recognizes the presence of feedback loops, where system outcomes influence future behavior, potentially leading to self-reinforcing or self-regulating dynamics.

Consider the example of an economic network, where consumer purchasing decisions can shape production levels, subsequently impacting employment and income. The interplay of consumer purchasing decisions and production levels creates feedback loops that resonate throughout the entire economy.

In Web3 networks, feedback loops occur as user interactions and changes in the network's state influence subsequent actions, contributing to self-regulation or evolving network dynamics. For instance, in a decentralized identity system, users providing attestations for others create a feedback loop, enhancing individuals' reputation and trustworthiness within the network.

10.1.2.6 Decentralized Decision-making

Network thinking supports decentralized decision-making by distributing decision authority across interconnected entities, promoting adaptability and responsiveness.

Web3 networks embrace decentralized decision-making through consensus mechanisms, enabling nodes to collectively determine the state of the blockchain without the need for centralized control.

10.1.2.7 Networked Innovation

Network thinking fosters innovation by encouraging collaborative problem-solving and knowledge-sharing within interconnected networks.

For example, in an open-source software development, which operates on a networked approach, contributors from around the globe collaborate to improve and innovate software projects.

In Web3 networks, the principles of network thinking drive innovation through collaborative development and contributions from a global community. Open-source blockchain projects like Ethereum illustrate networked innovation, with developers worldwide actively contributing to improve and expand the platform.

10.1.2.8 Dynamic Adaptation

Networks inherently have a dynamic and ever-evolving nature, and embracing network thinking involves adapting to system changes by understanding the dynamic interplay of relationships and interactions.

Decentralized finance protocols, for example, showcase adaptability by dynamically responding to changes in market conditions, adjusting interest rates and liquidity pools based on real-time data, and demonstrating a responsive and dynamic approach.

Okay, from the above discussion, it is evident that the quality of a Web3 system is not solely determined by the blockchain or decentralized ledger used. Instead, it results from the collective integration of various components, including storage, identity systems, oracles, and more. The effectiveness and resilience of a Web3 system are shaped by the collaborative and interconnected nature of these diverse elements.

10.2 Elements of Web3 Architecture

So, what are the basic elements of Web3 architecture?

10.2.1 Distributed Ledger (DLT)

Blockchain and other DLTs form the core of Web3 architecture by maintaining a decentralized and tamper-resistant record of transactions and data. This ensures transparency and trust among network participants.

10.2.2 On-chain Smart Contracts

On-chain smart contracts serve as the backbone of Web3 systems, providing the decentralized execution of programmable logic. These contracts enforce rules, enable trustless transactions, and ensure the integrity of the system.

In a decentralized finance (DeFi) application, for example, on-chain smart contracts facilitate trustless lending and borrowing. These contracts automate financial processes without the need for intermediaries, showcasing the power of on-chain execution.

We already discussed smart contracts in the chapter "Primer on Web3 and Distributed Systems."

By the way, "on-chain" is something that is on a blockchain, and "off-chain" means something that is not part of a blockchain.

10.2.3 Off-chain Decentralized Storage

Off-chain decentralized storage solutions, such as the InterPlanetary File System (IPFS), are integral to handling the limitations of on-chain storage. Storing large volumes of data or content on the blockchain itself can be impractical, making decentralized storage solutions an essential off-chain component.

Imagine a decentralized content-sharing platform. Storing large media files directly on the blockchain would be impractical (or impossible) due to blockchain storage limitations and cost. Instead, Web3 systems often leverage off-chain decentralized storage solutions like IPFS. This ensures efficient storage and retrieval of content without compromising decentralization.

We already have a whole chapter on decentralized storage.

10.2.4 Off-chain Centralized Storage

Including off-chain centralized storage recognizes the practical necessity for efficiency and cost-effectiveness in Web3 architectures. While decentralized storage is vital for data immutability and decentralization, off-chain centralized storage complements the architecture by offering scalable and accessible storage solutions.

For example, while designing a decentralized social media platform, off-chain centralized storage can play a vital role. User-generated content, such as profile pictures or smaller media files, can be stored in centralized servers, providing a balance between accessibility, scalability, and cost-effectiveness.

10.2.5 Third-party Elements

Third-party elements like oracles, scaling systems, privacy protocols, cross-chain bridges, and identity systems enhance the versatility and functionality of Web3 systems.

Now, the architecture of Web3 systems has transformed over time. Let us take the example of an architecture of Web3 gaming applications.

Earlier game applications such as Huntercoin and Crypto Kitties tried to store most of the game logic on a public blockchain. This makes the game truly decentralized. However, the blockchain throughput limitations and high cost of transactions limit the use of this approach to only simple games such as card games.

Advanced games require a more hybrid approach in which only transaction data is stored on a blockchain, game assets are stored on other kinds of decentralized databases such as IPFS, and the game logic is stored centrally by the game developers.

10.3 Third-party Elements in Web3 Systems

Third-party elements play a significant role in Web3 architecture and require some detailed discussion.

10.3.1 Scaling Solutions

Let us start with scaling solutions.

10.3.1.1 Why Talk about Scalability?

The scaling problem is arguably the most significant technical challenge limiting the widespread adoption of Web3.

Imagine a payment app built on the Ethereum blockchain achieving mass adoption, promising users to make in-store payments seamlessly. What user experience can we expect while using this app?

The Ethereum mainnet currently offers a throughput of about 15 transactions per second (TPS). Even on a peak day like December 9, 2022, with 1,932,711 daily transactions, the average TPS was approximately 22. Transactions per second (TPS) is a critical metric that measures a blockchain network's ability to process transactions within a second, indicating its scalability and efficiency.

Now, there are around 150,000 transactions consistently pending on the Ethereum network.

So, Ethereum has a throughput problem.

While blocks are generated every 15 seconds, transaction confirmations can take minutes, depending on the blockchain's demand. In high-demand situations, users may encounter delays in transaction confirmations.

Now, imagine using the payment app for grocery purchases in a crowded superstore with a long queue behind you. Waiting for minutes for payment confirmation could significantly impact the user experience.

Transaction confirmation time is not the only concern. The network fee (Gas fee in Ethereum) also rises with increased demand for transaction processing. Crucially, the network fee is not

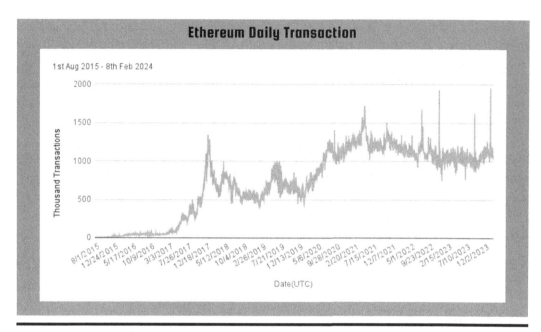

Figure 10.1   Ethereum daily transaction volume (in thousands).

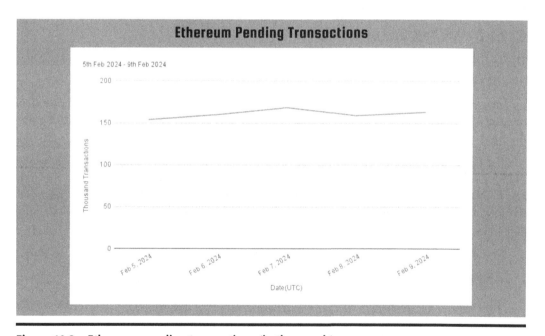

Figure 10.2   Ethereum pending transactions (in thousands).

determined by transaction value but rather by transaction complexity and demand on the ethereum network. Now, say you are paying US $50 for groceries. Based on demand on Ethereum blockchain the Gas fee can be anything US $0.5 or US $5 or more – there is no certainty.

To achieve predictability comparable to traditional applications, it is imperative for Web3 applications to tackle the scalability problem and implement solutions for blockchain scalability.

10.3.1.2 What Causes Scalability Challenges?

Addressing blockchain scalability is inherently challenging, given that these issues originate from the fundamental design of the blockchain protocol.

Two critical parameters in blockchain design determine the capacity of a blockchain network:

I. **Block Time:** This refers to the time required for a new block to be added to the blockchain.
II. **Block Size:** This is the maximum amount of data or transactions that a block can accommodate. It's important to note that Ethereum's block size is determined not by traditional kilobyte size but by the total gas value consumed by transactions within the block. Each transaction specifies a gas limit, and the cumulative gas value influences the block's size.

Anyways, block time and block size are fixed for a given blockchain, and any modification would require altering the blockchain protocol itself. Therefore, the maximum data or transactions that a blockchain can process is predetermined.

Modifying these parameters through protocol adjustments poses several challenges. For instance, reducing block time for quicker block creation requires careful consideration of the blockchain's distributed nature. With thousands of nodes distributed globally, faster block processing would demand more computing power for nodes. Similarly, increasing the block size requires nodes to process more data.

This challenge serves as the foundation of the blockchain scaling trilemma.

10.3.1.3 Blockchain Scaling Trilemma

Scaling a centralized system, like one hosted on AWS EC2, involves opting for a computing system with enhanced processing power and memory to handle increased traffic. However, scaling decentralized networks, especially blockchain networks, presents a distinct and challenging scenario, as articulated by Vitalik Buterin in his article "The Limits to Blockchain Scalability".

The scaling trilemma suggests that blockchain networks aim to achieve the three properties mentioned below, but only two can be achieved simultaneously with traditional methods.

10.3.1.3.1 Scalability

Scalability involves achieving faster finality and processing a higher number of transactions per second (TPS), essential for enhancing efficiency and promoting widespread blockchain network adoption. Finality in blockchain transactions refers to the point at which a transaction is considered irreversible and permanently recorded on the blockchain, ensuring it cannot be altered or undone.

10.3.1.3.2 Decentralization

Decentralization involves avoiding centralization, ensuring that a blockchain doesn't rely on a small group of large nodes. To maintain decentralization, becoming a node should be feasible with readily available and inexpensive equipment, such as a consumer laptop or even a cell phone.

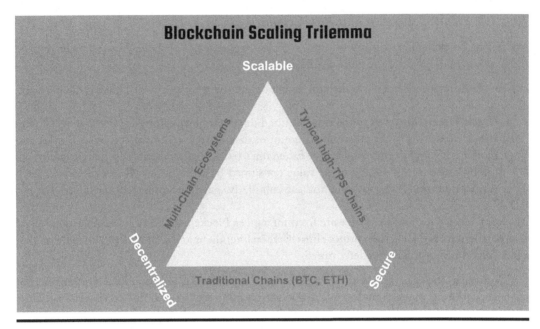

Figure 10.3   Blockchain scaling trilemma.

10.3.1.3.3 Security

Security in blockchain relates to preventing the hijacking of the consensus process, which, if compromised, could lead to unauthorized transaction additions.

For a secure blockchain consensus process, approval from the majority of full nodes is essential. This increases the difficulty of hacking, as it requires an attack on a substantial number of nodes.

As per the scaling trilemma, typical blockchain networks can achieve two out of three properties, leading to the classification of blockchain networks into three classes.

a. **Decentralized and secure:** Examples include traditional blockchains like Bitcoin and Ethereum, characterized by a large number of nodes. These networks require every node to verify every transaction, limiting scalability due to the significant amount of work involved.
b. **Scalable and secure:** Consists of blockchains using delegated proof of stake consensus mechanisms such as EOS, Lisk, and Tron. These chains rely on a small number of nodes (often 10–100) to maintain consensus, providing scalability and security. However, they are not decentralized as only a small number of nodes are involved, requiring users to trust a majority of these nodes.
c. **Decentralized and scalable:** Typically represented by multi-chain ecosystems where different applications operate on separate chains, and cross-chain communication protocols facilitate communication between them. While decentralized and scalable, smaller chains within these ecosystems may individually be vulnerable to attacks. An attacker only needs to control a consensus node majority in one of the many chains to cause damage across the entire network.

Okay, we understand the scaling problem – a little bit.

How do we solve this problem?

10.3.1.4 What is the Primary Goal of Blockchain Scaling?

The key objectives of blockchain scaling include achieving faster finality, indicating quicker transaction settlement, and increasing the number of transactions.

Finality refers to the assurance that blockchain transactions are immutable and impossible to alter, reverse, or cancel after completion. It is a measure of the time one must wait for a reasonable guarantee that executed crypto transactions on the blockchain will remain unchanged.

Now, coming to **TPS**. TPS implies the capability to process more transactions within a given timeframe.

While it may seem intuitive to enhance scalability by utilizing nodes with high computing power, this approach comes with drawbacks. It can increase the costs associated with hosting a node leading to centralization because now only a few resourceful entities, such as corporations, can afford to host nodes. This scenario may also foster collusion among the limited set of node hosts.

10.3.1.5 Ways to Scale a Blockchain

To illustrate various forms of blockchain scaling, consider an analogy of an automobile assembly line. Suppose the assembly line currently produces five cars per hour. Now, the company aims to boost production to 50 cars per hour.

What strategies can be employed?

At a broad level:

I. **Increasing the capacity of the assembly line**: This involves expanding the capacity of the main assembly process.
II. **Performing some assembly work off the main line**: This involves creating sub-assembly lines to handle a portion of the overall assembly process and then transferring partially assembled cars to the main line.

In the context of blockchain scaling:

I. The first option, increasing the capacity of the assembly line, is analogous to on-chain or layer-1 scaling.
II. The second option, carrying out some assembly work outside the main assembly line, is analogous to off-chain scaling.

10.3.1.5.1 On-chain Scaling

Continuing with the assembly line analogy, let's explore how we can increase the capacity of the assembly line –

I. **Utilize more powerful machines**: In the blockchain scaling context, this equates to requiring nodes to possess greater computing power. However, as previously discussed, this approach may have drawbacks, potentially impacting decentralization due to the limited number of entities able to afford powerful nodes.

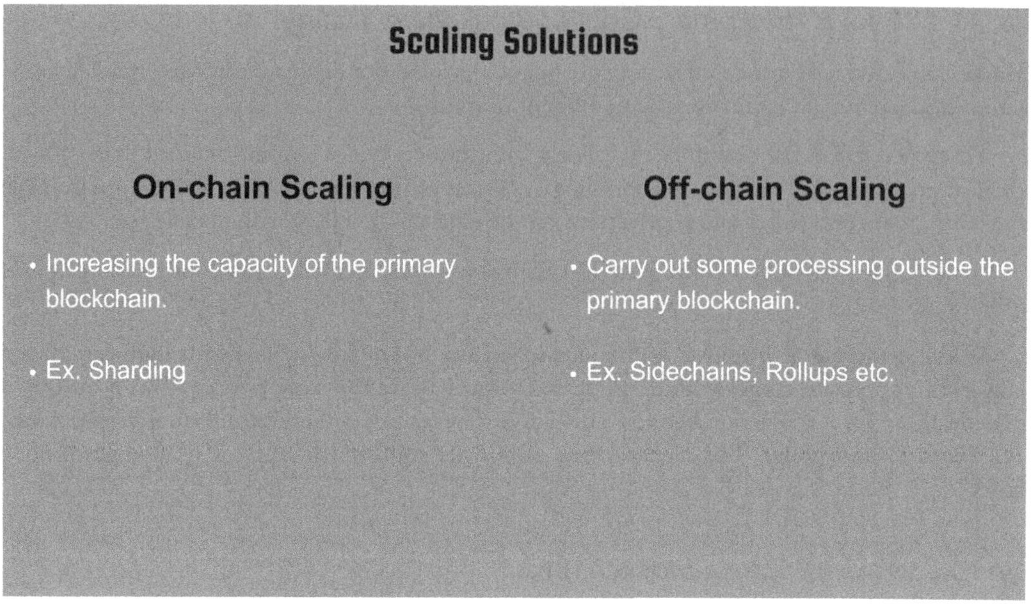

Figure 10.4 Classification of scaling solutions.

II. **Establish parallel assembly lines**: Creating additional assembly lines that operate in parallel can enhance production speed by allowing cars to be assembled concurrently.

Now, sharding is an on-chain scaling solution that operates on the principle of establishing parallel processing chains. Sharding fundamentally creates parallel chains that process transactions independently, boosting the overall capacity of the blockchain.

10.3.1.5.1.1 Sharding: Sharding is adapted from database management. In database management, sharding involves distributing a dataset across multiple machines for enhanced storage.

In blockchain, sharding is an on-chain scaling solution. It clusters active nodes into smaller groups called shards, sharing the transaction load. Each shard independently processes and stores specific transactions, allowing for increased transaction volume while maintaining security through verification by a sufficient number of nodes.

In its basic form, each shard maintains its transaction history, confining the impact of transactions on the state of that particular shard. In theory, sharding aims to reconcile the scaling trilemma, simultaneously achieving scalability, decentralization, and security.

The Ethereum team has previously planned to implement sharding in the Ethereum blockchain as part of their roadmap. However recently Ethereum has abandoned that plan and is currently adopting a new structure.

EIP-4844 (Proto-Danksharding) – Shard blob transactions is a step towards this new vision.

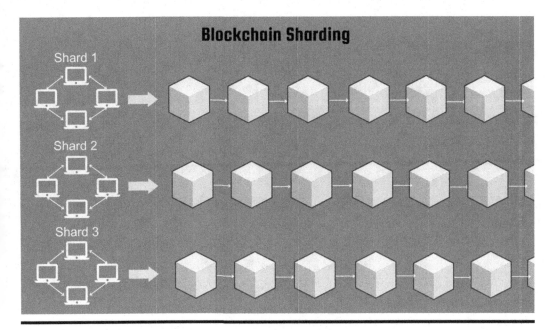

Figure 10.5   A very simplistic representation of blockchain sharding.

10.3.1.5.2 Off-chain Scaling

We've covered on-chain scaling solutions, which focus on increasing blockchain capacity through parallel transaction processing. Now, let's revisit the analogy of the automobile assembly line, where the second option involves carrying out some assembly work outside the main assembly line.

This approach is termed off-chain scaling. In off-chain scaling solutions, a portion of the processing occurs outside the primary blockchain. These solutions are typically developed by third parties. Off-chain scaling solutions can be further categorized based on whether they obtain security directly from the primary blockchain consensus or not.

Certain off-chain scaling solutions, like Sidechains and Plasma, employ their own consensus processes. On the other hand, solutions like Rollups and State Channels derive their security from the primary blockchain and do not operate with their own consensus mechanisms. These solutions are often termed as Layer 2 scaling solutions.

10.3.1.5.2.1 Sidechains: Sidechains are independent blockchains operating alongside the main chain, having autonomous consensus processes and block parameters. Two-way bridges enable seamless data transfer between the main chain and sidechains. Nodes on sidechains use dedicated client software, distinct from the main chain, and maintain their own consensus mechanisms.

Sidechains enhance blockchain scalability by offloading transactions from the main chain, allowing for parallel processing and faster confirmation times. With customized consensus mechanisms and specialized smart contracts, sidechains optimize efficiency, reduce congestion, and lower transaction costs on the main blockchain, contributing to an overall scalable blockchain ecosystem.

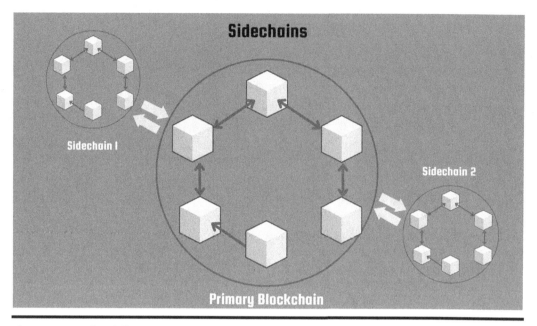

Figure 10.6 Visual illustration of sidechains.

Sidechains are crucially independent, not sending state changes and transaction data back to the mainnet. They have distinct block parameters, such as block time and size. For instance, the Polygon PoS, an Ethereum sidechain, uses Proof-of-Stake (PoS), different from Ethereum 1.0's Proof-of-Work (PoW). Ethereum 2.0 uses PoS.

Sidechains carry security risks due to autonomous consensus management and a limited number of nodes. Incidents like the Ethereum Ronin Sidechain security breach illustrate vulnerabilities, where compromising a small number of nodes can have a significant impact on the whole system.

Prominent examples of sidechains include Bitcoin's Liquid Network and Ethereum's Polygon PoS.

10.3.1.5.2.2 Plasma: Plasma is a framework designed to enhance scalability and security for smart contract platforms, primarily targeting Ethereum.

In the Plasma framework, individual sidechains, referred to as "Plasma chains," are linked to the main blockchain. These sidechains, also known as "child chains," independently process transactions and periodically update their state on the main blockchain.

Operating autonomously, Plasma chains enable assets to move between "child chains" and the main blockchain through a two-way peg. To ensure security, the architecture incorporates advanced measures like fraud proofs and exit mechanisms, maintaining the integrity of child chains while alleviating the main chain's load.

Plasma's architecture significantly improves scalability, reduces main chain congestion, and lowers transaction costs. It finds applications in decentralized exchanges, microtransactions, and scenarios requiring increased throughput.

E.g. OmiseGO (OMG Network).

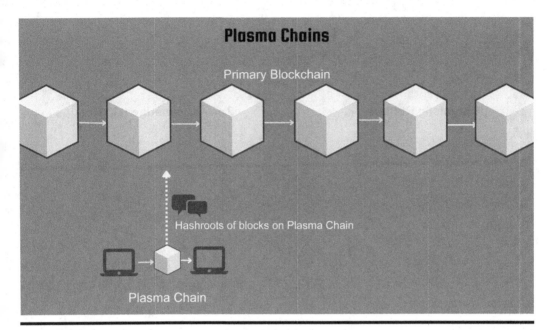

Figure 10.7   Visual illustration of Plasma chains.

10.3.1.5.2.3 Rollups: Rollups are scaling solutions that bundle multiple transactions into batches, sending only consolidated data to the main chain.

In Ethereum, Rollups are implemented as smart contracts on the main chain. These contracts store a state root, representing the Merkle root of the rollup's state, including account balances and contract code. Batches of transactions are presented in a compressed format, along with previous

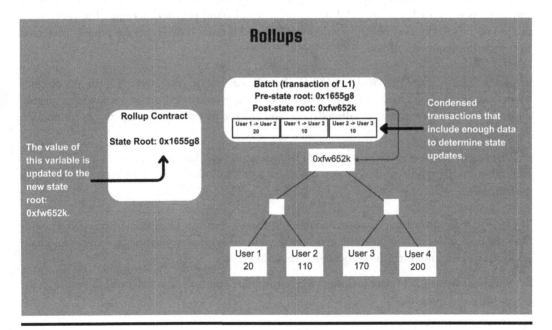

Figure 10.8   Visual illustration of Rollups.

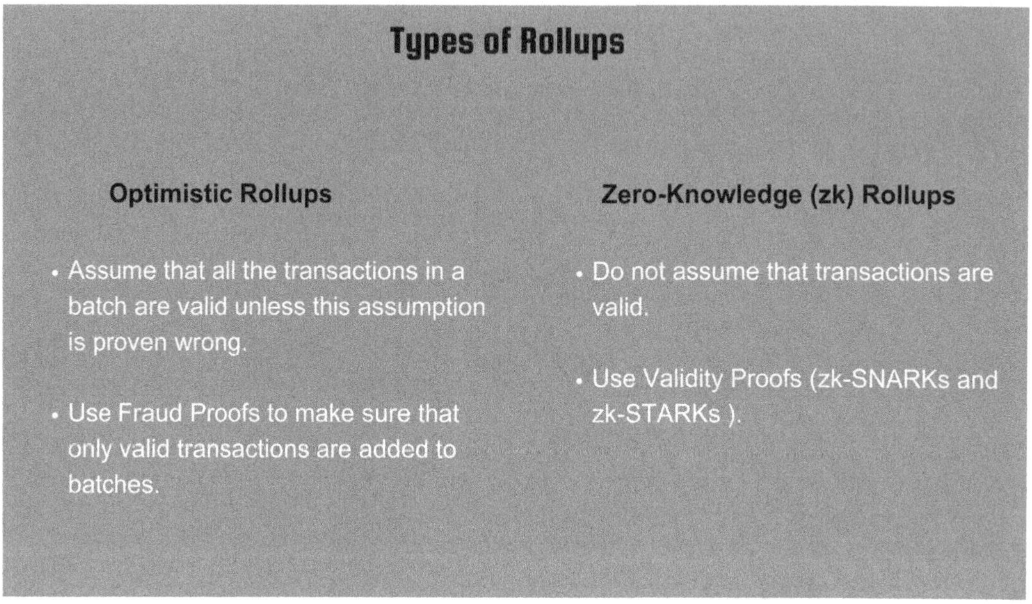

Types of Rollups

Optimistic Rollups

- Assume that all the transactions in a batch are valid unless this assumption is proven wrong.

- Use Fraud Proofs to make sure that only valid transactions are added to batches.

Zero-Knowledge (zk) Rollups

- Do not assume that transactions are valid.

- Use Validity Proofs (zk-SNARKs and zk-STARKs).

Figure 10.9   Classification of Rollups.

and new state roots. The smart contract validates the batch by comparing the state roots, and updating the state root if a change is detected.

Rollups are categorized based on their proof mechanisms, primarily falling into two types: Optimistic Rollups and Zero-Knowledge (ZK) Rollups.

10.3.1.5.2.3.1 Optimistic Rollups: Optimistic Rollups work on the presumption that all transactions within a batch are valid unless evidence of fraud proves otherwise. The verification process optimistically assumes transaction validity, and if fraud is detected, the proof is presented to contest the assumed validity.

10.3.1.5.2.3.2 Zero-Knowledge (ZK) Rollups: ZK Rollups differ from Optimistic Rollups by not assuming transaction validity. They use validity proofs based on zero-knowledge proofs, ensuring correctness without revealing details, and enhancing privacy and security in transaction verification.

The key distinction is in their approach to transaction validity assumptions, with Optimistic Rollups assuming validity unless proven otherwise and ZK Rollups relying on proofs to guarantee correctness.

10.3.1.5.2.4 Channels: Channels enable off-chain execution of multiple transactions, with only the final states recorded on the main blockchain. This off-chain approach reduces on-chain publishing needs and mitigates associated transaction risks.

Channels implement "state locking," where funds are committed as collateral to ensure channel security and integrity.

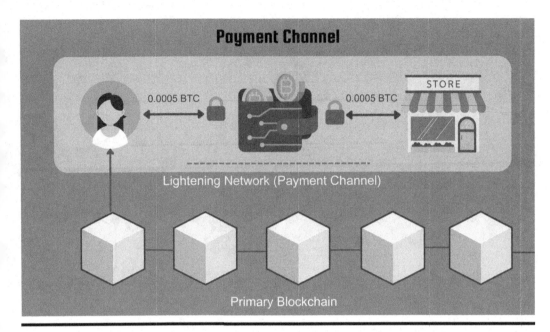

Figure 10.10   Visual illustration of a payment channel (Bitcoin's Lightning Network).

I. Payment channels, like Bitcoin's Lightning Network, facilitate off-chain transactions for faster and cheaper payments. They enable direct transactions between participants without involving the main blockchain for each payment, focusing on secure and efficient value transfer.

   Payment channels are used for micropayments, streaming payments, and scenarios with frequent transactions between participants.

II. State channels offer versatility beyond payments, accommodating various off-chain interactions. Suitable for applications like gaming, decentralized apps (DApps), and scenarios with frequent participant interactions, they involve participants initially "state locking" collateral in a multisig "channel contract." A multisig contract is a smart contract that allows multiple signers to review and agree on an action on the blockchain.

   The state that is "locked up" is called a state deposit. For instance, this might be an amount of ether or an ERC-20 token, but it could also be a CryptoKitty NFT or an ENS domain name. After the state deposit is locked, channel participants use off-chain messaging to exchange and sign valid transactions without deploying them to the main chain.

   The final agreed-upon state is then submitted to the main blockchain's smart contract for settlement, ensuring financial commitment, security, and dispute resolution on-chain, while most interactions occur off-chain for efficiency and scalability.

Let us end the discussion on scaling solutions here.

10.3.2 Blockchain Oracles

10.3.2.1 Why Do We Need Blockchain Oracles?

We understand the limitations of storing large amounts of data on-chain due to high costs and low throughput. Smart contracts, integral to decentralized applications (DApps), often require access

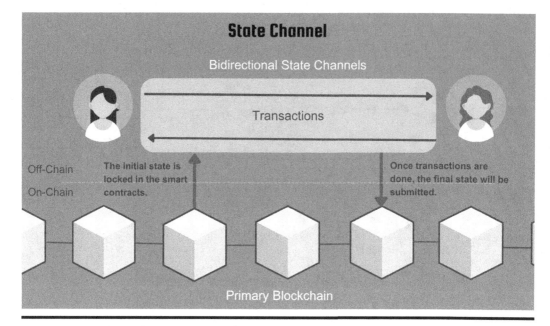

Figure 10.11 Visual illustration of working of state channels.

to various data types. Moreover, static data alone is not sufficient. For applications like weather or currency price updates, smart contracts need real-time information.

Developing applications dependent on real-time data, such as weather or live scores, requires smart contracts to have internet connectivity for accessing the latest information.

However, smart contracts lack direct connectivity to the conventional internet. This is where blockchain oracles play a crucial role.

10.3.2.2 What is a Blockchain Oracle?

Blockchain oracles act as intermediaries connecting smart contracts with external data, events, or computations.

Now, let's explore the utility of blockchain oracles through a few examples.

10.3.2.3 Blockchain Oracle Sample Use Cases

10.3.2.3.1 In Decentralized Finance (DeFi)

In the context of DeFi, applications often depend on real-time updates of price feeds, interest rates, and various financial data. The important role of blockchain oracles is to provide accurate and current information to these applications.

Consider the case of Stablecoins. Stablecoins require real-time price feeds to maintain stability and a close peg to a reference currency, like the US dollar. Blockchain oracles play a critical role in supplying precise and up-to-the-minute price information for the assets underlying stablecoins.

Furthermore, many stablecoins are backed by collateralized reserved assets. Blockchain oracles can retrieve real-time market values of these collateral assets, empowering the stablecoin protocol to dynamically adjust collateralization ratios. This dynamic adjustment ensures that the stablecoin maintains adequate collateralization, even in the middle of market fluctuations.

10.3.2.3.2 In Supply Chain Management

Oracles can enhance supply chain transparency by validating real-world events for blockchain smart contracts. For example, to monitor organic food authenticity, smart contracts, integrated with oracles, can fetch real-time data from trusted sources like certification authorities and weather stations. Oracles then can verify farm certification, sustainable practices, and environmental conditions during harvesting, ensuring data integrity.

The resulting immutable blockchain record provides consumers with real-time information on product origin, authenticity, and adherence to organic standards, fostering trust in the supply chain.

10.3.2.3.3 In Insurance and Risk Management

Oracles serve a crucial role in providing smart contracts with real-world information, such as weather conditions or flight delays, pivotal for triggering insurance payouts or managing risks.

In a decentralized insurance application, for example, oracles may fetch real-time weather data to assess adverse conditions affecting a policyholder's property. If predefined claim conditions, like severe storms or flooding, are met, the smart contract automatically triggers an insurance payout. This oracle-driven approach enhances claims efficiency, minimizes manual verification, and enables proactive risk management by automating responses to real-world events.

Now that we understand blockchain oracles a little bit, let's explore different types of oracles.

10.3.2.4 Classification of Blockchain Oracles

Blockchain oracles can be classified based on various attributes:

- **Purpose**: Does it supply data or conduct computations?
- **Source**: Is the data sourced from software, hardware, or humans?
- **Direction of information flow**: Is it inbound or outbound?
- **Trust**: Is it centralized or decentralized?

It's important to note that a single oracle can belong to multiple categories simultaneously.

10.3.2.4.1 Classification Based on the Purpose of the Oracle

10.3.2.4.1.1 Data Oracles: Data oracles are crucial for smart contracts, providing real-world information like prices, weather data, and sports scores. In decentralized finance (DeFi) applications, they play a vital role by providing accurate and current price feeds for various assets to smart contracts.

Prominent examples of data oracles encompass Chainlink and Band Protocol.

10.3.2.4.1.2 Computation Oracles: Computation oracles, also known as off-chain computation oracles, involve outsourcing complex computations to external systems and then incorporating the results back into the blockchain.

They are beneficial for handling resource-intensive computations that may be impractical or expensive to execute directly on the blockchain, addressing concerns related to scalability and costs. These tasks include complex data processing, AI/ML computations, or any computation requiring significant computing power.

Examples of computation oracles include iExec and Golem.

10.3.2.4.2 Data-source Based Classification

10.3.2.4.2.1 Software Oracles: Software oracles obtain data from software systems, including online databases, servers, websites, and various web-based sources.

E.g. Chainlink is an example of a software oracle.

10.3.2.4.2.2 Hardware Oracles: Hardware oracles source data from hardware systems such as sensors, IoT devices, scanners, RFID tags, etc.

Consider a weather station equipped with sensors measuring temperature and humidity, acting as a hardware oracle. The station collects real-world data and feeds it into the blockchain, ensuring accurate and current information about weather conditions.

10.3.2.4.2.3 Human Oracles: Occasionally, individuals possessing expertise in a specific field can function as oracles. They research and authenticate information from various sources, which is then utilized by smart contracts. Human oracles must validate their identity through cryptography to mitigate the risk of fraudulent attempts to impersonate them.

E.g. Augur.

10.3.2.4.3 Classification Based on the Direction of Information Flow

10.3.2.4.3.1 Inbound Oracles: Inbound oracles bring external data onto the blockchain using methods like APIs or databases. For example, an inbound oracle could supply a smart contract with temperature data collected by a sensor.

10.3.2.4.3.2 Outbound Oracles: Outbound oracles enable smart contracts to trigger actions in external systems, like interacting with web services or sending notifications. For instance, in a smart lock scenario, an outbound oracle could unlock the smart lock when funds are deposited to a specific address.

10.3.2.4.4 Trust-based Classification

10.3.2.4.4.1 Centralized Oracles: Centralized oracles rely on a single data source, which introduces risks like dependency on one entity, vulnerability to malicious interference, and a single point of failure, increasing susceptibility to attacks.

E.g. Provable (Oraclize).

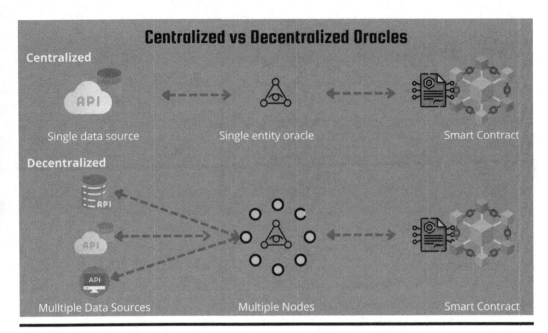

Figure 10.12   Classification of oracles – centralized and decentralized.

10.3.2.4.4.2 Decentralized Oracles: Decentralized oracles, also known as consensus-based oracles, enhance system reliability by avoiding dependence on a single data source.

They employ a consensus mechanism involving multiple data providers to reduce the impact of potentially malicious or inaccurate data.

Nodes in this decentralized structure collaborate to fetch and verify real-world data, ensuring the integrity of information transmitted to the blockchain. Oracle nodes are distributed computing entities across the network, often running on external servers or devices.

E.g. Band Protocol is an example of a decentralized oracle.

Okay, let us end our discussion on oracles here.

10.3.3 Privacy Protocols

10.3.3.1 What Is a Privacy Protocol?

Privacy protocols are a set of rules, processes, and technologies designed to safeguard sensitive information and ensure privacy in digital and communication channels. They focus on secure handling, processing, and transmission of data, protecting it from unauthorized access or disclosure.

Selective disclosure is a fundamental aspect of privacy protocols.

Selective disclosure empowers individuals to control and choose the information they share, allowing for the disclosure of specific details without revealing the entire information. This concept is vital in areas such as cryptography, data privacy, and identity management.

Blockchain Transactions

	Txn Hash	Method ⑦	Block		From		To		Value	
◉	0x53494949c1fa5df344...	Transfer	19192604	14 secs ago	0x264bd8...715997B5	→	0x0f077e...D94e70DF		0.20097836 ETH	0.00199078
◉	0x57eaa0b3083b762ba...	Transfer	19192604	14 secs ago	Bybit: Hot Wallet	→	0xE5c17f...3b99dF85		0.014 ETH	0.00193334
◉	0x77fb88daabb83adfa1...	Transfer	19192604	14 secs ago	Crypto.com 2	→	0x18B691...2c418dfA		0.45469 ETH	0.00213902
◉	0x4c11764f5d23a6ea8...	Transfer	19192604	14 secs ago	Crypto.com 2	→	Tether: USDT Stablecoin		0 ETH	0.00643837
◉	0x821d381d742eb688f...	Approve	19192604	14 secs ago	0xc7C6b2...67615BD8	→	Uniswap Protocol: Perm...		0 ETH	0.00274434
◉	0x89bc3c83569d91404...	Transfer	19192604	14 secs ago	() mostaccio.eth	→	BuildOnBeam: BEAM To...		0 ETH	0.00506129
◉	0xcf181c05a2e8d0f72c...	Transfer	19192604	14 secs ago	0xe5C0fa...Ba42E264	→	0x5A75c3...eDC5D306		0.1 ETH	0.00189243
◉	0xfbf906abcf0ffd19449...	0xca350aa6	19192604	14 secs ago	Coinbase: Deposit	→	Coinbase 10		0 ETH	0.05390503
◉	0xed9f41bcc43f23cc66...	Transfer	19192604	14 secs ago	Coinbase 12	→	0x5dfdf8...6b92928f		0.02810009 ETH	0.00191234
◉	0xba8bd68d034131d5a...	Transfer	19192604	14 secs ago	Coinbase 4	→	0x4d0660...74ADb0F7		0.04938196 ETH	0.00191234
◉	0xc6b96bdfba0ff91bc7...	Transfer	19192604	14 secs ago	0xb23360...C8D7c460	→	0x4e669A...DB21A1f0		0.04897503 ETH	0.00194313
◉	0x55d90cea3404eba51...	Transfer	19192604	14 secs ago	Stake.com	→	Tether: USDT Stablecoin		0 ETH	0.00426961

Figure 10.13 **Records of blockchain (Ethereum) transactions accessed from Etherscan.io.**

Web3 employs various privacy protocols that go beyond enhancing privacy. Zero-knowledge proofs, for instance, are integral to several blockchain scaling solutions.

Before delving into these protocols, it's crucial to understand the need for privacy in Web3.

10.3.3.2 Why Do we Need Privacy Protocols?

While blockchain transactions are often considered anonymous, they are not anonymous but pseudonymous. Transactions in Web3 use public addresses instead of user identity. Despite this, significant user information is still accessible, presenting a potential risk of de-anonymization.

Consider someone using a cryptocurrency wallet for multiple transactions, receiving funds from various sources and sending them to different destinations. Analysis of transaction patterns, including timing, frequency, and amounts, could reveal distinctive patterns associated with a specific user.

When a user verifies their identity on a service like a cryptocurrency exchange, the blockchain transactions can be linked to the user's identity through off-chain data.

External sources, such as social media or public forums, may also expose a user's identity if the users associate their blockchain address with these platforms. Additionally, blockchain analysis tools (e.g., CipherTrace and Scorechain) use clustering algorithms to group addresses controlled by the same entity, potentially compromising user anonymity.

ENS (Ethereum Name Service) can contribute to de-anonymization as it links human-readable names with Ethereum addresses.

If users associate real-world identities with these names, the pseudonymous nature of blockchain addresses is compromised. Registering identifiable ENS domains (e.g., "JohnDoe.eth") can lead to the association of Ethereum addresses with specific individuals.

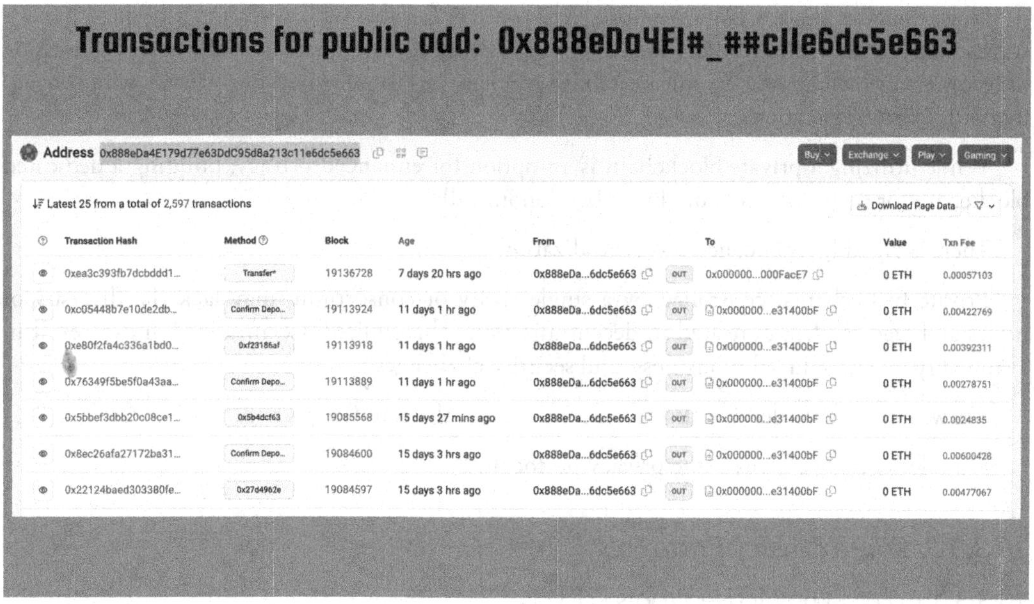

Transactions for public add: 0x888eDa4EI#_##cIIe6dc5e663

| Address 0x888eDa4E179d77e63DdC95d8a213c11e6dc5e663 | | | | | Buy ∨ Exchange ∨ Play ∨ Gaming ∨ |

⇅F Latest 25 from a total of 2,597 transactions   ⤓ Download Page Data ▽ ∨

⑦	Transaction Hash	Method ⑦	Block	Age	From		To		Value	Txn Fee
⊚	0xea3c393fb7dcbddd1...	Transfer*	19136728	7 days 20 hrs ago	0x888eDa...6dc5e663 ⎘	OUT	0x000000...000FacE7 ⎘		0 ETH	0.00057103
⊚	0xc05448b7e10de2db...	Confirm Depo...	19113924	11 days 1 hr ago	0x888eDa...6dc5e663 ⎘	OUT	⎗ 0x000000...e31400bF ⎘		0 ETH	0.00422769
⊚	0xe80f2fa4c336a1bd0...	0xf23185af	19113918	11 days 1 hr ago	0x888eDa...6dc5e663 ⎘	OUT	⎗ 0x000000...e31400bF ⎘		0 ETH	0.00392311
⊚	0x76349f5be5f0a43aa...	Confirm Depo...	19113889	11 days 1 hr ago	0x888eDa...6dc5e663 ⎘	OUT	⎗ 0x000000...e31400bF ⎘		0 ETH	0.00278751
⊚	0x5bbef3dbb20c08ce1...	0x5b4dcf63	19085568	15 days 27 mins ago	0x888eDa...6dc5e663 ⎘	OUT	⎗ 0x000000...e31400bF ⎘		0 ETH	0.0024835
⊚	0x8ec26afa27172ba31...	Confirm Depo...	19084600	15 days 3 hrs ago	0x888eDa...6dc5e663 ⎘	OUT	⎗ 0x000000...e31400bF ⎘		0 ETH	0.00600428
⊚	0x22124baed303380fe...	0x27d4962e	19084597	15 days 3 hrs ago	0x888eDa...6dc5e663 ⎘	OUT	⎗ 0x000000...e31400bF ⎘		0 ETH	0.00477067

Figure 10.14 Transaction records for a specific public address on Ethereum – accessed from Etherscan.io.

Publicly accessible ENS domain registrations on the Ethereum blockchain enable anyone to query the mapping between ENS domains and Ethereum addresses, potentially facilitating de-anonymization.

Users voluntarily connecting ENS domains to off-chain identities through social media or personal websites add context that aids de-anonymization, especially when publicly linked to identifiable information.

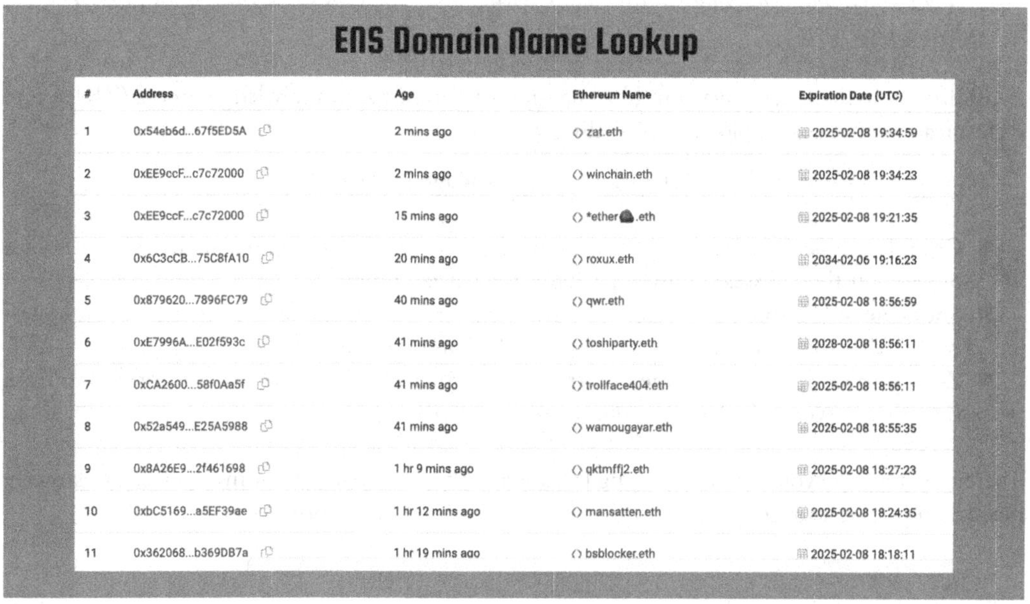

ENS Domain Name Lookup

#	Address	Age	Ethereum Name	Expiration Date (UTC)
1	0x54eb6d...67f5ED5A ⎘	2 mins ago	⟨⟩ zat.eth	2025-02-08 19:34:59
2	0xEE9ccF...c7c72000 ⎘	2 mins ago	⟨⟩ winchain.eth	2025-02-08 19:34:23
3	0xEE9ccF...c7c72000 ⎘	15 mins ago	⟨⟩ *ether●.eth	2025-02-08 19:21:35
4	0x6C3cCB...75C8fA10 ⎘	20 mins ago	⟨⟩ roxux.eth	2034-02-06 19:16:23
5	0x879620...7896FC79 ⎘	40 mins ago	⟨⟩ qwr.eth	2025-02-08 18:56:59
6	0xE7996A...E02f593c ⎘	41 mins ago	⟨⟩ toshiparty.eth	2028-02-08 18:56:11
7	0xCA2600...58f0Aa5f ⎘	41 mins ago	⟨⟩ trollface404.eth	2025-02-08 18:56:11
8	0x52a549...E25A5988 ⎘	41 mins ago	⟨⟩ wamougayar.eth	2026-02-08 18:55:35
9	0x8A26E9...2f461698 ⎘	1 hr 9 mins ago	⟨⟩ qktmffj2.eth	2025-02-08 18:27:23
10	0xbC5169...a5EF39ae ⎘	1 hr 12 mins ago	⟨⟩ mansatten.eth	2025-02-08 18:24:35
11	0x362068...b369DB7a ⎘	1 hr 19 mins ago	⟨⟩ bsblocker.eth	2025-02-08 18:18:11

Figure 10.15 Ethereum domain name lookup – accessed from Etherscan.io.

Now, imagine using a DeFi network. Are you comfortable with revealing all your financial transactions to the entire world? Indeed, for Web3 to achieve mainstream acceptance, addressing this concern is mandatory. We must establish mechanisms to safeguard our privacy while engaging with Web3 applications.

While utilizing a private blockchain is an option for enhanced privacy, building a dedicated blockchain for each app may not always be economically feasible.

There is an additional concern – centralization.

Private blockchains, controlled by a single entity or consortium, may lack the diversity of nodes and face challenges related to decentralization. This limited decentralization can result in availability issues, reduced robustness, and security challenges.

We will have a detailed discussion on private blockchain in Chapter 13.

Now, let's briefly explore some privacy protocols.

10.3.3.3 Some Privacy Protocols

10.3.3.3.1 Zero-knowledge Proofs (ZKPs)

Zero-knowledge proofs enable a party (the prover) to convince another party (the verifier) of the validity of a statement without disclosing any details about the statement itself.

The terms "prover" and "verifier" are frequently used in cryptographic contexts. The prover is the entity or program responsible for generating the cryptographic proof, while the verifier is the entity or program tasked with scrutinizing the proof's contents.

The paper "The Knowledge Complexity of Interactive Proof Systems" introduced zero-knowledge proofs as

> "those proofs that convey no additional knowledge other than the correctness of the propositions in question."

In addition to enhancing privacy in blockchain transactions, zero-knowledge proofs (ZKPs) find widespread application in blockchain scaling.

Now, the fundamental attributes of a zero-knowledge proof are:

- **Completeness**: If a statement is true, an honest verifier can be persuaded by an honest prover that they possess knowledge about the correct input.
- **Soundness**: If a statement is false, no dishonest prover can unilaterally convince an honest verifier that they possess knowledge about the correct input.
- **Zero-knowledge**: If a statement is true, the verifier gains no additional information from the prover beyond the fact that the statement is true.

Therefore, it goes beyond merely proving knowledge about something – it involves demonstrating possession of that knowledge without divulging any additional information.

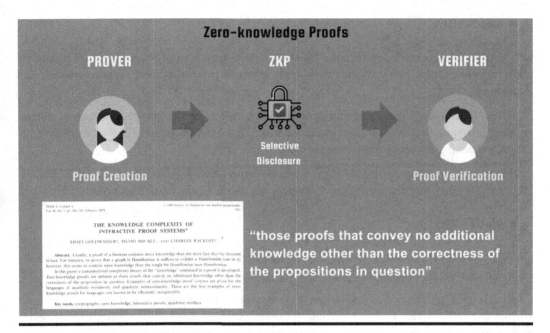

Figure 10.16   Visual representation of zero-knowledge proofs.

In a broader sense, zero-knowledge proofs, or ZKPs, revolve around proving a claim without revealing any confidential information.

Prominent examples of ZKPs include the Schnorr Protocol, zk-SNARKs (Zero-Knowledge Succinct Non-Interactive Argument of Knowledge), zk-STARKs (Zero-Knowledge Scalable Transparent Arguments of Knowledge), and Bulletproofs, among others.

Zero-knowledge proofs (ZKPs) can be categorized based on interaction – interactive ZKPs and non-interactive ZKPs.

Interactive ZKPs involve a series of messages exchanged between the prover and verifier, offering greater versatility to handle dynamic scenarios requiring additional information, as seen in the Schnorr Protocol. The Schnorr Protocol is a cryptographic protocol designed for secure and efficient digital signature generation.

On the other hand, **non-interactive ZKPs** can be verified with a single message from the prover, proving beneficial in applications where interaction needs to be limited or is impractical. Examples include zk-SNARKs and zk-STARKs.

Due to the non-interactive nature of these proof systems, specifically zk-SNARKs, they boast short prover times. This implies that these proof systems are swift in both proof generation and verification, rendering them suitable for use cases with time constraints, such as those encountered in blockchains.

Let us quickly discuss zk-SNARKS and zk-STARKs due to their widespread use in current web3 ecosystems.

■ zk-SNARKs

zk-SNARKs (Zero-knowledge Succinct Non-Interactive Argument of Knowledge) are non-interactive zero-knowledge proof systems with applications in privacy-focused cryptocurrencies like Zcash.

They enable the validation of transactions without revealing specific details, such as sender, receiver, or transaction amount. The succinct nature of zk-SNARK proofs allows for quick verification, enhancing efficiency in blockchain systems.

However, in the case of zk-SNARKs, a trusted setup phase is required, where initial parameters are generated, and the system's security depends on the integrity of this initial setup.

■ zk-STARKs

zk-STARKs (Zero-knowledge Scalable Transparent Arguments of Knowledge) are a type of non-interactive zero-knowledge proof designed for transparency and scalability in blockchain protocols.

Unlike zk-SNARKs, zk-STARKs have a transparent setup phase, eliminating the need for a trusted setup. zk-STARKs achieve scalability through efficient polynomial commitment schemes and recursive composition, making them suitable for verifying complex computations in large-scale systems.

Let us end our discussion on zero-knowledge proofs here.

10.3.3.3.2 Ring Signatures

A ring signature is a cryptographic protocol that offers a type of anonymous digital signature. It permits a member of a group (referred to as the ring) to sign a message on behalf of the group without disclosing which member's key was utilized to generate the signature.

For instance, the privacy-focused cryptocurrency Monero employs ring signatures to obscure the sender's address by blending it with multiple other addresses. This process makes it difficult to trace the origin of a transaction.

10.3.3.3.3 Enigma

Enigma is a privacy protocol employing homomorphic encryption to enable computations on encrypted data. This ensures the confidentiality of sensitive information while still facilitating computations to be executed.

As discussed in the "Decentralized Data Science" chapter, homomorphic encryption is a cryptographic method that enables computations on encrypted data without the need for decryption.

10.3.3.3.4 Differential Privacy

In simple terms, differential privacy is a method involving the introduction of noise to data, safeguarding individual privacy while still enabling meaningful statistical analysis.

We also discussed differential privacy in detail in the "Decentralized Data Science" chapter.

The privacy-focused blockchain platform Oasis Network utilizes differential privacy to shield user data, ensuring that statistical analysis on a dataset does not disclose information about any specific individual data point.

10.3.3.3.5 Secure Multi-party Computation (SMPC)

Secure Multi-Party Computation (SMPC) is a cryptographic technique facilitating multiple parties to collectively compute a function over their inputs while safeguarding the privacy of those inputs.

Again, we discussed SMPC in detail in the "Decentralized Data Science" chapter.

The Keep Network, serving as a privacy layer for public blockchains, facilitates the development of private and decentralized applications using SMPC. It enables multiple parties to collectively compute a function over their inputs while maintaining the confidentiality of those inputs.

10.3.3.3.6 Secure Hash Functions

Secure hash functions (SHFs) are essential for maintaining data integrity and privacy in Web3. They play a crucial role in blockchain systems by ensuring the integrity of data through the creation of secure chains. Each block in the blockchain includes the hash of the previous block, enhancing the overall security of the system.

While not directly addressing privacy concerns, these hash functions contribute to privacy in Web3 by representing user addresses as cryptographic hashes and protecting public keys' confidentiality.

Secure hash functions are essential in Web3 for various security purposes. They strengthen password hashing, safeguarding against plaintext exposure in data breaches. Additionally, they support digital signatures in decentralized systems, ensuring message authenticity and integrity via asymmetric cryptography. Furthermore, these functions play a role in privacy-preserving protocols like zero-knowledge proofs (ZKPs) and homomorphic encryption within Web3.

The two fundamental properties of these hash functions are:

- **Collision resistance**: Ensures that two different inputs won't produce the same hash value.
- **Preimage resistance**: Makes it computationally infeasible to reverse-engineer the original input from its hash output.

Let's conclude our discussion on privacy protocols here.

10.3.4 Communication Protocols

10.3.4.1 Why do we Need Communication Protocols in Web3?

We discussed earlier how Web3 adopts a networked structure. While this networked configuration enhances resilience, transparency, and collaboration among various entities, it also introduces technical challenges, particularly in establishing seamless communication between network elements.

Consider the block creation process. It entails all active nodes sharing the transactions they've received, sending the hash for the set of transactions, reaching a consensus, and managing various other information exchanges.

All these operations must occur seamlessly within milliseconds or seconds. Moreover, these network elements are often located across different geographic locations, may use diverse tech stacks, and can be controlled by different entities. The communication protocols must not only be efficient but also prioritize security and prevent any form of centralization at the same time.

Communication protocols are the set of rules and conventions governing the communication between different components within Web3 systems.

The role of communication protocols in Web3 is comprehensive, covering decentralization, security, interoperability, and efficiency.

Let's delve into the key roles that communication protocols play.

10.3.4.2 Key Roles of Communication Protocols in Web3

10.3.4.2.1 Decentralization

Communication protocols, especially those enabling peer-to-peer (P2P) communication, are crucial for the decentralized nature of blockchain networks. This direct communication between nodes eliminates the need for centralized intermediaries, fostering a distributed and trustless environment.

The stability of decentralization in blockchain and Web3 relies on secure and trustless communication among network elements.

10.3.4.2.2 Consensus and Network Integrity

Effective communication among nodes is essential for decentralized systems to achieve consensus on the blockchain's state, validate transactions, and maintain the integrity of the distributed ledger. Communication protocols play a crucial role in facilitating consensus among network participants.

10.3.4.2.3 Interoperability

Communication protocols are essential for facilitating interactions within a blockchain and promoting connectivity between diverse blockchains and ecosystem components like identity systems and storage networks. These protocols ensure interoperability, enabling a smooth exchange of assets and information among various network participants in Web3 systems.

10.3.4.2.4 Secure Transactions and Messaging

Blockchain networks often need to handle sensitive transactions and data. Secure communication protocols guarantee the confidentiality and integrity of the information exchanged among nodes and other network participants.

10.3.4.2.5 Smart Contract and DApp Communication

Communication protocols facilitate interaction between smart contracts and decentralized applications (DApps), allowing smart contracts to communicate, respond to external events, and exchange information within the blockchain ecosystem. DApps rely on protocols like JSON-RPC and GraphQL to query and retrieve blockchain data, simplifying the development process and improving user experiences.

10.3.4.2.6 Scalability

Scalability is emerging as a key factor in the design of blockchains and Web3 systems, evident in the ongoing development efforts within Ethereum.

With numerous scaling elements operating off-chain, ensuring efficient and secure communication with these scaling systems, such as Rollups, becomes crucial. Communication protocols play a significant role in this regard.

10.3.4.3 Classification of Communication Protocols

Okay, now let us learn about different types of communication protocols.

10.3.4.3.1 Classification Based on Functionality

10.3.4.3.1.1 Inter-blockchain Communication (IBC): Inter-bBlockchain communication (IBC) protocols are created to enable interoperability and communication among diverse blockchains. The capability for blockchains to communicate and exchange information is essential for establishing a connected and interoperable decentralized ecosystem. Numerous IBC protocols have been developed to fulfill this requirement, enabling the transfer of assets and data across distinct blockchain networks.

Examples include gRPC, Tendermint RPC, AMQP, etc.

10.3.4.3.1.2 P2P Communication Protocols: These protocols facilitate peer-to-peer communication among nodes within a blockchain network, enabling the exchange of transactions, block information, and other relevant information.

Examples include Whisper, Ethereum RLPx, and Libp2p, etc.

10.3.4.3.2 Classification Based on Use Cases

10.3.4.3.2.1 Messaging Protocols: Examples include protocols like Whisper in Ethereum or Secure Scuttlebutt for decentralized and private messaging.

10.3.4.3.2.2 Blockchain Transaction Propagation: These protocols facilitate the propagation of transactions and blocks within a blockchain network, ensuring the synchronization of the distributed ledger.

E.g. Gossip Protocol, Whisper Protocol, Flooding (Broadcast) Protocol, Compact Block Relay (BIP 152), XThin Protocol, Falcon Relay Network (FRN), and Parallel Validation and Propagation.

10.3.4.3.2.3 Smart Contract Communication: These protocols facilitate communication between smart contracts and decentralized applications (DApps) within a blockchain network.

Okay, now let us discuss some specific protocols.

10.3.4.4 Libp2p

Libp2p is a modular network stack and protocol collection designed for constructing peer-to-peer (P2P) applications. It offers a versatile set of tools and libraries essential for developing decentralized and distributed systems.

Libp2p, aligning with decentralization and peer-to-peer principles in Web3, stands out for its modular design. Its modularity allows developers to customize functionalities, making it versatile for diverse Web3 applications. The framework emphasizes decentralized connectivity, supporting direct peer-to-peer communication without intermediaries.

Libp2p is transport-agnostic, working across protocols like TCP, UDP, and WebSockets, ensuring adaptability to various network conditions. Security is a priority, with cryptographic protocols, secure channels, encryption, and authentication for robust data protection in Web3.

The incorporation of decentralized peer discovery in Libp2p enables autonomous node connections, a crucial element for establishing peer-to-peer networks in Web3 applications. Libp2p's versatility extends across decentralized storage, content distribution, identity management, and blockchain networks, making it adaptable to the specific requirements of various decentralized applications within the Web3 ecosystem.

10.3.4.5 JSON-RPC (JSON Remote Procedure Call)

JSON-RPC, using JSON as its serialization format, offers a lightweight and human-readable approach for easy parsing and comprehension. While this aids in debugging, the human-readable aspect may be less efficient in size and speed compared to binary formats.

JSON-RPC follows a stateless approach, ensuring independence for each client request, and simplifying communication.

Versatile and adaptable to various transport protocols, JSON-RPC is commonly used over HTTP, making it ideal for web communication. Its language-agnostic nature enables communication between services implemented in different programming languages.

In the blockchain context, JSON-RPC serves as a vital communication protocol between clients (wallets, dApps) and blockchain nodes. Platforms like Ethereum extensively use JSON-RPC for interacting with smart contracts, allowing clients to send transactions, invoke smart contract methods, retrieve states, or deploy new contracts.

10.3.4.6 gRPC (Google Remote Procedure Call)

gRPC, created by Google, is an open-source RPC framework that simplifies communication and data exchange among distributed systems. It streamlines the development of scalable microservices architectures by adhering to the RPC paradigm for intuitive interactions. With support for

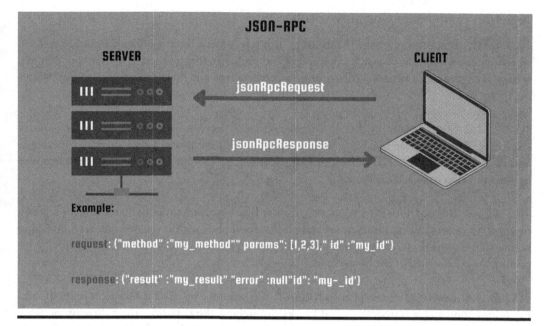

Figure 10.17   Visual representation of JSON-RPC.

multiple programming languages, gRPC promotes interoperability in polyglot (written in different programming languages) microservices architectures.

gRPC is valuable for constructing efficient and scalable auxiliary services, tools, or middleware that interact with smart contracts or blockchain nodes. While JSON-RPC or REST are commonly used for core interactions with blockchain networks, gRPC is suitable for developing additional services in a more efficient and scalable manner.

10.3.4.7 Gossip Protocol

A gossip protocol is a decentralized communication protocol used by network nodes to share information in a peer-to-peer manner. It operates by allowing nodes to randomly exchange data with their peers. When a node engages in this process, it becomes a source of information for others, establishing a distributed and fault-tolerant communication pattern.

Gossip protocols operate in a decentralized manner without a central authority, allowing nodes to communicate directly for a resilient and distributed system.

Functioning asynchronously with random peer selection, these protocols ensure well-distributed data dissemination and provide fault tolerance, making them suitable for expanding networks.

Widely implemented in blockchain and peer-to-peer systems, gossip protocols play a crucial role in establishing resilient and scalable decentralized communication patterns.

Gossip protocols are used for various purposes – enabling consensus processes, peer discovery, event broadcasting, state synchronization, fault detection, etc.

10.3.4.7.1 Examples of Gossip Protocols

10.3.4.7.1.1 Epidemic Gossip Protocol: This represents a basic version of a gossip protocol, where nodes consistently choose random peers and exchange information in a recurring manner. It finds extensive use in situations demanding a decentralized and scalable approach to disseminating information.

10.3.4.7.1.2 Scuttlebutt Protocol: Scuttlebutt is a decentralized communication protocol employing a peer-to-peer approach with a gossip-style mechanism for propagating messages. Specifically crafted for social networking applications, it enables users to share messages and updates in a decentralized fashion.

10.3.4.7.1.3 Bitcoin Gossip Protocol: In the Bitcoin context, the network utilizes a gossip protocol for disseminating transactions and blocks. Each node within the network communicates with a subset of its peers, sharing information about new transactions and blocks, thereby maintaining the consistency of the blockchain.

10.3.4.7.1.4 Ethereum Gossip Subprotocol: Ethereum employs a gossip protocol to distribute information about transactions and blocks throughout the network. The Ethereum network depends on peer-to-peer communication to achieve consensus and uphold a consistent state.

10.3.4.7.1.5 Hashgraph Gossip Protocol: Hedera Hashgraph, a distributed ledger technology, utilizes a gossip protocol to disseminate information regarding transactions and achieve consensus. This design aims to deliver high throughput and fairness within a decentralized network.

Various gossip protocols, such as the Cassandra Gossip Protocol in Apache Cassandra, SWIM, and Rumor Mongering in Amazon DynamoDB, are employed in different distributed systems for efficient communication and fault tolerance.

10.3.4.8 Flooding (Broadcast) Protocol

The flooding protocol, or broadcast protocol, is a simple communication method used in computer networks to distribute information from one node to all others. In this approach, a message is broadcasted to neighbors, and each receiving node rebroadcasts it until all nodes have received it.

While effective in small, well-connected networks for initial peer discovery, challenges like broadcast storms and scalability issues arise in larger networks due to redundancy and resource consumption.

A broadcast storm is a network issue characterized by an excess of broadcast or multicast messages, overwhelming the network's bandwidth and causing performance degradation or network collapse.

In controlled Web3 environments, flooding protocols can be manageable with careful management to avoid inefficiencies.

10.3.4.9 Compact Block Relay (BIP 152)

Compact Block Relay, introduced in Bitcoin Improvement Proposal 152 (BIP-152), is a protocol enhancement for the Bitcoin network designed to optimize block transmission among nodes.

It achieves efficiency and reduces bandwidth usage by employing a "header-first" approach, initially sending a compact block with essential information. This allows nodes to request only missing transactions, minimizing redundant data transmission.

BIP 152 aims to improve Bitcoin network efficiency, supporting scalability and resilience. In the context of Web3, such efficient block relay mechanisms contribute to faster and more reliable data propagation, crucial for staying synchronized with the latest blockchain state.

10.3.4.10 XThin Protocol

Xtreme Thinblocks (XThin), associated with the Bitcoin Unlimited client, is a technology aimed at improving the efficiency of block propagation within the Bitcoin network. XThin optimizes network performance by minimizing data requirements during block transmission.

It specifically targets the efficient dissemination of new blocks across the network, reducing redundant data and enhancing bandwidth efficiency. This optimization contributes to faster block propagation, addressing scalability concerns and improving overall network performance.

10.3.4.11 Ethereum RLPx (Recursive Length Prefix Multiplexing)

RLPx is the communication protocol for Ethereum nodes, establishing the Ethereum peer-to-peer network. Combining the encoding principles of RLP (Recursive Length Prefix) and the framework of DevP2P (Dev Peer-to-Peer), RLPx facilitates efficient communication among Ethereum nodes.

RLP, a binary encoding method, serializes data structures in Ethereum. On the other hand, DevP2P provides the framework for peer-to-peer protocols in Ethereum. RLPx introduces multiplexing, enhancing communication efficiency, and includes encryption and authentication for secure data exchange between nodes. Multiplexing refers to the ability to handle multiple data streams or transactions simultaneously over a single network channel, optimizing resource usage and improving network efficiency.

Vital for Ethereum operations, RLPx supports functions like transaction broadcasting, block propagation, and blockchain state synchronization, ensuring reliable interaction for decentralized applications (dApps) with the Ethereum blockchain.

10.3.4.12 Whisper Protocol

Whisper, an Ethereum messaging protocol, supports decentralized and secure communication in line with the Web3 vision. Integral to Ethereum, it enables private peer-to-peer messaging within the network. Prioritizing privacy, Whisper encrypts messages for only the intended recipient's access.

Supporting asynchronous messaging, it allows flexible communication without a simultaneous online presence. Nodes can subscribe to specific topics for relevant messages. From user communication to decentralized application transactions, Whisper is crucial for coordinating Web3 ecosystem components.

10.3.4.13 AMQP and GraphQL

AMQP (Advanced Message Queuing Protocol) facilitates asynchronous communication in distributed environments, supporting loose coupling between applications. It enables message queueing for scalability and fault tolerance, using exchanges to route messages based on rules.

GraphQL, developed by Facebook, serves as a query language for APIs and a runtime for data queries. Offering efficiency over traditional REST APIs, GraphQL provides a unified endpoint for data manipulation, reducing unnecessary network usage.

Okay, let us end our discussion on communication protocols here.

10.3.5 Interoperability in Web3

10.3.5.1 Interoperability in the Traditional Internet

To appreciate the importance of interoperability in Web3, it's helpful to draw a comparison with the seamlessly interconnected nature of the traditional Internet.

Consider the marvel of plugging in a server from any corner of the globe and instantly possessing an identity, expressed through an IP address, that is universally recognized by all other servers worldwide.

The traditional internet's multistakeholder model involves entities like IANA, ICANN, and IETF. IANA (Internet Assigned Numbers Authority) manages global IP address allocation, ICANN (Internet Corporation for Assigned Names and Numbers) coordinates DNS and domain names, and IETF (Internet Engineering Task Force), a community-driven organization, develops internet standards.

The seamless communication and cooperation facilitated by these entities have been fundamental to the internet's success, and as we transition to Web3, ensuring similar levels of interoperability becomes paramount for the continued growth and functionality of the decentralized web.

However, the internet, developed over the span of 40 years, exhibits a distinct characteristic: centralized control.

ICANN holds significant influence through managing the DNS root zone file and approving Top-Level Domains (TLDs), including the centralized process for introducing new gTLDs (Generic top-level domains). It plays a crucial role in overseeing IP address allocation, DNS root zone management, and protocol parameter assignment.

Concerns have been raised regarding the centralization of control within ICANN, highlighting the need for checks and balances in overseeing critical Internet resources.

10.3.5.2 Why Do we Need Interoperability in Web3?

Web3 is not a homogeneous ecosystem. It comprises diverse public blockchains (e.g., Ethereum, Solana) and private blockchains like those built using Hyperledger Fabric or Corda.

These blockchains do not readily talk to each other.

Apart from that, beyond handling information, blockchains also manage funds, requiring efficient and secure transfers between different blockchains. This process of secure transfers must ensure trust among entities without relying on a central authority.

Contrasting with the centralized financial system where central banks act as trusted authorities in fund transfers between banks, Web3 can't afford such centralization.

So, Web3 does not only need interoperability but decentralized interoperability.

10.3.5.3 *What Is Interoperability?*

Interoperability in the context of blockchains pertains to the seamless communication, information sharing, and transactions between different blockchain networks.

For blockchain technology to achieve widespread adoption and scalability, interoperability is crucial.

10.3.5.4 *Types of Interoperability*

There are different types of interoperability.

10.3.5.4.1 Protocol Interoperability

Ensures effective communication among different blockchain networks by adhering to shared communication protocols and standards.

10.3.5.4.2 Asset Interoperability

Enables smooth movement of assets (e.g., cryptocurrencies, tokens) across different blockchains, preserving their attributes and value across various platforms.

10.3.5.4.3 Data Interoperability

Facilitates the seamless exchange and sharing of data between blockchain networks, empowering decentralized applications (dApps) to access and utilize data from multiple sources.

10.3.5.5 *Benefits of Blockchain Interoperability*

10.3.5.5.1 Enhanced Accessibility and Expanded Ecosystem

Interoperability broadens user access to assets and data across different blockchains, fostering inclusivity in blockchain applications. It encourages collaboration and integration among platforms, contributing to the growth of a diverse ecosystem with a broader range of applications and services.

10.3.5.5.2 Asset Portability and Cross-platform Tokenization

Interoperability allows for the smooth transfer of digital assets, such as tokens or cryptocurrencies, across different blockchains, improving liquidity and flexibility in asset management. It contributes to the development of a unified token economy, promoting greater liquidity and dynamism in the digital asset ecosystem.

10.3.5.5.3 Cross-chain Smart Contracts

Interoperability facilitates the execution of smart contracts across multiple blockchains, empowering decentralized applications to leverage unique platform features. This fosters innovation and efficiency in the development of complex, cross-chain applications.

10.3.5.5.4 Scalability Solutions and Improved Efficiency

Interoperability can address scalability challenges by facilitating transactions across multiple blockchains, distributing network load, and enhancing overall transaction throughput.

10.3.5.6 Interoperability Mechanisms

Now, let us dive into various interoperability mechanisms.

10.3.5.6.1 Cross-chain Communication Standards

Cross-chain communication standards are crucial for achieving interoperability between diverse blockchain networks. These standards define protocols and conventions to enable smooth communication, asset transfer, and data exchange among different blockchains.

The goal is to create a unified framework that promotes trustless interaction across various blockchain platforms, and multiple projects are actively involved in developing these standards.

Examples of cross-chain communication protocols include the Interledger Protocol (ILP) and Cosmos Inter-Blockchain Communication (IBC).

The Interledger Protocol (ILP) facilitates interoperability between payment networks and ledgers, including blockchains. It establishes a standard for routing payments across different systems, enabling seamless value transfer. ILP is used in cross-border payments and financial transactions, connecting various payment networks and blockchains.

The Inter-Blockchain Communication (IBC) protocol, part of the Cosmos network, enables communication and asset transfer among independent blockchains. IBC standardizes message exchange within the Cosmos ecosystem, facilitating the transfer of tokens between connected blockchains.

10.3.5.6.2 Cross-chain Bridges

Cross-chain bridges act as protocols or mechanisms enabling asset transfer between separate blockchain networks. Their primary role is to connect isolated blockchain ecosystems, promote interoperability, and enable seamless token or data movement across diverse networks.

Unlike cross-chain communication protocols that facilitate information sharing, cross-chain bridges specifically facilitate the transfer of assets (tokens) between blockchains. They use smart contracts or validators to lock assets on one blockchain and mint equivalent assets on another. This process employs secure and trustless mechanisms to ensure asset integrity during the transfer.

Some examples of cross-chain bridges include Wormhole and Avalanche Bridge.

Wormhole serves as a cross-chain bridge, enabling the transfer of assets across numerous blockchains like Ethereum, Solana, BNB Chain, Polygon, Avalanche, Polkadot, and more. Its functionalities include seamless token transfer, NFT transfer across blockchains, user deposits on supported chains, and support for multi-chain apps.

The Avalanche Bridge, integral to the Avalanche network, facilitates interoperability and asset transfer between the Avalanche C-Chain and other blockchains. As a cross-chain bridge, it allows the movement of assets, including tokens and digital assets, across diverse blockchain ecosystems.

10.3.5.6.3 Notary Schemes

Notary schemes, also known as notary-based inter-blockchain protocols, employ a trusted entity known as a notary to facilitate interoperability across different blockchains.

In a notary-based cross-chain transaction mechanism, the notary acts as an intermediary, validating the state or legitimacy of transactions on one blockchain and enabling another blockchain to accept this information without direct communication. The notary, acting as a centralized authority, establishes trust and coordination between the involved blockchains.

When a user initiates a cross-chain transaction, the notary verifies the transaction details, creates cryptographic proof of its validity, and transmits this proof to the other blockchain, allowing it to proceed with the necessary actions based on the notary's confirmation.

10.3.5.6.4 Atomic Swaps

Atomic swaps, also known as atomic cross-chain swaps, represent a mechanism enabling users to directly exchange cryptocurrencies across different blockchains without relying on intermediaries or trusted third parties.

These swaps prioritize trustlessness, security, and decentralization, ensuring that the asset exchange occurs atomically – either completing the transaction entirely or not at all. This is to avoid the risk of partial fulfillment or the risk of one party not receiving their assets.

Atomic swaps eliminate the need for trust between parties. The exchange occurs in a way that neither party can cheat or back out of the trade once it has been initiated.

Atomic swaps commonly utilize smart contracts, specifically Hashed TimeLock Contracts (HTLCs), incorporating cryptographic hash functions for conditions and time locks to define specific windows for swap completion.

Atomic swaps can be classified into on-chain atomic swaps and off-chain atomic swaps.

- **On-chain atomic swaps** are the traditional form of atomic swaps where the entire process occurs on the blockchain.
- **Off-chain atomic swaps** occur off the main blockchain and are often facilitated by layer-2 scaling solutions like the Lightning Network. Off-chain swaps enable faster and more scalable transactions by keeping most of the exchange details off the main blockchain.

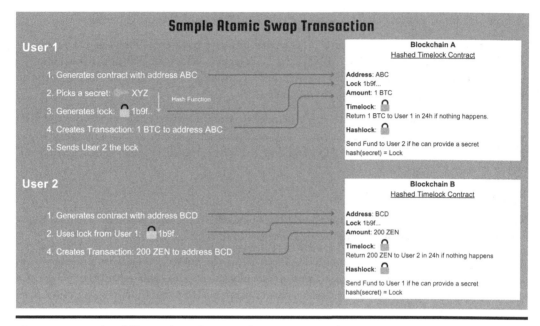

Figure 10.18 Visual illustration of an atomic swap transaction.

Atomic swaps are used in decentralized exchanges (DEXs) where they enable peer-to-peer trading without relying on centralized exchanges. Users can swap cryptocurrencies across different blockchains without the need for an intermediary.

These swaps are also used for cross-chain payments where merchants or service providers can accept payments in different cryptocurrencies, and the payer can make a payment using a different blockchain.

Let us end this chapter with a brief discussion of the role of decentralized identity solutions on Web3 networks. We have dedicated a whole chapter to this topic and hope you have already gone through the chapter.

10.3.6 Decentralized Identity Solutions on Web3 Networks

Web3 networks are supposed to be all about openness, but lately, we've seen some serious security issues. To beef up security, we need an authentication layer. But using the usual centralized username/password setup seems like a step backward. It creates a single point of failure and raises privacy red flags.

Decentralized identity solutions empower users to manage their identity without relying on a central authority, enhancing security in Web3 networks. By leveraging blockchain technology and encryption, these solutions secure data without centralizing sensitive information. Users can selectively share necessary details, reducing the risk of significant data breaches and providing increased privacy control.

Beyond security, decentralized identity contributes to resilience, eliminating the risk of catastrophic failures associated with centralized databases. Even if one component fails, the decentralized nature ensures continued functionality.

In summary, decentralized identity solutions are a strategic choice for Web3 networks, prioritizing user control, privacy, and security in the decentralized web landscape.

In the next chapter, we will discuss how we can incorporate these Web3 elements into traditional architectures to bring qualities of Web3 systems (especially decentralization) to traditional technical systems.

Bibliography

AMQP. (n.d.). AMQP: Home. Retrieved February 2, 2024, from https://www.amqp.org/

The Apache Software Foundation. (n.d.). *Frequently Asked Questions | Apache Cassandra Documentation.* Apache Cassandra. Retrieved February 2, 2024, from https://cassandra.apache.org/doc/stable/cassandra/faq/

Avalanche. (n.d.). *Avalanche Bridge™.* Avalanche Support. Retrieved February 6, 2024, from https://support.avax.network/en/collections/3073022-avalanche-bridge

Bagdasaryan, E. (n.d.). *Gossip Protocols.* Cornell CS. Retrieved February 2, 2024, from https://www.cs.cornell.edu/courses/cs6410/2016fa/slides/19-p2p-gossip.pdf

Band Protocol. (n.d.). Band Protocol. Retrieved February 2, 2024, from https://www.bandprotocol.com/

Beniiche, A. (n.d.). *A Study of Blockchain Oracles.* arxiv.org. Retrieved February 5, 2024, from https://arxiv.org/pdf/2004.07140.pdf

Beyer, S. (2019, April 5). *What is Ethereum Whisper? A Detailed Guide.* Mycryptopedia. Retrieved December 28, 2023, from https://www.mycryptopedia.com/ethereum-whisper-a-detailed-guide/

Bitcoinwiki. (n.d.). *Hashed TimeLock Contract – BitcoinWiki.* BitcoinWiki. Retrieved February 2, 2024, from https://bitcoinwiki.org/wiki/hashed-timelock-contracts

Bitcointalk. (2016, June 8). *[Fundamentals] Pre-announce: FALCON, Fast Relay Network for Bitcoin Blocks.* Bitcoin Forum. Retrieved February 2, 2024, from https://bitcointalk.org/index.php?topic=1503970.0

Bulletproofs | Stanford Applied Crypto Group. (n.d.). Applied Cryptography Group. Retrieved December 28, 2023, from https://crypto.stanford.edu/bulletproofs/

Bünz, B., Bootl, J., Boneh, D., Poelstra, A., Wuille, P., & Maxwell, G. (n.d.). *Bulletproofs: Short Proofs for Confidential Transactions and More.* Cryptology ePrint Archive. Retrieved January 4, 2024, from https://eprint.iacr.org/2017/1066.pdf

Buterin, Vitalik. The Limits to Blockchain Scalability, 23 May 2021, https://vitalik.eth.limo/general/2021/05/23/scaling.html. Accessed 13 June 2024.

Buterin, V. (2022, August 29). *Demystifying the Technical Properties of Sharding: Why it is Great.* HackerNoon. Retrieved January 4, 2024, from https://hackernoon.com/demystifying-the-technical-properties-of-sharding-can-tell-us-why-it-is-great

Chainlink. (n.d.). Chainlink: The Industry-Standard Web3 Services Platform. Retrieved February 2, 2024, from https://chain.link/

CipherTrace. (n.d.). Crypto Intelligence and Blockchain Analytics - Data Analysis. Retrieved February 2, 2024, from https://ciphertrace.com/

Corallo, M. (n.d.). *BIP-152.* Bitcoin Cash Protocol. Retrieved February 2, 2024, from https://reference.cash/protocol/forks/bip-0152

Cosmos. (n.d.). *IBC - Ecosystem.* Cosmos. Retrieved February 6, 2024, from https://cosmos.network/ibc/

Costa, P. (2023, September 25). *Oracles | ethereum.org.* Ethereum. Retrieved December 28, 2023, from https://ethereum.org/en/developers/docs/oracles/

Danksharding | ethereum.org. (n.d.). Ethereum. Retrieved December 28, 2023, from https://ethereum.org/en/roadmap/danksharding/

Das, A., Gupta, I., & Motivala, A. (n.d.). *SWIM: Scalable Weakly-consistent Infection-style Process Group Membership Protocol.* Cornell CS. Retrieved February 2, 2024, from https://www.cs.cornell.edu/projects/Quicksilver/public_pdfs/SWIM.pdf

Ethereum. (n.d.). *devp2p/rlpx.md at master · ethereum/devp2p*. GitHub. Retrieved February 2, 2024, from https://github.com/ethereum/devp2p/blob/master/rlpx.md

Ethereum. (n.d.). *ethereum/devp2p: Ethereum Peer-to-Peer Networking Specifications*. GitHub. Retrieved February 2, 2024, from https://github.com/ethereum/devp2p

Etherscan. (n.d.). Ethereum (ETH) Blockchain Explorer. Retrieved February 2, 2024, from https://etherscan.io/

Etherscan. (n.d.). *Ethereum Daily Transactions Chart*. Etherscan. Retrieved January 4, 2024, from https://etherscan.io/chart/tx

Etherscan. (n.d.). *Ethereum Network Pending Transactions Chart*. Etherscan. Retrieved January 4, 2024, from https://etherscan.io/chart/pendingtx

Ethereum. (n.d.). *State Channels | ethereum.org*. Ethereum. Retrieved January 4, 2024, from https://ethereum.org/en/developers/docs/scaling/state-channels/

Ethereum. (2022, February 25). *EIP-4844: Shard Blob Transactions*. Ethereum Improvement Proposals. Retrieved January 4, 2024, from https://eips.ethereum.org/EIPS/eip-4844

Ethereum. (2023, September 29). *Plasma Chains | ethereum.org*. Ethereum. Retrieved January 4, 2024, from https://ethereum.org/en/developers/docs/scaling/plasma/

Ethereum. (2023, October 25). *Recursive-Length Prefix (RLP) Serialization | ethereum.org*. Ethereum. Retrieved February 2, 2024, from https://ethereum.org/developers/docs/data-structures-and-encoding/rlp

A., Esteban, J., & Barabonkov, D. (n.d.). Ring Signatures - Analysis and Implementation. Retrieved February 2, 2024, from https://courses.csail.mit.edu/6.857/2020/projects/17-Barabonkov-Esteban-Fabrega.pdf

Goldwasser, S., Micali, S., & Rackoff, C. (n.d.). The Knowledge Complexity of Interactive Proof-Systems. . Retrieved February 2, 2024, from https://people.csail.mit.edu/silvio/Selected%20Scientific%20Papers/Proof%20Systems/The_Knowledge_Complexity_Of_Interactive_Proof_Systems.pdf

The GraphQL Foundation. (n.d.). GraphQL | A Query Language for Your API. Retrieved February 2, 2024, from https://graphql.org/

gRPC.io. Retrieved February 2, 2024, from https://grpc.io/

gRPC Authors. (2023, February 16). *Introduction to gRPC*. gRPC. Retrieved February 2, 2024, from https://grpc.io/docs/what-is-grpc/introduction/

Harvard University. (n.d.). *Differential Privacy*. Harvard University Privacy Tools Project. Retrieved February 2, 2024, from https://privacytools.seas.harvard.edu/differential-privacy

Hedera Hashgraph. Hedera https://hedera.com/learning/hedera-hashgraph. Accessed 13 June 2024.

Herlihy, M. (n.d.). *Atomic Cross-Chain Swaps*. arxiv.org. Retrieved February 6, 2024, from https://arxiv.org/pdf/1801.09515.pdf

IEEE. (2023, October 21). *What Is Homomorphic Encryption?* IEEE Digital Privacy. Retrieved February 2, 2024, from https://digitalprivacy.ieee.org/publications/topics/what-is-homomorphic-encryption

IETF HTTP Working Group. (n.d.). HTTP/2. Retrieved February 2, 2024, from https://http2.github.io/

Interledger Foundation. (n.d.). *Interledger Protocol® | Interledger*. Interledger Foundation. Retrieved February 6, 2024, from https://interledger.org/developers/get-started/

IPFS. (n.d.). IPFS Tech. Retrieved December 28, 2023, from https://ipfs.tech

Keep SEZC. (n.d.). Keep Network: Keep. Retrieved February 2, 2024, from https://keep.network/

Layer 2 | ethereum.org. (n.d.). Ethereum. Retrieved December 28, 2023, from https://ethereum.org/en/layer-2/

Lightning Network. (n.d.). Lightning Network. Retrieved January 4, 2024, from https://lightning.network

Lindell, Y. (n.d.). *Secure Multiparty Computation (MPC)*. Cryptology ePrint Archive. Retrieved January 4, 2024, from https://eprint.iacr.org/2020/300

Liquid Network. (n.d.). Liquid Network: Purpose-Built for Asset Issuance. Retrieved February 2, 2024, from https://liquid.net/

Mark Newman, Albert-László Barabási, & Duncan J. Watts. (2023). *The Structure and Dynamics of Networks*. Princeton University Press. Retrieved December 28, 2023, from https://books.google.co.in/books/about/The_Structure_and_Dynamics_of_Networks.html?id=xLfQCwAAQBAJ&redir_esc=y

Monero. (n.d.). Home | Monero - Secure, Private, Untraceable. Retrieved February 2, 2024, from https://www.getmonero.org/

MPCM Technologies LLC. (n.d.). JSON-RPC. Retrieved February 2, 2024, from https://www.jsonrpc.org/

Musharraf, M. (2021, November 15). *What is the Blockchain Trilemma?* Ledger. Retrieved December 28, 2023, from https://www.ledger.com/academy/what-is-the-blockchain-trilemma

Nikolaev, M Y., & Fortin, C. (2023, October 30). *Systems Thinking Ontology of Emergent Properties for Complex Engineering Systems.* IOPscience. Retrieved December 28, 2023, from https://iopscience.iop.org/article/10.1088/1742-6596/1687/1/012005/pdf

NIST. (n.d.). *Preimage Resistance - Glossary | CSRC.* NIST Computer Security Resource Center. Retrieved February 2, 2024, from https://csrc.nist.gov/glossary/term/preimage_resistance

Oasis Network. (n.d.). Oasis Network. Retrieved February 2, 2024, from https://oasisprotocol.org/

OMG Network. OMG Network Docs, 26 January 2021, https://docs.omg.network/ Accessed 13 June 2024.

Optimistic Rollups | ethereum.org. (2023, October 15). Ethereum. Retrieved December 28, 2023, from https://ethereum.org/en/developers/docs/scaling/optimistic-rollups/

O'Reilly Media. (n.d.). *Whisper - Mastering Blockchain - Second Edition [Book].* O'Reilly. Retrieved February 2, 2024, from https://www.oreilly.com/library/view/mastering-blockchain/9781788839044/179582cb-9b26-4f60-b176-7e577ed9a325.xhtml

Packt. (n.d.). *Learn Ethereum.* Learn Ethereum. Retrieved February 2, 2024, from https://subscription.packtpub.com/book/data/9781789954111/11/ch11lvl1sec64/ethereum-messages-whisper

Polygon Labs. (n.d.). *Polygon PoS | The Most Efficient Blockchain Protocol.* Polygon Technology. Retrieved January 4, 2024, from https://polygon.technology/polygon-pos

Protocol Labs. (n.d.). libp2p. Retrieved February 2, 2024, from https://libp2p.io/

Protocol Labs. (n.d.). libp2p Connectivity. Retrieved February 2, 2024, from https://connectivity.libp2p.io/

Provable. (2019, August 28). Provable Documentation. Retrieved February 2, 2024, from https://docs.provable.xyz/

Response: Xthin Block ("xthinblock"). Bitcoin Cash Protocol. Retrieved February 2, 2024, from https://reference.cash/protocol/network/messages/xthinblock

Rizun, P. R. (2016, May 30). *Towards Massive On-Chain Scaling: Presenting Our Block Propagation Results With Xthin.* Medium. Retrieved February 2, 2024, from https://medium.com/@peter_r/towards-massive-on-chain-scaling-presenting-our-block-propagation-results-with-xthin-da54e55dc0e4

Sarkar, R. (n.d.). Epidemics and Gossip Algorithms. Retrieved February 2, 2024, from https://www.inf.ed.ac.uk/teaching/courses/stn/files1819/slides/epidemics.pdf

Schnorr, C. P. (n.d.). Schnorr's Protocol. Retrieved February 2, 2024, from http://www.lsv.fr/Software/spore/schnorr.pdf

Scorechain S. A. (2017, November 9). scorechain.com. Retrieved February 2, 2024, from https://lp.scorechain.com/demo/blockchain-compliance-intro

Scuttlebutt Protocol Guide. (n.d.). SSBC. Retrieved December 28, 2023, from https://ssbc.github.io/scuttlebutt-protocol-guide/

Secure Scuttlebutt. (n.d.). Scuttlebot. Retrieved January 4, 2024, from https://scuttlebot.io/more/protocols/secure-scuttlebutt.html

Sharma, T. K. (n.d.). *Centralized Oracles Vs. Decentralized Oracles.* Blockchain Council. Retrieved December 28, 2023, from https://www.blockchain-council.org/blockchain/centralized-oracles-vs-decentralized-oracles/

Sidechains | ethereum.org. (n.d.). Ethereum. Retrieved December 28, 2023, from https://ethereum.org/en/developers/docs/scaling/sidechains/

State Channels | ethereum.org. (2023, January 19). Ethereum. Retrieved December 28, 2023, from https://ethereum.org/en/developers/docs/scaling/state-channels/

Tendermint. (n.d.). Tendermint RPC v0.34 OAS3. Retrieved February 2, 2024, from https://docs.tendermint.com/v0.34/rpc/

Thurman, Andrew. "Axie Infinity's Ronin Network Suffers $625M Exploit." CoinDesk, 29 March 2022, https://www.coindesk.com/tech/2022/03/29/axie-infinitys-ronin-network-suffers-625m-exploit/. Accessed 13 June 2024.

Vadhan, S. (n.d.). Collision-Resistant Hash Functions. Retrieved February 2, 2024, from https://people.seas.harvard.edu/~salil/cs127/fall13/lec18.pdf

What Is A Cross Chain Bridge? (2023, August 9). Chainlink. Retrieved December 28, 2023, from https://chain.link/education-hub/cross-chain-bridge

Willkomm, D. (n.d.). Flooding. Retrieved February 2, 2024, from https://doc.omnetpp.org/inet/api-current/neddoc/inet.networklayer.flooding.Flooding.html

Wormhole. (n.d.). The Best Way to Build cross-chain. Retrieved February 6, 2024, from https://wormhole.com

Wormhole. (n.d.). Wormhole - Simple, Private File Sharing. Retrieved January 4, 2024, from https://wormhole.app

Xiong, A., Liu, G., & Zhu, Q. (2023, May 19). *A Notary Group-based Cross-chain Mechanism.* sciencedirect.com. Retrieved February 6, 2024, from https://www.sciencedirect.com/science/article/pii/S235286482200061X

Zcash. Zcash: Privacy-protecting digital currency, https://z.cash/. Accessed 13 June 2024.

Zero-knowledge proofs | ethereum.org. (n.d.). Ethereum. Retrieved December 28, 2023, from https://ethereum.org/en/zero-knowledge-proofs/

Zero-Knowledge rollups | ethereum.org. (2023, November 17). Ethereum. Retrieved December 28, 2023, from https://ethereum.org/en/developers/docs/scaling/zk-rollups/

Zyskind, G., Nathan, O., & Pentland, A. (n.d.). *Enigma: Decentralized Computation Platform with Guaranteed Privacy.* MIT Living Lab. Retrieved February 2, 2024, from http://livinglab.mit.edu/wp-content/uploads/2016/01/enigma_full.pdf

Chapter 11

Decentralization of Traditional Architectures with Decentralization Layers

Sam Ghosh

11.1 What Is a Decentralization Layer?

A decentralization layer, as defined in this book, refers to a set of structural elements, including APIs, interfaces, and databases, that facilitate the integration of decentralization enablers – such as decentralized identity systems, decentralized storage, and distributed ledgers – into centralized systems as support networks.

A decentralization layer serves as the foundation for incorporating key Web3 qualities, such as decentralization, immutability, and trustlessness, into centralized technical infrastructures.

Now, before we discuss how we can bring Web3 qualities to traditional architectures, we need to be clear on what we can achieve and what we cannot.

11.2 What Can We Achieve with Decentralization Layers?

11.2.1 Decentralized Support Networks

The primary use of decentralization layers is to add a decentralized support network to a traditional centralized system. For example, a technical architect may want to store some media files on decentralized storage and manage the index and access records using a blockchain. We will discuss more on this later in this chapter.

DOI: 10.4324/9781003507352-11

11.2.2 Immutability of Records

We already discussed that blockchain records are immutable, i.e. once a record becomes part of a blockchain, it cannot be edited without consensus of the whole network. This property has various use cases such as in intellectual property management, supply chain, and managing content ownership, etc.

11.2.3 Trustless Access Controls

Trustless access control, facilitated by decentralized identity solutions, allows resource or service access without the need for verification by a central authority.

Trustless access control will allow the creation of products that can perform verifications, such as KYC, without the need to collect sensitive information. Users are often hesitant to share personal details with unrecognized services. Trustless access control will remove this friction by eliminating the need for users to provide sensitive information.

11.2.4 Privacy Focused Systems

The integration of decentralized identity systems enhances privacy in conventional systems by reducing reliance on centralized entities for identity verification. Self-sovereign identity allows selective disclosure of relevant information, reducing exposure of unnecessary details.

Verifiable credentials and zero-knowledge proofs in decentralized systems provide identity proof without disclosing sensitive data, enhancing privacy. These systems promote interoperability, reducing data silos and mitigating the impact of large-scale breaches.

Decentralized identity systems often include robust consent mechanisms, allowing users to explicitly grant permission for the use of their identity information. Users have more transparent control over how their identity data is used, fostering a privacy-centric approach where consent is a fundamental aspect of information sharing.

11.2.5 Global and Permissioned Transparency

Public blockchains offer global transparency by showing transactions publicly. This transparency can revolutionize government processes like tax collection and allocation of public resources. Tax payments and government expenditures recorded on the blockchain create tamper-proof ledgers. Public oversight allows citizens to monitor spending, reducing corruption risk.

The immutability of public blockchains prevents fraudulent activities.

In cases requiring higher privacy for the transaction records, private blockchains can be used. Say, for healthcare records or financial records, we can use private or permissioned blockchain-based "decentralization layers." We will discuss more about private blockchain-based "decentralization layers" in a later chapter.

11.3 What We Cannot Achieve with Decentralization Layers?

Okay, so we have some understanding of what we can achieve with decentralization layers and will discuss some use cases in detail later in this chapter but first let us understand what decentralization layers cannot do.

11.3.1 Use of Blockchain as Primary Storage

As we have discussed earlier, blockchains are very inefficient and expensive as storage.

However, we can incorporate a decentralized storage network (such as IPFS) in the "decentralization layer" for storage. Still, decentralized storage solutions may not match the performance of centralized storage. Decentralized storage may be slower, can be less scalable, and may be lacking in user experience. Apart from that, decentralized storage may introduce security and privacy challenges. The novel nature of these systems may also introduce adoption challenges.

Decentralization layers are not meant to convert a centralized system to a completely decentralized system but rather enhance effectiveness and performance with the use of decentralized systems.

11.3.2 Decentralized Governance

As mentioned above, decentralization layers are not meant to convert centralized systems to decentralized ones. So, we are only talking about technical decentralization here and not governance decentralization.

Decentralization layers are not meant to decentralize the network ownership and control through decentralized governance.

> *"Technical decentralization" arises from the node-based structure of DLTs and brings in higher availability and robustness to technical architectures.*
>
> *"Governance decentralization" refers to decentralized regulations of Web3 platforms with the use of DAOs or other decentralized governance mechanisms.*

11.3.3 Use of Crypto-assets as Currency and for Fundraising

As decentralization layers are not meant for decentralization of control, they are not supposed to use crypto-assets as currency and for fundraising as in the case of Web3 platforms.

Tokens and NFTs can be used to facilitate non-economic functionalities and record keeping. NFTs, especially, can add enormous value to "decentralization layers" without being used for economic purposes. For example, solbound tokens can be used to build decentralized reputation and credential systems.

11.4 Sample Implementations of Decentralization Layers

Okay, now let us discuss some sample implementations where decentralization layers can add value. These use cases are only representative and not meant for real-life implementations.

11.4.1 Decentralization Layer for Decentralized Access Management

11.4.1.1 Use Case

Imagine a centralized healthcare system where patient data is traditionally managed by a central authority, leading to concerns about data breaches, identity theft, and limited patient control over personal health information.

We want to enhance data privacy, security, and user control over health data by integrating a decentralized identity system into the existing centralized healthcare infrastructure.

Now, we can build a decentralization layer with the use of Hyperledger Indy that provides a decentralized identity framework, Ethereum blockchain for storage of decentralized identifiers and cryptographic proofs, a mobile wallet for managing decentralized identity credentials, and a react web interface that allows patients to manage their consent preferences. We can follow HL7 FHIR to ensure interoperability between the centralized healthcare system and the decentralized identity system. HL7 FHIR (Fast Healthcare Interoperability Resources) is a standard for exchanging healthcare information electronically, designed to facilitate interoperability between different healthcare systems and applications.

Solidity-based smart contracts can be implemented to manage access control. Patients' consent and authorization are encoded into smart contracts, allowing them to control who can access their health data and for what purposes.

zk-SNARKs-based zero-knowledge proofs can be employed to enable patients to prove specific health attributes (e.g., vaccination status) without revealing the underlying data. This enhances privacy during data sharing.

11.4.1.2 User Journey

11.4.1.2.1 Identity Creation

Patients download a healthcare app that integrates with the decentralized identity framework (Hyperledger Indy). They create decentralized identifiers (DIDs) and obtain verifiable credentials related to their health history from trusted issuers.

11.4.1.2.2 Blockchain Registration

Patients register their DIDs and cryptographic proofs on the Ethereum blockchain, ensuring the integrity and security of their identity records.

11.4.1.2.3 Access Control Setup

Smart contracts are deployed to manage access control. Patients set preferences for who can access their health data and under what conditions.

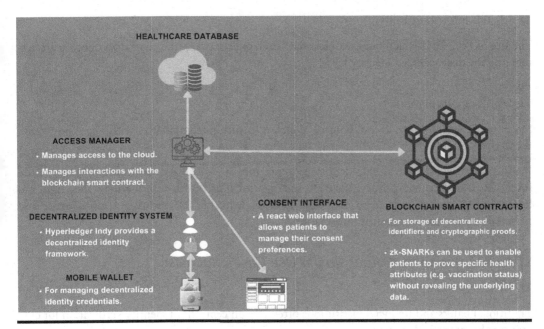

Figure 11.1   Sample decentralization layer for access management systems for a healthcare database.

11.4.1.2.4 Health Data Sharing

When visiting a healthcare provider, patients use their mobile wallet to selectively share verifiable credentials and zero-knowledge proofs for specific health attributes without revealing unnecessary details.

11.4.1.2.5 Consent Management

The react-based consent management interface allows patients to review and manage access permissions in real-time. They can revoke or grant access based on their preferences.

11.4.1.3 So, What Are the Benefits of such a System?

11.4.1.3.1 Enhanced Privacy

Patients have granular control over their health data, sharing only necessary information with trusted entities.

11.4.1.3.2 Security

Blockchain ensures the immutability and security of decentralized identifiers, reducing the risk of identity theft.

11.4.1.3.3 User Empowerment

Patients actively participate in managing their health data, promoting a sense of ownership and control.

11.4.1.3.4 Interoperability

The use of HL7 FHIR facilitates seamless data exchange between the centralized healthcare system and the decentralized identity layer.

11.4.1.3.5 Compliance

Smart contracts enforce access control policies, ensuring compliance with data protection regulations.

Incorporating decentralized identity systems into a centralized healthcare infrastructure improves patient-centric privacy, security, and control over health information. This addresses longstanding concerns related to data management in healthcare, ensuring a more secure and personalized approach to patient information.

11.4.1.4 There can Be other similar Use Cases, such as:

11.4.1.4.1 Banking

Traditional banks and financial institutions often rely on centralized identity verification for customer onboarding and transactions.

We can build a decentralization layer encompassing decentralized identity systems to enhance customer privacy, reduce the risk of identity theft, and streamline cross-border transactions.

11.4.1.4.2 Government Services

Centralized government databases hold citizens' identity information for various services such as voting, licenses, and social welfare programs.

We can build a decentralized layer encompassing decentralized identity to give citizens more control over their personal data, reduce the risk of data breaches, and enhance the efficiency of government service delivery.

11.4.1.4.3 Human Resources and Workforce Management

Centralized HR systems manage employee records, including personal information, certifications, and work history.

We can integrate a decentralization layer encompassing decentralized identity to empower employees to manage and selectively share their credentials during job applications, reducing the need for redundant background checks.

11.4.1.4.4 Legal and Notary Services

Centralized legal systems manage legal documents, contracts, and notary services.

We can add a decentralization layer encompassing decentralized identity to enhance document authenticity, reduce fraud, and streamline notary services with verifiable credentials.

11.4.2 *Decentralization Layer for Storing Transaction Data*

11.4.2.1 *Use Case*

The use of a decentralization layer for the storage of transaction data can add transparency, security, immutability, and a certain amount of decentralization to a conventional tech architecture.

Here is a potential use case in **supply chain management:**

Blockchain can be used to track the source and movement of goods in supply chains. Each step of the supply chain process is recorded as a transaction, providing visibility and transparency into the origins, handling, and quality of products.

So, we can add a new web interface that uses Web3.js to interact with say Ethereum blockchain on which smart contracts are triggered by predefined conditions, automating data recording on the blockchain. Web3.js is a JavaScript library that allows interaction with Ethereum blockchain networks, enabling developers to build decentralized applications (DApps) and integrate blockchain functionality into web applications.

We need to remember that storing data on Ethereum can be expensive due to gas fees (network fee) and can be slow due to low throughput. So, we need to use a scaling solution.

Say, we use an Optimistic Rollup. As mentioned earlier, Optimistic Rollup is a layer 2 scaling solution for Ethereum that addresses the network's scalability challenges by enabling more transactions to be processed off-chain while maintaining the security and decentralization of the Ethereum mainnet.

Optimistic Rollup allows most transactions to be processed off-chain in a separate layer, referred to as the "rollup" layer. Transactions in the rollup layer are processed optimistically, assuming that they are valid. This optimistic assumption allows for faster and more efficient transaction processing. Multiple off-chain transactions are aggregated into a single batch, reducing the amount of data that needs to be submitted to the Ethereum mainnet. This aggregation helps in saving transaction fees and mitigating congestion on the mainnet. While optimistic execution assumes the validity of transactions, participants have the opportunity to submit "fraud proofs" if they detect any malicious activity. These proofs challenge the optimistic assumption and trigger an on-chain dispute resolution process on the Ethereum mainnet.

A smart contract is deployed on the Ethereum mainnet to represent the rollup. This contract stores a compressed version of the transaction data, ensuring that the mainnet remains the ultimate source of truth and security.

11.4.2.2 *So, What Are the Benefits of such a System?*

Such a system will provide transparency to the whole supply chain and be decentrally accessible to various stakeholders. Modern supply chains are complex and may involve stakeholders from various countries with access to different technologies. As the data is stored on a blockchain, the system becomes highly interoperable, and different stakeholders may build individual systems to access the same data.

As blockchain data is immutable and tamper-proof, all stakeholders can be assured of the legitimacy of the data, ensuring that all stakeholders, including customers, can confidently verify

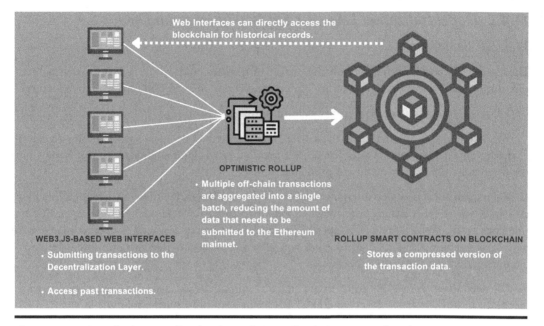

Figure 11.2 Sample decentralization layer for supply-chain transaction data storage.

the source of the products. This transparency builds trust and can be particularly valuable in industries prone to counterfeiting.

The system offers real-time tracking of products from their origin through each step of the supply chain. This end-to-end visibility helps identify the source of issues, such as defects or contamination, facilitating more effective recalls.

Smart contracts can also record checkpoints, such as compliance checks, to foster trust among all stakeholders that these checkpoints have been met. Financiers who fund sourcing can have transparent tamper-resistant data sources to evaluate the real-time economic health of the supply chain network.

11.4.2.3 Similar Decentralization Layers Can Be Built for

- Financial services for recording financial transactions, including settlements, cross-border payments, and trade finance.
- Healthcare for recording patient medical records.
- Real-estate transactions to record title deeds/land registries.
- Intellectual property records.

11.4.3 Decentralization Layer for Storage of Object Metadata

11.4.3.1 Use Case

Objects stored in Cloud Storage are accompanied by associated metadata. This metadata serves to identify the characteristics of the object and outlines specific instructions on how the object should be managed upon access. The metadata is structured in the form of "*key: value*" pairs.

Note that, "objects" refer to discrete units of data that are stored as files, say video or audio files. Unlike traditional file storage systems that organize data in a hierarchical structure (folders and directories), object storage uses a flat address space where each piece of data, known as an object, is uniquely identified by a key or a unique identifier.

Decentralization layers can be used to facilitate the use of blockchains for the storage of object metadata, providing a secure, tamper-resistant, and transparent way to manage and verify information about digital objects. Object metadata typically includes details about an object's characteristics, ownership, history, and other relevant attributes.

The objects can be stored in centralized storage or decentralized storage based on primary system design.

Smart contracts can be used to store and manage object metadata on the blockchain. Also, smart contracts can include details such as object ID, ownership information, timestamps, and references to centralized or decentralized cloud storage.

Now, to implement such a system we need to build a system of APIs. These APIs will connect the primary cloud system with the decentralized metadata storage. We can use libraries such as Web3.js and GraphQL for building such a system.

Apart from that, we also need to build a scaling solution to manage the throughput and cost of using blockchain for storage.

NFTs can be tied to object metadata to further enable ownership transfers through token transactions.

So, the decentralization layer would comprise the API system, the smart contracts, the scaling solution, any related NFT, and other supporting components.

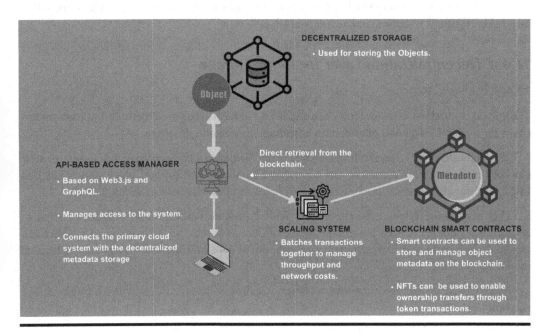

Figure 11.3   Sample decentralization layer for object metadata storage.

11.4.3.2 So, What Are the Benefits of such a System?

Accessing metadata is a more frequent requirement than accessing the actual files, especially for applications like image or video galleries, menu interfaces, and search functionalities. Storing metadata on blockchains enhances availability due to decentralization and reduces overhead by eliminating the need to access the actual media files.

Storing metadata on a blockchain in a standardized format encourages interoperability, enabling various systems and applications to effortlessly retrieve and interpret the metadata, and facilitating smooth integration across diverse platforms.

Once information is recorded on a blockchain, it becomes immutable and impervious to unauthorized alterations. This characteristic guarantees the integrity of object metadata over time, providing utility for source tracking and auditing purposes.

Blockchains offer dependable and cryptographically verifiable timestamps for object metadata. This feature holds significance in determining the time of creation, modification, or transfer of an object, proving crucial for legal, regulatory, or historical purposes.

The blockchain can log ownership changes and transfers of objects, treating each transfer as a transaction on the blockchain. This approach offers a transparent history of ownership transitions.

Blockchain utilizes cryptographic techniques to safeguard data, guaranteeing that only authorized parties have access to and can modify the metadata. This enhances the overall security of the data.

The decentralized nature of blockchain reduces dependence on intermediaries for data verification and storage, streamlining processes and potentially lowering costs.

Smart contracts offer automation capabilities for tasks related to object metadata, including ownership transfers, royalties, and access control.

11.4.4 Decentralization Layer for Index Storage

11.4.4.1 Use Case

Traditional cloud databases store indices using B-tree or hash-tree-based methods but using blockchain for storing indices can offer certain advantages in specific situations.

We can build such a decentralization layer using blockchain (Ethereum or any programmable blockchain) based smart contracts, any centralized databases that support block storage (such as EBS) or optionally decentralized (IPFS, etc) storage, and libraries such as Web3.js.

The smart contracts manage the indices with a suitable replication strategy, centralized or decentralized storage is used for storage of actual data as blocks, an API system to connect this system with the primary storage system, and an optional decentralized identity system can be used to manage access.

As discussed before, we also need to build a scaling solution to deal with throughput and network fees.

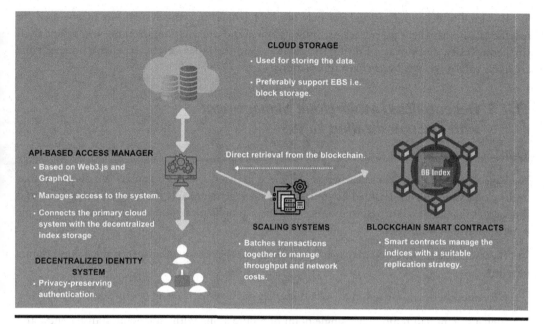

Figure 11.4 Sample decentralization layer for index storage.

11.4.4.2 So, What Are the Benefits of such a System?

As blockchain offers higher availability, this decentralization layer can lead to higher availability and higher robustness for the cloud database as it removes a single point of failure.

In many cases, indices are frequently accessed for different operations such as search, etc. Indices on a blockchain can expedite data retrieval, especially when users need to quickly access specific subsets of data. Blockchain's decentralized and transparent nature can enhance the efficiency of querying.

Another advantage is the immutability of blockchains. Blockchain's immutability ensures that once index data is recorded on the blockchain, it cannot be altered or deleted without consensus from the network participants. This property guarantees the integrity of the index. Any update of the index will require consensus among the network participants, enhancing security and reducing the risk of unauthorized or fraudulent changes.

Apart from that, The transparent and auditable nature of blockchains provides visibility into the history of index updates and changes. Auditors and database administrators can easily verify the index's integrity and track any modifications.

Blockchain's decentralized nature enables global access to indices, enabling participants from different regions to access the data efficiently.

Smart contracts can automate operations based on index changes, streamlining processes and reducing manual interventions.

Yes, we cannot forget that all this will cost network fees and will have to deal with latency issues. We also may need to implement an encryption system to increase privacy.

This kind of decentralization layer may not be a general-purpose system but can be used for specific situations where global access, immutability, and automation are more important than cost, complexity, and privacy. Editing the database and the index can be expensive because edits are likely to involve new blockchain transactions.

11.4.5 Decentralized Multi-cloud Management with Decentralization Layers

11.4.5.1 Use Case

We have discussed multi-cloud earlier in the "decentralized storage" chapter. We discussed that multi-cloud strategies are enabled by multi-cloud management tools which are a set of tools and procedures that allow a business to monitor and secure applications and workloads across multiple public cloud environments.

The issue with multi-cloud management tools is that they inadvertently introduce single points of failure.

We can build decentralized multi-cloud management systems using decentralization layers.

Such a system will remove any single point of failure along with enhancing transparency, and security, and enabling automation of cloud resource management across multiple cloud service providers.

Such a system will require smart contracts on public blockchains such as Ethereum or Solana, libraries such as Web3.js to communicate with the blockchain, decentralized identity systems such as Sovrin or uPort, optional decentralized storage systems, cloud provider APIs, optional data oracles, and optional blockchain explorers.

Smart contracts form the heart of this decentralization layer. Smart contracts can be used to manage multi-cloud resources, automate provisioning, and execute operations based on pre-defined rules.

Decentralized identity solutions can be used to ensure secure and verifiable access to the multi-cloud management system. Users and entities can have unique, blockchain-based identities.

Decentralized storage such as IPFS can be used to store and retrieve files related to cloud configurations, policies, and other relevant information in a decentralized and resilient manner.

Cloud provider APIs can be used to manage and orchestrate multi-cloud resources.

Oracles can be used to track demand for the cloud services and economic factors affecting the cloud budget (if applicable) and feed the data to the smart contracts.

The smart contracts can be coded to enable optimized allocations based on the data provided by Oracle. The multi-cloud management system can query the smart contract periodically to track changes in the optimal allocation and execute cloud allocation based on that.

At last, blockchain explorer APIs can be used to monitor and visualize transactions, smart contract interactions, and the state of the decentralized multi-cloud management system.

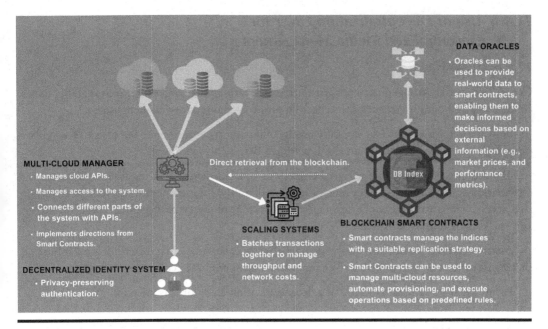

Figure 11.5 Sample decentralization layer for decentralized multi-cloud management.

11.4.5.2 So, What Are the Benefits of such a System?

All transactions and operations are recorded on the blockchain, providing transparency into resource management, access control, and system activities. Blockchain's transparent ledger facilitates efficient auditing of resource provisioning, usage, and compliance with predefined policies.

Smart contracts can automate cost optimization strategies, such as choosing the most cost-effective cloud provider or scaling resources based on demand.

Integrating a cross-cloud replication strategy alongside a decentralized index is instrumental in constructing cloud architectures with high availability and resilience, capable of handling the failure of a single cloud provider seamlessly. Smart contracts can play a crucial role in implementing automated processes such as access control, load balancing, data replication, data retrieval, and search logic within multi-cloud systems.

Additionally, smart contracts can initiate data synchronization procedures across diverse cloud environments, guaranteeing data consistency and redundancy to enhance overall system availability.

As mentioned before, in current multi-cloud architectures, the multi-cloud management system itself can become a single point of failure. The use of blockchain can solve that issue as blockchains are decentralized.

Further, integrating decentralized identity solutions enhances user privacy and security, allowing for verifiable and self-sovereign identities.

11.4.6 Use of Decentralization Layer for Decentralized Media Management

11.4.6.1 Use Case

Centralized media management and distribution face various challenges such as availability issues, content theft, unauthorized access, intellectual property and security challenges, etc.

Downtime for these systems not only results in lost short-term revenue but also affects reputation. Who wants to subscribe to an OTT platform that is "always down?"

The use of a decentralization layer can help us build decentralized media management and distribution systems that can offer much higher availability, limit content theft, reduce unauthorized access, and streamline processes such as intellectual property management, access tracking, and tracking pay-per-view revenue.

Apart from that, we can also create media management systems that foster interoperability, i.e. sharing of media content among service providers for a share in fee collected.

Let us discuss a sample structure of a decentralization layer for this purpose.

11.4.6.2 So, What Are the Components of such a System?

11.4.6.2.1 Blockchain Platform and Smart Contracts

Ethereum or any other suitable blockchain platform supporting smart contracts can be used for transparent and immutable record-keeping, ensuring transparency in media transactions and content ownership.

Smart contracts can manage media transactions, content licensing, and royalty distribution. Smart contracts can also automate and enforce rules for content usage.

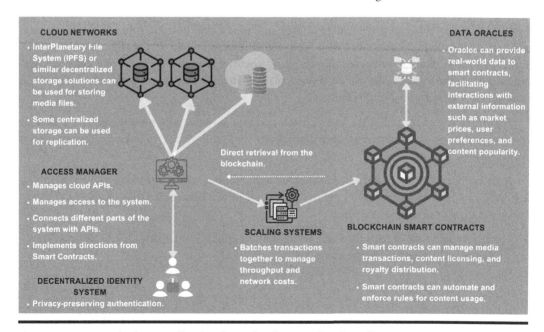

Figure 11.6 Sample decentralization layer for decentralized media management.

11.4.6.2.2 Decentralized Storage

InterPlanetary File System (IPFS) or similar decentralized storage solutions can be used for storing media files, ensuring data availability, and reducing reliance on centralized servers.

We can also keep some centralized storage in the mix for replication.

11.4.6.2.3 Decentralized Identity Solutions

Sovrin, uPort, or other decentralized identity platforms can be used to implement decentralized identity for users, content creators, and distributors. Decentralized identity ensures secure and verifiable user authentication and content ownership.

11.4.6.2.4 Decentralized Data Science

Federated learning and decentralized AI networks can be used to analyze user preferences, recommend content, and enhance the overall user experience without compromising user privacy.

11.4.6.2.5 Blockchain Oracles

Chainlink oracles or similar solutions can provide real-world data to smart contracts, facilitating interactions with external information such as market prices, user preferences, and content popularity.

11.4.6.2.6 Scaling Solution

As mentioned earlier, storing data on the blockchain can be expensive and slow. So, we need to incorporate a suitable scaling solution.

11.4.6.2.7 APIs and other Infrastructural Components

Obviously, we need to build an intricate and secure API system to connect various components.

11.4.6.3 Some Benefits and Features this kind of System Can Bring

11.4.6.3.1 Higher Availability

As mentioned before, downtime can kill media distribution businesses. The use of the above-mentioned decentralization layer can increase the availability of media distribution significantly. Higher availability will not only reduce revenue loss but also may give a competitive edge building a better reputation.

11.4.6.3.2 Global Access

Media management and distribution may involve distribution to different jurisdictions and dealing with varied technologies. These systems often struggle to deal with such complexity.

The use of such a decentralization layer may enable the separation of the media storage infrastructure layer from the distribution interfaces (apps, web interfaces, etc.). The infrastructure layer can be designed to be accessed from all the distribution channels.

However, we need to think about latency and data localization regulations if any.

11.4.6.3.3 Transparency

The use of a decentralization layer may increase the transparency of the media management system drastically.

- Transparency can be brought to content access records. This can help in dealing with unauthorized access and credential sharing.
- Transparency can be brought to transactions such as pay-per-view transactions.
- Transparency can be brought to the whole content flow.

11.4.6.3.4 Content Ownership and Copyright Management

The creator economy has made managing intellectual property a whole lot more complicated.

While engaging with creators may provide a continuous supply of fresh and relevant content, tracking ownership and intellectual property for the content becomes much more complicated.

The chances of copyright infringement become much higher with an increasing amount of content to process on the system.

It is possible to build automated intellectual property verification systems using Soulbound tokens representing content ownership, smart contracts automating various processes, oracles connected with third-party IP verification APIs such as YouTube Content ID API or Audible Magic API, AI-based content recognition systems, etc.

We can also build a reputation system for the content creators. Apart from the use of decentralized identities for content creators, the reputation system can use an incentive mechanism for marking stolen content.

11.4.6.3.5 Cross-platform Licensing

An exciting possibility with a decentralization layer is cross-platform licensing.

We have discussed the separation of the content storage infrastructure layer and distribution layer. Now, we can attach NFTs to each content. NFTs enable interoperability within the blockchain on which it is issued.

Further, cross-chain interoperability solutions enable cross-blockchain access to NFTs.

These NFTs can facilitate managing automated cross-platform content requests, verification of content requesters, content access approval, tracking and executing revenue sharing, etc.

Smart contracts embedded in the NFTs may contain predefined licensing terms and conditions. When a cross-platform content request is initiated, these smart contracts can automatically validate the request against the licensing terms, granting or denying access based on predefined criteria.

NFTs can include programmable logic to track the usage of licensed content across platforms using data oracles. This includes views, downloads, or any other predefined metrics.

So, we have discussed a basic framework for decentralization layers and then discussed some sample implementations.

Now, let us get into further nitty-gritty such as regulatory aspects, privacy aspects, and economic aspects of decentralization layers.

Bibliography

Ethereum. "web3.js - Ethereum JavaScript API." web3.js - Ethereum JavaScript API — web3.js 1.0.0 documentation, https://web3js.readthedocs.io/en/v1.10.0/. Accessed 10 June 2024.

HL7 FHIR. (n.d.). HL7.org. Retrieved December 29, 2023, from https://www.hl7.org/fhir/

Indy. (n.d.). Hyperledger. Retrieved December 29, 2023, from https://www.hyperledger.org/projects/hyperledger-indy

Zero-knowledge Proofs | Ethereum.org. (n.d.). Ethereum. Retrieved December 30, 2023, from https://ethereum.org/en/zero-knowledge-proofs/

Chapter 12

Regulatory Considerations for Decentralization Layers

Sam Ghosh

Yes, the use of blockchains brings many regulatory challenges as regulators around the world are trying to regulate the sector, especially crypto-assets.

But, this is only one side of the story. The use of these technologies can reduce compliance costs especially related to privacy and personal data management regulations.

This chapter will look into the potential increase and decrease in compliance burden as an effect of the use of "decentralization layers."

The actual impact on compliance burden will depend on the actual structure of the "decentralized layer," jurisdictions the platform will be accessed from, industry, and several other factors.

12.1 Factors Increasing Compliance Burden

Let us first cover how "decentralization layers" can increase compliance burden.

12.1.1 Financial Regulations

One of the concerns associated with the use of blockchains, smart contracts, and especially tokens (NFTs or fungible tokens) is that it may inadvertently attract financial regulations such as anti-money laundering (AML) – Know Your Customer (KYC) regulations, regulations related to security issuance, etc.

This is one of the primary reasons we suggest avoiding the use of tokens as currency, raising funds, and governance of decentralization layers. Decentralization layers are not supposed to act as standalone Web3 systems.

But, for some specific purposes, we may need to use tokens, especially NFTs. The problem is even if we use tokens for non-financial purposes, often the burden-of-proof and burden of

 DOI: 10.4324/9781003507352-12

compliance falls on the hands of the platform builders. So, we need to be aware of these financial regulations and how they could impact us in the context of decentralization layers.

12.1.2 Anti-money Laundering (AML) and KYC Regulations

These regulations are used to prevent the use of cryptocurrencies for money laundering and illicit activities. Some examples of such regulations are the Bank Secrecy Act (BSA) of the US and the EU's AML directives (such as the Fourth and Fifth AML Directive).

Compliance requirements involve collecting and verifying user identification information before providing services, in addition to transaction monitoring and reporting suspicious activities.

12.1.3 Securities Regulations

These regulations are employed to govern the issuance and trading of securities. An example is the Securities Act of 1933 in the US, which mandates companies to register securities offerings with the Securities and Exchange Commission (SEC) before selling them to the public.

Compliance with these regulations involves registration of securities offerings and disclosure requirements.

Some jurisdictions have defined regulations around ICO (initial coin offering) and STO (security token offering). For example, the Liechtenstein Blockchain Act provides a legal framework for the tokenization of securities and defines requirements for token issuers and service providers.

The use of crypto-assets may attract compliance requirements with these regulations.

12.1.4 Payment Services Regulations

These regulations regulate payment services. The use of crypto-assets for payments may attract compliance with these regulations.

Compliance may involve licensing, specific security measures, and adherence to other payment regulations.

An example of such regulation is the Revised Payment Services Directive (PSD2) in the EU. This directive governs payment services within the EU, including those related to cryptocurrencies, and mandates Strong Customer Authentication (SCA) for secure access and transactions.

12.1.5 Cross-border Transactions and Remittance Regulations

Public blockchains by nature are global as the nodes can be located in different countries and the blockchain can be accessed from anywhere in the world. The use of crypto-assets on these blockchains may inadvertently attract cross-border transactions and remittance regulations (such as international money transfer laws in the US) as these crypto-assets can be accessed from anywhere in the world.

12.1.6 Taxation of Crypto-assets

Jurisdictions around the world are bringing various regulations to tax earnings from crypto-assets and even to the holding of crypto-assets. For example, as per US Internal Revenue Service (IRS) guidance, crypto-assets are treated as property for tax purposes, and in the UK crypto-asset transactions are subject to capital gains tax.

The use of crypto-assets on the decentralization layers may inadvertently result in a visit from the taxman.

Even though you are not designing the decentralization layer for transactions or for raising funds, it is worthwhile to be aware of the relevant taxation laws in the jurisdictions the platform will be accessible from.

12.1.7 Data Localization Regulations

Data localization regulations, also known as data sovereignty regulations, mandate certain types of data to be stored, processed, and managed within the geographical boundaries of the country of origin. These laws vary across jurisdictions and influence how organizations handle data.

Data localization regulations primarily target personal data due to its sensitive nature and privacy and security concerns. The scope of these regulations can vary by jurisdiction, with some extending to other data types beyond personal information.

Some of the most important data localization considerations appear in the General Data Protection Regulation (GDPR) of the EU. GDPR technically is not a data localization regulation but GDPR places restrictions on the transfer of personal data outside the EU unless certain conditions are met.

Another example is China's Cybersecurity Law which imposes data localization requirements, particularly on critical information infrastructure operators.

Now, public blockchains by nature are global as they are open networks and anyone from anywhere can join them. This raises questions about compliance with data localization laws.

It is important to study the prevailing data localization laws and their requirements. In general, Decentralization layers do not necessarily involve storing personal data because we can always use decentralized identity systems for user authentication.

In extreme cases, we can use private blockchains especially designed for the decentralization layer. We will discuss private blockchains later in this book.

12.1.8 Other Regulations

12.1.8.1 Consumer Protection Regulations

The use of crypto-assets may attract compliance with various consumer protection regulations. Compliance with these regulations may involve various disclosure requirements along with the implementation of internal policies.

12.1.8.2 Smart Contract Legal Recognition

It is important to note that the legal status of smart contracts as formal contracts is often obscure in most jurisdictions.

So, it will probably be a good idea not to consider smart contracts as an alternative to traditional contracts but as automated programs on blockchains. Even if you use smart contracts on a decentralized layer for legal purposes, it is a good idea to have a backup system in line with respective regulations to deal with compliance requirements.

Okay, now let us discuss how the use of a decentralization layer may reduce the compliance burden.

12.2 Factors Decreasing Compliance Burden

12.2.1 Regulations Related to User Privacy

User privacy regulations, such as the General Data Protection Regulation (GDPR) in the EU and the California Consumer Privacy Act (CCPA) and HIPAA (Health Insurance Portability and Accountability Act) in the US, are designed to protect individuals' personal information and give them control over how their data is collected, processed, and shared.

Decentralized identity systems and decentralized data science, especially approaches like federated learning and edge computing, can offer solutions to help organizations reduce compliance burdens associated with these regulations.

A decentralization layer that incorporates these tools helps minimize the personal data collection required for the system. For example, the use of a decentralized identity system removes the need for the collection of personal data for identity verification and authentication. On the other hand, as federated learning makes it possible to train models on-device, user data does need to be accumulated in a centralized server.

12.2.2 KYC (Know Your Customer) and AML (Anti-money Laundering)

Although the use of decentralized identity may not completely remove the need for AML-KYC regulations, the use of decentralized identity solutions with smart contracts can help us streamline these processes.

Smart contracts can automatically trigger the AML-KYC process when a new user registers and the verification steps can be embedded in the smart contract logic.

Upon a new user's registration, the smart contracts engage with decentralized identity systems to authenticate the information provided by the user.

For instance, identity information could be presented as verifiable credentials, and smart contract verification could then utilize on-chain registries to confirm these credentials. This integration streamlines the AML-KYC validation process, making it more efficient.

12.2.3 Consumer Protection Laws

The use of decentralization layers may help reduce the compliance burden linked with consumer protection laws such as the Federal Trade Commission (FTC) Act in the US and the Consumer Rights Directive in the EU.

We have discussed how we can use decentralization layers to bring end-to-end transparency to the supply chains.

The use of a decentralized identity can make sure that only authorized entities can interact with the supply chain system. Transparent and immutable transaction records may help consumers trace the origin, production, and distribution of products, fostering confidence in the supply chain.

Apart from that, smart contracts can help automate various processes such as warranty claims, returns, and refunds.

Another side of consumer protection is the protection of consumer privacy. Many businesses collect too much user data for consumer profiling. The use of federated learning allows analysis of consumer behavior to personalize consumer experience without compromising individual privacy. As data is never accumulated in a centralized system, the chances of consumer data breaches can be minimized.

Okay, let us end this chapter here. In the next chapter, we will discuss the possibility of the use of dedicated private blockchains for decentralization layers.

Bibliography

Bank Secrecy Act (BSA) | OCC. (n.d.). OCC.gov. Retrieved December 30, 2023, from https://www.occ.treas.gov/topics/supervision-and-examination/bsa/index-bsa.html

Cybersecurity Law of the People's Republic of China. Retrieved December 30, 2023, from http://www.lawinfochina.com/Display.aspx?LookType=3&Lib=law&Id=22826&SearchKeyword=&SearchCKeyword=&paycode=

EU Anti-Money Laundering Directives (AMLD). (n.d.). LSEG. Retrieved December 30, 2023, from https://www.lseg.com/en/risk-intelligence/financial-crime-risk-management/eu-anti-money-laundering-directive

European Commission. (n.d.). *Consumer Rights Directive - European Commission*. European Commission. Retrieved December 30, 2023, from https://commission.europa.eu/law/law-topic/consumer-protection-law/consumer-contract-law/consumer-rights-directive_en

Federal Trade Commission & Ritchie, A. (n.d.). *Federal Trade Commission Act*. Federal Trade Commission. Retrieved December 30, 2023, from https://www.ftc.gov/legal-library/browse/statutes/federal-trade-commission-act

General Data Protection Regulation (GDPR) – Official Legal Text. Retrieved December 30, 2023, from https://gdpr-info.eu

Liechtenstein's Parliament Approves Blockchain Act Unanimously | Embassy of the Principality of Liechtenstein in Washington, D.C. (n.d.). Embassy of Liechtenstein. Retrieved December 30, 2023, from https://www.liechtensteinusa.org/article/liechtensteins-parliament-approves-blockchain-act-unanimously

Revised Rules on Payment Services. (2023, June 28). European Commission. Retrieved December 30, 2023, from https://ec.europa.eu/commission/presscorner/detail/en/qanda_23_3544

SECURITIES ACT OF 1933 [References in Brackets ф¿ Are to title 15, United States Code] [As Amended Through P.L. 117–263, Ena. (n.d.). GovInfo. Retrieved December 30, 2023, from https://www.govinfo.gov/content/pkg/COMPS-1884/pdf/COMPS-1884.pdf

State of California Department of Justice. (2023, May 10). *California Consumer Privacy Act (CCPA) | State of California - Department of Justice - Office of the Attorney General*. California Department of Justice. Retrieved December 30, 2023, from https://oag.ca.gov/privacy/ccpa

U.S. Department of Health and Human Services. (n.d.). *Health Information Privacy*. HHS.gov. Retrieved December 30, 2023, from https://www.hhs.gov/hipaa/index.html

Chapter 13

Public vs Private Blockchains for Decentralization Layers

Sam Ghosh

We discussed how blockchain transactions are transparent. But, this transparency can be a problem too.

While discussing privacy protocols in the chapter "Web3 Architectures," we discussed how transactions on public blockchains are pseudonymous and not anonymous. There are various de-anonymization techniques using which the identity of the entities involved in the transaction can be tracked down.

It is pretty understandable that many entities, especially corporations will not be very happy with this kind of transparency.

So, what is the solution?

One way to handle this situation is using private blockchains specifically designed for the decentralization layer we want to build. There are some benefits and some pitfalls in this approach.

Let us discuss.

13.1 What Is a Private or Permissioned Blockchain?

Private blockchains are a type of blockchain network that operates with restricted access and is typically used within a specific organization or among a consortium of organizations.

Unlike public blockchains, where anyone can participate and access the network, private blockchains are permissioned, meaning participants need explicit permission to join and participate in the network.

DOI: 10.4324/9781003507352-13

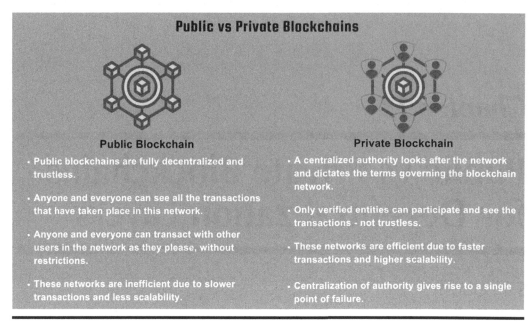

Figure 13.1   Comparison of public and private blockchains.

13.2 Benefits of Private Blockchains

13.2.1 Higher Privacy

Private blockchains offer higher privacy compared to public blockchains, where transactions are visible to the world. Permissioned access on private blockchains only allows authorized users to view transactions without making them public. This ensures the confidentiality of transaction details.

13.2.2 Faster Transactions and Scalability

Private blockchains provide better control over transaction visibility as well as the technical structure of the blockchain. The organization or the consortium can define block size and block time, impacting blockchain throughput.

In the case of public blockchains, users do not really have any control and forecasting ability over the demand for the blockchain as users around the world can openly join the blockchain anytime they want. This causes significant volatility and uncertainty in blockchain demand, affecting transaction speed, as throughput is fixed by block size and block time.

Private blockchains provide control over throughput and transparency on blockchain demand, thanks to permissioned access.

13.2.3 Customizable Consensus Process and Reduced Technical Complexity

Private blockchains can tailor consensus mechanisms for efficiency. With fewer participants, less resource-intensive mechanisms like Practical Byzantine Fault-tolerance (PBFT) or Raft can be used for faster transaction confirmation.

In private blockchains, built-in trust minimizes the need for extensive validation checks, expediting transaction verification. Simpler smart contracts with reduced complexity can be agreed upon, contributing to faster execution.

Smaller network size in private blockchains leads to significantly reduced block propagation times, ensuring quicker dissemination of transaction information.

13.2.4 Predictable Cost Structure

We discussed network fees earlier in this book. In simple words, the network fee (Gas fee in Ethereum) is the fee collected for transactions to pay the node providers. Basically, a network fee is a fee for the infrastructure.

In a centralized system, the centralized authority covers the cost of infrastructure. In a decentralized system, anyone can provide infrastructure for the nodes. The transaction fee, which is collected as a network fee, serves as a form of compensation or reward for node providers who provide the network's infrastructure.

Anyways, as private blockchains are controlled by a centralized entity or a consortium, the network fee is not applicable in the case of private blockchains.

In private blockchains, transaction validation is often handled by a select group of known and trusted participants.

Private blockchain costs are typically covered by consortium entities or the organization managing the blockchain. Instead of a network fee, operational costs like server maintenance, infrastructure, and security measures are incurred. Additionally, private blockchain solutions may include licensing fees for underlying technology or platforms.

13.3 Limitations of Private Blockchains

We discussed the benefits that private blockchains can bring. Now, let us discuss the limitations that private blockchains can introduce.

13.3.1 Centralization Concerns

So, why are we implementing a decentralization layer?

The primary reason for implementing a decentralization layer is, well, decentralization.

Effective decentralization in blockchain relies on node diversity, including geographical separation, varied technical environments, and distribution of control among different entities. Private blockchains, controlled by one entity or consortium, face challenges in achieving node diversity, potentially limiting the benefits of decentralization.

To address this, it's crucial to ensure an adequate number of nodes, promote diverse technical environments (e.g., different operating systems and programming languages), and consider geographic diversity through various strategies, such as outsourcing node hosting. Consortiums can significantly enhance node diversity in private blockchains by bringing together multiple participants for distributed governance and operation.

13.3.2 Upfront Investments and Operating Costs

Setting up a private blockchain entails significant upfront investments, covering infrastructure, technology, security measures, and potential licensing fees. Beyond computing resources, achieving node diversity requires organizational efforts and employee hours.

Operating costs for private blockchains include server acquisition and maintenance costs, cloud service expenses, licensing fees, node maintenance costs, and the cost of security protocol implementation to mitigate cyber threats. The specific costs depend on factors like blockchain scale, feature complexity, and chosen infrastructure.

13.4 Implementing Private Blockchains

Setting up a private blockchain involves choosing the right technology, infrastructure, and configuration to meet specific business requirements. There are several ways to set up private blockchains, each with its own advantages and considerations.

13.4.1 Framework-based Setup

Framework-based setups utilize established blockchain frameworks like Hyperledger Fabric, Corda, or Quorum. These frameworks provide modular and scalable solutions, allowing organizations to tailor private blockchains to their specific needs. With a permissioned model, access control ensures restricted participation.

13.4.1.1 Hyperledger Fabric

Hyperledger Fabric, hosted by the Linux Foundation, is an open-source enterprise-grade blockchain framework. It offers a modular and scalable platform for developing permissioned blockchain networks, making it suitable for businesses requiring a controlled and private environment.

With versatility and robustness, Hyperledger Fabric is well-suited for enterprise-grade blockchain solutions in various industries such as finance, supply chain, and healthcare, emphasizing privacy, permissioning, and modularity.

13.4.1.2 Corda

Corda, developed by the R3 consortium, is an open-source blockchain platform tailored for financial services and privacy-sensitive industries. It uniquely addresses business application needs, emphasizing data privacy, regulatory compliance, and interoperability with existing systems.

Corda has applications in diverse industries, including trade finance, healthcare, and supply chain.

13.4.1.3 Quorum

Quorum, developed by JP Morgan and now owned by Consensys, is an open-source, enterprise-grade blockchain platform. Built upon the Ethereum protocol, it prioritizes privacy, performance, and scalability.

With customized modifications, Quorum caters to the distinct needs of businesses, particularly in finance. Widely used in financial applications like trade finance and supply chain finance, Quorum is recognized for its focus on addressing enterprise requirements, especially in industries with critical concerns about data privacy and regulatory compliance.

13.4.2 Blockchain as a Service (BaaS)

Blockchain as a Service (BaaS) streamlines the deployment of private blockchains through cloud providers such as Azure, AWS, and IBM. These platforms simplify network permissioning and enhance scalability, making it easier to create and manage secure blockchain networks.

13.4.2.1 Azure Blockchain Service

Azure Blockchain Service is a fully managed blockchain service by Microsoft Azure, facilitating easy development, governance, and expansion of blockchain networks.

With versatile tools and services, it caters to organizations across various sectors, streamlining the utilization of blockchain technology for purposes like supply chain management and financial services.

13.4.2.2 Amazon Managed Blockchain

Amazon Managed Blockchain, a service by Amazon Web Services (AWS), simplifies the creation, management, and scaling of blockchain networks.

It enables organizations to build scalable applications without the complexities of setting up and maintaining blockchain infrastructure. With a managed approach, it eliminates the need for extensive expertise, making blockchain accessible to developers and enterprises.

13.4.2.3 IBM Blockchain Platform

The IBM Blockchain Platform, a BaaS offering by IBM, streamlines the development, governance, and operation of multi-cloud blockchain networks.

Designed with enterprise-grade features, security, and multi-cloud support, it provides a comprehensive set of tools and services for organizations across various industries to leverage blockchain technology.

13.4.3 On-premises Deployment

On-premises deployment of private blockchains involves setting up and managing a network within an organization's physical infrastructure, providing control over participation and access. However, this approach is more complex compared to other options as it involves capital expenses and management of various physical and digital resources.

On-premises deployment with custom nodes provides organizations with granular control over their private blockchain networks, enabling tailored solutions that meet specific organizational needs and compliance requirements. Regular maintenance and adherence to security best practices are essential for the ongoing success of the deployment.

Okay, let us end this chapter here.

Bibliography

Amazon Web Services. (n.d.). *Distributed Ledger Software & Technology - Amazon Managed Blockchain.* AWS. Retrieved December 30, 2023, from https://aws.amazon.com/managed-blockchain/

Castro, M., & Liskov, B. (n.d.). *Practical Byzantine Fault Tolerance.* Programming Methodology Group. Retrieved December 30, 2023, from https://pmg.csail.mit.edu/papers/osdi99.pdf

Consensys. (2020, August 25). *Consensys Acquires Quorum® Platform from J.P. Morgan.* Consensys. Retrieved December 30, 2023, from https://consensys.io/blog/consensys-acquires-quorum-platform -from-jp-morgan

Consensys Quorum. (n.d.). Consensys. Retrieved December 30, 2023, from https://consensys.io/quorum

Corda. (n.d.). Corda | The Open Permissioned Distributed Application Platform. Retrieved December 30, 2023, from https://corda.net

The Corda Platform: An Introduction. (n.d.). Corda. Retrieved December 30, 2023, from https://www.corda .net/content/corda-platform-whitepaper.pdf

Hyperledger Fabric. (n.d.). Hyperledger. Retrieved December 30, 2023, from https://www.hyperledger.org /projects/fabric

IBM Blockchain Platform: Hyperledger Fabric Support Edition. (n.d.). IBM. Retrieved December 30, 2023, from https://www.ibm.com/products/blockchain-platform-hyperledger-fabric

Microsoft Azure. (n.d.). *Web3 – Developer Solutions.* Microsoft Azure. Retrieved December 30, 2023, from https://azure.microsoft.com/en-in/solutions/web3

Ongaro, D., & Howard, H. (n.d.). *The Raft Consensus Algorithm.* Raft Consensus Algorithm. Retrieved December 30, 2023, from https://raft.github.io

Chapter 14

Economics of Decentralization Layers

Sam Ghosh

Now, let us discuss the economics around decentralization layers.

To effectively assess the economic costs and benefits associated with decentralization layers, it is essential to recognize that integrating such layers can impact not only the individual organizations but also the wider ecosystem within which the organization operates.

So, let us divide our discussion into micro-economic considerations (for the organization implementing the decentralization layer) and macro-economic considerations (for the broader ecosystem).

Please note that the actual economic effects of decentralization layers may be drastically different for different designs of the decentralization layer, industry environment, the maturity of the organization, etc.

So, the below discussion is aimed at inducing a basic understanding rather than acting as a tutorial. Ultimately, an economic model for a specific project needs to be built taking into consideration the unique, idiosyncratic characteristics of the decentralization layer and the circumstances around the implementation.

14.1 Micro-economic Impact

Micro-economic effects of decentralization layers are often readily visible and realized in the short term.

14.1.1 Direct Economic Costs

Let us first cover the direct economic costs of decentralization layers.

DOI: 10.4324/9781003507352-14

14.1.1.1 Cost of Implementation

The composition and magnitude of implementation costs vary significantly between public and private blockchains. Public blockchains may require access to node-service providers like Alchemy or Infura, and for increased reliability, hosting a blockchain node might be required.

Development costs in these projects go beyond the core technology, covering scaling solutions, smart contracts, decentralized identity integration, and decentralized storage. Specific solutions, such as Sovrin's decentralized identity, may have additional charges like fees for DID write, Schema, and credential definition.

The cost of implementing a private blockchain-based decentralized layer varies based on the implementation approach. A framework-based implementation involves development costs and potential licensing fees, while custom node deployment requires substantial resources, including computing infrastructure, real estate, architectural design costs, development expenses, and engineering work.

14.1.1.2 Operating Cost

Similar to implementation costs, operating costs may vary significantly based on whether we are using a public or a private blockchain.

Public blockchains incur network fees like Gas fees in Ethereum.

Private blockchains, based on implementation, can have various types of costs. Framework-based and Blockchain-as-a-Service involve hourly charges. Custom node deployments may include licensing, rent, power, maintenance, and personnel costs.

Apart from running the blockchain, utilization costs for decentralized identity and storage solutions may also apply based on architecture.

14.1.1.3 Compliance Cost

As we have discussed earlier, the use of blockchain may introduce various compliance requirements such as periodic disclosure requirements. These regulatory requirements will involve some cost.

14.1.2 Direct Economic Benefits

So, what are we getting in return for the implementation and operating costs?

We have already discussed the benefits that decentralization layers can bring – such as higher availability, automation, increased resilience, etc. The direct economic benefits stem from these qualities that decentralization layers bring to the tech architecture.

14.1.2.1 Higher Availability

The decentralized nature of blockchains and other decentralized components can result in significantly increased availability of the system.

Depending on the implementation, the higher availability may directly result in increased revenue (say, in the case of a decentralized media distribution system) or result in increased reputation and trust for the service among the users.

14.1.2.2 Increased Resilience

Another quality of decentralized systems is increased resilience due to the removal of single points of failure. Increased resilience results in lower maintenance costs and increased availability.

14.1.2.3 Automation

Smart contracts, along with other decentralized components such as decentralized identity systems, allow us to automate various functionalities such as user authentication, etc.

This kind of automation is likely to reduce human resources costs.

14.1.2.4 Reduced Storage Requirements

One important benefit of using decentralized support systems such as decentralized identity systems and decentralized data science (such as federated learning) is that we need to store less user data, especially sensitive user data.

We can expect a significantly lower storage bill due to the use of a decentralization layer.

14.1.2.5 Reduced Compliance Cost

As previously discussed, storing user data is subject to various compliance requirements, including privacy regulations (like GDPR) and data localization regulations.

As the use of decentralized identity solutions and privacy-preserving decentralized data science removes the need for storing sensitive personal data, they reduce compliance costs as well.

14.1.2.6 Lower Security Cost

The decentralized nature of blockchain networks and identity systems reduces vulnerability to common cyber attacks, such as single-point-of-failures, DDoS attacks, and unauthorized access.

Also, by using a decentralized identity and avoiding centralized repositories of sensitive information, the risk of large-scale data breaches is significantly reduced. Even if one node is compromised, it does not compromise the entire system.

Okay, now let us discuss the economic impact of decentralization layers on the broader ecosystem in which the organization operates.

14.2 Macro-economic Impact

The macroeconomic effects are often obscure and generally realized in the medium to long term. Let us divide our discussion into two parts – collective costs and collective benefits.

14.2.1 Collective Costs

14.2.1.1 Integration Costs

Organizations do not operate in a vacuum and implementing a decentralization layer within an organization's ecosystem may require integration changes across the value chain, impacting suppliers and users.

This is especially notable when the organization holds a significant role in the value chain. Integration costs, including training expenses and potential customer churn, may arise as the ecosystem adapts to the decentralization layer.

For example, say a B2B player incorporates a decentralization layer and it includes the use of a decentralized identity solution. Earlier to the implementation of the decentralization layer, the user authentication was based on the ID/password system. So, the customer organizations used to access the services through an API-based system that used the ID/password. Now, as their service provider migrates to a decentralized identity-based system, they need to build API systems that are compatible with decentralized identity-based systems.

These collective integration costs may come back to the organization in terms of training expenses, requests for discounts, and even lost customers, etc.

14.2.1.2 Regulatory Uncertainty

We have discussed earlier in this book that the regulatory implications of the use of blockchains are not clear right now. This regulatory uncertainty can spill over to the whole ecosystem.

Other ecosystem members may not be subjected to legal actions but disruption of the services by the organization (implementing a decentralized layer) for legal reasons may impact the whole ecosystem. This is especially relevant when the organization holds an important position in the value chain.

14.2.1.3 Technological Uncertainty

Blockchains and other decentralized systems are emerging technologies and are not totally stable.

Other members of the ecosystem may be impacted by the technological uncertainty associated with the decentralization layer in two ways. Any technological disruption in the organization implementing the decentralization layer is likely to impact the whole ecosystem in the form of service disruptions. Apart from that, if the other ecosystem members have systems connected with the said organization, technical disruption may propagate through the whole ecosystem.

14.2.2 Collective Benefits

So, what are the collective benefits?

As we have discussed earlier in this book, the use of a decentralization layer is expected to bring various benefits to the whole ecosystem – transparency, automation, increased privacy for users, etc.

These ecosystem benefits will likely benefit the organization implementing the decentralization layer through increased brand value, greater negotiating power with other value chain members, increased trust in the ecosystem, lower cost of quality assurance, etc.

14.2.2.1 Transparency – Reduced Information Asymmetry

One of the primary benefits of using blockchains is the immutable and transparent transaction history. This transparency can be enormously beneficial for the whole ecosystem.

Let us explain this point through the theory – "The Market for Lemons."

"The Market for Lemons" is a concept introduced by economist George Akerlof in his seminal 1970 paper "The Market for 'Lemons': Quality Uncertainty and the Market Mechanism," which discusses how information asymmetry can lead to market inefficiencies.

Akerlof's idea revolves around the presence of information asymmetry, where sellers possess more information about the quality of a product than buyers. In such markets, the quality of goods tends to degrade because buyers are unable to distinguish between high-quality and low-quality products.

Blockchain technology introduces transparency and immutability to transactions. Every transaction is recorded on a decentralized ledger that is accessible to all participants in the network. This transparency reduces information asymmetry, as the entire transaction history of a product or service is available for verification.

By addressing information asymmetry and fostering trust, blockchains can lead to efficiency gains in various industries. For instance, in supply chains, the ability to quickly verify the origin and authenticity of products can streamline logistics, reduce fraud, and cut costs.

14.2.2.2 Automation

Smart contracts can automate various processes such as quality assurance, warranty claims, payment approvals, etc.

For example, smart contracts can be used to enforce certain conditions or quality standards. If a product's quality falls below a specified threshold, a smart contract can automatically trigger actions such as refunds or penalties.

This kind of automation is likely to improve the efficiency of the whole ecosystem and lower various costs related to manual processes.

14.2.2.3 Security and Privacy

The use of decentralized identity solutions, federated learning, etc. limits the amount of data that needs to be collected. As much less or no amount of sensitive personal data needs to be collected in the case of a decentralized system, the security of the whole ecosystem improves.

At the same time, users gain control over their identity as well as their personal data.

So, now we have some understanding of the economic costs and gains that an organization may be exposed to due to the implementation of a decentralization layer.

But, how can we put all these together for decision-making?

We can use various financial modeling tools to evaluate a proposed decentralization layer project. Let us discuss a couple of those tools here.

14.3 Project Evaluation

Before we discuss these tools, we need to have a basic understanding of some financial concepts.

14.3.1 Financial Concepts

14.3.1.1 Opportunity Cost

Say, you have US $1,000. Now, you can keep that money in your purse, deposit it in a savings account, or invest in an exchange traded fund (ETF).

If you keep that money in your purse it will remain safe but at the same time, it will not earn any return. So, US $1,000 will remain US $1,000.

Now, if you deposit that money in a savings account you earn some interest. Depending on where you live in the world and the kind of financial institution you deposit your money into, interest rates can vary a lot – maybe zero or 3-4% on an annualized basis.

While you earn a little interest, the risk also increases a little bit. Depending on the deposit insurance from the government, the financial health of the government itself, and the type of financial institution, the risk may be negligible to significant.

Anyways, you can also invest your US $1,000 in an ETF. As stock market investments are fundamentally risky – your risk increases significantly, but at the same time, you can expect to earn significantly higher returns. The average annual return can be 10% or 20% if you invest for the long term.

The point is that you have various "opportunities" for what you can do with your money.

Now, say we think that a particular savings account investment involves more or less the same level of risk as that of keeping the money in your purse. So, by not keeping the money in the savings account you are losing the savings account interest rate – say 2.5%.

This cost that is associated with not opting for an opportunity that can give you a higher return for the same risk is called opportunity cost.

14.3.1.2 Cost of Capital

To implement a new project, an organization needs financial resources. Now, financial resources are not free even if an organization is using resources from their own reserves – due to the opportunity cost associated, i.e. the reserves could have been used for some other purpose.

This cost associated with financial resources that are to be used for a project is called the cost of capital.

Now, in general, organizations can raise capital in two forms: by taking a loan and by selling equity.

The interest rate for a loan is called the cost of debt.

The cost of equity represents the minimum return on equity that fund providers would typically expect from investments with similar risk exposure. The equity return expectations are estimated with frameworks like CAPM (capital asset pricing model).

Now, we can estimate the aggregate cost of capital using WACC – weighted average cost of capital.

The formula for WACC is as follows:

$$WACC = \left(\frac{E}{V} \times R_e\right) + \left(\frac{D}{V} \times R_d \times (1 - T_c)\right)$$

Where:

- E is the market value of the company's equity,
- D is the market value of the company's debt,
- V is the total market value of the company's debt and equity, i.e. (E + D),
- R_e is the cost of equity,
- R_d is the cost of debt,
- T_c is the corporate tax rate.

14.3.1.3 Marginal Cost of Capital

The cost of debt or cost of equity does not remain fixed for an organization. If an organization keeps on raising funds, it is understandable that investors and lenders will ask for higher returns for future investments due to increased risk.

So, the cost of capital for a project may not be equal to the cost of raising funds for past projects. Instead, we need to consider the cost of capital for acquiring additional funds, which is known as the marginal cost of capital.

We need to adjust our WACC calculations to the marginal cost of debt and the marginal cost of equity.

$$WACC_{Marginal} = \left(Marginal\ Cost\ of\ Equity \times \left(\frac{E}{V}\right)\right)$$

$$+ (Marginal\ Cost\ of\ Debt \times \left(\frac{D}{V}\right) \times (1 - T_c)$$

Where,

- Marginal Cost of Equity is the cost of new equity.
- E is the market value of the company's existing equity.
- V is the total market value of the company's equity and debt, i.e. (E + D).

- Marginal Cost of Debt is the cost of new debt.
- D is the market value of the company's existing debt.
- T_c is the corporate tax rate.

14.3.1.4 Time Value of Money

The time value of money (TVM) is a fundamental financial concept that recognizes the idea that a sum of money has a different value today compared to its value in the future. In other words, the value of money changes over time due to various factors such as inflation, opportunity cost, and risk.

Say, instead of investing the US $1,000, you decided to give it to a friend of yours. Your friend promised to return the US $1,000 after a year.

Will the US $1,000 that you will receive after a year be of the same value as the US $1,000 you now have?

Can you buy the same amount of goods and services with that US $1,000 after one year?

No. In general, you will receive a little less amount of goods and services using the US $1,000 after one year compared to the amount of goods and services you can receive now.

So, the value of money changes over time.

Not only that, but because you do not have the US $1,000 with you now, you may face problems in case of an urgent need for cash. This is called liquidity cost. Also, an exciting investment opportunity may show itself which you will not be able to participate in because you do not have the money with you. So, there is an opportunity cost as well. Also, we cannot ignore the possibility that your friend fails to pay you back – this is the counterparty risk factor.

So, it is not only inflation that affects the value of money.

We can quantify the time value of money as follows.

Say, PV represents the present value and FV is the future value – i.e., the amount that would get us the same amount of goods and services after say "n" years.

$$FV = PV \times (1+r)^n$$

Where r is called the discounting rate. The discounting rate is estimated based on counterparty risk, liquidity risk, and expected inflation. This is not a finance book so I am not going into details here.

14.3.1.5 Sunk Cost

A sunk cost is a cost that has already been incurred and cannot be recovered. In business and economics, recognizing and understanding sunk costs is crucial for making rational and forward-looking decisions. Sunk costs should not be considered in the decision-making process, as they are irrelevant to future costs and benefits.

Okay, now that we understand some basic financial concepts, let us discuss some tools that will help us evaluate decentralization layer projects from an economic perspective.

14.3.2 Net Present Value (NPV) Analysis

Net present value (NPV) analysis is a method used in financial decision-making to evaluate the feasibility of an investment or project and considers the time value of money.

It computes the present value of anticipated future cash flows associated with the project decision, minus the present value of investment costs. The basic premise of NPV analysis is that cash received or paid in the future is worth less than cash received or paid today due to the time value of money.

Below is a simplified equation for NPV analysis. Simplified because it assumes that there is only a one-time investment requirement at time t = 0.

$$NPV = \sum_{t=0}^{T} \frac{CF_t}{(1+r)^t} - CF_0$$

Where:

- NPV is the net present value,
- T is the total number of periods,
- CF_t is the net cash flow during period t,
- r is the discount rate (the rate used to discount future cash flows to their present value),
- Variable t is the time period, and
- CF_0 is the initial investment or cash outflow at time t = 0.

A project is acceptable if the NPV is positive.

For the microeconomic analysis of the impact of the decentralization layer on an organization, we can calculate the cash flows relevant to direct costs (implementation, operating costs, etc) and direct benefits (increased revenue due to higher availability, savings from lower data storage cost, savings due to a lower security threat, etc), and then use them for NPV analysis. The cost of implementation is obviously the initial investment cost.

While NPV analysis is generally used for cash flow, we can estimate the economic value generated and destroyed due to the implementation of the decentralization layer and calculate an economic NPV.

Collective costs can be used in place of negative cash flows and collective benefits can be in lieu of positive cash flows.

So, this economic NPV would suggest the net economic value that a decentralization layer brings to the whole ecosystem.

14.3.3 Internal Rate of Return (IRR) Analysis

The internal rate of return (IRR) is a financial metric used to evaluate the attractiveness of an investment or project. It is the discount rate that makes the net present value (NPV) of the project's cash inflows and outflows equal to zero. In other words, it is the rate of return at which the present value of future cash flows equals the initial investment.

$$NPV = \sum_{t=0}^{T} \frac{CF_t}{(1 + IRR)^t} - CF_0 = 0$$

In this formula:

- NPV is the net present value,
- T is the total number of periods,
- CF_t is the net cash flow during period t,
- IRR is the internal rate of return, and
- CF_0 is the initial investment or cash outflow at time t = 0

If the IRR is greater than the required rate of return or the hurdle rate, the project is considered financially viable.

If the IRR is equal to the required rate of return, the project is expected to break even (NPV is zero).

If the IRR is less than the required rate of return, the project may be considered less attractive.

We can use IRR analysis similarly to how we talked about the use of NPV analysis to evaluate the micro-economic and macro-economic impact of a decentralization layer.

Okay, let us end this chapter here. In the next chapter, we will cover case studies covering various industries and how Web3 is impacting those industries through decentralization.

Bibliography

Alchemy - the Web3 Development Platform. Retrieved December 31, 2023, from https://www.alchemy.com

Web3 Development Platform | IPFS API & Gateway | Blockchain Node Service. Retrieved December 31, 2023, from https://www.infura.io

The Market for "Lemons": Quality Uncertainty and the Market Mechanism. (2023, October 30). JSTORE. Retrieved December 31, 2023, from https://www.jstor.org/stable/1879431

Sharpe, W. F. (2023, November 7). *Capital Asset Prices: A Theory of Market Equilibrium Under Conditions of Risk.* Wiley Online Library. Retrieved December 31, 2023, from https://onlinelibrary.wiley.com/doi/full/10.1111/j.1540-6261.1964.tb02865.x

Sovrin Price Plan - Sovrin. (n.d.). Sovrin Foundation. Retrieved December 31, 2023, from https://sovrin.org/sovrin-price-plan/

Chapter 15

Industry Case Studies

Sam Ghosh

We have talked about the theoretical aspects of decentralization. Now, let us cover some case studies on the kind of roles decentralization plays in different industries. Hopefully, this will inspire the readers to implement decentralization layers in their industries.

15.1 Gaming Industry Case Study

A group of teenagers in my locality is heavily engaged in Free Fire, a popular battle royale game created by 111Dots Studio and published by Garena.

Free Fire follows a free-to-play model, allowing gamers to acquire virtual goods, character skins, and various customization options through in-game purchases. These virtual goods, including skins and weapons, are important for improving one's rankings within the game.

Presently, players require the in-game currency called "diamonds" for such purchases. Diamonds can be acquired through different avenues, such as buying them with real currency or earning them as rewards during regular gameplay, events, and various in-game activities.

Anyway, these teenagers were thrilled to have approximately US $2,000 "invested" in a collection of Free Fire accounts.

So, what makes Free Fire accounts a form of investment?

Despite Garena, the publisher of Free Fire, explicitly stating that trading and selling accounts violate their policies, there is a thriving market for Free Fire accounts. Notably, e-commerce platforms like Eldorado and PlayerAuctions facilitate the trading of Free Fire accounts.

I found it surprising that Garena is not aligning itself with the apparent user motivation, which revolves around the trading of accounts.

However, users aren't necessarily seeking to trade entire accounts – instead, their focus is on trading in-game virtual assets such as skins and weapons.

DOI: 10.4324/9781003507352-15

Many modern-day gaming platforms recognized this market gap and have since not only allowed users to trade in-game assets but actively encouraged such transactions.

While talking to the teenagers, I couldn't help but wonder about the fate of their significant in-game "investments" if Free-Fire were to suddenly shut down. Wouldn't these investments become worthless?

I did not get any answer.

I'll return to this question later, but for now, let's take some time to delve into some gaming industry concepts.

15.1.1 The Video Gaming Industry

According to Grand View Research, the global video game market reached a valuation of approximately US $217 billion in 2022, with a projected compound annual growth rate (CAGR) of around 13%. The proliferation of smartphones, rapidly growing internet penetration, and the widespread availability of games online are considered to be key contributors to the market's continued growth.

15.1.1.1 Evolution of the Video Gaming Industry

The gaming industry has undergone significant evolution over the years. In the early days of the gaming industry, revenue primarily came from publishing and direct sales, exemplified by Atari's success with the Pong series in the 1970s.

In the traditional gaming model, the primary source of profit used to be the "content business," involving activities like IP licensing and direct game sales, with profits going to publishers and content creators.

In the early 2010s, a new earning model emerged with professional gamers participating in official leagues, often established as marketing channels by major publishers. This concurred with the rise of professional influencers who used personality-driven content on platforms like Twitch and YouTube Gaming. Their success showcased the potential for individuals to profit through gaming, either by playing or leveraging game-related content, often with heavy sponsorship or publisher involvement.

In the 2020s, a new paradigm emerged – the era of "play to earn." The blockchain game industry introduced a rewarding system where gamers could monetize game content simply by playing. This shift resulted in unprecedented growth.

Now, let's delve into some gaming-related concepts.

15.1.1.2 Gaming Concepts

15.1.1.2.1 Gaming Revenue Models

15.1.1.2.1.1 Pay to Play: In this case, players pay an upfront cost or a subscription fee to gain access to the game. This model is prevalent in many console and PC games.

Figure 15.1   Gaming revenue models.

15.1.1.2.1.2 Free to Play (Freemium):   In this case, games are free to download and can be played without any initial cost. Revenue is generated through in-app purchases, microtransactions, and advertisements. This model is extensively utilized in mobile games, offering optional real-money purchases for in-game items or features.

15.1.1.2.1.3 Play-to-Earn: This revenue model motivates players with the prospect of earning in-game currency or valuable digital assets. Often associated with blockchain technology, this model may entail an initial investment, such as purchasing digital assets or tokens.

Play-to-earn represents a newer and evolving model in the industry.

Each model comes with its unique advantages and considerations, designed to cater to diverse player preferences and game genres. The gaming industry is in a constant state of evolution, with emerging models reflecting technological advancements and shifts in player expectations.

15.1.1.2.2 "Player vs Player" and "Player vs Environment"

In video games, two primary gameplay types are "player vs player" (PvP) and "player vs environment" (PvE).

PvP entails players competing against each other, while PvE involves players encountering challenges presented by the game's artificial intelligence, which may include non-playing characters or the game's environment.

15.1.1.2.3 Single-Player, Multiplayer Games, and Massively Multiplayer Online Games

Single-player games focus solely on PvE (player vs environment) gameplay, whereas multiplayer games incorporate both PvE and PvP (player vs player) elements.

A massively multiplayer online game (MMOG) is a video game genre that enables a large number of players to simultaneously engage over the internet. These games typically unfold in a shared world accessible to gamers after acquiring or installing the game software.

15.1.1.2.4 User-Generated Content (UGC) in Gaming

In gaming, user-generated content (UGC) refers to changes made to the game environment by people outside the original development team. These modifications can include adding new elements, altering visuals, or creating entirely new levels.

User-generated content can involve items like weapons, armor, clothing, and entire game levels. For example, a notable case is the transformation of Spacewar through the addition of a sun object, which significantly changed the game's dynamics.

15.1.2 Decentralization in the Gaming Industry before Web3

15.1.2.1 Rise of Decentralization in Gaming

In the past, gaming companies generally discouraged user-generated content (UGC), and UGC trades often occurred in underground markets. Early games lacked developer support for UGC creation, limiting such endeavors to skilled developers•or unintentional occurrences, commonly referred to as "modding."

Figure 15.2   The "mod" of Space War contains a sun object at the center.

At times, these modifications, or mods, gained even more popularity than the original games. Notably, Counter-Strike originated as a mod for Half-Life and eventually became one of the most influential games in the industry.

Recognizing the advantages of user-generated content (UGCs), game developers have progressively embraced them by incorporating support for UGCs on their platforms.

However, it is not only about UGCs.

While the term "Web3" may seem new, the concepts linked to decentralization, platform-native currencies, tokens, and in-platform trading were not alien to the gaming industry even in the early days of online gaming. Even before the widespread acceptance of Web3 principles, platforms such as Roblox, Minecraft, Second Life, and even traditional games like World of Warcraft demonstrated aspects of decentralization.

It's essential to note that games such as Free-Fire, despite incorporating features like in-game currency, did not embrace decentralization. As discussed earlier, Free-Fire lacks support for in-game trading and maintains centralized control over game components.

Roblox and Minecraft transformed the gaming landscape. How?

Let's begin by exploring Roblox.

15.1.2.2 Roblox

Roblox features a decentralized economy within its platform, allowing users to create their own games, design virtual items, and participate in trading with others.

Figure 15.3   Gaming platforms without blockchains that offer some level of decentralization.

The platform operates with its exclusive virtual currency called "Robux," serving as the native currency. Players can earn Robux through various avenues, such as game development, and use it for in-game purchases or trading with fellow players.

Renowned for its emphasis on user-generated content, Roblox empowers players to create games using the platform's development tools. Player-generated games can gain popularity and widespread play without direct involvement from the central game developer. This decentralized content creation model stands as a pivotal element contributing to Roblox's success

15.1.2.3 Minecraft

While predating the Web3 era, Minecraft stands out as a noteworthy example of a game that flourished through user-generated content. Players have the ability to develop their mods, skins, and customized maps. The Minecraft community enthusiastically engages in crafting and exchanging content, playing a significant role in sustaining the game's enduring popularity.

15.1.2.4 Second Life

Second Life is an early virtual world platform that champions a decentralized virtual economy. Participants were empowered to produce and trade virtual goods and services, with the in-game currency, Linden Dollars (L$), being exchangeable for real-world currency on external markets. This pioneering approach closely resembles the virtual economies seen in certain blockchain-based games in recent times.

15.1.2.5 World of Warcraft

In World of Warcraft, players have long engaged in decentralized trading. The in-game auction house facilitates the buying and selling of items using in-game currency, showcasing a player-driven market that embodies decentralized economic interactions within the gaming environment.

15.1.2.6 Limitation of Pre-blockchain Gaming Systems

As we see, even before blockchain gaming, traditional gaming platforms allowed users to create and trade user-generated content (UGC) and in-game assets. However, these assets were tied to specific platforms, lacking portability and interoperability.

If these platforms were to shut down, the fate of all in-game assets would become uncertain. Additionally, the ownership structure lacks transparency and heavily relies on the decisions made by the platform owners.

Blockchain gaming addresses at least some of these issues.

15.1.3 Blockchain Gaming

15.1.3.1 Introduction

Blockchain gaming refers to a type of online gaming application that incorporates a distributed database, often utilizing blockchain technology.

The decision regarding which components of the gaming system to store on a blockchain depends on the chosen game architecture. This choice, particularly when opting for a public blockchain for decentralized access, carries long-term consequences.

Currently, blockchains are used to streamline in-game asset transactions and to establish a financial system within online gaming platforms. This differs from earlier blockchain games like Huntercoin, where the entire gaming logic was on the blockchain. In modern blockchain games, most gaming components reside off-chain.

So, what benefits does the use of a blockchain or any other distributed database provide in this context?

Previously, we discussed user-generated content (UGC) and highlighted that the exchange of UGCs primarily occurred in unofficial channels.

However, this paradigm shifted with the emergence of gaming platforms like Minecraft and Roblox. Users now have the ability to conduct transactions involving in-game assets directly within the gaming platform, allowing them to acquire these items using real currency.

However, there is a problem.

As these gaming platforms are centralized, the ownership of in-game assets is tied to the gaming system. In the event of the game going offline, users face the risk of losing their in-game assets with no way of recovering their investments.

Blockchain-based NFTs are addressing this issue.

NFTs serve as evidence of ownership for these in-game assets. Non-fungible tokens or NFTs represent a form of crypto tokens wherein the value of each unit can differ from the others.

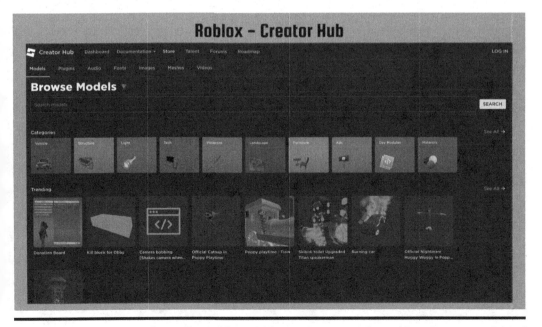

Figure 15.4   Creator Hub on the Roblox platform. Creator Hub enables the transaction of UGCs.

Now, NFTs enable the tracking of uniquely identifiable items, with the codes behind these assets often stored in various decentralized data stores, such as IPFS, in the form of Voxel or Unity models.

This fosters unparalleled transparency and interoperability. A common challenge in trading in-game digital assets lies in the absence of proof of authenticity. The incorporation of NFTs ensures transparent and easily auditable transfer records for these assets.

Furthermore, as the game assets are stored decentrally and represented by NFTs, they can be theoretically used on other gaming platforms.

Leveraging blockchain technology decentralizes the transactions involving these game assets. The exchange of these assets occurs through NFT transactions, establishing independence from the gaming platform.

Now, let's cover some blockchain gaming platforms.

15.1.3.2 Huntercoin

Many may not be familiar with Huntercoin, often considered the pioneer in blockchain-based gaming, launched in 2014, before the advent of Ethereum.

In Huntercoin, all game logic was embedded directly into the blockchain. Notably, Huntercoin originated as a fork of Namecoin, itself a fork of Bitcoin.

The game involves players collecting coins on a map, incorporating elements of player vs player combat to compete for resources.

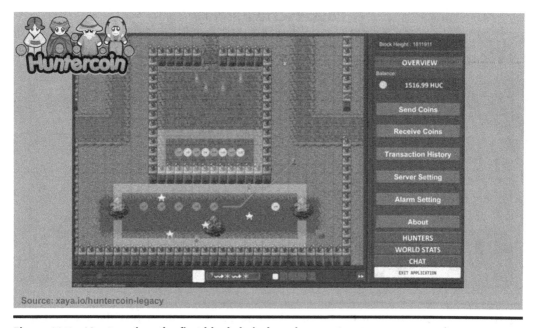

Source: xaya.io/huntercoin-legacy

Figure 15.5   Huntercoin – the first blockchain-based game. Image source: xaya.io

With the entire game logic residing on the blockchain, Huntercoin stands out as one of the most decentralized blockchain games. However, this characteristic also adds to its scalability challenges.

15.1.3.3 CryptoKitties

Introduced in 2017 by Dapper Labs, a Canada-based company, CryptoKitties gained prominence as the first widely known blockchain game. The game revolves around digital cats, allowing users to collect, breed, and trade these unique virtual felines.

CryptoKitties are unique digital collectibles represented as non-fungible tokens (NFTs) on the Ethereum blockchain. Each Kitty's appearance is determined by its distinct set of genes, which include both visible traits and hidden characteristics. Breeding two CryptoKitties produces offspring with a new combination of genes, influencing their rarity and value.

The value of a CryptoKitty depends on factors like rarity and cooldown speeds, with lower-generation Kitties possessing rarer traits and shorter cooldown periods, increasing their value. The cooldown period is the waiting time a cat must undergo after breeding before it can be bred again.

The game's logic is primarily governed by smart contracts on the Ethereum network.

While CryptoKitties is fairly decentralized, playing the game on the Ethereum network incurs high transaction costs.

15.1.3.4 Axie Infinity

Axie Infinity stands out as a prominent play-to-earn game created by the Vietnamese studio Sky Mavis.

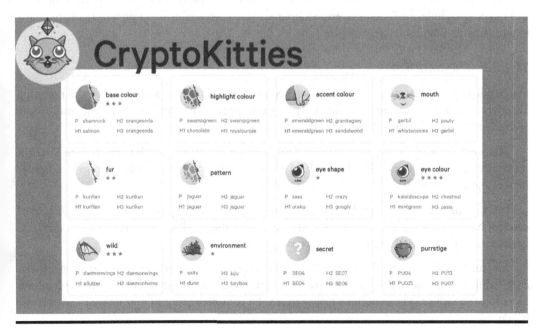

Figure 15.6 Genes that determine the appearance of the cats in CryptoKitties. Image Source: cryptokitties.co

Figure 15.7   The Axies are defined by the traits they carry. Image Source: axieinfinity.com

Axie Infinity operates on the Ronin sidechain of Ethereum, addressing Ethereum's scaling challenges. The game draws inspiration from Nintendo's Pokémon series and allows players to collect and battle monsters called Axies. Each Axie has seven body parts with distinct shapes.

Axies are represented as NFTs, and players assemble teams of three Axies to participate in gameplay. Lunacia, the game's virtual world, consists of NFT plots of land that serve as residences and operational hubs for Axies. Players can upgrade these plots using in-game resources and crafting ingredients found during gameplay.

15.1.3.5 The Sandbox

The Sandbox is a Metaverse that empowers players to construct, own, and monetize their gaming experiences on the Ethereum blockchain. The Metaverse is a collaborative, enduring, and openly accessible 3D virtual universe, essentially comprising multiple virtual worlds.

The Sandbox is a user-generated content ecosystem where users create 3D objects with Voxedit, trade them as ERC-721 and ERC-1155 NFTs, and use the Game Maker application to build experiences and gameplay for others.

LANDS in The Sandbox are blockchain-secured virtual tokens, following the ERC-721 standard for NFTs. These tokens represent specific parcels in The Sandbox Metaverse, allowing players to own part of the virtual world and host content.

In The Sandbox's virtual real-estate ecosystem, users can create and share gaming experiences while having the option to monetize their crafted games. This dynamic environment allows users to earn SAND, The Sandbox's utility token, by completing quests and missions within the Metaverse.

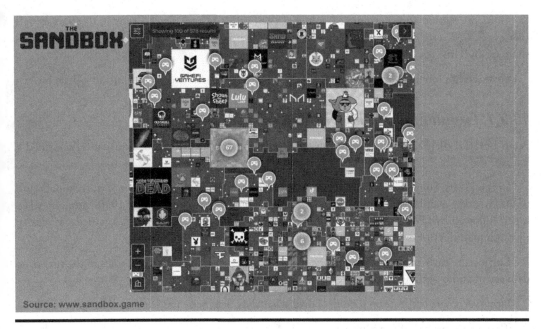

Source: www.sandbox.game

Figure 15.8   The Sandbox LANDS NFTs representing virtual real estate. Image Source: sandbox .game

15.1.4 Conclusion

We observed that blockchain-based gaming platforms significantly enhance decentralization by moving the ownership and transaction layer of user-generated content (UGC) to the blockchain.

However, is this sufficient decentralization?

No.

In a fully decentralized gaming ecosystem, user-generated content (UGC) and other in-game assets, like characters, weapons, or skins, would be interoperable. This implies the ability to seamlessly use in-game assets from one gaming platform on other platforms. While blockchains ensure the perpetual ownership of digital assets, the real value that blockchains bring lies in interoperability, allowing assets to be utilized across diverse platforms.

Enjin and similar platforms are dedicated to advancing the interoperability of gaming assets. However, achieving complete decentralization in the gaming ecosystem remains a distant goal.

Achieving complete decentralization in the gaming ecosystem demands not only the perpetual ownership of digital assets but also widespread interoperability among diverse platforms.

How do you believe we can create such an ecosystem using a decentralization layer?

15.2 Media Distribution Case Study

Doesn't it seem like everyone is getting into content creation lately?

Data supports this epiphany.

Content creation and sharing are booming. The DOMO Data Never Sleeps 10.0 report reveals that as of 2022, every minute, 500 hours of video are uploaded to YouTube, and Instagram users share 66,000 images.

Now, before moving forward, let us discuss the evolution of media distribution a little bit.

15.2.1 Evolution of Media Distribution

From physical distribution to streaming services, the media distribution industry transformed a lot over the years.

In the 1980s, Sony revolutionized audio distribution with the introduction of the compact disc (CD), marking a shift to digital formats. For video content distribution, the 1970s brought VHS tapes, followed by DVDs in the 1990s. JVC led the VHS format, while DVDs gained popularity through manufacturers like Sony and Toshiba.

During the early to mid-20th century, radio and television played pivotal roles in the real-time delivery of audio and visual content, fostering a shared cultural experience.

However, users had minimal control over what they watched, and their choices were limited.

Then came the era of the internet.

In the 1990s, the internet became more accessible, primarily through slow-speed dial-up connections. The digitization of content gave rise to online publishing. However, dial-up connections proved insufficient for quality media distribution. High-speed internet started gaining traction in the late 1990s and early 2000s, addressing these limitations.

Early pioneers like MP3.com and Napster revolutionized music distribution through peer-to-peer sharing. MP3.com, founded by Michael Robertson in 1997, and Napster, founded by

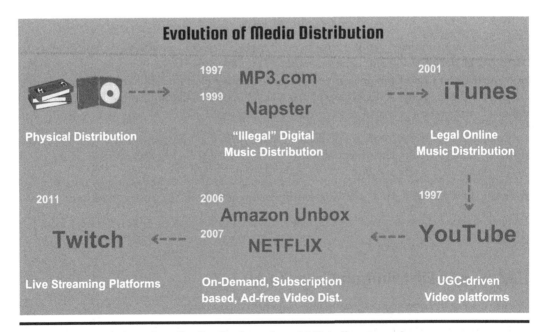

Figure 15.9   Evolution of media distribution – from VHS to live streaming.

Shawn Fanning and Sean Parker in 1998–99, played crucial roles in reshaping the landscape of music distribution. Both faced legal challenges related to copyrighted material, with Napster's model encouraging copyright violations, and MP3.com facing legal challenges for its My.MP3.com service.

In 2001, Apple launched iTunes as a legal online music store. Successfully negotiating licensing agreements with major record labels, iTunes allowed users to legally purchase and download individual songs or albums. Operating within copyright law and securing necessary licenses helped iTunes avoid the legal challenges faced by platforms like Napster and MP3.com.

The online video distribution era began with the founding of YouTube in 2005. Netflix, established in 1997, only entered video streaming in 2007, while Amazon launched Amazon Unbox in 2006.

Hulu, a collaboration of NBC Universal, Fox Entertainment Group, and ABC Inc., started in 2007, officially launching in 2008 with a free, ad-supported streaming model. Twitch, founded in 2011, specializes in live-streaming video games and esports content. Platforms like Disney+ and Peacock also emerged in this evolving landscape.

With the evolution of the business models, various revenue models also emerged. Let us have a quick discussion.

15.2.2 Revenue Models in Media Distribution

15.2.2.1 Advertising-supported Models

Let's begin with the ad-supported business model.

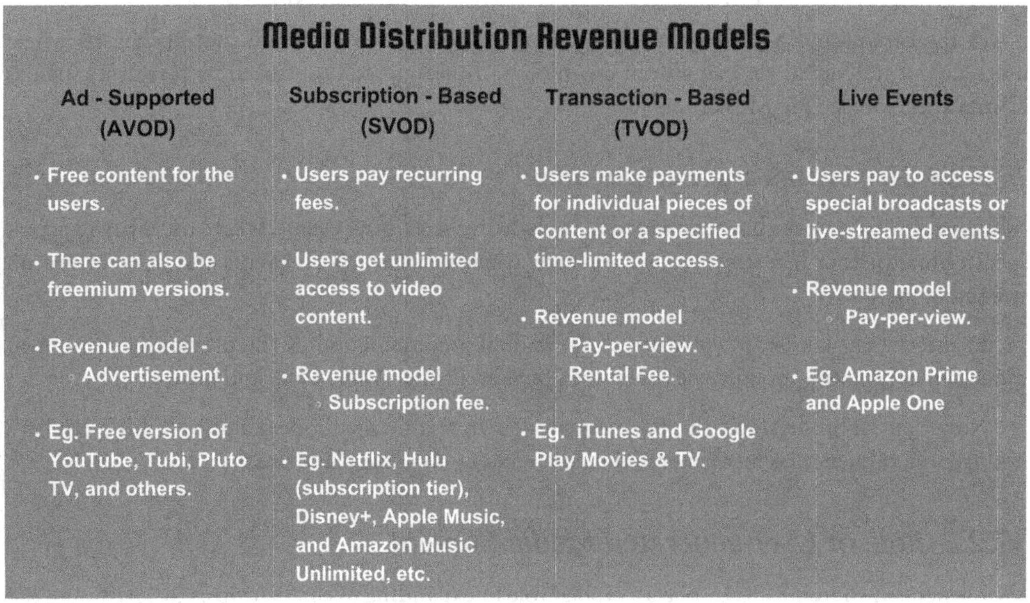

Media Distribution Revenue Models			
Ad - Supported (AVOD)	**Subscription - Based (SVOD)**	**Transaction - Based (TVOD)**	**Live Events**
• Free content for the users.	• Users pay recurring fees.	• Users make payments for individual pieces of content or a specified time-limited access.	• Users pay to access special broadcasts or live-streamed events.
• There can also be freemium versions.	• Users get unlimited access to video content.		• Revenue model Pay-per-view.
• Revenue model - Advertisement.		• Revenue model Pay-per-view.	
	• Revenue model Subscription fee.	Rental Fee.	• Eg. Amazon Prime and Apple One
• Eg. Free version of YouTube, Tubi, Pluto TV, and others.	• Eg. Netflix, Hulu (subscription tier), Disney+, Apple Music, and Amazon Music Unlimited, etc.	• Eg. iTunes and Google Play Movies & TV.	

Figure 15.10   Media distribution revenue models.

The ad-supported video on demand (AVOD) model offers free access to content monetized through ads, seen on platforms like the free version of YouTube, Tubi, and Pluto TV.

Similarly, the freemium music streaming model provides limited free access with ads, with options for ad-free premium subscriptions, as seen in Spotify and Pandora.

The ad-supported model serves as a means to attract users to the platform, often evolving into a freemium model, as seen in YouTube's introduction of YouTube Premium, which offers an ad-free experience for a monthly fee.

15.2.2.2 Subscription-based Models

Now, let's delve into subscription-based models.

In the subscription video on demand (SVOD) model, users subscribe by paying a recurring fee, granting them unlimited access to a comprehensive library of video content. Notable platforms employing this model include Netflix, Hulu (subscription tier), Disney+, etc.

Similarly, in the music streaming subscription model, users pay a subscription fee for unrestricted access to an extensive music library, with examples including Spotify Premium, Apple Music, and Amazon Music Unlimited, among others.

Hybrid platforms like Amazon Prime offer a combination of audio and video subscriptions, encompassing Prime Video and Amazon Music.

15.2.2.3 Transaction-based Models

Now, turning to the transactional video-on-demand (TVOD) model. Users make payments for individual pieces of content or a specified time-limited access.

Notable platforms employing this model include iTunes and Google Play Movies & TV.

In the case of audio delivery, a similar model operates on downloads and purchases, where users pay for individual song or album downloads. This approach is utilized by platforms such as iTunes and Google Play Music.

15.2.2.4 Live Events and Pay-per-view

Many streaming services have expanded to include live streaming events, where users pay to access special broadcasts or live-streamed events, such as pay-per-view sports events and live concerts on streaming platforms.

In the current landscape, platforms often adopt a combination of the previously mentioned models, incorporating bundled services like Amazon Prime, Apple One, and others.

Now that we understand the business models in online media distribution a little bit, let's evaluate the influence of user-generated media content on these platforms.

15.2.3 Role of User-generated Media Content

User-generated content (UGC) plays a crucial role in expanding Web2 platforms by leveraging the power of network effects. Network effects occur when the value of a platform increases with the number of users, creating a positive feedback loop.

15.2.3.1 *How Does UGC Fuel Platform Growth?*

15.2.3.1.1 Building User Traction

User-generated content plays a key role in attracting users to platforms through diverse and relevant content, often shared through word-of-mouth recommendations. Content providers promote their creations beyond the platform, advertising the platform itself.

For example, when you upload a video on YouTube, it's common to share the video link across all your social media profiles, as well as through emails and messages. This process actively drives traffic to the platform and enhances search engine rankings, facilitating rapid platform growth.

15.2.3.1.2 Increased Engagement

User-generated content (UGC) fosters a sense of community among users with shared interests, boosting engagement and retention as individuals connect with like-minded peers.

Platforms often integrate interactive features such as comments, likes, shares, and collaborations, elevating the user experience and encouraging prolonged platform interaction.

15.2.3.1.3 Trend Following in Content Creation

Content creators strive to cultivate an audience by producing content aligned with current "hot" and "trending" topics. This ensures that platforms consistently offer not only pertinent content for their visitors but also a constant stream of fresh material.

Consider this – if a significant event occurs today and you visit YouTube, you are likely to find content creators already producing videos on that topic. Traditional media may need a lot longer to catch up with the trend.

So, we understood that user-generated content is not only significant for these platforms but vital for their existence and growth.

YouTube recognized the importance of UGC early on and embraced this trend with the Youtube Partner Program.

15.2.3.2 *YouTube Partner Program (YPP)*

YouTube's Partner Program (YPP), launched in 2007, revolutionized content creation by allowing creators to monetize their videos through advertising. Unlike other attempts by platforms like Revver and Blip.tv, YPP achieved unprecedented success.

Creators in YPP earn revenue from ads displayed alongside or within their videos based on factors like ad impressions and viewer engagement. This program empowered creators to turn their passion into income, fostering diverse and engaging content on the platform.

To join YPP, creators need to meet specific criteria like attaining a minimum number of subscribers and watch hours, incentivizing them to produce high-quality content, and growing their audience.

YPP transformed YouTube into a viable career choice for creators, encouraging full-time content creation and contributing to the platform's evolution into a dynamic content ecosystem.

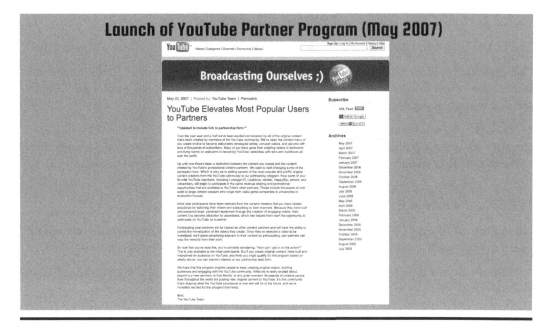

Figure 15.11   Launch of Youtube Partner Program in May 2007. Image Source: <u>web.archive.org</u> <u>(youtube.com)</u>

Overall, YPP has been instrumental in fostering content growth, content diversity, and economic opportunities within the YouTube community, positioning the platform as a leading destination for content creators worldwide.

Alright, so far, we've examined the industry from the viewpoint of platform development – observing the evolution, revenue generation, and utilization of UGC for growth.

Now, let's delve into the industry from the standpoint of content providers.

Content creation is no longer just a hobby, it has evolved into a primary source of income for many individuals. According to Linktree's report, there are approximately 200 million creators worldwide as of 2022. Goldman Sachs predicts that the creator economy could reach US $480 billion by 2027.

In the existing centralized model of online content distribution, the priorities of creators frequently take a back seat to the interests of platform providers.

This is where the concept of decentralization comes into play.

15.2.4 What Would Decentralization of Media Distribution Mean for Content Creators?

15.2.4.1 Control over Content

Arguably, the most significant aspect of decentralization would entail content creators gaining meaningful control over their created content. While creators legally own the content they create on digital platforms, in practice, content providers often lack meaningful control over how their content is distributed and utilized.

15.2.4.2 Brand Preservation for the Content Creators

The dynamism between content providers and platforms is typically framed with platforms positioning themselves as service providers, as outlined in user agreements. However, there's a prevailing sense that content creators are implicitly working for these platforms, resulting in the assimilation of content providers' brands into the platform itself.

Decentralization could offer a solution to protect the brand value of content providers.

15.2.4.3 Interoperability and Portability

Consider this scenario: You upload a video on YouTube, which stores the video in its databases and distributes it to users. Now, if you want to distribute the same video on Instagram, you must upload it again on Instagram. For each platform where you wish to distribute the video, you need to repeatedly upload the same video.

In a decentralized solution, the need for repeated uploads should be minimized.

15.2.4.4 Disintermediation

Decentralization involves disintermediation and the removal of intermediaries.

In the centralized media distribution model, platforms act as intermediaries, hindering direct contact between content creators and consumers. Creators are often restricted from connecting directly with the audience, limiting their ability to move the audience to other platforms. This poses challenges, as creators lack granular audience insights and direct engagement.

A decentralized solution should avoid restricting creators' ability to connect with their audience in any way.

15.2.4.5 Access Control

If I request the deletion of a video on YouTube, and YouTube confirms its deletion, do I have a way to verify if it's truly removed from YouTube's databases? How can I be sure that YouTube isn't keeping a copy of my data?

This concern may seem theoretical but it is not. For example, Tiktok was banned from India in 2020 but it has been reported by several media outlets that still in 2023, employees of ByteDance, the parent company of Tiktok, had access to data of over 150 million Indian accounts and users. Remember that TikTok is often accused of sharing data with the Chinese Communist Party.

In a decentralized solution, content providers should have the ability to control and restrict content access, ensuring transparency about where their content resides and who has access to the content.

15.2.4.6 Transparency

Centralized platforms often lack transparency, especially in content recommendation algorithms, content moderation policies, and revenue-sharing practices. Content creators may face challenges in understanding how their content is evaluated, the reasons for moderation actions such as removal or flagging, and the distribution of generated revenue.

In conflicts, these platforms often act unilaterally, leaving content providers with minimal authority over their own content.

15.2.5 Decentralization without Web3

When considering the decentralization of media distribution without Web3 on a broader scale, platforms like MUVI come into mind.

Muvi is an Infrastructure as a Service (IaaS) platform offering comprehensive solutions for content creators to launch their streaming services. It operates on a business-to-business (B2B) model, serving businesses, organizations, and individual content creators.

Rather than controlling revenue streams and taking a percentage, MUVI charges subscription fees directly from content creators. MUVI presents diverse monetization choices for content creators, encompassing subscription models, pay-per-view, and ad-based revenue within their tailored streaming services.

Despite offering brand control through white-label services, platforms like MUVI still function as intermediaries in transactions between creators and their audiences.

15.2.6 Decentralization with Web3

Blockchain-based platforms like Hive-Tube, LBRY, and BitTube have taken significant strides toward decentralization.

Hive-Tube, operating on the Hive blockchain, is a decentralized streaming platform providing content creators with the freedom to monetize and distribute their media without censorship or fees, serving as an alternative to mainstream platforms like YouTube and Spotify.

LBRY is a blockchain-driven content-sharing platform prioritizing decentralization. Content creators can publish directly on the LBRY blockchain, enabling users to discover and tip creators using cryptocurrency.

BitTube is a blockchain-powered platform that incorporates the cryptocurrency TUBE for content monetization. Blending video streaming with a decentralized social media platform enables users to earn TUBE tokens for both content creation and engagement.

Now, let us compare MUVI, a decentralized media distribution platform that does not use blockchain, and LBRY, a blockchain-based media distribution platform.

Muvi functions within a centralized technical architecture, where the platform's infrastructure is controlled by a central authority. This centralization poses potential vulnerabilities and dependencies on the platform provider.

In contrast, LBRY operates on a decentralized blockchain, eliminating the necessity for a central authority. Content is stored across a distributed network of computers, boosting resilience and minimizing the risk of single points of failure.

Although Muvi provides multiple monetization options for content creators, it functions as an intermediary in transactions.

In contrast, LBRY enables direct monetization between content creators and viewers through cryptocurrency LBC. This direct interaction is facilitated by smart contracts on the blockchain, minimizing the reliance on intermediaries.

LBRY's resistance to censorship is higher due to its decentralized nature. Content information resides on a blockchain, and the protocol is designed to grant content creators greater control over their work, mitigating the risk of arbitrary removal.

In the case of MUVI, content ownership, and distribution are overseen by the platform provider, leaving users and creators with limited insight into the platform's internal operations. LBRY's decentralized model, on the other hand, guarantees transparency in content ownership and distribution. The blockchain serves as an immutable record, documenting ownership and transactions, thereby enhancing transparency and accountability.

15.2.7 *Limitations of Current Blockchain-based Solutions*

While blockchain-based solutions contribute to decentralization in media distribution, there is still a significant journey ahead.

15.2.7.1 *User Adoption Challenges*

Cryptocurrency is a rapidly evolving technology, and its usage may not be universally accepted. Blockchain-based media distribution solutions, relying on cryptocurrencies for payments, encounter a substantial challenge in scaling their platforms to a critical mass.

15.2.7.2 *Content Discovery and Search*

While blockchain-based solutions aim to decentralize content discovery, the user experience may not match the refinement of centralized platforms. Users accustomed to sophisticated recommendation algorithms on mainstream platforms may find content discovery on blockchain-based platforms less intuitive.

15.2.7.3 *Monetization and Financial Integration*

Integrating cryptocurrency monetization may pose challenges for content creators accustomed to traditional payment systems. Some creators may prefer platforms that offer more straightforward financial integration.

Another related concern is that creators receive payment in cryptocurrencies, such as LBC on LBRY. As the prices of these cryptocurrencies constantly fluctuate, creators are exposed to price risk associated with these crypto-assets.

15.2.7.4 *Regulatory Uncertainties*

Cryptocurrencies worldwide are subject to evolving regulations, introducing uncertainties for platforms utilizing them. The future of these platforms may face existential crises with the introduction of new regulations.

15.2.8 Way Forward

Did you notice that the challenges mentioned are primarily associated with distribution – user adoption, payments, etc.?

A potential solution could involve separating the infrastructure layer (used for storage and maintenance of media objects) from the distribution layer as discussed in Chapter 11, "Decentralization of Traditional Architectures with Decentralization Layers."

The utilization of blockchain can be limited to the infrastructure layer, with traditional Web2 technologies employed for the distribution layer.

This approach allows leveraging the user adoption and network effect benefits of Web2 solutions while enabling creators to maintain control over their media assets through the use of blockchains. Viewers do not need to deal with cryptocurrencies, and creators retain control over their media assets, with only metadata and thumbnails shared with the distribution layer.

Decentralized storage can be employed for storing media, blockchain with smart contracts for managing access and tracking ownership of the media, and decentralized identity for secure authentication of the content creators.

As blockchains enable transparent and immutable records, content access logs become more auditable and reliable for creators.

Various cryptographic techniques can be employed to identify content theft and the upload of stolen content.

In this manner, creators can maintain command over their media assets and leverage various channels for distribution without the need for repetitive content uploads. This significantly enhances interoperability without compromising the security of the content.

What type of decentralization layer do you believe would facilitate the development of such a system?

15.3 Social Media Case Study

Let us begin this case study with a scene from David Fincher's 2010 movie *The Social Network*.

Eduardo Saverin, portrayed by Andrew Garfield, is providing testimony about the moment when Mark Zuckerberg approached him with the concept of "The Facebook."

Eduardo was attending the "Alpha Epsilon Pi Caribbean Night, 2003" when Zuckerberg approached him and requested to step outside.

Zuckerberg, portrayed by Jesse Eisenberg, shares the concept of "The Facebook" with Eduardo.

Prior to this, Mark Zuckerberg had created "Facemash," a platform similar to "Hot or Not" for Harvard students. He allegedly obtained images of female students by hacking into various Harvard websites, leading to a summons from the Harvard Administrative Board.

At the same time, he received an offer from the Winklevoss twins to work together on developing an exclusive dating website for Harvard students.

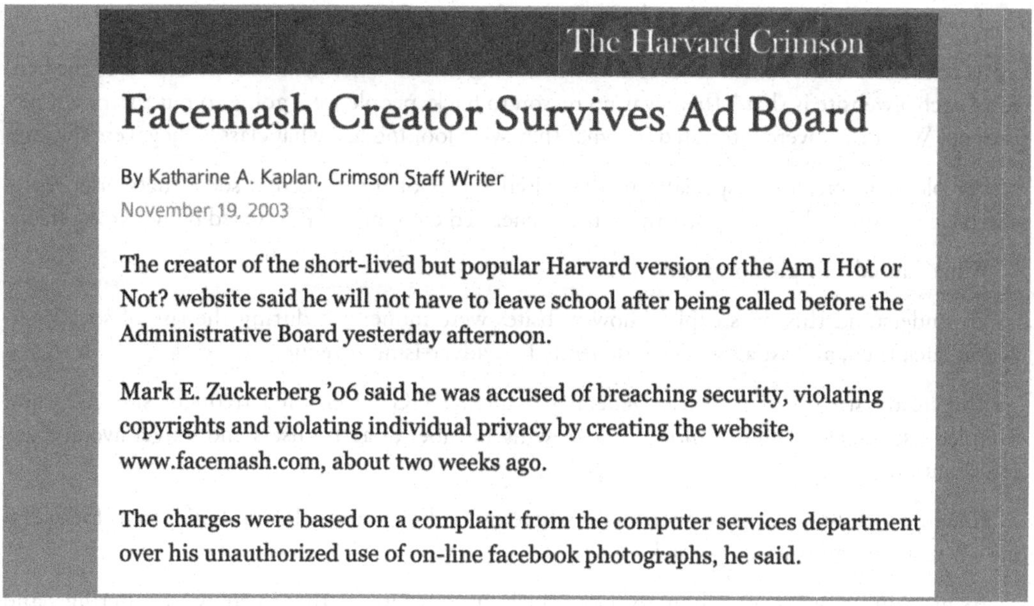

The Harvard Crimson

Facemash Creator Survives Ad Board

By Katharine A. Kaplan, Crimson Staff Writer
November 19, 2003

The creator of the short-lived but popular Harvard version of the Am I Hot or Not? website said he will not have to leave school after being called before the Administrative Board yesterday afternoon.

Mark E. Zuckerberg '06 said he was accused of breaching security, violating copyrights and violating individual privacy by creating the website, www.facemash.com, about two weeks ago.

The charges were based on a complaint from the computer services department over his unauthorized use of on-line facebook photographs, he said.

Figure 15.12 Article on The Harvard Crimson dated November 19, 2003, covering Facemash .com. Image source: thecrimson.com

Now, returning to the Caribbean Night scene.

Mark describes the platform as "an online community of friends." People would be able to click into pictures and profiles and browse around. He described the platform as "taking the entire social structure of college and putting it online."

Eduardo understood the value of the idea pretty quickly. He realized that there was no reason to hack, people were going to put their own pictures up.

Okay, now let's delve into our discussion on social media.

15.3.1 What Is a Social Network?

Social networks have undergone transformations over the years (we will explore their evolution in the next section), but the core essence of social networks is succinctly captured in the previously mentioned scene from *The Social Network* movie.

As Mark Zuckerberg describes it "an online community of friends … taking the entire social structure of college and putting it online."

The essence of social networks, especially in their early days, was centered on community participation through social presence and communication channels.

Alright, this encapsulates the user perspective of social networks.

15.3.1.1 But, What Is a Social Network for Platform Builders?

Let us refer back to the same scene from the *The Social Network* movie. Eduardo describes the benefit of such a website is that "There was no reason to hack, people were going to put their own pictures up. What they were interested in, what they were looking for, what classes they were taking."

For platform creators, especially in the initial stages of social media, social networks represented a constant and growing stream of user-generated content (UGC) fueled by network effects.

What caused this phenomenon?

To understand this, let's explore how websites were monetized during the rise of social networks. Back then, almost all websites depended on advertising revenue.

The steady stream of new user-generated content (UGCs) ensured frequent site visits and extended user engagement, resulting in a growing number of active users and longer average session durations.

Imagine social networks as open parks where individuals can gather and offer food for everyone – a vast and continuous potluck.

As more individuals contribute to the potluck, more people gather to enjoy the offerings, and in turn, they also bring their own contributions. This cycle continues, leading to a continuous growth of the gathering.

The park management maintains the park. When there is a large enough gathering in the park, the management starts allowing businesses to put up their billboards around the park and the management starts earning revenue from the billboard ads.

The willingness of businesses to pay for advertisements depends on the number of visitors to the park and the time spent by these visitors. Therefore, the continuous influx of free food is crucial, as it attracts more people to consume and spend time at the food stalls.

In the case of social media, instead of food, it's content – "free content."

It is essential to highlight "free content" because, prior to the rise of UGC (and Web2), content was not easily accessible for free. Website builders had to curate and source content for their websites.

Social media paved the way for a continuous flow of free content.

Now, to assess social networks and understand the impact of Web3 on them, we must first examine their evolution over the years.

15.3.2 A Brief History of Social Networks

15.3.2.1 Emergence of Early Social Networking (1997–2004)

Six Degrees, launched in 1997, is considered the first social media platform enabling users to create profiles, connect with friends, and send messages. Subsequently, Friendster (2002) and MySpace (2003) pioneered features like profile customization and photo sharing.

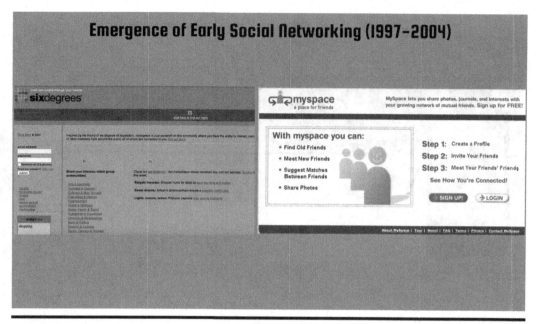

Figure 15.13 Early social media networks. Source: web.archive.org (sixdegrees.com and myspace.com)

15.3.2.2 *Rise of Mainstream Social Media (2004–2010)*

The launch of Facebook (as thefacebook.com) in 2004 marked a significant turning point in the evolution of social media.

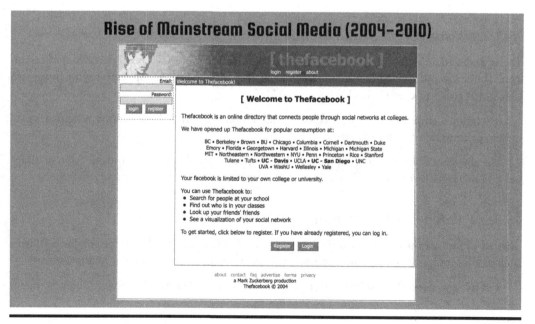

Figure 15.14 Early days of Facebook as thefacebook.com. Source: web.archive.org (thefacebook.com)

Figure 15.15 Visual content and mobile-first era. Source: web.archive.org (instagram.com and snapchat.com)

The introduction of News Feed in 2006 transformed content consumption dynamics, propelling Facebook to global dominance.

YouTube (2005) revolutionized video sharing, and Twitter (2006) popularized microblogging, introducing new methods for content creation and real-time information sharing.

15.3.2.3 Visual Content and Mobile-first Era (2010–2015)

The widespread adoption of smartphones played a crucial role in social media's continued expansion. The newfound accessibility led to the emergence of mobile-centric applications like Instagram (2009–10) and Snapchat (2011–12).

Instagram's emphasis on visual content and Pinterest's curated collections reshaped social media, gaining significant popularity.

The emergence of messaging apps like WhatsApp (2010) and Snapchat's introduction of disappearing messages disrupted traditional communication, prioritizing privacy and immediacy.

15.3.2.4 Video Content Dominance (2015–Present)

The rise of live streaming on platforms like Periscope (2015), integrated later into major platforms such as Facebook and Instagram, emphasized the significance of real-time, authentic content.

TikTok popularized short-form, user-generated content, ushering in a new era of viral content and trends.

Figure 15.16 Rise of video content. Source: web.archive.org (pscv.tv and tiktok.com)

15.3.2.5 Social Commerce and Integration (2020s)

In the 2020s, social media platforms, including Instagram and Facebook, smoothly incorporated e-commerce features like Instagram Shopping and Facebook Shops, introducing social commerce. This integration went beyond traditional advertising, enabling platforms to earn commissions on e-commerce sales.

Figure 15.17 Rise of social commerce. Source: about.fb.com

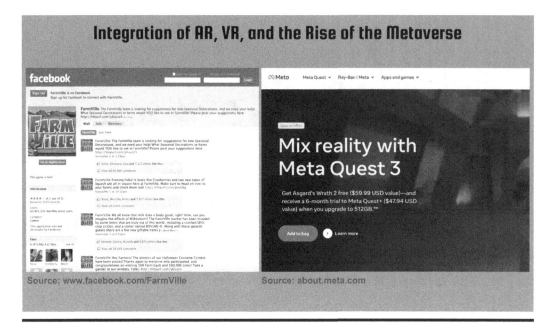

Figure 15.18 Integration of AR, VR, and the rise of Metaverse. Source: web.archive.org (facebook.com/FarmVille) and meta.com.

15.3.2.6 Integration of AR, VR, and the Rise of the Metaverse

Gaming and social networks have shared a deep connection, particularly evident on platforms like Facebook. During the mid-2000s, social media platforms opened their doors to third-party developers, fueling the emergence of social gaming.

Games such as FarmVille and Mafia Wars achieved iconic status by leveraging users' social connections for collaborative play, shared achievements, and friendly competition, thereby enhancing the social aspect of the platforms.

Presently, advanced technologies like augmented reality (AR), virtual reality (VR), and the emergence of the metaverse are reshaping social media.

Meta's rebranding in 2021 and its vision for the Metaverse signify this transformative era. The Metaverse, a collective virtual space, is fueled by AR and VR, revolutionizing user engagement with digital content.

This shift blends the digital and physical worlds, offering users unparalleled opportunities for creativity, collaboration, and shared experiences, marking an exciting phase in the ongoing evolution of social gaming and digital interconnectedness.

15.3.3 Limitations of Traditional Social Networks

15.3.3.1 Handling of UGC

While user-generated content (UGC) is vital for social networks, users often struggle to maintain control over their content. Although many platforms offer privacy controls, the algorithms dictating content visibility are opaque and entirely under the control of platform providers.

For example, if you have 1,000 followers, not all will likely see your content due to opaque visibility algorithms.

Additionally, interoperability is limited, content uploaded on one platform is generally inaccessible on others, with few exceptions, like Facebook and Instagram under the same parent company.

15.3.3.2 Monetization of UGC

Now, let's delve into monetization. Over the last decade, social media has transformed with the rise of professional content creators. Social media has evolved into a significant income source for these content creators, with over 200 million globally, according to Linktree's 2023 Creator Report.

Despite creators contributing significant economic value, many platforms fail to fully acknowledge their impact. Creators often monetize through avenues such as brand endorsements, affiliate marketing, sponsored content, and direct audience contributions.

In the last few years, some platforms have introduced creator subscription programs, such as Facebook Fan Subscriptions and the Medium Partner Program, offering creators additional earning avenues. Although, technically Medium is not a social network.

15.3.3.3 Failure to Appraise Influence

While user-generated content (UGC) is crucial for social network traffic, the influence of users is equally important. A notable example is Warren Buffett, who has a Twitter profile with 1.7 million followers despite posting only nine tweets. Engagement is driven by the influence and reputation of users, not necessarily the frequency of their content.

Most social networks lack the tools to accurately assess influence and assign economic value to influence.

Real-life influential figures, such as actors and singers, bring substantial value to networks by attracting users and boosting engagement.

Centrality measures, including degree centrality, betweenness centrality, and closeness centrality, assess an individual's position in the network. Influential figures typically have high centrality scores, signifying their central role in information flow and connections.

Influential individuals act as key nodes for information diffusion. When they share content or express opinions, information rapidly spreads through the network, reaching a broad audience – a concept aligned with "broadcast" nodes in network theory.

Social networks often have community structures, where nodes are more densely connected internally. Influential individuals may bridge different communities, fostering information flow between diverse user groups.

Influential individuals have the ability to initiate viral content and cascades. When they share a post or endorse a product, a domino effect occurs as their followers continue to share the content. This cascading effect is a distinctive feature of influential nodes in network dynamics.

In summary, influential individuals play a crucial role in drawing a crowd to social networks and contributing to the overall health of these networks. However, traditional social media platforms often fall short in recognizing and assigning economic value to their influence and impact.

15.3.3.4 Deceptive Social Presence

The prevalence of fake profiles, artificial engagement, trolling, and the dissemination of fake news pose substantial reputation risks to social networks.

Fake profiles are not only used for deceiving job seekers or phishing attacks but also by spies from certain countries to collect information.

Artificial engagement, often orchestrated through automated processes, distorts genuine user activity, compromising authenticity and real-time communication. Instances of acquiring fake followers erode the credibility of social media metrics.

Trolling, marked by provocative or offensive behavior, creates a toxic online environment and discourages open dialogue, particularly affecting minority groups.

Additionally, the widespread occurrence of fake news undermines the credibility of social networks, as misinformation erodes public trust and contributes to confusion. For instance, during the 2016 US presidential election, it was uncovered that Russian troll farms had established fake profiles on Facebook and Twitter to disseminate disinformation and manipulate public opinion. These fabricated accounts participated in divisive political discussions.

Existing social media platforms lack the necessary tools to effectively tackle these challenges, presenting considerable difficulties for social networks.

15.3.3.5 Content Theft

Content theft, ranging from copying LinkedIn posts to downloading and hosting videos for revenue, poses a threat to professional content creators. Unauthorized use poses a threat to the economic value of carefully crafted content aimed at engaging audiences and generating revenue.

Addressing content theft remains a significant challenge for most social media platforms.

15.3.3.6 Privacy and Safely Challenges

I am addressing the most important issues at the end – privacy and safety.

What sort of information do you believe Facebook owns about you?

If you assume that Facebook only retains fundamental details like your name, age, location, and data related to your Facebook usage, you are greatly underestimating the privacy concerns associated with social networks.

Facebook and many other social networks not only store identity-related information such as names, ages, locations, and employment details but also hold biometric data like facial recognition, online behavioral data (including browsing history), and even details about individuals in your contact list if you use their mobile applications.

You've likely come across notifications like "X from your contacts has joined this network as Y."

Let's delve into the lawsuits these social networks faced over the years to comprehend the extent of the issue.

15.3.3.6.1 Cambridge Analytica Scandal (2018)

The Cambridge Analytica Scandal remains ingrained in our memory. Facebook faced legal troubles for inappropriate data sharing with the political consulting firm Cambridge Analytica, resulting in unauthorized access to user data. Consequently, Facebook encountered various legal issues, culminating in a US $5 billion settlement with the US Federal Trade Commission (FTC).

15.3.3.6.2 Various GDPR Investigations (2018 Onward)

Facebook is confronted with accusations of General Data Protection Regulation (GDPR) violations in the EU, including concerns about user consent and data processing. Numerous European data protection authorities are conducting antitrust investigations on Facebook, with some imposing fines on Facebook.

15.3.3.6.3 Biometric Privacy Lawsuits

Facebook is currently facing multiple legal actions related to its use of facial recognition technology without obtaining proper consent, thereby violating biometric privacy laws. A significant case in point is a class-action lawsuit filed by Facebook users in Illinois, US, which concluded with a US $550 million settlement.

15.3.3.6.4 WhatsApp Data Sharing Controversy (2016 Onward)

Facebook allegedly revised WhatsApp's privacy policy, allowing for the sharing of data with Facebook without adequate user consent. Consequently, Facebook faced fines and regulatory investigations in several countries, including Germany and the UK.

15.3.3.6.5 Child Safety on Social Media

Let us now discuss the matter of child safety on social media.

On January 31, 2024, CEOs of many social media platforms were grilled on the safety of children on social media in a dramatic senate hearing.

The discussion ranged from the kind of abuse children face on these platforms, to the distribution of child-pornographic material on these platforms, to possible revocation of section 230 of the Communications Decency Act, 1996.

Data shows that social media is absolutely not safe for children.

According to leaked Meta documents, as reported by *The Guardian*, approximately 100,000 children using Facebook and Instagram face online sexual harassment daily, which includes exposure to images of private parts.

According to John Shehan, head of the exploited children division at the National Center for Missing and Exploited Children, reports of child sexual abuse material on online platforms increased from 32 million in 2022 to a record high of over 36 million in 2023.

We may soon see some significant changes in social media regulations, including the Revised Kid's Online Safety Act.

Apart from these, there are multiple allegations of inadequate security measures leading to data breaches and exposure of user information, resulting in various investigations.

The point is that traditional social media platforms failed to uphold user privacy to an expected standard.

15.3.4 Web3 Social Networks

Over the years, many blockchain-based social networks have emerged, each offering distinct features and strategies to harness decentralized technology, aiming to address some of the challenges mentioned above.

Let us talk about some of those platforms here.

15.3.4.1 Steemit

Steemit is a social network built on the Steem blockchain, utilizing its native cryptocurrency STEEM to reward users for content creation and curation.

This network provides a decentralized and incentivized approach to content creation.

15.3.4.2 Minds

Minds is an open-source, blockchain-based social network emphasizing user privacy and control. Utilizing blockchain technology, it rewards users with tokens for engagement and content creation, while also offering support for encrypted messaging.

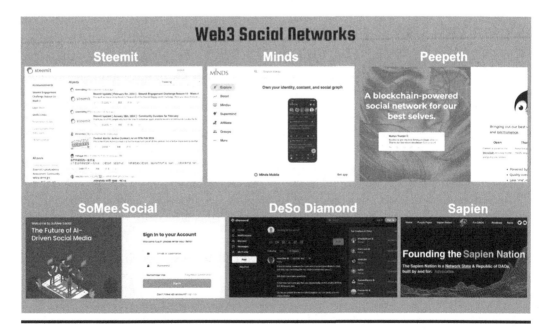

Figure 15.19 Examples of Web3 social media networks.

15.3.4.3 Peepeth

Peepeth, built on the Ethereum blockchain, strives to establish a more ethical and accountable social network. Leveraging smart contracts, it facilitates features such as tip-based rewards for content creators and prioritizes positive interactions.

15.3.4.4 SoMee.Social

SoMee.Social is a blockchain-based social network dedicated to utilizing blockchain for social good, providing users with control over their data and privacy settings.

15.3.4.5 DeSo Diamond App

The DeSo Diamond serves as a Web3 alternative to Twitter, positioning itself as a decentralized social media platform powered by the DeSo blockchain.

Some attributes of DeSo Diamond include:

I. **NFTs**: Creating and sharing digital collectibles on the DeSo Blockchain is simplified through one-click NFT minting for users.
II. **Tipping System**: Diamond offers a tipping system that empowers users to send cryptocurrency tips (diamonds) to their preferred creators, attaching tangible value to content. This encourages a more direct and rewarding relationship between creators and their audience.
III. **Creator Coins**: On this platform, creators receive their own Creator Coin upon setting up their profile. These coins represent a form of social token uniquely associated with the creators. Other users on the platform can purchase these Creator Coins using cryptocurrency. The purchase of Creator Coins directly supports the creator financially. The value of the Creator Coin may be appreciated as the creator's popularity and influence increase.
IV. **Community Focus**: The Diamond team places a high priority on cultivating an active and engaged community. They encourage participation through various means, such as offering bounties for user tasks. Additionally, the team is dedicated to continuously enhancing the platform by incorporating new features based on valuable feedback from the community.

15.3.4.6 Sapien

Sapien operates as a decentralized social platform on the Ethereum blockchain, featuring a reputation system that enables users to establish credibility through their contributions. The platform utilizes its native token, SPN, for transactions and rewards.

15.3.4.7 Diaspora

Diaspora is a decentralized social network operating on a distributed network of servers, known as pods. It places a strong emphasis on user privacy and control, enabling users to share content with specific pods or the entire network.

Okay, let us end this chapter here.

Bibliography

111dots Studio. (2023, October 30). *111dots Studio*. Google.com. Retrieved January 1, 2024, from https://g. co/kgs/PssanP

Alphabet. (2021, September 22). *Google Play Music*. Google Play. Retrieved January 2, 2024, from https:// music.youtube.com/googleplaymusic

Amazon Music Unlimited | 100 Million Songs ad-free. (n.d.). Amazon.com. Retrieved January 2, 2024, from https://www.amazon.com/music/unlimited/

Amazon Prime. (n.d.). Amazon.com. Retrieved January 2, 2024, from https://www.amazon.com/ amazonprime

Apple Music - Web Player. Retrieved January 2, 2024, from https://music.apple.com/us/browse

Apple One. (n.d.). Apple. Retrieved January 2, 2024, from https://www.apple.com/apple-one/

Axie Infinity. (n.d.). *494425 | App.Axie*. Axie Infinity. Retrieved January 1, 2024, from https://app.axiein-finity.com/marketplace/axies/494425/

Axie Infinity. (n.d.). Axie Infinity - Battle, Collect, and Trade Collectible NFT Creatures. Retrieved January 1, 2024, from https://axieinfinity.com/

Axie Infinity. (n.d.). *Lunacia SDK*. Axie Infinity. Retrieved January 1, 2024, from https://whitepaper.axie-infinity.com/gameplay/land/lunacia-sdk

BitTube. (2021, February 26). *BitTube. You Own Your Content. - Apps on Google Play*. Google Play. Retrieved January 2, 2024, from https://play.google.com/store/apps/details?id=app.fedilab.bittube&hl=en_US

Blizzard. (n.d.). *Explore*. World of Warcraft. Retrieved January 1, 2024, from https://worldofwarcraft.bliz-zard.com/en-us/

Blumenthal, S. R., & Blackburn, S. M. (n.d.). A BILL. Retrieved February 6, 2024, from https://www.blu-menthal.senate.gov/imo/media/doc/kids_online_safety_act_-_bill_text_-_2023.pdf

Cadwalladr, C., & Graham, E. (2018, March 17). *Revealed: 50 Million Facebook Profiles Harvested for Cambridge Analytica in Major Data Breach*. The Guardian. Retrieved January 2, 2024, from https:// www.theguardian.com/news/2018/mar/17/cambridge-analytica-facebook-influence-us-election

Coinmarketcap. (n.d.). *BitTube Price Today, TUBE to USD Live Price, Marketcap and Chart*. CoinMarketCap. Retrieved February 15, 2024, from https://coinmarketcap.com/currencies/bit-tube/

Coinmarketcap. (n.d.). *LBRY Credits Price Today, LBC to USD Live Price, Marketcap and Chart*. CoinMarketCap. Retrieved February 15, 2024, from https://coinmarketcap.com/currencies/library -credits/

Coinmarketcap. (n.d.). *Steem Price Today, STEEM to USD Live Price, Marketcap and Chart*. CoinMarketCap. Retrieved February 15, 2024, from https://coinmarketcap.com/currencies/steem/

Corera, Gordon."'Chinese spy' targeted thousands over LinkedIn." *BBC*, 23 August 2023,https://www.bbc .com/news/uk-66599376. Accessed 14 June 2024.

Crunchbase. (n.d.). *Revver*. Crunchbase. Retrieved January 2, 2024, from https://www.crunchbase.com/ organization/revver

CryptoKitties | Collect and Breed Digital Cats! Retrieved January 1, 2024, from https://www.cryptokitties .co/

The Diaspora* Project. Retrieved January 2, 2024, from https://diasporafoundation.org/

DOMO. (n.d.). *Data Never Sleeps 10.0*. Domo. Retrieved January 1, 2024, from https://www.domo.com/ data-never-sleeps

Eldorado. (n.d.). *Garena Free Fire Accounts For Sale*. Eldorado.gg. Retrieved January 1, 2024, from https:// www.eldorado.gg/free-fire-accounts/a/46-1-0

Enjin. (n.d.). *Enjin Coin (ENJ)*. Enjin.io. Retrieved January 1, 2024, from https://enjin.io/enjin-coin

Ethereum. (2023, April 7). *ERC-1155 Multi-Token Standard | ethereum.org*. Ethereum. Retrieved January 1, 2024, from https://ethereum.org/en/developers/docs/standards/tokens/erc-1155/

Ethereum. (2023, June 23). *ERC-721 Non-Fungible Token Standard | ethereum.org*. Ethereum. Retrieved January 1, 2024, from https://ethereum.org/en/developers/docs/standards/tokens/erc-721/

Facebook (Meta). (2022, August 30). *Thefacebook.com as of April 2003*. Wayback Machine. Retrieved January 2, 2024, from https://web.archive.org/web/20040524063031/http://www.thefacebook.com/

Feed - Diamond. Retrieved January 2, 2024, from https://diamondapp.com/browse?feedTab=Hot

Firstpost. (2023, March 23). *Despite Getting Banned in 2020, TikTok Still Has Access to Data of Indian Users*. Firstpost. Retrieved February 15, 2024, from https://www.firstpost.com/world/despite-getting -banned-in-2020-tiktok-still-has-access-to-data-of-indian-users-12339972.html

Fowler, B. (2023, February 11). *Scammers Targeting Job Seekers as Layoffs Mount*. CNET. Retrieved January 2, 2024, from https://www.cnet.com/tech/services-and-software/fake-online-recruiters-looking-to -scam-job-seekers/

Free Fire. (n.d.). Garena Free Fire. Best Survival Battle Royale on Mobile! Retrieved January 1, 2024, from https://ff.garena.com/en/

Garena. (n.d.). *Garena*. Garena. Retrieved January 1, 2024, from https://www.garena.sg/

Garena. (2022, March 30). *Account Trading – Garena Free Fire*. Garena Free Fire. Retrieved January 1, 2024, from https://ffsupport.garena.com/hc/en-us/articles/4501218599066-Account-Trading

Goldman Sachs. (2023, April 19). *The Creator Economy Could Approach Half-a-Trillion Dollars by 2027*. Goldman Sachs. Retrieved January 2, 2024, from https://www.goldmansachs.com/intelligence/pages /the-creator-economy-could-approach-half-a-trillion-dollars-by-2027.html

Goolge Play Movies and TV. (n.d.). Android Apps on Google Play. Retrieved January 2, 2024, from https:// play.google.com

Grand View Research. (n.d.). *Video Game Market Size, Share And Growth Report, 2030*. Grand View Research. Retrieved January 1, 2024, from https://www.grandviewresearch.com/industry-analysis/ video-game-market

The Guardian. (2022, November 8). *TikTok's ties to China: Why Concerns Over Your Data Are Here to Stay*. The Guardian. Retrieved February 15, 2024, from https://www.theguardian.com/technology/2022/ nov/07/tiktoks-china-bytedance-data-concerns

The Guardian. (2024, January 18). *Meta Documents Show 100000 Children Sexually Harassed Daily on its Platforms*. The Guardian. Retrieved February 6, 2024, from https://www.theguardian.com/technol- ogy/2024/jan/18/instagram-facebook-child-sexual-harassment

Hirst, N. (2017, December 19). *Facebook's Data Collection Faces Antitrust Charge in Germany*. POLITICO .eu. Retrieved January 2, 2024, from https://www.politico.eu/article/facebook-data-collection-could -be-an-antitrust-abuse-in-germany/

Hive Tube. (n.d.). *Hive-Tube - The Free Plugin That Monetizes Any Streaming Media, Censorship-free, P2P, via the Hive Blockchain. Zero Fees. Passive Income. Use it and Earn!* Retrieved January 2, 2024, from https://hive-tube.com/

Hulu: Stream TV and Movies Live and Online. Retrieved January 2, 2024, from https://www.hulu.com/ welcome

IMDB. (n.d.). *Spacewar! (Video Game 1962) - Plot*. IMDb. Retrieved January 1, 2024, from https://www .imdb.com/title/tt0396224/plotsummary/

IMSDb. (n.d.). *The Social Network*. The Internet Movie Script Database (IMSDb). Retrieved January 2, 2024, from https://imsdb.com/scripts/Social-Network,-The.html

Instagram (Meta). (n.d.). *Instagram as of March 2005*. Wayback Machine. Retrieved January 2, 2024, from https://web.archive.org/web/20110411160704/http://instagram.com/

Internet Archive. (2012, September 4). *Space War '95 : Advanced Computer Technology : Free Download, Borrow, and Streaming*. Internet Archive. Retrieved February 24, 2024, from https://archive.org/ details/SpaceWar95_1020

IPFS. (n.d.). *IPFS*. IPFS: An Open System to Manage Data without a Central Server. Retrieved January 2, 2024, from https://ipfs.tech/

Isaac, M. (2020, January 29). *Facebook to Pay $550 Million to Settle Facial Recognition Suit (Published 2020)*. The New York Times. Retrieved January 2, 2024, from https://www.nytimes.com/2020/01/29/tech- nology/facebook-privacy-lawsuit-earnings.html

iTunes. (n.d.). Apple. Retrieved January 2, 2024, from https://www.apple.com/itunes/

JVC. (n.d.). *VHS*. JVCKENWOOD USA Corporation. Retrieved January 2, 2024, from http://pro.jvc .com/

Kaplan, K. A. (2003, November 19). *Facemash Creator Survives Ad Board | News*. The Harvard Crimson. Retrieved January 2, 2024, from https://www.thecrimson.com/article/2003/11/19/facemash-creator -survives-ad-board-the/

Krishnan, A. (2023, July 26). *How to Avoid LinkedIn Phishing Attacks in the Enterprise.* TechTarget. Retrieved January 2, 2024, from https://www.techtarget.com/searchsecurity/tip/How-to-avoid-LinkedIn-phishing-attacks-in-the-enterprise

LBRY. (n.d.). LBRY - Content Freedom. Retrieved January 2, 2024, from https://lbry.com/

Linktree. (n.d.). *2022 Creator Report by Linktree.* Linktree. Retrieved January 2, 2024, from https://linktr.ee/creator-report/#Chapter-1

Medium. (n.d.). *Medium Partner Program.* Medium. Retrieved January 2, 2024, from https://medium.com/partner-program

Meta. (n.d.). *FarmVille.* Facebook. Retrieved January 2, 2024, from http://www.facebook.com/FarmVille/

Meta. (n.d.). *Subscriptions | Meta for Creators.* Facebook for Creators. Retrieved January 2, 2024, from https://creators.facebook.com/tools/subscriptions/?locale=en_US

Meta. (2020, May 19). *Introducing Facebook Shops: Helping Small Businesses Sell Online | Meta.* Meta. Retrieved January 2, 2024, from https://about.fb.com/news/2020/05/introducing-facebook-shops/

The Metaverse is the Future of Digital Connection. (n.d.). Meta. Retrieved January 2, 2024, from https://about.meta.com/metaverse/

Minds. Retrieved January 2, 2024, from https://www.minds.com/

Minecraft. (n.d.). *Get Minecraft.* Welcome to the Minecraft Official Site | Minecraft. Retrieved January 1, 2024, from https://www.minecraft.net/en-us

MP3.com. (n.d.). *MP3.com.* MP3.com. Retrieved January 2, 2024, from http://mp3.com/

Mp3.com. (n.d.). *Mp3.com as of July 1997.* Wayback Machine. Retrieved January 2, 2024, from https://web.archive.org/web/19981212031130/http://mp3.com/

Muvi. Best Video Streaming Solution | On-Demand, Live, Apps & Monetization,https://www.muvi.com/. Accessed 11 June 2024.

Myspace. (n.d.). *myspace.com as of February 2002.* Wayback Machine. Retrieved January 2, 2024, from https://web.archive.org/web/20031004101518/http://myspace.com/

Napster. (n.d.). *Napster.com as of October 1998.* Wayback Machine. Retrieved January 2, 2024, from https://web.archive.org/web/19991127080306/http://www.napster.com/

Netflix – Watch TV Shows Online, Watch Movies Online. (n.d.). Netflix. Retrieved January 2, 2024, from https://www.netflix.com/

Newman, J., & Ritchie, A. (2019, July 24). *FTC Imposes $5 Billion Penalty and Sweeping New Privacy Restrictions on Facebook.* Federal Trade Commission. Retrieved January 2, 2024, from https://www.ftc.gov/news-events/news/press-releases/2019/07/ftc-imposes-5-billion-penalty-sweeping-new-privacy-restrictions-facebook

Newman, L. H. (2021, January 8). *WhatsApp Has Shared Your Data With Facebook for Years, Actually.* WIRED. Retrieved January 2, 2024, from https://www.wired.com/story/whatsapp-facebook-data-share-notification/

Pandora: Music and Podcasts, Free and On-Demand. Retrieved January 2, 2024, from https://www.pandora.com/

Peacock: Stream TV and Movies Online, Watch Live News and Sports. Retrieved January 2, 2024, from https://www.peacocktv.com/

Peepeth. Retrieved January 2, 2024, from https://peepeth.com/welcome

Periscope. (n.d.). *pscp.tv as of April 1026.* Wayback Machine. Retrieved January 2, 2024, from https://web.archive.org/web/20170501080223/https://www.pscp.tv/

Pinterest. (2022, August 30). Pinterest. Retrieved January 2, 2024, from https://www.pinterest.com/

PlayerAuctions. (n.d.). *Free Fire Accounts for Sale | Buy FF ID.* PlayerAuctions. Retrieved January 1, 2024, from https://www.playerauctions.com/freefire-account/

PR Newswire. (2014, February 19). *Huntercoin: The Online Game That Earns You Money.* PR Newswire. Retrieved January 2, 2024, from https://www.prnewswire.com/news-releases/huntercoin-the-online-game-that-earns-you-money-246237231.html

Roblox. (n.d.). *Buy Robux.* Roblox. Retrieved January 1, 2024, from https://www.roblox.com/upgrades/robux

Roblox. (n.d.). *Creator Hub.* Models - Creator Marketplace. Retrieved January 2, 2024, from https://create.roblox.com/marketplace/models

Roblox. (n.d.). *SIGN UP AND START HAVING FUN!* Roblox. Retrieved January 1, 2024, from https://www.roblox.com/

The Sandbox. (n.d.). The Sandbox Game — User-Generated Crypto & Blockchain Games. Retrieved January 1, 2024, from https://www.sandbox.game/en/

The Sandbox. (2021, September 22). *The Sandbox Metaverse Map*. The Sandbox. Retrieved January 1, 2024, from https://www.sandbox.game/en/map/?lat=-12&lng=26&zoom=1

Sapien | Homepage. Retrieved January 2, 2024, from https://www.sapien.network/

Satariano, A. (2021, June 4). *Facebook Faces Two Antitrust Inquiries in Europe*. The New York Times. Retrieved January 2, 2024, from https://www.nytimes.com/2021/06/04/business/facebook-eu-uk-antitrust.html

Satariano, A. (2023, May 22). *Meta Fined $1.3 Billion for Violating E.U. Data Privacy Rules*. The New York Times. Retrieved January 2, 2024, from https://www.nytimes.com/2023/05/22/business/meta-facebook-eu-privacy-fine.html

Second Life. (n.d.). *Explore*. Official Site | Second Life - Virtual Worlds, Virtual Reality, VR, Avatars, and Free 3D Chat. Retrieved January 1, 2024, from https://secondlife.com/

Second Life. (2022, September 10). *How to Earn Linden Dollars in Second Life*. Second Life Wiki. Retrieved January 1, 2024, from https://wiki.secondlife.com/wiki/How_to_Earn_Linden_Dollars_in_Second_Life

Singer, Natasha. "What You Don't Know About How Facebook Uses Your Data (Published 2018)." *The New York Times*, 11 April 2018,https://www.nytimes.com/2018/04/11/technology/facebook-privacy-hearings.html.Accessed 14 June 2024.

Sixdegrees, inc. (n.d.). *sixdegrees.com as of April 1998*. Wayback Machine. Retrieved January 2, 2024, from https://web.archive.org/web/19991013030457/http://www.sixdegrees.com/

Starks, Tim, et al."Russia's manipulation of Twitter was far vaster than believed." *Politico*,5 June 2019.

Stream Disney, Pixar, Marvel, Star Wars, Nat Geo | Disney+. Retrieved January 2, 2024, from https://disneyplus.com/

TechCrunch. (2006, September 7). *Amazon Unbox Goes Live*. TechCrunch. Retrieved January 2, 2024, from https://techcrunch.com/2006/09/07/amazon-unbox-goes-live/

Tiktok. (n.d.). *Tiktok*. TikTok - Make Your Day. Retrieved January 2, 2024, from https://www.tiktok.com/

Trending posts — Steemit. Retrieved January 2, 2024, from https://steemit.com/

Tubi: Watch Free Movies and TV Shows Online | Free Streaming Video. Retrieved January 2, 2024, from https://tubitv.com/

Twitch.tv. Retrieved January 2, 2024, from https://www.twitch.tv/

VoxEdit. (n.d.). VoxEdit Website. Retrieved January 2, 2024, from https://www.voxedit.io

The Washington Post. (2024, January 28). *The internet's CSAM Problem Keeps Getting Worse. Here's Why*. The Washington Post. Retrieved February 6, 2024, from https://www.washingtonpost.com/technology/2024/01/28/csam-ncmec-senate-hearing-child-porn/

Web Player: Music for Everyone. Retrieved January 2, 2024, from https://www.spotify.com

Welcome to SoMee Social. Retrieved January 2, 2024, from http://somee.social/

WhatsApp (Meta). (n.d.). *WhatsApp*. WhatsApp | Secure and Reliable Free Private Messaging and Calling. Retrieved January 2, 2024, from https://www.whatsapp.com/

Xaya. (n.d.). *Huntercoin*. Xaya. Retrieved January 1, 2024, from https://xaya.io/huntercoin-legacy

YouTube. (n.d.). *YoutTube.com as of April 2005*. Wayback Machine. https://web.archive.org/web/20051101000000*/https://www.youtube.com/

YouTube. (2017, November 9). *Launch of YouTube Partner Program (May 2007)*. Wayback Machine. Retrieved January 2, 2024, from https://web.archive.org/web/20070516073101/http://youtube.com/blog?entry=4b3PkL8HQcw

YouTube Gaming. (n.d.). *Gaming*. YouTube. Retrieved January 1, 2024, from https://www.youtube.com/gaming

Chapter 16

Epilogue: Decentralization as a Separate Industry

Sam Ghosh

Let us discuss the type of service offering prevalent in the blockchain and Web3 space.

16.1 Services in the Web3 Space

16.1.1 Public Blockchain API Platforms

E.g. Alchemy, Infura.

API for Public Blockchains – These platforms provide a simple API that allows developers to interact with the public blockchain without running a full node. It abstracts away the complexities of running and maintaining blockchain infrastructure.

16.1.2 Blockchain Cloud Providers

E.g. Microsoft Azure Blockchain, Amazon Managed Blockchain, and IBM Blockchain Platform.

These services involve providing cloud-based platforms and tools for deploying and managing blockchain networks. They typically support various blockchain protocols and frameworks.

16.1.3 Infrastructure as a Service (IaaS) with Blockchain

E.g. Oracle Blockchain Cloud Service.

These services involve integrating blockchain capabilities into existing cloud infrastructure services, allowing businesses to deploy and manage blockchain networks as part of their overall cloud strategy.

 DOI: 10.4324/9781003507352-16

16.1.4 Blockchain Development Platforms

E.g. R3 Corda Enterprise, Chainstack.

These services involve providing development platforms that enable businesses to create, test, and deploy blockchain applications without the need for extensive in-house infrastructure.

16.1.5 Managed Blockchain Solutions

E.g. Kaleido, Blockdaemon.

These services involve offering fully managed blockchain networks, including node deployment, maintenance, and updates, simplifying the operational aspects for businesses.

16.1.6 Decentralized Storage API Services

E.g. Pinata, Textile ThreadDB, etc.

These platforms offer easy-to-use APIs for decentralized file storage solutions (such as IPFS).

16.1.7 Decentralized Identity API services

E.g. 3Box Labs - Ceramic Network

These services involve offering APIs for building decentralized and verifiable identities. They abstract away the complexities of building on decentralized identity protocols.

16.2 Decentralization as a Service (DaaS)

A proposed service model that offers decentralization out of the box. The concept of DaaS is not limited to blockchain and Web3 but incorporates other decentralized solutions such as self-sovereign identity, federated learning, decentralized storage, SMPC, etc.

But, how can DaaS be different from the above-mentioned service models?

16.2.1 Comprehensive Solution

Decentralization as a Service (DaaS) should provide a decentralization layer as a single entity that gets connected to the primary infrastructure through a set of APIs as an abstraction. The decentralization service provider should take care of the complex interconnections among blockchain, smart contracts, decentralized identity, decentralized data science, etc. The user organization should not have to bother about any coding (including smart contract writing) except for the APIs.

16.2.2 Tailored Solutions

The DaaS should be able to cover the most predictable use cases of decentralization that an organization may require.

16.2.3 Standardization

At the same time, the DaaS solutions should be standardized, i.e. the client organization can easily pick a decentralization service suitable for them without bothering much about the technical details.

16.2.4 Flexible Packages

Clients should be able to choose from any combination of decentralization services they require – with or without decentralized identity, with or without federated learning, etc.

Also, the clients should be able to choose from various blockchains (e.g. Ethereum, Solana, etc.), various decentralized storage solutions, various decentralized identity technologies and service providers, various decentralized data science technologies, etc.

16.2.5 Portable and Interoperable Solutions

Keeping the fundamental philosophy of decentralization alive, the DaaS services would be interoperable, i.e. the clients should not lose access to their data if they switch services.

DaaS as a whole should act like a network connecting various decentralized services (such as blockchains, decentralized identity services, etc.) rather than a centralized platform.

So, switching to a DaaS service would involve acquiring the specifications of decentralized services (say Ethereum addresses, DID addresses, etc) from existing DaaS services and then providing the specifications to the new DaaS service provider.

Okay, let us conclude the book here. Hopefully, you will find the concepts learned in this book useful.

Subhasis and I would like to thank you for considering this book. If you have any comments or feedback, feel free to reach out to us.

Index

Printed in the United States
by Baker & Taylor Publisher Services